DELEUZE AND ENVIRONMENTAL DAMAGE

Advances in Criminology
Series Editor: David Nelken

Titles in the Series

Re-Thinking the Political Economy of Punishment: Perspectives on Post-Fordism and Penal Politics
Alessandro De Giorgi

Globalization and Regulatory Character: Regulatory Reform after the Kader Toy Factory Fire
Fiona Haines

Family Violence and Police Response: Learning From Research, Policy and Practice in European Countries
Edited by Wilma Smeenk and Marijke Malsch

Crime and Culture: An Historical Perspective
Edited by Amy Gilman Srebnick and René Lévy

Power, Discourse and Resistance: A Genealogy of the Strangeways Prison Riot
Eamonn Carrabine

Hard Lessons: Reflections on Governance and Crime Control in Late Modernity
Edited by Richard Hil and Gordon Tait

Informal Criminal Justice
Edited by Dermot Feenan

Becoming Delinquent: British and European Youth, 1650–1950
Edited by Pamela Cox and Heather Shore

Migration, Culture Conflict and Crime
Edited by Joshua D. Freilich, Graeme Newman, S. Giora Shoham and Moshe Addad

Critique and Radical Discourses on Crime
George Pavlich

Contrasting Criminal Justice: Getting from Here to There
Edited by David Nelken

Deleuze and Environmental Damage

Violence of the Text

MARK HALSEY
University of Melbourne, Australia and
Flinders University of South Australia, Australia

ASHGATE

Published by
Ashgate Publishing Limited
Gower House
Croft Road
Aldershot
Hampshire GU11 3HR
England

Ashgate Publishing Company
Suite 420
101 Cherry Street
Burlington, VT 05401-4405
USA

Ashgate website: http://www.ashgate.com

British Library Cataloguing in Publication Data
Halsey, Mark
Deleuze and environmental damage. - (Advances in criminology)
1.Deleuze, Gilles - Knowledge - Environmental law
2. Environmental law - Philosophy
I.Title
344'.046

Library of Congress Cataloging-in-Publication Data
Halsey, Mark.
Deleuze and environmental damage : violence of the text / by Mark Halsey.
p. cm. -- (Advances in criminology)
Includes bibliographical references and index.
ISBN 0-7546-2491-9
1. Offenses against the environment. 2. Environmental degradation. 3. Ecology -- Philosophy. 4. Human ecology. 5. Criminology. 6. Deleuze, Gilles. I. Title. II. Series.

HV6401.H35 2005
364.1'8--dc22

2005028883

ISBN-10: 0 7546 2491 9

Printed and bound in Great Britain by MPG Books Ltd. Bodmin, Cornwall.

Contents

List of Figures *viii*
Acknowledgements *ix*

Introduction 1
The case of Goolengook 3
Telling the story 4

PART A

1 Modernity and Ecological Thought: A Brief Critique 11
Modernity, humanity, rationality 12
Modernity, nature, ecophilosophy 14
In sum 34

2 Environment and Criminological Thought 41
Review and critique 43

3 Ecology and Machinic Thought: Deleuze/Guattari 57
Precedents to machinic thought 61
Deleuze/Guattari 68

4 Event, Method, Lexicon 81
Event 82
Method 85
Lexicon 90

PART B

5 Becoming Known 97
18,000 BCE: site of Aboriginal occupation 98
1770: site within the British Empire 99
1788: site within the waste lands of the Colony of New South Wales 99
1836: site within the Pastoral District of Port Phillip 100
1847: site within unsettled districts 101
1848–55: site of depasturing 101
1851: site within the Pastoral District of Gippsland, Colony of Victoria 106
1855: site within the sovereign state of Victoria 106
1856–60: site of depasturing 107

1865: site of potential reservation of timber 111
1869: site of prevalent timber 111
1871: site within the County of Croajingolong 112
1872: site of depasturing 113
1876: site of remnant 'wild people' 116
1885: site of alleged payable gold-field 118
1887: site of unknown qualities 122
1889: site of botanical exploration 126
1888–91: site of geodetic survey 130

6 Becoming Forest 135
1908 (March): site of protected forest 135
1917: site exterior to chief saw-milling localities 141
1921: site within the Orbost Forest District 142
1924–25: site of potential conservation 143
1928 (June): site lacking commercial value 145
Interlude 146
1959: site of forest produce 152
1960 (April): site of permanently reserved forest (stage 1) 154
1972: site of forest management block 155

7 Becoming Contested 161
1977 (March): site of uncommitted land 161
1977: site of Stringybark forests 164
1981: site of invisibilities 164
1981: site of botanical significance 165
1981: site of global zoological significance 168
1982: site for supply of 'defective material' 168
1982 (March): site of permanently reserved forest (stage 2) 170
1983: site of institutionalised conflict 171
1986: site within East Gippsland forest management area 171
1986 (July): site within the Bemm River Water Supply Catchment 172
1986 (December): site of multiple use 173
1988 (May): site of national park 178
1989 (May): site subject to code of forest practices 179
1990: site for the realisation of sustainable yields 181
1991 (March): site of cyanide anomalies 182
1991 (April): site of national park extension 183
1991 (June): site of hydrological conservation 183
1991 (November): site of biological significance 186
1992: site of heritage river 189
1992 (October): site of acid dyke sampling 190
1993 (June 7): site of hardwood forest resources 190
1993 (June): site of uneconomic mineralisation 193

1994: site of old-growth forest and ecological vegetation classes 194
1995 (July): site of Commonwealth intervention 197
1995 (December): site of multiple forest management 198
1996 (July): site of resource inventory 204
1996 (October): site of national park management strategy 205
1996 (November): site subject to revised code of forest practices 206
1996 (December): site of logging reprieve 207
1997 (January): site of protester base camp 207
1997 (February): site subject to regional forest agreement 208
1997 (March): site of police presence 208
1997 (April): site of arrests (round 1) 208
1997 (May): site earmarked for timber harvesting 209
1997 (June): site of 'scientific lament' 210
1997 (June): site of arrests (round 2) 210
1997 (July): site of public relations exercise 211
1997 (July): site of arrests (round 3) 213
1997 (August): site of geological destruction/indigenous desecration 213
1997 (November): site of 'concluded' logging operations 213
1997 (December): site of police publicity 214
1998 (February): site subject to Magistrates Court decision 214
1998 (March): site of continuing conflict 215
1998 (May): site subject to statutory amendment 215
1998 (May): site of forest operation zone 215
1998 (October): site subject to Supreme Court decision 218
1998 (November): site of flora and fauna reserve 220
1998 (December): site of corporate concern 221
1999 (January): site for immediate timber extraction 221
1999 (February): site invoked at Senate Inquiry 222
1999 (April): site displaying signs of conflict 222
1999 (November): site subject to statutory repeal 223
2000 (February): site of increased conflict 223
2000 (May): site subject of feature article 223
2000 (October): site of police raid 224
Interruption 224

PART C

8 On the Unsaid: Text, Nature(s), Damage 229
Modalities of 'Nature' 229
(Some) criminological implications (toward the acategorical) 250

Conclusion 253

References 259
Index 273

List of Figures

Figure 1	Map displaying location and distribution of forest stands and compartments for Goolengook forest management block, 1992. Sourced from Department of Natural Resources and Environment, Orbost, Victoria	62
Figure 2	Photograph of author standing on the track dividing the northeastern portion of Goolengook forest block from Ada block. The featured tree is most likely a Messmate (eucalyptus obliqua) and stands about 70 metres (220 feet) tall. Photography: Adam Biggs	63
Figure 3	Map displaying sites of biological significance within Goolengook forest management block, 1991. Extracted from Lobert, B.O., Gillespie, G.R., Lunt, I.D., Peacock, R.J. and Robinson, D. (1991) Ecological Survey Report no 35 Flora and Fauna of the Goolengook Forest Block, East Gippsland, Victoria, East Melbourne: Department of Conservation and Environment	127
Figure 4	Photograph of block 839, Goolengook, compartment 513, stand 10, post-logging operations, April 1999. Still held to be sacred by descendants of the Bidwell tribe, the rock was blown apart by forestry workers in order to make room for a logging road approximately 400 metres from the rock debris. For a sense of scale, note the figure sitting on top of the rock abutting the track. Photography: Mark Halsey	191

Acknowledgements

An author writes not from the standpoint of a solitary individual, but from the perspective of a force marked by countless events. In the writing of this book, the following events have mattered to me: visiting the forests of the Errinundra Plateau in South Eastern Australia; learning of the plight of the Powerful Owl, the Spot Tailed Quoll, and the ecosystems they rely upon; and knowing something of the damage likely to occur whenever forests are mapped according to their prescribed functions as opposed to their unknown qualities. Kate Dorsey, John Fitzgerald, Benjamin Pederick, Michael Garrod, Adam Biggs, Simon Holmes, and Mark Rosenthal all, in their singular ways, influenced the writing of this story. Sincere thanks to Ms Antonia Quadara for her assistance in preparing the manuscript.

Publication of this work was assisted by a publication grant from the University of Melbourne.

Versions of chapters 2, 3 and 8 have appeared, respectively, as:

- Halsey, M. (2004) 'Against "Green" Criminology', *British Journal of Criminology*, Vol. 44, No. 6, pp. 833–53, by permission of Oxford University Press;
- Halsey, M. (2005) 'Ecology and Machinic Thought: Nietzsche, Deleuze, Guattari', *Angelaki: Journal of the Theoretical Humanities*, Vol. 10, No. 3, pp. 33–56, by permission of Routledge;
- Halsey, M. (2004) 'Environmental Visions: Deleuze and the Modalities of "Nature"', *Ethics & the Environment*, Vol. 9, No. 2, pp. 33-64, by permission of Indiana University Press.

For Mum, Dad and Nicky.

Introduction

Early in 2001 I visited an exhibition at the South Australian Museum devoted to the extinct thylacine – also known as the 'Tasmanian Tiger'. One display in particular caught my eye – a text from 1886 which ran as follows,

> It is quite time some other name was commonly adopted for the comparatively harmless marsupial, generally spoken of as 'The Tiger'. It is not the tenacious brute the name implies, and under no circumstances would it attack ever a child. On two occasions I have met with recently arrived emigrants who objected to leave town to secure work in the country for fear they or their children might be devoured (*The Tasmanian Mail*, September 1886).

I cite this text because it is a clear example of how words can significantly alter the course of events. Indeed, writers such as Friedrich Nietzsche and Michel Foucault contend that words are themselves events since they are the acoustical outcome of (violent) struggles, impositions, and forgettings (see Nietzsche, 1992; Foucault, 1980a, pp. 139–64). No one knows precisely how many 'tigers' there were prior to Europeans arriving in 1788 in 'Australia'. What is known is that these animals once roamed not just the island of Tasmania but across the mainland of Australia and probably numbered somewhere in the low tens of thousands. Due predominantly to their perceived threat to people and livestock, successive governments of the late nineteenth and early twentieth centuries issued bounties to anyone who could produce a dead tiger. By 1900, around 2000 such bounties had been paid in Tasmania alone. The tiger is believed to have been driven into extinction on the mainland around 3000 years ago. On July 10, 1936, the Tasmanian Government passed legislation to protect 'its' Tasmanian Tigers. However, less than two months later, the last known tiger died in captivity at the Hobart Zoo.

At this point, it is important to ask: What's in a name? In the above example, it would seem necessary to say that the name 'tiger' brought with it nothing less than the urge toward the decimation of a species. And it did so largely because the term 'tiger' took the form of an overcoded signifier – a word capable of projecting (however erroneously) a very particular series of imaginings based around such terms as 'ferocity', 'danger', and 'unpredictability'. In some cultures, though, such as parts of India and Siberia, the tiger signified (and continues to signify) everything majestic and noble. This, of course, was not the case in Australia where it was ascribed demonic characteristics (savage, cunning, ruthless). Ironically, the scientific name given the Tasmanian 'Tiger' was *Didelphis cynocephalus*, which means, literally, 'marsupial with a *dog*-like head'. Being a marsupial, this 'tiger' had a pouch and suckled its young. Although portrayed in folklore and newspapers as preying 'mercilessly' on sheep and other livestock, it is now believed to have spent most of its time eating other small marsupials and birds and even insects when food was particularly scarce. But even this is conjecture since, due to its 'early' extinction, scant little is known about the social habits and life cycle(s) of the thylacine. In short, the capacity to inquire and become acquainted with this animal's various flows (of movement), speeds (of maturation) and intensities (of play, hunting, aggression), was irrevocably interrupted by the will to locate and destroy it. This is not to say that the fate of the thylacine would have been better if it had been spoken of as a kind of dog or a marsupial rather than as a member of the giant cat family. But it is to contend that its fate would have been *different* – perhaps even preferable to the present state of affairs.

The purpose of this brief recounting is to suggest that naming is far from being a neutral or simple process. Instead, naming matters. Names levy effects. They either preclude or leave open particular kinds of potentials, capacities and juxtapositions of bodies. Within sociological and criminological circles, this is something that has been known for some time (see Becker, 1963; Goffman, 1963; Lemert, 1967). But in the main such work has confined itself to an examination of the effects which flow from the application of juridical categories (criminal, delinquent) or from the social categories which signify some kind of marginal existence (deviant, queer, abnormal). Whilst in no way wishing to downplay the importance of such work, I want to suggest that an analysis of such labels generates a fairly limited understanding of the factors which contribute to 'social harm'. On a first count, labels (names, categories – call them whatever) need themselves to be put into critical relief – they need, in other words, to be given a genealogy (a body capable of displaying the struggles and costs that belie their usage in 'everyday speech'). Secondly, I think there are a whole raft of processes which contribute *en masse* to social, and in particular, ecological harm (the two most often infusing the other) (see Guattari, 2000). Such processes remain under-theorised by labelling theorists as well as criminological and socio-legal theory more generally. Accordingly, one of the key purposes of this book is to offer a micropolitical account of the evolution of such taken-for-granted concepts as 'Nature', 'sustainability', and 'environmental harm'. For what law prescribes as permissible in respect of Nature, and *ipso facto*, what it deems to be ecologically criminal, is intimately linked to how such terms have been spoken of, imagined, and otherwise deployed over time. To believe other than this is to turn away from the ethical, and at times violent, dimensions that go along with speaking and writing the world.

It is *the process, impact, and ethics of naming Nature* that is the subject of this book. In more specific terms, this book is centred around a study of the categories and thresholds used over time to map and transform a particular area of what can loosely be termed 'forested terrain'. And it is a study of the socio-ecological costs arising from such thresholds and transformations. Although written from a criminological and socio-legal perspective, this is not, however, a study specifically about 'crime' nor indeed about 'environmental crime'. It is instead about the way such terms as 'harm', 'sustainability', 'ecological significance', 'value', and 'right', have been coded, decoded, and recoded by various means, at various times, with particular results. Further, this is not a study about 'justice' – at least, not in the transcendental sense of the term. But it is most certainly about the way law marks the earth. More particularly, it is about the composition of the various knowledges law calls upon to justify its 'justness', its 'rightness', and its 'comprehensivity' when it permits, for instance, the conversion of a 10,000 year old ecosystem into scantling for houses or paper for copying machines. In simple terms, this is a book about the modes of envisaging and enunciating a particular geopolitical space over time and the violences which make such visions and enunciations possible. As shall become clear, such violence has little if anything to do with traditional weapons such as guns, fists, or knives. Instead, it is *a violence borne by way of the slow and largely inaudible march of the categories and thresholds associated with using and abusing Nature*. This, therefore, is a work intended to (further) challenge orthodox framings of the relationships spanning crime, law, and environment.

The case of Goolengook

Since late 1996, a dedicated group of persons (sometimes called protesters, other times called 'ferals', 'greenies', 'dole bludgers', and the like) have agitated against the logging activities carried out in Goolengook forest block located in far eastern Victoria, Australia. During such time, there have been verbal and physical confrontations, hundreds of arrests, dozens of court hearings (including one at Supreme Court level), and numerous attempts by authorities to divide the body of Goolengook up in a manner deemed fair and equitable to all parties. At the time of writing, protesters are taking up position in and around coupes scheduled for logging in 2005. Whether arrests will occur is difficult to say. What is certain, though, is that the forest in this part of the world will be further depleted of processes and relationships little understood by governments, scientists, foresters and even by protesters and environmental groups.

Ostensibly, there are many ways to write about this conflict. Typically, however, this has involved talking about Goolengook and other such forest conflicts in terms of greenies versus loggers, or greenies versus government, or, on occasion, loggers versus government. Like most David and Goliath narratives, such accounts make for interesting reading. But stories based on dichotomies such as those just mentioned do not, arguably, sufficiently articulate the nuances contributing to forest conflict as *event* – that is, as something which is both a discursive invention (i.e. an object of our policies, laws, imaginings) *and* a body consistently eluding efforts to frame, categorise, think, speak – in short, *represent*, 'its' aspects.

In an attempt to write forest conflict as event (as a site of intensities permanently oscillating between a becoming-the-same and a becoming-other), this book applies the ideas of French poststructuralist writers Gilles Deleuze and Felix Guattari to what is now the longest running forest conflict to occur in Australia since European settlement/occupation. As will become clear, the conflict at Goolengook is about something much more than 'forests' – Australian or otherwise. Indeed the struggles taking place in and over this area raise critically important questions concerning who we are (subjectivity), what we can do (power), what we can know (epistemology), and who we might become (desire). Moreover, it raises questions as to the ontological consistency and ecological utility of terms like 'we', 'society', 'global', 'Nature', 'environment', 'forest block', 'old-growth', 'truth', 'harm', 'right', 'crime' and so forth. A primary aim of this book, therefore, is to demonstrate how a geopolitical terrain has been *textually configured* over time (by law, by management plans, by mining leases, by Indigenous knowledges, and other) in order to subsequently show how, why and for whom it 'works', as well as how, why and for whom it recurs as a problematic site.

Writing a micropolitical account of forest conflict will involve three interrelated tasks. In the first instance, it will mean *tracing* the various texts (or abstract machines) which have heralded the imposition of particular modes of environmental regulation. In the second, it will mean *articulating* how various of Deleuze and Guattaris' concepts impact the dichotomies underpinning such regulatory policies. And in the third, a micropolitics of environmental (forest) conflict will involve *mapping* the kinds of assemblages and abstract machines capable of creating new configurations of bodies and ecologies – a configuration which might allow a becoming-the-same (becoming-anti-ecological) to find the space to become-other (to become-subsistent).

Telling the story

The book is assembled in the following way. Chapter 1 offers an overview of modernist accounts of environmental damage/conflict. I demonstrate that each of the five main ecological schools of thought underpinning contemporary environmental regulatory mechanisms are unable to account for the highly complex relationships pertaining between language, power, knowledge and various identities/social roles. More specifically, I argue that modern accounts of environmental damage proceed in monolithic fashion (the irresponsible consumer monolith under liberal ecology, the capitalist monolith under ecomarxism, the patriarchal monolith under ecofeminism, the hierarchical monolith under deep ecology, and the domination monolith under social ecology) and that this produces a hypostatised rendering of the 'causes' and 'effects' of ecological ruin. Here, a range of problems (concerning chiefly language, subjectivity, and the textual production of damaged or 'pristine' terrains) are shown to disappear below the grid of intelligibility made possible by modernist ecologist thought.

Chapter 2 explicates the way in which environmental issues have been constructed and theorised within criminology to date. Three broad crimino-ecophilosophical approaches are identified (spanning the five ecological schools discussed in Chapter 1) and the shortcomings associated with each are discussed. Critically, I show how 'green' criminology has largely neglected to address the micropolitical forces which contribute *en masse* to environmental problems (and, indeed, to what is framed as ecological damage). These micropolitical forces (identified later in the book as 'Modalities of Nature') have to do with the way Nature is *envisioned*, the *speed* at which Nature is transformed, the *categories* or lexicon used to 'build' Nature, and the *proximities* (or relations between bodies) which stem from the preceding modalities. I suggest that in order for criminology to know something of environmental conflict and regulation it must first understand the limits embedded within its own discourse concerning a) what counts as a criminological problem, and b) what might be done about such issues. The chapter concludes by calling for a theoretical approach capable of addressing these issues and the impact these have on the legal and extra-legal limits of environmental damage.

Chapter 3 is centred around the concept of *machinic thought* and its significance for thinking through the sources of environmental conflict and new forms of environmental regulation. Here, a way of thinking-acting is advanced that regards as futile all programmes aimed at the final resolution of the struggle between humans and Nature, science and opinion, or, in Nietzsche's terms, good and evil. The chapter therefore introduces the notion of difference (or the acategorical) and shows how and why such a concept is critical to ecological matters. Chiefly, I argue that modern modes of environmental regulation are built around systems of representation which do violence to the production of difference – the difference immanent to persons, rivers, deserts, forests, invertebrates – in short, the difference immanent to life itself. It is in this context that the work of Nietzsche (who, with the possible exception of Thales, can be regarded as the philosopher of flows/becoming-immanent par excellence) is surveyed. In particular, Nietzsche's work on rhetoric and culture is used to open up the isomorphic relationship between words and things such that questions which ask 'What is Nature?' or 'What is environmental harm?' become, at least temporarily, unanswerable – perhaps even (given a genealogical standpoint) non-sensical.

The chapter then moves to a substantive discussion of the work of Deleuze and Guattari – two writers who have contributed significantly to the creation of a lexicon capable of subverting the binaries (humans/Nature, cause/effect, harm/benign conduct, crime/order, law/disorder) characteristic of modern thought. Several of their key concepts are clearly explicated and their relevance to environmental matters made plain. Particular emphasis is placed on their notion of a *plane of consistency* since it is this concept which allows such terms as 'Nature', 'environment', 'wilderness' – all those 'things' which form the traditional objects of ecological struggles and crimino-ecophilosophical discourse – to be placed to one side. This strategy fits with one of the central aims of the book – namely, to move away from categorical accounts of environmental damage (where all things are known ahead of time) in order that Nature might be conceived as something problematic, as something fleeting, as something which eludes efforts to quantify, capture or code. Overall, then, the chapter is designed to convey the basic premises and strengths of poststructuralist thought with respect to problems of Nature/Naturing.

The fourth chapter briefly contextualises the key site for analysis (that is Goolengook forest block) and clarifies the methodology and terminology engaged to bring this site into (and out of) relief throughout the remainder of the book. This is a critically important chapter as it sets out the technique used to 'free' particular sites of environmental contestation from the political, legal, scientific and popular renderings that traditionally constrain the shape of environmental discourse. I show how and why disputed terrains are best conceived as *events* and that each event needs to be written in terms of its multiplicities in place of its prescribed functions. In keeping with Deleuze's reading of Spinoza, the question of what each disputed area *is* or is not (essence) is replaced by the question of what each terrain can or cannot *do* (affect) subsequent to the production of different texts (historic, legal, scientific, corporate). When matched with those given in Chapter 3, the concepts outlined in this chapter (machine, assemblage, fold) facilitate the production of a *chirographic machine*. In essence, the function of this machine will be to produce an archive of naming and envisioning capable of dislodging orthodox renderings of Nature and its so-called 'proper' relationship to Man over time. This machine – this meticulous documenting of major and minor texts with respect to a 'single' terrain – assists the emergence of the *becoming-other* of Goolengook as event.

The production of the chirographic machine occurs over the course of Chapters 5, 6 and 7 which collectively serve to relay something of the impact of two centuries of (European) textual incorporation of the site in question. Chapter 5 shows – to a particular chronological moment – the ways in which various texts named, categorised, and ascribed different 'values' to this space. It portrays, in other words, the texts which contributed to Goolengook 'becoming-known' (to Europeans) (beginning with archaeological evidence of Aboriginal occupation around the time of the last ice age and concluding with the geodetic survey documents which heralded the arrival of roads and industrialisation).

Chapter 6 cites and deconstructs the texts that helped to configure Goolengook as exhibiting one – and only one – kind of quality. That is, it demonstrates the changes in the mode of envisioning, transforming, and speaking Nature which contributed to Goolengook 'becoming-forest'. It begins with the *Forests Act* 1907, moves to an examination of the impact of technological advances (chainsaw, footed track, articulated vehicle), international events (World War II, housing construction boom), as well as 'natural disasters' (the Great Fire of 1939), and concludes with a discussion of the instruments which allowed south eastern Victoria to be converted into a series of forest blocks (thus signifying the privileging of industrial processes over geological speeds and rhythms).

Chapter 7 details the texts which have subsequently conferred upon Goolengook a multitude of possible qualities, values and uses. Here, I examine the different methodologies and epistemological assumptions embedded in these textual encodings and their subsequent role(s) in producing Goolengook as a site of conflict (as 'becoming-contested'). The chapter begins with a text which constructs portions of Goolengook as a place of unremarked potential and concludes with a reference to this site a place subject to police raids.

The final chapter of the book explicates the implications of preceding discussions for orthodox accounts of environmental harm/conflict. In particular, it examines the relationship spanning a) the modernist 'scopic' regimes within which Nature has been seen or sensed, b) the way in which Nature is named or spoken of, c) the speed at which Nature is textually (re)produced, and d) the lived effects and *a*ffects of such Natures on various bodies (human and nonhuman). It does this by drawing from Deleuze's own work as well as his collaborations with Guattari. The chapter shows how law and science (as well as other discursive regimes) propound a spurious (if not potentially lethal) conception of Nature due to the inability of each to grapple with the acategorical – which, for Deleuze, equates to the inability to account for 'the differences borne by individuals' as against 'individual differences'. A call is made for modernist conceptions of Nature to be put aside in order that various bodies (chiefly those of criminologists) might better understand the problematics attending any and all texts purporting to speak authoritatively/categorically about the world. Following Deleuze's lead – and building on evidence and ideas presented in previous chapters – it is argued that modern environmental discursive frames have envisioned Nature in terms of populations and species (and, more rarely, sub-species) at the expense of developing a lexicon or mode of seeing/communicating which is capable of accounting for the temporal, spatial and physical particularities of seemingly 'similar' bodies and the affective relations they are capable of entering into.

In this way, the final chapter responds to questions which have seldom if ever been posed with regard to environmental regulation: namely, What has it been possible and impossible to see and say with regard to Nature?; Which units of environmental management are politically tolerable and which threaten to throw state expertise into disarray?; What is the relationship between the rate and type of texts which speak of various terrains and the associated contestations which arise over such territories?; And, finally, to paraphrase Deleuze and Guattari, *Who* does environmental conflict think it is? (meaning, in effect, who names environmental damage and at what cost has such naming occurred?).

Overall, my aim in this book is to engage the events occurring at and around Goolengook forest block in a way that allows each of us to think through precisely what it is we do when we 'interact' with, write about, monitor, test, and legislate for or against, Nature. For criminology, for socio-legal theorists, for philosophers – indeed for anyone with an interest in environmental regulation, thresholds of ecological harm, and the like – the complexities surrounding the management of this terrain will hopefully demonstrate both the violence and untenability of the ontological assumptions that presently inform our views about 'forests', 'rivers', 'endangered species' and so forth. More specifically, my hope is that the current work contributes to a wider appreciation of the costs associated with imposing binary schemas not just on each other, but on other species and environs as well.

PART A

Chapter 1

Modernity and Ecological Thought: A Brief Critique

> Nature is always value-less, but has been *given* value.
>
> Nietzsche, *The Gay Science*, 1974, §301

> We're tired of trees. We should stop believing in trees, roots, and radicles. They've made us suffer too much. All of aborescent culture is founded on them, from biology to linguistics ... Many people have a tree growing in their heads, but the brain itself is much more a grass than a tree.
>
> Deleuze and Guattari, *A Thousand Plateaus*, 1996, p. 15

Unlike philosophy, the discipline of ecology is a very recent phenomenon emerging at a time when the tenets of modernity – faith in scientific reason, acceptance of the ontological legitimacy of categories dividing organisms, desire for rational and detached observation – were heavily entrenched. According to Foucault (1997), 'life' itself – the very thing of which ecology tries to speak – did not exist prior to the nineteenth century (see also Doyle, 1997). Life and the study of its interrelations (that is, ecology) are therefore decidedly late arrivals among humanity's accoutrements. But like most sciences, ecology has had little problem believing in the outright ontological validity of its key concepts – Nature, deleterious effect, organism, population, to name several. These are, according to ecology, *things in themselves*. They exist in spite of the prejudices and desires of scientists. They have, in other words, an essential (Aristotelian) status.

Or do they? Perhaps these and other taken-for-granted concepts (such as cause, effect, species, bioregion) are less rigid and less familiar than they first appear. Perhaps these concepts in fact bear *no* intrinsic relation to the world they seek to illuminate. Perhaps, in short, ecology is an *affect* of modernity – an affect, that is, of the modern episteme and its incessant search for *certainty* (of existence), *closure* (around organisms and inert matter), and *foundation* (of life). Deleuze (1986, p. 99) writes, 'The affect is independent of all determinate space-time; but it is none the less created in a history which produces it as the expressed and the expression of a space or a time, of an epoch or milieu ...'. Ecology can be considered an affect of modernity insofar as it is something intangible (we cannot touch ecology, hold ecology, hear ecology, and so on) *yet* 'knowable' (since it charts by way of scientific discourse its own series of relations, speeds, thresholds, and so on). We do not relate to an 'essential' ecology (an ecology in and of itself) but to an idea, to a force, to a moment which induces in us a certain combination of feelings and emotions (that is, affections) about Nature and its potentials, attributes, powers and limits. If this is so, it becomes necessary to ask questions *not* so much about 'ecology' but about how *modernity* has characterised Man and the problem of Nature. For it is modernity that rises up through ecological thought and holds it ransom to the quest for complete knowledge of earth and all its 'beings'. Arguably, repeated attempts to meet this quest have helped build some of the most ecologically damaging alliances and processes of the last 10,000 years – the time when sedentary social relations first emerged. But how, precisely, does modernity relate to practices of human-induced environmental damage – damage perpetuated, as Nietzsche would say, on a 'grand scale'? Moreover, how has modernity impacted various socio-ecological perspectives? These are the questions examined below.

Modernity, humanity, rationality

Modernity, as opposed to modernism or modernisation, stretches back to the Renaissance (see Featherstone, 1993, p. 3). This, of course, was a time when humanity's assumed place at the centre of the universe was looking increasingly precarious due largely to the work of Galileo (Man as peripheral force). But with the discovery of a rational, purposive subject (via Descartes' infamous *cogito*) in the eighteenth century, and the subsequent rise of the human sciences in the nineteenth, humanity (read Man) again assumed prime position in the great scheme of (words and) things (Foucault, 1997).[1] The work of Darwin, however, again problematised the human condition. Here, Man was revealed to be little more than a deterritorialised ape (see generally Deleuze and Guattari, 1994a). Nietzsche added to this decentring by writing Man in terms of 'a piece of fate' and as a *problem to be overcome* rather than admired. Taken together, these were serious blows to the burgeoning disciplines of, amongst others, psychiatry, psychology, and criminology. In attempting to locate the salient aspects of the modern subject each of these instead produced variation upon variation concerning such matters as pain thresholds, susceptibility to disease, metabolic rate, morphology, propensity toward offending, and so forth (see Foucault, 1997). Despite this setback, the modernist project continued to thrive. Only it did so along quite different lines.

With the transition from feudalism to capitalism well on its way, writers such as Comte, Marx, Durkheim and Weber – all of whom were working at a time when Man's essential nature was found to reside neither in his soul, his mind, nor his physicality – sought instead to reveal the essential features of *society*. If the 'enduring' structures of society could be located, this, it was thought, would reveal something of the immutable qualities of Man as well. And, continuing this line of thought, if Man's essence could be found this would provide the *grund* on which to build the 'good society' (including, of course, a model set of criminal codes and

1 The 'founding' of consciousness would later prompt Foucault to observe that 'man is a recent invention' not yet three hundred years old (1997, p. 386).

laws). In other words, sociology – the scientific study of groups and social structures – would attempt to do for/to Man what psychology, (positivist) criminology and psychiatry could not. In relation to those writers mentioned above, society was said, respectively, to reflect the dictates of 'evolution', 'the economic base', 'social facts' and 'status groups'. And the essence of Man was given to reside in his biology, in his interactions with Nature (the forces of production), in his ability to use language or law, and in his desire for prestige or particular modes of consumption. Again, Man emerged here as a fragmented phenomenon. Indeed, from this point (around the late nineteenth century), Man, somewhat illogically, would be attributed *many* 'essences' (consciousness, rationality, will, aggression, sentience) and aligned to *numerous* teleologies (to become self-aware, to act in accordance with preordained rules, to engage in purposeful activity, to resist violence, to avoid pain). Where modernity had sought, via a broad spectrum of positivist methods, to locate a comforting and lasting foundation, it instead produced a disconcerting *aporia*. Man had neglected to understand one thing – that not only does,

> [s]cience transform[ ] the living; it pulverizes it. Instead of turning [life] into a *base* on which it could find support, science makes it more and more artificial. The more the living learns about itself through biology, [and one might say psychology, criminology, sociology and so forth] the more it knows it will never be able to draw any information about the way it *should* live. The split between what is [i.e. ontology] and what should be [i.e. ethic] has never been as strong as today (Ewald, 1995, p. 283 emphases added).

The summations of Comte, Marx, Durkheim, and, to a lesser extent, Weber, epitomise(d) the modernist project – both in terms of their subject matter and the epistemological assumptions underpinning it (assumptions concerning subject and object, word and world, truth and falsity, science and rhetoric, and so forth). In conjunction with much earlier work by Descartes, Locke, Hume, Rousseau, and Hobbes, this 'oeuvre' produced conceptions of subjectivity and, correspondingly, notions of knowledge and power, very much akin to those which inform the political systems and environmental regulatory strategies currently operating throughout the western world. As one commentator has remarked, 'Modernity … may be in crisis but it continues to shape the contours of our lives' (Seidman, 1994, p. 1).

Carrington (1994, p. 263), following the work of Hebdige, has tendered three defining characteristics of modernity: 'its essentializing conception of history, politics, society and the transcendental subject, its teleological search for origins or causes, and its utopian solutions to the problems of modern[ity]'. As if speaking to all three of these, Turner (1995, p. 24) has remarked,

> We are probably prone to consider our age not only as uniquely special but also as unmatched in the pervasiveness and depth of its crisis. Our age is struck forcefully and self-consciously by its modernity, its secularization and its nihilism. Perhaps the conflict between the modernists and the postmodernists should be seen precisely in the context of such global crises, namely that it is no longer clear that dependence on human rationality will be sufficient in principle to respond to these global crises, precisely because there is

> the suspicion that the crises are actually produced by the same instrumental rationality. There is now the widespread suspicion that global disasters such as the holocaust [and one might also add nuclear accidents, ozone depletion, deforestation, acid rain, salinization] are not an abnormal or perverted digression in the unfolding of western rationality, but in fact the primary and ordinary illustration of instrumental rationalism in practice.

It is clear that modernity is characterised by many things. However, and as indicated here, one of its defining features – one that guides and constrains the overall composition of the modernist project – is its abiding faith in the ability of *instrumental reason* to resolve any and all problems thrown up by society or Nature. As Bauman (1995, p. 8) puts it, 'Modernity is about conflict-*resolution*, and about admitting of no contradictions except conflicts amenable to, and awaiting, resolution'. Modernity, in other words, is that which seeks to expunge all semblance of ambiguity by invoking or, more accurately, *imposing* its own particular 'will to truth' as the universal means by which to 'improve' society (see generally Nietzsche and Foucault). Modernity is the age in which all things contingent and particular are (re)presented as necessary and universal. In this sense,

> The era of modernity had been marked by an active superiority: part of the world constituted the rest as inferior – either as crude, still unprocessed 'raw material' in need of cleaning and refinement, or a temporarily extant relic of the past. Whatever could not be brought up to the superior standards, was clearly destined for the existence of subordination. Western practices defined the rest as pliable or malleable substance still to be given shape. This active superiority meant the right of the superior to proselytize, to design the suitable form of life for the others, to refuse to grant authority to the ways of life which did not fit that design (Bauman, 1988, p. 220).

The rush to colonise, proselytise, and hypostatise earth – that is, the urge to subdue and make Nature known through the scientific method and the structures of modernity more generally – are key processes contributing to environmental conflict. As shall be seen, what is particularly unsettling is the degree to which these same processes are invoked as its (re)solution.

Modernity, nature, ecophilosophy

The great majority of academic and governmental work on environmental regulation embodies (consciously or otherwise) the methods and epistemologies of modernity (for overviews of the main environmental perspectives see O'Riordan, 1976; Dobson, 1990; Eckersley, 1992; Vincent, 1993). Typically, Nature is spoken of in a manner that assumes the earth is ontologically unproblematic. Nature is cast as a given, as a discrete entity, as already 'there'. It is presented socially, legally and politically as something knowable and ultimately controllable in *all* its aspects. And it becomes the task (or, more accurately, the unfulfilled promise) of 'value-free' science to equip administrators with the technologies for such control. As will become apparent, modernist environmental accounts tend to carry quite rigid templates about what can and should form the object of environmental regulatory policies, and indeed what can and should be the focal points of environmental struggle. This is arguably the case for the five main environmental perspectives presently informing programmes for 'ecological renewal' in various parts of the world – *liberal ecology* (World Commission on Environment and Development, 1987; Barbier, 1989; Pearce et al., 1989; Barde and Pearce, 1991; Pearce, 1991), *ecomarxism* (Bahro, 1984; Castillina, 1985; Dunkley, 1992; Pepper, 1993), *ecofeminism* (Plumwood, 1986), *deep ecology* (Leopold, 1970; Naess, 1973, 1989; Devall and Sessions, 1985; Tobias, 1985), and *social ecology* (Bookchin, 1986, 1987; Clark, 1990; Merchant, 1992).

The buzz word or concept informing each of these philosophies is 'ecological sustainability'. This notion, it might be said, is the *raison d'être* of modern environmental theorising. Ecological sustainability has to do with uncovering the precise combination of social policies, economic principles, cultural practices and legal rules that will ensure the viability of ecosystemic processes over the short and long term. Another way of saying this is that the search for ecological sustainability translates into the search for an enduring equilibrium between humans and Nature. Modern forms of environmental regulation (whether this be polluter pays programmes, bioregionalism, or whatever) attempt to put everything in its 'rightful' place. Where once the sole objective was to control the insane, the young, the feminine, the vagrant and the deviant, the objective in recent times has been to arrest the nonhuman, the inorganic, the inert – in short, the so-called 'natural world'. This should not be taken to mean that modernity has a monopoly over the vicissitudes of what is ecologically sustainable and what is not. The flow of waste – the presence of an undesired excess of matter-energy – has been secreted in various quantities and guises for all peoples (Markham, 1994). But what is utterly unique to modernity is the *speed*, *scale* and *intensity* of such secretions (for example acid rain, dioxin, nuclear radiation, salinisation). It could be said that modernity has been forced to confront the flow of waste as a *globally* recurring event rather than as a localised or clearly delineated problem (Beck, 1992). Of course, the paradoxical trait of modernist environmental perspectives is that they continue to view the sum of the latter as equivalent to the former. The critical point here is not that the whole is greater than the sum of its parts. It is, rather, that the composition of the part and the whole have more to do with the comings and goings of discursive and political inventions than with a knowable, stable or eternal circumstances. In the remainder of this chapter, therefore, the basic tenets and problems of the five perspectives previously mentioned will be discussed. Such an explication should provide a useful point from which, in subsequent chapters, to set out the relative strengths of a poststructuralist approach to environmental conflict.

Liberal ecology

For liberal ecologists, environmental conflict tends to be reduced to problems of participatory democracy and unresponsive market mechanisms – to a lack, that is, of direct public influence over environmental decisions and of economic models capable of 'costing' environmental damage. Typical here a remark, made by such bodies as the Resource Assessment Commission of Australia, stating that '... the main "cause" of pollution is commonly known as market failure – that is, the failure of the market to correctly signal the cost of the pollution activity ...' (1989, p. 25). In all instances liberal ecology views as *compatible* both the long-term health of ecosystems *and* the maintenance of the structures inherent to liberal democratic/late-capitalist societies. 'Ecology', in this scenario, is taken to be a discrete field of knowledge whose foundations for observing, knowing and predicting events is construed as ontologically consistent as opposed to politically, historically and socially conditioned. Science, therefore, is ascribed a privileged position in terms of its ability to understand and address environmental problems. The corollary of this is that lay or minor knowledges of, say, air pollution or toxic waste, are taken to be secondary, deviant or otherwise unqualified to speak (on the relationship between 'lay' and 'expert' knowledge of environmental problems see Litfin, 1994, pp. 78–176; Wynne, 1996).[2] For the most part, liberal ecology is likely to reside in the armatures of government where the main task is to study and report on (predefined) ecological issues in politically sensitive ways – that is, in ways which do not fundamentally challenge the will and authority of the (capitalist) state.

In Australia, the 'classic' texts embodying liberal ecology were first disseminated under the federal Labor Government during the late 1980s/early 1990s (see Ecologically Sustainable Development documents for relevant industrial sectors). The concept of ecologically sustainable development gained formal recognition in the World Commission on Environment and Development's publication called *Our Common Future*. In this report ecologically sustainable development is defined as 'meeting the needs of the present without compromising the ability of future generations to meet their own needs' (World Commission on Environment and Development, 1987, p. 8). As a set of principles – embodying such ideals as 'optimum sustainable yield', 'reasonable precautionary measures', 'an environment adequate to [*human*] health and well-being' – ecologically sustainable development constitutes a refrain which governments, businesses and environmental groups alike come back to time and time again – as if to ensure that the ship of sustainability is on course and well clear of dangerous waters (that is other environmental philosophies) (World Commission on Environment and Development, 1987, pp. 348–49). Indeed, one commentator cites evidence that ecologically sustainable development has become 'the environmental mandate for the world' and, therefore, 'the central pivot around which all environmental law will ultimately revolve' (Tranter, 1999, pp. 292–93).

Presently, the principles of ecologically sustainable development inform the work of such bodies as Environment Australia, the Commonwealth Scientific and Industrial Research Organisation (CSIRO), the Victorian Department of

2 Witness, for instance, the marginalisation of residential concerns over particulate pollution from City Link tunnel stacks in Richmond, Victoria, or the efforts by the Victorian government to quell fears over the siting of a toxic waste repository amongst market gardens at Werribee.

Sustainability and Environment (DSE) and their State and Territory equivalent(s), and the various Environment Protection Authorities/Agencies (EPAs) throughout the country. At first glance, the issues addressed by such bodies appear to be of a very serious kind – greenhouse gas emissions, biodiversity, salinisation, water quality and so forth. However, in the majority of instances what ultimately counts as 'ecological sustainability' is whatever fits into the ebb and flow of commodity production/consumption. One liberal ecological strategy even frames its object in terms of 'sustaining *our* living *wealth*', perpetuating in typical fashion, a thoroughly anthropocentric and economistic model of biota (Department of Natural Resources and Environment, 1997). What matters to liberal ecology, therefore, is such things as more efficient kinds of transport (instead of the elimination of the combustion engine), stronger reinforced steel for oil tankers (instead of elimination of oil production), temporary reductions in fishing quotas (instead of the elimination of drift-nets and longlines), safer tailings dams (instead of the elimination of uranium mining), longer-lasting light bulbs (instead of the elimination of coal production) and so forth (see, for instance, South Australian Government, 1996; State of the Environment Advisory Council, 1996; National Greenhouse Gas Inventory Committee, 1997; Victorian Environment Protection Authority, 1998; Environment Australia, 1998; State Government of Victoria, 'Cleaner Production/Clear Profit').

In addition to (consciously?) helping the state to maintain the conditions for the exponential (if marginally more 'efficient') consumption of resources, liberal ecology aims first and foremost to effect the desires (or consumption habits) of the middle class or 'typical consumer'. Here, there is the liberal contention that the (conspicuous) consumption patterns of the middle class are the primary cause of the environmental crisis (which is in fact many crises). And further that the burden of environmental recovery should ideally be borne by those who consume most (for example government departments, big business, young up-and-coming professionals). The message to each of these groups is that being a good environmental citizen is *easy*. Indeed all one need do is 'turn off lights', 'use water sparingly', 'recycle goods', 'keep engines tuned' and so forth. This is the environmental message emanating, in the main, from Environment Protection Authorities across Australia, the US and elsewhere (see Victorian Environment Protection Authority, 'Managing Air Quality') to the conspicuous or well-to-do consumer. But in reality, the brunt of environmental problems and their day to day solution typically ends up residing in the fears, demands and knowledges of particular groups of citizens – the poor, the geographically isolated, the young, and the uneducated (see Williams, 1996). That is, liberal ecology tends to frame the 'solution' to environmental problems without due regard to the range and type of ecological dilemmas that flow from differences in race, geography, gender and class. This is, of course, yet another example of how the intended 'address' of liberalism is often discontinuous with its lived impact.

Under liberal ecology, then, 'ecological renewal' equates to how effectively those with medium and high level incomes can sort their garbage into its constituent parts (plastics, papers, metals, and so forth). Relatedly, the advent of environmental renewal becomes – just like the problem of crime prevention, unemployment, and public health – a personalised issue (which in one sense it is) rather than the undesired effect of the confluence of a range of structural/social and subjective processes. In its attempt to diagnose the cause of environmental problems liberal ecology neglects to understand that *all* of us – not just any one class, gender, race or geographic location – are immersed in highly complex cycles of environmental damage. The problem – which, in contorted fashion, actually recurs as a 'solution' for the materialist ethic of liberal ecology – is that these are framed as *anything other* than 'ecologically harmful' (for example eating breakfast as divorced from growing wheat and clearing native vegetation; buying a gold wedding ring as logically distinct from mineral exploration and heap-leach/cyanide mining; wearing a tea-shirt as unrelated to irrigating cotton farms and depleting freshwater rivers; turning on a light as separate to mining coal and producing greenhouse gases; using copy paper as a process distinct from clearfelling forests and fragmenting and simplifying habitat). What is needed, then, is a sense of how people *frame* and *neutralise* the ecological implications flowing from their conduct with earth on a daily indeed hourly basis. Not only is liberal ecology uninterested in this task, it also lacks the theoretical lens through which to view such an issue. Liberal ecology thus speaks 'in vain' of ecological sustainability. It is vanity.

Ecomarxism

Ecomarxism is the antithesis of liberal ecology. Marx himself, of course, rarely mentioned environmental problems. But the few passages in which he (and Engels) did speak of the environmental degradation have, somewhat predictably, been invoked as 'proof' of Marx's (and the marxist) commitment to environmental issues and values (Parsons, 1977; Benton, 1989, 1992; Grundmann, 1991; Raskin and Bernow, 1991; Luzon, 1992; Vaillancourt, 1992; Leff, 1993). For ecomarxists the primary cause of environmental conflict is capitalism, or indeed any system based on exponential material growth and antagonistic class relations. There are, according to this perspective, strict limits to the carrying capacity of the planet and these are in danger of being permanently transgressed due to the unrestrained private production, circulation, consumption and accumulation of goods and services beyond 'immediate human need'. Behind exploitative relations of production, contend ecomarxists, lurks not just the alienation and degradation of Man (or (his) 'species being') but the alienation and degradation of Nature as well. The 'solution' to environmental degradation is therefore framed in terms of common ownership of the means of production and the application of 'objective' scientific data to environmental problems like the greenhouse effect, hazardous waste and deforestation. Significantly, ecomarxists believe the *only* kind of society capable of delivering ecological sustainability is socialism (state) or, better still, communism (stateless). Marx himself writes, 'Communism as completed naturalism is humanism and as completed humanism is naturalism. It is the genuine solution of the antagonism between *man* and *nature* and between man and man … It is the solution to the riddle of history and knows itself to be this solution' (Marx, 1988, p. 89 emphases added).

As a tool for understanding and pulling apart the *macro* dynamics and trends of capitalism, marxism (still) stands as a considerable force. However, as a means of diverting ecological conflict or elucidating the micropolitical aspects of ecological damage, *eco*marxism contains a number of problematic elements. The first of these has to do with the conception of humanity (or Man) pervading the marxist oeuvre. Marx was firmly of the Aristotelian view that what separated Man from all other species was 'rationality', or, in Marx's own words, the capacity for 'free conscious activity' (Marx, 1977, p. 73). For ecomarxists, the deployment of rationality toward 'benign ends' stands as a key component of programmes aimed at environmental renewal. Here, reason – just like consciousness and truth – is assumed to be a force capable of exposing the ideologies and untruths that prevent the 'essence' or 'underlying cause' of *the* environmental crisis being fully revealed. This, needless to say, is a highly dubious epistemological position to take. As Foucault has aptly demonstrated, rationality (in addition to being a discursive invention) is a *technology of power* that suppresses and marginalises as many possibilities as it creates. 'Discursive practices', Foucault writes, 'are characterized by the delimitation of a field of objects, the definition of a legitimate perspective for the agent of knowledge, and the fixing of norms for the elaboration of concepts and theories. Thus, each discursive practice implies a play of prescriptions that designate its exclusions and choices' (Foucault, 1980a, p. 199).

The concerns raised here extend also to the ecomarxist contention that there is or ever could be such a thing as 'objective scientific data'. Under such a scenario, science (with its rhetorically problematic assumptions concerning cause, effect, salient variables, and peripheral occurrences) becomes the metanarrative for the framing and solution of environmental problems. Witness the following remark by Engels, '… [W]e, with flesh, blood, and brain, belong to nature, and exist in its midst, and […] all our mastery of it consists in the fact that we have the advantage over all other creatures of *being able to know and correctly apply its laws*' (quoted in Parsons, 1977, p. 179 emphases added). Passages such as this extol an unbridled faith in the capacity of scientific reason to both decipher Nature's secrets and provide a blueprint for social relations (the 'good society'). And yet, arguably, such faith has come at considerable socio-ecological cost. Indeed, far from alleviating environmental pressures, the study and subsequent application of Nature's 'laws' to various problems (the problem of war, the problem of durability, the problem of reproduction, the problem of pleasure, the problem of supply, the problem of communication, the problem of construction, the problem of energy, the problem of mobility, the problem of consumption) has *facilitated* all manner of hazardous events (nuclear weapons testing, asbestos, thalidomide, cigarettes, genetically modified foods, pulp mill effluents, clearfell logging, coal dust, photochemical smog, ozone depletion). What is thoroughly unsettling here is that each of these events (in addition to countless others) were, at various stages, held by science – that metanarrative of and for Truth – to be harm*less*. Of course, this is not to suggest that all science is bad science. It is however to argue that any perspective placing the discursive possibilities arising from the deployment of scientific methods above all competing knowledges, is likely to be a perspective that *produces* as many social and environmental problems as it 'resolves'.

Wedded to this idea is the fact that ecomarxists tend – despite their materialist origins – to forget that science and subjectivity do not occupy discrete universes but mutually inform one another. It is not a matter of Man (*qua* subject) wielding and freely directing an independent object (*qua* scientific knowledge). As Foucault puts it,

> [I]n scientific practice, wouldn't the subject as much as the object of knowledge be constituted? And isn't the historical origin of a science to be found precisely in this reciprocal genesis of the subject and the object? What is the truth-effect that is produced in this way? Its consequence would be that there isn't just one truth that is 'given'. And this doesn't carry with it the affirmation of an irrational history, and even less of the falsity of a science; on the contrary, it confirms the presence of a real and intelligible history, of a series of collective rational experiences (which respond to a set of quite precise and identifiable rules) in the course of which the knowing subject is constructed as much as the object which is known (Foucault, 1991a, pp. 63–4).

For all its claims to 'scientificity', (eco)marxism – if indeed there be such a unified body of thought – is in fact a site of rhetorical acrobatics, a locale for the production of *truth effects*. The point is that these effects (consistently mistaken for dogma) have no intrinsic or necessary relationship to ecological sustainability. Indeed, 'ecological sustainability' has proved to be one of the most elusive and mobile concepts of the late twentieth and early twenty-first centuries. There is no good reason, therefore, for thinking that the contradictions of capitalism nor the serious scientific (that is, rational) study of the conditions for reconciling Man and Nature will, or should, lead to it being permanently aligned to one politico-social system in place of all others.

One further problem in need of explication concerns the ecomarxist belief that communism will *automatically* guarantee ecological sustainability. The most obvious point to be made here is that the environmental record of 'communist' countries – such as China, Cambodia, Vietnam and the former USSR – is quite poor. Protagonists argue that this is due to the combination of 'exterior forces' like war and/or flooding rather than something *inherent* to communism itself. Arguments have also been advanced to the effect that ecological damage witnessed in such countries is evidence that the state had not, in the words of Engels, sufficiently 'withered away' to allow the 'environmentally friendly fruits of communism' to take hold. There is, of course, probably some merit in both these contentions. However, in the first instance it is clear that neither war nor flooding can be blamed for all or even a substantial portion of the ecosystemic damage occurring in these and other 'communist' countries. The depletion of China's and Russia's forests, for instance, owed/owes as much to the human desire for fuel, food and shelter under Asiatic (that is, non-capitalist) modes of production as it does to the ravages wrought by successive natural disasters (which, in any case, can no longer be viewed as independent of human conduct). Indeed, there is evidence to suggest that locking capitalism 'out' of the East, has often served to lock massive state-induced ecological damage 'in'.

Just as East and West are *both* capable of perpetrating nuclear annihilation, so communism – no less than capitalism – is a system perfectly capable of nurturing processes of ecosimplification and ecofragmentation.

In relation to the second instance (that is the question of bureaucratic form and subsequent effects on ecological sustainability), it is highly doubtful that 'stateless' societies are possible or indeed have ever existed. Deleuze and Guattari, drawing on archaeological evidence, go so far as to suggest that the state has always been present in one form or another. '*[T]here has always been a State*, quite perfect, quite complete … [T]he State itself has always been in a relation with an outside and is inconceivable independent of that relationship'. Moreover, '[t]he law of the State is not the law of All or Nothing (State societies *or* counter-State societies) but that of interior and exterior' (1996, p. 360 emphases added). By this reckoning, it is the height of naiveté to think, firstly, that the state is the cause of all ecological problems, and secondly, that it is possible to demolish every last semblance of it. There has and always will be a necessary relation between *Urstaat* and *Nomos*, between sedimentation and flow. The question, therefore, is properly one of *thresholds* – of what gets captured and repelled by society's organs at any one moment. For a state *will* rise up and things *will* get captured – however fleetingly and to whatever effect. Whenever humans seek to classify, number or otherwise denote the earth, a state will have been instituted. But as illustrated by Deleuze and Guattari, along with the founding of a state – of an organ which captures bodies – come those things which problematise the intended alignment or ordering of events. For example, in addition to isolating high quality timbers, the marking out of logging zones also brings into focus the plight of endangered species, the remains of Indigenous culture, the problems with high intensity burning, and so forth. *The 'enemy', therefore, is not the state. Rather the enemy is the belief in the permanency or legitimacy of that which the state erects*. As Foucault writes,

> [T]he political, ethical, social, philosophical problem of our days is not to try to liberate the individual [nor Nature] from the state, and from the state's institutions, but to liberate us [and Nature] both from the state and from the type of individualization which is linked to the state. We have to promote new forms of subjectivity [and ecology] through the refusal of this kind of individuality [and 'Naturing'] which has been imposed on us for several centuries (1982, p. 216).

The marxist dismissal of the state as inherently repressive along with a hankering for the permanent resolution of Man and Nature under communism (or stateless circumstances) is problematic. At best it represents the height of wishful thinking since the urge to mark out, regulate, and defend territory has been a characteristic of most, if not all, societies. At worst, such a programme is a recipe for the *demise* rather than promotion of cultural and ecological diversity since everything is expected to fall under the *same* politico-social design.

Ecofeminism

Ecofeminism – a term first used in France in 1974 – has developed into a discourse with many strands and permutations (see Plumwood, 1986, especially p. 121). Merchant (1992, pp. 183–210), for instance, speaks variously of liberal, marxist, cultural, social and socialist ecofeminism. Each of these draws on ideas formulated in classic feminist texts by, for instance, Marilyn Waring, Simone De Beauvoir, Marilyn French, and Gloria Steinem. Out of these works has emerged a critique of environmental damage based around androcentric themes and terms. Generally, ecofeminists consider environmental damage or conflict to be symptomatic of entrenched patriarchal social relations. The domination of Nature is merely the logical extension of the domination of women by men. In this sense, it is *men* (specifically, the knowledges and practices they embody and perpetuate), and not just economic *systems* per se (feudalism, capitalism, socialism, anarchism), that are held to be the catalyst of environmental destruction. As one Russian woman, speaking in the wake of Chernobyl put it, 'Men do not think of life, they only want to conquer nature and the enemy, whatever the costs may be!' (quoted in Mies and Shiva, 1993, p. 93). Taking this sentiment a little further, Mies comments '[m]en seem to be experts for technology, women for life, men make war, women are supposed to restore life after wars' (in Mies and Shiva, 1993, p. 93).

On this account, men not only dominate aquatic bodies, terrestrial bodies and atmospheric bodies but those of women as well. And they do so in ways which ensure conceptions of 'right', 'progress', 'good', 'justice', 'economy' and 'sustainability' are construed along distinctly *masculine* lines. Here, *biological* differences are used by men to provide the logical and natural basis for the perpetuation of *social* differences between 'men' and 'women'. Masculinity – that is, cultural conceptions of what 'being male' means – is typically aligned to such traits as rationality, activity, thought, reason, culture, power, objectivity and abstraction. Femininity, on the other hand, is said to be the exact opposite of this, embodying such characteristics as irrationality, passivity, feelings, emotions, Nature, sensitivity, subjectivity and context (see Olsen, 1990). Through a complex web of (c)overt violences, the former (that is masculine) traits have, according to feminists (at least those of the 'second' and 'third' wave variety) been presented as *intrinsically* superior to the latter (that is feminine) variety (see Naffine, 1990). Ecofeminists enter the fray here by arguing that Nature has typically been ascribed the qualities of woman. As such, it should come as no surprise that Nature is a force which must be subjugated in favour of that which is masculine. On this count, Woman *is* Nature and Nature *is* Woman, and everything that does or ever could happen to, or within, such bodies must by necessity be irrational, passive, emotional, subjective and so forth. Conversely, Man is *not* Nature or Woman and must *ipso facto* be superior, objective, scientific, rational, active and so on. By excluding women from key debates and issues, men, it is contended, can *only* reinforce androcentrism and, its necessary corollary, ecocide.

At first glance, ecofeminist critiques appear to powerfully and succinctly capture the 'essence' of environmental problems (and, by default, the 'essence' of women's subjugation). And yet on closer inspection it is apparent that there are several problems that need addressing. Firstly, and with few exceptions, ecofeminists have tended to demonise the knowledges and practices of men *qua* men. Rather than focusing on the lived effects of *particular configurations or varieties of masculinity*, it is men *tout court* who are cast (out) as Other, as the force to be admonished and (perhaps even) despised for developing and upholding systems of government and economy which legitimise the domination and subjugation of women and Nature. Indeed, men, under this scenario, can do little else than entrench the dichotomy men/women=Nature (see Salleh, 1997, pp. 53–68). Such a strategy allows little if any scope for *forming alliances* with the millions of men who *do* strive to improve environmental conditions. At a very basic level, it needs to be remembered that organisations such as Greenpeace, Friends of the Earth, The Wilderness Society, and The Australian Conservation Foundation all have *broad based memberships* which cut across race, socio-economic *and* gender lines. Further, there are also men in positions of state bureaucratic power who are actively pushing for more stringent environmental standards and regulations in areas such as air pollution, water pollution and hazardous waste transportation and who, at the same time, often realise that such efforts fundamentally gloss over many of the key sources of ecological ruin (such as the structures and habits which view the domination of women and Nature as the norm).

Another problem arising from ecofeminist thought is its general unwillingness to remark upon *women*'s agency in the production of environmentally damaging practices. Here the question becomes: Is there not a sense in which each sex (male, female, hermaphrodite, transsexual) consciously *desires* environmental damage – that is, is a willing participant in the flows and practices leading to the damage of ecosystems? Further, isn't there good reason to think this occurs despite fairly widespread if carefully scripted knowledge of the factors exacerbating environmental problems? Arguably, we can no longer afford to ignore the degree to which *all* of us (regardless of sex, gender or credit rating) gain pleasure from desiring and participating in practices we *know* to be environmentally damaging (for example buying clothes, watering the garden, driving a car, having a shower, purchasing CDs, taking photos and having them developed). The incessant flows of desire and pleasure seriously complicate the relation between gender and sustainability. Each of us – irrespective of being ascribed a sex or performing the rituals of gender – desires. Indeed, bodies exist only insofar as they are desired by (an)other body. Whatever the case, desire is a productive force. There is no such thing as a desire free from effects. Even the mundane desire for a clean set of dishes produces all manner of impacts – on waterways, on beaches, on vegetation. Desire (as conceived by Deleuze and Guattari) and, to a lesser extent, pleasure (as conceived by Foucault) function rhizomatically rather than dynamically which means they are rarely if ever amenable to the categories and knowledges of environmental damage produced at the molar level. Ecological sustainability therefore requires more than the 'death' of the masculine. It requires also the fall of femininity – at least that which feeds into a molarised subject. Massumi, following Deleuze and Guattari, remarks,

> 'Man' and 'Woman' as such have no reality other than that of logical abstractions. What they are abstractions of are not the human bodies to which they are applied, but habit-forming whole attractors to which society expects its bodies to become addicted (love, school, family, church, career: artificially closed energetic systems revolving around subtypes of each gender category) ... Gender is a form of imprisonment, a socially functional limitation of a body's connective and transformational capacity (Massumi, 1992, pp. 86–7).

Accordingly, and as will be mentioned later, 'The end of gender politics, for Deleuze and Guattari, is the destruction of gender (of the molar organization of the sexes under patriarchy) – just as in their view the end of class politics is the destruction of class (of the molar organisation of work under capitalism). The goal would be for every body to ungender itself, creating a nonmolarising socius that fosters carnal invention rather than containing it, however evenhandedly: from difference to hyperdifferentiation, in a locally-globally correlated cascade of supermolecular self-inventions' (Massumi, 1992, p. 89). Of course, with respect to anglophone circles, issues surrounding desire, pleasure and the sex-which-is-not-one have been addressed extensively in feminist debates since at least the 1980s. However, *eco*feminism seems to have remained largely immune to such discussions.

In addition to the above, there are certain epistemological problems that need to be addressed within ecofeminist thought. Summarily, there are two main issues. The first concerns the desire for 'wholeness' or a complete (that is feminised) understanding of the order of (all) things. Birkeland (1993, p. 19), for example, goes so far as to say that 'Ecofeminism is [...] a holistic value system'. In a slightly more autocratic tone, Gaard (1993a, p. 3 emphases added) writes, 'Ecofeminists' interconnected sense of self *requires* us to create a *theory* that will provide, as fully as possible, an inclusive and *global* analysis of oppression'. What such views tend to imply is that ecofeminism not only *knows* the key variables 'causing' social and environmental ruin but also has implicit within it the makings of a comprehensive, indeed transcendental solution. There is a somewhat worrying parallel to the modernist project here and its quest to locate a *grund* on which to base all future discourse surrounding personhood and ecology. But what if a different kind of question was posed – a question that revelled in the fact that the search for wholeness is, as Nietzsche would say, laughable. What if, in other words, instead of the whole being greater than the sum of its parts, there were no 'whole', no *grund*, no lasting foundation? What if the search for a *grund* – whether this be the strictures of femininity or something else – was in fact *entrenching* rather than alleviating socio-environmental problems? Wouldn't this give cause to abandon such a project? For poststructuralism the answer necessarily falls in the affirmative. Indeed, as a matter of history, it is certain that modernist projects can do nothing other than fall well short of their mark. We live in the aftermath of a disaster – of science pushing aside public opinion, of men subordinating women, of so-called everyday citizens exterminating those with impure bloodlines, of the west converting parts of the east into a toxic wasteland. In the face of all this, modernist programmes appear at best conceited and at worst reactive. As Deleuze and Guattari put it,

> We no longer believe in a primordial totality that once existed, or in a final totality that awaits us at some future date. We no longer believe in the dull gray outlines of a dreary, colorless dialectic of evolution, aimed at forming a harmonious whole out of heterogeneous bits by rounding off the edges. We believe only in totalities that are peripheral. And if we discover such a totality alongside various separate parts, it is a whole *of* these particular parts but does not totalize them; it is a unity *of* all of these particular parts but does not unify them; rather, it is added to them as a new part fabricated separately (Deleuze and Guattari, 1994a, p. 42).

The second epistemological issue relates to the way ecofeminism conceives of the relation between men, women, and Nature. Generally, there has been a tendency to configure women as 'naturally' closer to Nature (as part of the 'inside') since they themselves are, biologically speaking, 'bearers of life' (just like 'Mother' earth). Along with this idea runs the view that women's natural affinity with Nature means that *only* they can 'truly' discern the impacts of environmental problems and their 'solution'.[3] For instance, Mies (1993, p. 92) comments '... [C]hildren and many women [...] experience [the] sudden separation from nature as a deep, almost physical pain. They feel a sense of deprivation, of loss'. In the same, oft cited work, it is contended,

---

3 This is certainly not to deny the ongoing contributions that many women make to environmental matters. Witness, for instance, the work of Diane Fossey, Joy Adamson and Rachel Carson (1956, 1965). Indeed, consider the farming/agricultural practices of millions of women in parts of the third world that have helped to sustain some of oldest cultures on earth (see, for instance, Shiva, 1988; Sontheimer, 1991). One could invoke the actions of such persons as Ruth Clements, Joanne Ryan and Jill Redwood, who have led long and complex campaigns concerning, respectively, air pollution, toxic waste, and old-growth forest destruction. One could point to the numerous women who have actively campaigned 'on site' around Australia at such places as the Franklin River, Hinchinbrook, Lord Howe Island, Beverley Uranium Mine, Jabiluka Uranium Mine, Wilson's Promontory, Hindmarsh Island and so forth. Similarly, one could point to the series of court actions in the US in the 1960s brought by women campaigning against such bodies as Pacific Gas, the Nuclear Regulatory Commission, and the Dresden Nuclear Power Plant (see Salleh, 1997, pp. 17–23). Clearly, undeniably, and thankfully, women have worked, and continue to work, for what Carolyn Merchant has termed a more 'liveable world'. What such contributions do to the 'universal victim' status ascribed to women by many ecofeminists is, however, another issue. Perhaps this 'contradiction' between women's 'agency' and women's 'oppression' is one that feeds all too easily into the rhetoric of conservatism. For if it is indeed 'true' that hundreds of thousands of women *are* actively engaging in processes of environmental renewal then it becomes nonsensical (for government) to speak on behalf of women's 'universal' subjugation. Conversely, if women are *not* carrying out such tasks, then this can – in line with neo-classical ideas on responsibility – be put down to a lack of (women's) individual will rather than, as might otherwise be argued, sustained structural oppression. Whatever the case, both of these situations are likely to impact the relation between subjectivity, environment and ecofeminist strategy.

> Wherever women acted against ecological destruction or/and the threat of atomic annihilation, they immediately became aware of the connection between patriarchal violence against women, other people and nature, and that: In defying this patriarchy we are loyal to future generations and to life and this planet itself. *We have a deep and particular understanding of this both through our natures and our experiences as women* (Mies and Shiva, 1993, p. 14, emphases added).

And again, '[O]ur basic understanding of ecofeminism as a perspective [...] starts from the fundamental necessities of life; we call this the subsistence perspective. Our opinion is that *women are nearer* to this perspective than men ...' (Mies and Shiva, 1993, p. 20 emphases added). Of course, not all ecofeminists cast men in such a light. Salleh (1997, p. 111), for one, seems to offer an olive branch to all men by declaring, 'Ecofeminism loves and needs its radical brothers. For despite our socially constructed and other differences, one thing we all want is a new intersubjectivity between men, women, nature – hitherto divided by old and arbitrary labels'. This sounds promising, but in the same work she asserts,

> Women's restorative labors and knowledges cut across all classes – middle, working, peasant – and may yet prove the dissolution of old industrial concepts of class as such. Feminine suffering is universal because wrong done to women and its ongoing denial fuel the psychosexual abuse of all Others – races, children, animals, plants, rocks, water, and air. Ecofeminists make no particular claim for themselves, but a claim in general. *An emancipation of the relational sensibility of women and its reclamation by men will release earth energies* (Salleh, 1997, p. 14).

At the risk of a serious misreading, this last passage sounds remarkably like a plea to elevate the desires and experiences of women *above* those of men. However, men's 'relational sensibility' to earth is not 'less' than women's, nor 'more' than women's, nor exactly 'like' women's, but merely *different* from women's. Standpoint epistemology establishes here the importance of resurrecting the voice of the subjugated – in this instance, women. To this extent, such an epistemology is necessary. But the difficulty has tended to be that the notion of subjugation or oppression is then identified with the plight of women rather than humans/cultures *tout court*. In addition, it also needs to be said that the epistemology at work here – indeed any epistemology – elides what might be termed the differential ontology of events. In simple terms, 'women' (just like the term 'men'), has a unity and a cogency only as it is written or spoken and not as it is lived by 'each' body or subject.

The idea that women carry 'inside them' some kind of *transcendental* if hitherto historically repressed and/or socially oppressed ecological panacea is an idea premised on a remarkably unsophisticated conception of subjectivity. Nietzsche, Foucault, Deleuze and others have all illustrated that who we are and what we can become relates not to some latent structure of the body or mind but to the always already heterogeneous composition of circumstance and desire. In their view, all pretences toward locating the foundation or essence of the subject (Man *or* woman) are little more than the audible or chirographic aspects of competing and ever-evolving wills to power, discursive formations and stratifications. What ecofeminism hankers after here, then, is the resolution of (wo)man and Nature via *dialectical* means. This, of course, is not only impossible but politically and socially dangerous. As Deleuze puts it, 'History progresses not by negation and the negation of negation, but by deciding problems and *affirming differences*. It is no less bloody and cruel as a result ... Contradictions are not "resolved", they are dissipated by capturing the problem of which they reflect only the shadow' (1994, p. 268, emphases added). Dialectics tends therefore to masquerade as the 'end of history' (or the 'completion' of enlightenment) and in so doing, seeks desperately to quell any and all experimentation with the 'real' (since the real, by all accounts, should/would have reached its limit).

What is generally in evidence within ecofeminist writing, then, is the substitution of one hierarchy (that is Man/woman/Nature or, better still, Man vs. woman=Nature) for another (that is woman/Nature/Man or woman=Nature vs. Man). It is difficult to see how the maintenance of this kind of hierarchy can aid environmental, not to mention, social problems. Hierarchies, as ecofeminists are keenly aware, set up and reinforce artificial divisions between people and things and thus place strict boundaries around *who* can know, *what* can be known, and what can or should be *done*. Although ecofeminists are correct in arguing that the alienation and subjugation of women has been a primary cause of environmental crises, it is nonetheless very difficult to see how *the alienation and subjugation of men* could lead to their resolution(s). The problem, in other words, is the positing of hierarchies *tout court* and not the groups that happen to fall on either side of the dividing line or threshold. Perhaps what is needed, then, is the elimination of hierarchy and the inception of what Deleuze and Guattari term the *plane of consistency*. This is the plane where nothing but speeds and intensities pass – a moment where bodies/identities are *un*made and where potentials rather than actualities or realities predominate (this concept will be further explicated in Chapter 3).

One final, and somewhat curious, problem within ecofeminist writing is the lexicon used to denote the planet on which we (and others) live. Mies and Shiva (1993, pp. 18–19), for instance, speak variously of 'a celebration of our dependence to Mother Earth', 'heal[ing] Mother Earth', and that 'the term Mother Earth does not need to be qualified by inverted commas, because [...] the earth [is] a living being which guarantees [...] survival'. Elsewhere, Vance (1993, pp. 130–136) talks of 'Mother Nature' and 'Sister Nature'. And Shiva (1993) views the 'soil as a sacred mother'. The issue here has not so much to do with the choice of terms (which are wholly reflective of a feminist standpoint epistemology) but with how terms work – that is, with the kinds of terrains opened up and closed off by particular phrases. A lexicon that includes such references as 'Mother Earth', 'Sister Nature' and so forth arguably undermines a good part of ecofeminist efforts to move *away* from, rather than toward, hierarchies. For if, as is often contended, environmental destruction *is* the result of androcentric practices and frameworks, and, further, that such practices and frameworks tend automatically to correlate the feminine with everything deserving of subordination, then it is difficult to see how continued reference to *Mother* (that is female, feminine, submissive, conniving, Other) Earth could do anything except *perpetuate* masculine framings of women and/as Nature. As one commentator has put it, 'We should check carefully whether we really want to view our relationship with Earth through genderized lenses' (Garb quoted in Gaard, 1993b, p. 303). The project of Irigaray for example is one which, while often accused of essentialism, actually helps to reinscribe our lexicon (of maternity in particular) beyond the Nature/culture divide. As shall be seen in subsequent chapters, Deleuze and Guattari also go to great lengths to implode such dichotomies developing what might be termed a both/and or *immanent* conception of the social and 'natural' world.

Deep ecology

For deep ecologists, environmental conflict is viewed as the product of widespread ignorance of 'the interconnectedness of all things' – particularly of the individual (or 'small' self) to the world (or 'larger' Self). In an attempt to move beyond crude anthropocentric accounts, deep ecology ascribes intrinsic value and indeed moral consideration to ecosystems writ large (called 'biocentric egalitarianism'). The way clear of environmental problems, according to deep ecology, is via a process of 'self-realisation' – of slowly coming to terms with the fact that humans are *part* of Nature and not some abstraction presiding over and above it/her. Here, Indigenous knowledges of various terrains are configured as overarching panaceas to ecological (and social) dilemmas.

As a site for coming to know the sources of environmental conflict, deep ecology exhibits a number of problematic elements. The first has to do with the proclivity to configure environmental problems in terms of a *lack* of a consciousness of interconnectivity. Such an idea is predicated on a misunderstanding of the political, cultural (gendered), economic and scientific constraints which confront vast numbers of the population on a daily basis. It is perfectly possible – indeed all too common – for someone to feel a 'deep' affinity with ecological processes (say with the sea, or a forest, or a particular kind of animal) and yet for this same person to be immersed in structural/routinised forms of environmental damage. To take an example. Cattle breeders in Brazil *know* that clearing rainforest to make way for pasture and beef production is environmentally damaging. They also know that this damage has repercussions not just for people in Brazil but for the world over – in short, they have a sense of 'the interconnectedness of all things'. But additionally, and most significantly, they know that short of walking off their land and slowly starving to death, the solution to this damage is one that predominantly resides with those who produce the social structures and constraints associated with third-world debt.

The accumulation of this debt has in turn to do with decades of Eurocentric policies (including wars fought in their name) designed to privilege the knowledges and practices of one part of the world (the first) over all remaining parts of the world (the second and third). These policies, of course, are premised on a particular *teleology* – one that says the 'goal' of human existence is/should be to create global conditions for the accumulation and consumption of as many material items as possible. Here 'moving forward' or 'progressing' involves leaving 'behind' the old or 'backward' ways of feudalism, or worse, 'primitivism' (the tribal customs of Brazilians). And this should be done in order to openly embrace industrialisation and its concurrent technological, social and economic 'advantages' or 'revolutions'. Continuing this scenario, it is apparent that this last process has relied for its efficacy not only on *increased divisions of labour* (leading to overspecialisation of roles and a heightened sense of boredom and social alienation for millions of people) but also on *increased divisions and hierarchies between sexes* (men as distinctly rational and active, women as inherently irrational and passive; rationality and activity as always superior to irrationality and passivity).

With all this in mind, it is difficult to see how either 'self-realisation' or 'biocentric egalitarianism' is likely to assist the farmer in Brazil or, for that matter, persons in similar circumstances in other regions. Idealism (which is very different to inventing and operationalising new concepts within new epistemes) cannot fundamentally impair capitalist modes of accumulation and consumption. Even the personal environmental ethics of econocrats such as the President of the World Bank or the leaders of G7 are constrained by the dictates of the 'free'-market and globalisation. And this is where deep ecology really begins to lose its purchase on environmental dilemmas. For *capitalism has no centre*. 'There is no universal capitalism, there is no capitalism in itself; capitalism is at the crossroads of all kinds of formations, it is neocapitalism by nature. It invents its eastern face and western face, and reshapes them both – all for the worse' (Deleuze and Guattari, 1996, p. 20). The insidious paradox of capitalism, therefore, is that it has always recognised the 'interconnectedness of all things'. How else does one explain the value it places on roles as geographically and socially distinct as the US President, Iraqi oil barons, Brazilian cattle farmers, Chinese fast food workers, Australian indigenous artists, and Taiwanese outworkers? *Lack* of interconnectivity, therefore, is not the rallying point for ecological problems. Indeed, along with Virilio, one could safely portend the opposite – that ecological dilemmas result from *too much* contact with the Other (rivers, forests, soils, 'exotic' cultures). Except possibly for the bottom of the deepest oceans, the furthest point on earth can now become the nearest in a matter of milliseconds. This, of course, extended/extends to an intolerable 12 (Concorde) and 24 (regular jet) hours respectively if one wishes to do more than merely gaze at images on a screen.

A second major problem with deep ecology is its desire to write humans (*back*?) into Nature's workings and laws – to a time when Indigenous customs and knowledges held sway and human induced ecological problems where few if any. This is, arguably, an excessively romantic view of the past/Indigenous culture.[4] Romanticism, one should note, posits a belief not only in a divided subject (self/other, self/Nature, self/God) but in the fact that such divisions can and should be

4 For an excellent discussion of the manner by which certain individuals/groups (including David Suzuki) have uncritically elevated nomadic or Indigenous knowledges to the position of 'ecological saviour', see Fuller, 2000.

permanently overcome. For deep ecologists, Indigenous cultures are taken to be models for bringing about the union of humans and Nature. However, such cultures are known to have suffered many (human induced) environmental problems. For example, the knowledges and practices of Indigenous Australians led to all kinds of extinctions and extensive habitat manipulation (Flannery, 1994). Certain of the tribes in Papua New Guinea are known to have hunted the Giant Moa into extinction. Accordingly, nomadic and semi-nomadic tribes did not 'solve' ecological dilemmas so much as they were able to physically remove themselves from their immediate proximity as they arose. They had, literally, the (geographical) space to flee. This socio-environmental 'strategy' owed as much to an economy of tribal numbers as any *intrinsic* conception of 'ecological sustainability'. 'Pollution', 'environmental harm', 'toxicity', 'deleterious effects' – call it whatever – was therefore in no way a foreign force but an effect destined to arrive at very different rates and intensities to those pressing us at present. In short, Indigenous cultures hold no monopoly over the solution(s) to ecological dilemmas. As Foucault remarks, '[Y]ou can't find the solution of a problem in the solution of another problem raised at another moment by other people' (1991, p. 343). This is why Nietzsche talked about a 'return to a nature' as necessarily having to involve an *ascendancy* (an active creation of the yet-to-be) rather than a turning back (a reactive invocation of a state of affairs located in the past). In any case, one needs to seriously question whether, at the beginning of the twenty-first century, the proportion of arable land to the human population would sustain the modality of life practised by most Indigenous cultures. This modality is/was, of course, nomadism. It may in fact be the case that certain traits of the modernist modality of fixity – particularly those of becoming sedentary, slowing down, becoming less mobile – are better ecological strategies than urging six billion humans to become mobile. There is more to nomadism, in other words, than the constant physical movement from one geographical territory to the next. Indeed, for Deleuze and Guattari, nomadism has always had to do with speed and intensity of the flow of bodies across two kinds of spaces – geographical and *cerebral*. Perhaps, then, the greatest and most intense ecological movement humans could immerse themselves in would be *no* movement at all. Perhaps, in other words, we are moving too fast in relation to certain types of bodies' ongoing vitality – forests, rivers, oceans, atmospheres, mountains, birds, marsupials, reptiles, insects, and micro-organisms.

In addition to these points, something also needs to be said about the phrase 'deep ecology'. This term was coined by Arne Naess – the founder of deep ecology – to signify a 'profound' as opposed to 'shallow' understanding of the interconnections between Man and Nature. Such terminology, however, arguably places this perspective within a highly questionable epistemological, as well as social, purview. The problematic assumption here is that there resides somewhere 'out there', a *perfectible* set of meanings capable of dictating (via a transcendental rather than contextualised ethic) what should be done to reconcile humans and Nature. But what if, after a life time of searching and interpreting Nature, one finds that at the most 'profound' or deepest ecological level, lies not a solution or a reconciliation but a conglomeration of problems and variables that elide capture or hypostatisation?

What if, in other words, the 'hermeneutics of the deep' turns out to be nothing other than a genealogy (Foucault, 1990) or a *schizoanalytic of surfaces, affects, machines and bodies* (Deleuze and Guattari, 1996)? This would entail, would it not, a serious re-examination of the conceptions of identity, language, rationality and so forth that underpinned such a programme.

Social ecology

Social ecology is a perspective that tries to take account of the problems embedded within the aforementioned standpoints. In doing so, social ecologists view environmental problems not only as the logical extension of the domination of women by men, but also of men by men – particularly of those men who hold and wield political and economic power over those who do not. There is thus an explicit acknowledgement of the role of structural constraints in perpetuating environmental damage. And there is, further, a very real concern to absolve political and social worlds of the kinds of hierarchies that have led to the privileging of Man over woman and of Man over Nature. In this regard, social ecology favours an anarchist conception of society – hardly surprising since the founder of social ecology is the Spanish anarchist Murray Bookchin.[5] Social ecology has received much attention from ecologists and sociologists/cultural theorists alike and it is therefore important to understand something of its shortcomings.

A first problem concerns the idea that non-antagonistic or non-hierarchical (that is anarchist) *social* relations will *ipso facto* result in non-antagonistic relations with Nature. Fox (1989, p. 15) points out that it is in fact 'possible for a relatively egalitarian human society to be extremely exploitative ecologically'. Further, there are numerous examples of hierarchical societies that have treated Nature with due reverence and economy. Eckersley (1992, p. 151) cites 'Benedictine communalism, feudalism and many preliterate societies' as examples. One could also add the Eskimo, the Tibetan monk, the nomads of Mongolia's steppes, as well as the tribes remaining in highland Papua New Guinea. Each of these works 'with' rather than against Nature but also retain strict hierarchies dividing men's work from women's, custom from deviance, and so forth.

A second problem has to do with the idea that it is possible to read or discern from Nature the 'correct' or best way of organising social relations. Such an idea – echoing the project of Comte – goes hand in hand with the belief that the world has, beneath all its veneers, surfaces, appearances and impressions, an essential and timeless body

5 More recently, Merchant (1992, p. 9) has described her own radical ecological perspective (which includes just about every theory that has as its goal the overthrow of the capitalist state) as nothing less than 'the cutting edge of social ecology'. And yet in the conclusion to her work she seems explicitly to align herself to *deep* ecology, saying that 'Deepest ecology is both feminist and egalitarian. It offers a vision of society that is truly free' (1992, p. 107). In light of the fact that social ecologists – at least those adhering to the work of Bookchin – hold out nothing but disdain to deep ecologists, it is difficult to know how to read or place Merchant's work.

of signs waiting to be read by Man. This, of course, is a highly problematic notion. It implies the continuation of a strict separation of subject and object, of viewer and viewed, of interpreter and interpreted. In turn, such dichotomies have led to all kinds of disastrous projects being implemented on the basis that they are designed to do 'what Nature intended'. Consider the following example. Once a year, in certain of the rivers of North America, schools of schnook salmon swim upstream against the current to spawn. At certain points in their journey it is necessary – in order to have a chance of reaching their destination – that they momentarily leap clear of the water over the rocks, branches and accumulated debris which form the various plateaus or levels of the riverbed. Importantly, and historically, only the strongest fish make it over these obstacles to pass on their genes to the next generation. However, humans – and more tellingly, late-capitalist subjectivities – also reside near and use the rivers in which salmon spawn. In particular, they use the river as a means of supplying fresh water to their crops. Weirs, as most people know, are an integral part of dam construction and design. They control the rate of flow and volume of water along different stretches of the river. However, weirs are also much greater in height and of a much steeper gradient than the 'natural' plateaus created by rocks and wood. Despite this, numerous weirs have been erected within rivers inhabited by schnook salmon. In a short time, the salmon population dramatically declined. After much research, the reason given for such declination was that the weirs were found to be of such a height and gradient that *none* of the salmon – let alone the strongest – were able to make it to their breeding grounds. The objective of policy makers/scientists then became twofold – to replenish numbers of fish whilst retaining *all* weirs. After testing many different scenarios (removing the weirs was not one of them!), a 'solution' was found. This consisted of erecting at the base of each weir a series of electronic lifts/nets capable of gathering up large numbers of salmon and depositing them in the waters lying upstream. This was done for all weirs leading to breeding grounds.

Not only is the mechanical migration of schnook salmon actually occurring, it is happening on the basis that this is 'what Nature intended'. When all the contestations and public dissent concerning the intrusion of civilisation into the wilderness had passed, Nature was invoked as a means of legitimising this mechanical solution. For what Nature ultimately 'intended' was that fish be able to get from one end of a river to the other in order to spawn. The fact that *all* fish – instead of just the strongest – are now able to complete the journey becomes merely an unfortunate by-product of the trade-off that must occur between economic progress and 'nonhuman' ecosystems (that is, Nature). The subsequent impact on the *diversity of other species* in the food chain which have suddenly to compete with ever larger populations of salmon becomes a *necessary* evil.

This is, quite clearly, a prime example of how reading or studying Nature can lead to monstrous ends. Again, the instrumentalist ethic comes to the fore. This ethic obscures the notion that attempts to manipulate Nature in accordance with some preordained or essential function (for example to grow trees, to produce fish, to yield wheat) is to mistake an infinite and unknowable complexity of flows, speeds and intensities for the routine simplicity of a substance (for example wood, flesh, fibre). In reading, deciphering and manipulating Nature we are inventing not an exterior or an other, so much as the possibilities of creating and destroying ourselves. There are, in short, no transcendental or omnipresent messages to be gained from studying Nature – other than, of course, the message that there is no message. Nature is a contested terrain, a product of discourse, a semblance of our imaginations and desires. This is what social ecology fails to grasp.

A third and major problem with social ecology is that it espouses a free-willing, purposive view of subjectivity. Bookchin writes, 'Every organism is in some sense "willful", insofar as it seeks to preserve itself, to maintain its identity, to resist a kind of biological entropy that threatens its integrity and complexity … [M]etabolic activity is coextensive with the notion of activity as such and imparts an identity, indeed, a rudimentary "self", to every organism' (1986, pp. 72–3). Here it is the positing of a stable 'rudimentary' self that provides the basis for instrumental rationality. This rationality, it might be recalled, is one that has brought with it all manner of sufferings – for women, migrants, the insane, the elderly, the Indigenous, and the homeless, but also for the so-called 'average' citizen. Further, this 'rudimentary self' is one and the same self that has functioned as the foundation on which to erect neo-classical conceptions of crime and punishment, as well as bourgeois (Western) notions of freedom and equality. It is now known – and certainly was always known by those who bore the brunt of the policies and programmes conceived under rationalist and paternalist pretences – that the kinds of freedoms and equalities spawned by liberalism, are in reality a continuation of the war of all against all carried on by other means (whether by seduction (Featherstone, 1991), panopticism (Foucault, 1977), governmentality (Barry et al., 1996; Rose, 1999) or, on occasion, the overt physical force of the state (Bauman, 2000)). If history, or more accurately, the various counter-memories emerging from it, is indicative of anything, it is perhaps that those who seek to erect a new kind of society on the basis of stable identities (rather than difference), inevitably produce something akin to fascism – that is, a will to the same (see Bauman, 1991; Deleuze and Guattari, 1994a). And here fascism should be understood not merely as something which centralised government practises on constituents. Rather, the fascism in need of most vigilance is that which exists 'in us all, in our heads and in our everyday behaviour, the fascism that causes us to love power, to desire the very thing that dominates and exploits us' (Foucault in Deleuze and Guattari, 1994a, p. xiii). There is a type of fascism not just in the desire to see an 'Other' become like an 'Us' (East like West, Blacks like Whites, Greenies like Capitalists), but also in what is conceived to be the appropriate method of doing so – means such as reason, logic, truth, god, law, right, and so forth.

With all this in mind it is interesting to note what Bookchin says about reason and its role in resolving environmental dilemmas. He comments, 'We cannot avoid the use of conventional reason, present-day modes of science, and modern technology … But we can establish new *contexts* in which these modes of rationality, science, and technology have their proper place – an *ecological* context that does not deny other, more qualitative modes of knowing and producing which are participatory and emancipatory' (1986, p. 75). The lexicon is modernist in the extreme – 'modes of rationality', 'emancipatory', 'conventional reason', 'proper place'. As such, reason retains its position as the great emancipator of humanity. But as Bauman has shown, there is an *aporia* at work here that is consistently mistaken for something resolvable. This aporia is one which tries to marry the '[a]utonomy of rational individuals [with the] heteronomy of rational management [of subjects and objects (earth)]'. Each, of course, '[can]not do without [the] other; but they [can]not cohabit peacefully either' (Bauman, 1995, p. 7). And yet,

> It [is] a characteristic, perhaps the defining, feature of modernity that the aporia [is] played down as a conflict not-yet-resolved-but-in-principle-resolvable; as a temporary nuisance, a residual imperfection on the road to perfection, a relic of unreason on the way to the rule of reason, a momentary lapse of reason soon to be rectified, a sign of not-yet-fully-overcome ignorance of the 'best fit' between individual and common interests. One more effort, one more feat of reason, and the harmony would be reached – never to be lost again. Modernity kn[ows] it [is] deeply wounded – but th[inks] the wound curable. And thus it never cease[s] to look for a healing ointment. We may say that it remain[s] 'modernity' as long, and in as far as, it refuse[s] to abandon that belief and those efforts (Bauman, 1995, p. 8).

What social ecology refuses to understand is that danger lurks as much in the formulation and implementation of 'solutions' as in recognising an initial problem. No matter what the context, rationality (or 'conventional reason') is likely to function as a socially and ecologically damaging force since its model for judging 'causes' and 'effects' is that of the tree (arborescence), rather than the rhizome (flow). Trees, as everybody (except possibly for Plato) knows, require each branch and leaf to pay eternal homage to a central organising principle (that is the system of roots). And it is the requirement to incessantly revisit foundations that manifests itself as the death of becoming-other.

In sum

Each of the perspectives outlined above (and a good many others such as romantic ecology – see Bate, 1991), fall well short of addressing or even acknowledging the aporia of which Bauman speaks. Indeed attempts at doing this have arguably seen environmental problems (or, more accurately, the discourses which frame their nature and limits) *increase*. The 'sources' of modernity's inability to come to grips with environmental problems are, of course, to be found in the 'solutions' it proffers. Such solutions include: a privileging of transcendental unities (subject, object, Nature) over immanent processes (dividuals, multiplicities, flows of matter-energy); the search for universal foundations from which to legitimise programmes of ecological renewal (laws of Nature, god, social justice); the positing of teleologies which promise to permanently resolve socio-environmental conflict (ecologically sustainable development, subsistence living, anarchism, ecosocialism); and the production of binary oppositions (culture/Nature, men/women, science/opinion, capitalism/communism, ecologically significant/ecologically insignificant).

In more general terms, the problems with modernist conceptions of environmental damage are twofold. Firstly, there has been a tendency to write the 'causes' of environmental problems in *monolithic* fashion – the irresponsible consumer monolith under liberal ecology, the capitalist monolith under ecomarxism, the patriarchal monolith under ecofeminism, the hierarchical monolith under deep ecology, and the domination monolith under social ecology. The (unintended) consequence of these monoliths has been the proliferation of precisely the kinds of configurations and dichotomies that have long underpinned the processes of environmental damage and its discursive production. *Configurations* such as: ecologically benign policies versus irresponsible citizens; economically powerful owners of the means and forces of production versus environmentally conscious but powerless labourers; ecologically destructive men versus environmentally mindful women; ecologically damaging humans versus ecologically benign nonhumans; humans as creatures of domination versus Nature as symbiotic entity. *Dichotomies* like: lay/expert; Nature/economy; woman/Man; nonhuman/human; order/chaos. The problem here is one which neatly typifies the modernist project and involves what might be termed the *stochastic modelling of the world into discrete bodies* – bodies of proximity (here/there), speed (fast/slow), scale (large/small), space (full/empty), envisioning (colonial/postcolonial) and so forth. Deleuze and Guattari contend that such a schema is based around the belief in the utility of an *arborescent* model of social relations. 'Arborescent systems', they write, 'are hierarchical systems with centers of signifiance and subjectification, central automata like organized memories' (Deleuze and Guattari, 1996, p. 16).[6] Arborescence holds sway precisely to the extent that active forces are made into subjects of one kind or another (greenie, forester, judge) and that there exists a belief in the ontological validity and utility of binary modes of thought. The problem with binary modes of thought is not just that the complexity of the world is forsaken in favour of a recognisable and repeatable series of dichotomies (self/other, culture/Nature, capitalism/communism, endemic/foreign, timber/habitat), but that one side of the dichotomy tends to be privileged (and therefore more highly desired) than the other.

Such privileging has been named by Deleuze and Guattari as adhering to a molar semiotics – that is, to a system of signification where one term 'fully' constitutes and subordinates its 'other'. But 'there is such diversity in the forms of expression, such a mixture of these forms, that it is impossible to attach any particular privilege to the form or regime of the "signifier"' (Deleuze and Guattari, 1996, p. 111). Dichotomies 'work' only to the extent that one term (that is lay, Nature, woman, nonhuman, chaos) consistently differs from and, more importantly, *defers* to another (that is expert, economy, Man, human, order). The major problem with the perspectives outlined above, therefore, is that they merely *reverse* the process of deference rather

6 See also (1996, plateau one) for further elaboration of the distinction between arborescent and rhizomatic thought.

than extirpate it. So, where 'lay' knowledge once deferred to 'expert' knowledge, the reverse is expected to occur. Where Nature once deferred to 'economy', economy should now defer to Nature. Where 'woman' once deferred to Man, Man should now defer to woman. And so forth. The undeniable result of this continued deference is the (re)construction of *the image of thought* – of a preconceived schema dictating ahead of time what can and should be said and done (about environmental problems) (see Deleuze, 1994, pp. 129–67; Chapter 2 of present book). Modernist environmental perspectives therefore inadvertently elevate and mistake 'structure' and 'hierarchy' for, over, and above, *flow* and *difference*. In doing this, the kinds of divisions initially viewed as so problematic tend to be exacerbated.

A second problem with modernist accounts of environmental problems is their relative inability to take account of the *mobility of discourse* that defines and structures environmental regulatory policies and practices through time. Specifically, the process of *dichomotisation* is apt to create a very narrow series of heuristic devices and responses to socio-ecological problems. The disjunction between, on one hand, the conceptual frames emerging out of modernist environmental accounts, and, on the other, the mobility of environmental discourse, can be illustrated with respect to the following. Up until the early 1980s woodchipping was commonly thought to be a necessary, ecologically benign, and profitable activity. Since this time, however, numerous polls have shown strong opposition to such activity. One of these, a Morgan poll taken in July 1996, showed 90% of Australians to be firmly against the woodchipping of old-growth forests. Despite this opposition (which exists to the present), around 85% of woodchips (that is five million tonnes) are still sourced from Australian native old-growth forests each year (Halsey, 1997b). The question is: How would each of the above environmental philosophies account for the apparent division between 'thought' (popular opinion) and 'practice' (government policy) in this instance.

Liberal ecology would advocate that forest production is carried out under the gaze of experts and that such production is not only sustainable but satisfying a known demand. Here, public opinion is conceived as 'lay' opinion and should stay clear of the technical and complex job of managing Nature. However, there are many 'experts' who think woodchipping and clearfelling old-growth forests is unsustainable (see Scotts, 1991; Lobert et al., 1991). And further, there are firm indications that the demand for (hardwood) woodchips is *falling* (see Australian Bureau of Agricultural and Resource Economics, 2001). Ecomarxism would say government is putting profit and jobs before ecological sustainability. But if one surveys the financial dimensions of woodchipping it becomes clear that native forest operations result in an annual net economic *loss* and that forestry related jobs – due largely to technological interventions – have declined 60% over the last two decades (Resource Assessment Commission, 1992). Ecofeminism would submit that woodchipping continues because it reflects the masculine need to dominate Nature – what better way to do this than to reduce thousands of five-hundred year old trees to millions of tiny pieces no bigger than a matchbox? And yet there are female forest supervisors, administrators, and family members who fully condone such activity.

Is it really sufficient, therefore, to merely contend that such women have been either forcibly coerced or 'tricked' into masculine roles? Conversely, there are men in each of the aforementioned positions who *oppose* woodchipping and advocate something other than a masculinist view of the environment.[7] Deep ecologists would contend that there is a failure on behalf of government to understand the way humans are connected to Nature. But places such as national parks, wilderness areas and the like are extremely well patronised by those (including forest policy makers) who see little or nothing wrong with woodchipping (for example Head Forester, Orbost District, Victoria). Social ecologists would argue that dissent over woodchipping could be quelled by the application of scientific principles to forest production processes. And yet, the rational scientific management of other 'resources' (such as the atmosphere, the sea, the soil) has arguably *increased* the nexus between humans and Nature to the point where Nature is cast in the role of an Other, 'out there', or as something subordinate or separate to humans (see Halsey, 1999).

Another example that illustrates the inability of modernist environmental perspectives to explain the mobility and meaning(s) of environmental issues, concerns the naming of the department responsible for the management of Victoria's natural resources (including forests). Over the last decade and a half, this department has changed its name and mission statement many times, and each change has heralded a different emphasis on certain key terms/phrases like 'wealth production', 'conservation' and so forth. The following passages drawn from various Departments' annual reports illustrates this point,

1988/89: DEPARTMENT OF CONSERVATION, FORESTS AND LANDS

No mission statement

1991/92: DEPARTMENT OF CONSERVATION AND ENVIRONMENT

Mission statement:

To protect Victoria's land and water environments, conserve Victoria's natural and cultural heritage, manage and promote sustainable use of resources in ways which are environmentally sound, socially just and economically efficient.

1993/94: DEPARTMENT OF CONSERVATION AND NATURAL RESOURCES

Mission statement:

The DCNR will:

- *protect Victoria's land and water environments,*
- *utilize Victoria's natural resources for sustainable use by the community,*

7 In conversation, Keith Gidley, April 1999.

– conserve Victoria's natural and cultural heritage, in ways which are socially fair and economically efficient.

1994/95: DEPARTMENT OF CONSERVATION AND NATURAL RESOURCES

Mission statement:

To manage the conservation and sustainable use of natural resources and rural and urban public land, to maintain their long-term values and promote Victoria's competitiveness and attractiveness.

1995/96: DEPARTMENT OF NATURAL RESOURCES AND ENVIRONMENT

Mission statement:

The staff of the DNRE are committed to efficiently and effectively delivering high quality products and services to our customers, to generate wealth through the sustainable development of primary industries and natural resources, and to conserve and protect our natural and cultural heritage.

1997/98: DEPARTMENT OF NATURAL RESOURCES AND ENVIRONMENT

Mission statement:

The Department ... is charged with managing Victoria's public lands, natural resources and assisting primary industries maximize sustainable production of value added products and services for Australian and international markets.

2002/03: DEPARTMENT OF SUSTAINABILITY AND ENVIRONMENT

Our Vision:

DSE is committed to a future in which all Victorians are living sustainably within their natural and built environments.

Our Objectivies:

[...] Improve the management of public and private land to enhance, protect and restore bio-diversity assets and ecosystem services.

In just over a decade, therefore, the department 'progressed' from being called the 'Department of Conservation, Forest and Lands' to the 'Department of Sustainability and Environment'. The jettisoning of the terms 'conservation' and 'forest' is not insignificant in the context of what has been happening to Victoria's forests – something that will become clearer in subsequent chapters. However, the 'causes', and subsequent environmental effects of this change in lexicon are not, as many would have it, the result of expertise, capitalism, patriarchy, problems of hierarchy, or systems of domination. Instead, and at the risk of sounding trite, it is the result of *all* these things and much *more* – more in the sense that the structures just mentioned are supported by all manner of processes typically deemed marginal to the 'serious' study of environmental conflict. Accordingly, a primary goal of this study is to interrupt this trend by examining four interrelated processes – the mode of envisioning Nature (or its scopic regime, Foster, 1988; Simington, 1997); the thresholds and categories used to name Nature (Deleuze, 1990, 1994; Foucault, 1997); the speed at which Nature is transformed (Virilio, 1986; 1999); and the effects and affects of transforming Nature (Deleuze, 1992, especially pp. 217–34; Massumi, 1996).

Arguably, the frameworks discussed earlier on and indeed any of those which seek to theorise environmental crises in terms of one 'dominant' or 'ultimate' factor – risk (Beck), distorted speech patterns (Habermas), administration (Dryzek), regulatory capture (Grabosky and Braithwaite), economic growth (Pepper), patriarchy (Mies and Shiva), anthropocentrism (Eckersley), hierarchy (Devall and Sessions), domination (Bookchin) – are incapable of depicting how each of the four processes just mentioned impact both the forms and intensities of environmental conflict. Put differently, a range of problems (concerning chiefly the relationship between language, subjectivity, environment and the discursive construction of damaged or 'pristine' terrains) disappears below the grid of intelligibility made possible by modernist ecological thought. The task in the next chapter, therefore, will be to introduce a philosophical perspective capable of making such relationships intelligible. In contrast to modernist accounts, the aim will be to move away from dialectics – from the search for closure, for (economic and ecological) certainty, and for the permanent resolution of (environmental) conflict. For the problem resides not in environmental damage or conflict *per se*, so much with as those bodies that try to limit Nature to a single form or function.

Chapter 2

Environment and Criminological Thought

Like previous decades, the first few years of the twenty-first century have heralded the notion that global depletions of biodiversity as well as human-induced declinations in air, water and soil quality are chronic processes rather than fleeting events. These are not, it now seems clear, the result of some inexplicable 'blip' in (supposedly predictable) weather patterns, breeding cycles, market forces or the like. Instead they are fundamentally linked to the 'normal' operation of various political, cultural and economic practices (United Nations Environment Programme, 2002). As a result, and with the possible exception of terrorism and the (in)actions of so-called 'rogue' states, investigating the causes and possible remedies of environmental harm (however defined) are now key priorities for most western nations.[1] Environmental problems are, in short, recognised to be of a central and serious kind such that those who trivialise or downplay the fate of the globe are increasingly being asked by governments, by law, by green groups, by 'average' citizens to justify their (improbable/imprudent) position.

In this context – and as a discipline intimately concerned with the geographies, intensities, frequencies and visibilities of harm – it would be reasonable to assume that the vicissitudes of environmental damage and environmental crime (two very different things) would by now constitute central objects of criminological thought (Cohen, 1988). For, make no mistake, environmental harms do markedly impact the capacities of particular populations to actively and benignly engage with the flows of matter-energy conducive to what might be termed 'non-toxic lives'. Sound evidence of this can be found in what remains the most comprehensive study on global ecosystemic health conducted by some 175 scientists on behalf of the United Nations Development Programme, the United Nations Environment Programme, the World Bank and the World Resources Institute. The report shows that,

> Half of the world's wetlands were lost [during the twentieth century]; Logging and conversion have shrunk the world's forests by as much as half [to around 3 billion

---

1 See, for example, documents emerging from the UN Commission on Sustainable Development, Eleventh Session, New York, 28 April – 9 May 2003. Evidence of further commitment toward resolving particular kinds of environmental damage is (despite the lack of support from countries such as the US and Australia) reflected in text 'Kyoto Protocol – Status of Ratification, 10 July 2003' (84 Signatures, 111 Ratifications, Acceptances, Approvals and / or Accessions) (available at: http://unfccc.int/resource/kpstats.pdf).

> hectares]; Some 9 percent of the world's tree species are at risk of extinction; Tropical deforestation may exceed 130,000 square kilometers per year; Fishing fleets are 40 percent larger than the ocean can sustain; Nearly 70 percent of the world's major marine fish stocks are overfished or are being fished at their biological limit; Soil degradation has affected two-thirds of the world's agricultural lands in the last 50 years; Some 30 percent of the world's original forests have been converted to agriculture; Since 1980, the global economy has tripled in size and [the] population has grown by 30 percent to 6 billion people; Dams, diversions or canals fragment almost 60% of the world's largest rivers; Twenty percent of the world's freshwater fish are extinct, threatened or endangered (Media Release, 17 April 2000, Washington, DC, summarising key trends emerging from *World Resources 2000–2001: People and Ecosystems: The Fraying Web of Life*).

Despite such disturbing trends – whose truth effects will always be subject to the power of particular discourses to (re)construct the limits of harm – criminological concern for the environment is, quite demonstrably, by far and away the exception to the rule (but see Goff and Geis, 1993; Edwards et al., 1996; Williams, 1996; Beirne, 1998; Halsey and White, 1998; Pearce and Tombs, 1998; A-Khavari, England and Godden, 1999; Halsey, 1997a, 1997b, 1999; Seis, 1999; Walters, 2004). A key question, therefore, is this: Why, at a time when most disciplines (for example politics, economics, history, cultural studies) have built or extended their *oeuvres* to include an analysis of environmental problems, has criminology seen fit *not* to do so? Alternatively, why are there so few criminologists writing about environmental harm/crime as opposed to the multitude prepared to discuss such issues as illicit drug taking, rape, robbery, homicide and other so-called 'orthodox' crimes?

Such questions stand to generate many important insights about criminology as well as those working within (and beyond) its confines. In the final chapter I respond to these issues and look specifically at the relationship between criminology, andro/anthropocentrism, and the marginalisation of Nature as the Other of 'real' criminological work. For the moment though, I want to examine how criminology has talked about environmental crime/harm to date and the problematic dimensions of such discourse. Specifically, I want to argue that green criminologists have, with few exceptions, drawn implicitly or explicitly upon one or a combination of the five (competing) environmental perspectives outlined in the previous chapter. My intention is to show that adherence to any of these streams of thought necessarily leads to highly questionable renderings of Nature, society, subjectivity and, concomitantly, of what causes and what might be seen to prevent environmental damage. Green criminology does not, I will argue, possess the lexicon required to move beyond modernist conceptions of harm and reparation.

In addition, I want to suggest that when criminologists engage the term 'green' they necessarily manifest the kind of political baggage which comes with dividing the world into distinct – one might say, polar – domains. Getting better at socio-ecological relations will not, I contend, be simply a matter of siding with the green or red, the anthropocentric or ecocentric, the classical view of offending or the positivist, the constructionist take on 'reality' or the essentialist (Platonic), and so forth. Rather, improved functioning of socio-ecological worlds needs to be tied to ways of thinking-acting which subvert binary modes of thought (that is thought which results from the habit of segmenting the world into polar opposites and unified categories). Indeed, I want to suggest that *the term 'green' should be jettisoned from socio-environmental discourse* primarily because it does not adequately capture the inter-subjective, inter-generational, or inter-ecosystemic processes which combine to produce scenarios of harm. There are particular costs associated with thinking and writing the world in various ways, and green criminology, I will suggest below, misunderstands the nature and extent of the task at hand.

Review and critique

The problem of anthropocentrism

Perhaps the most worrying trend emerging from recent criminological work on environmental issues is that such efforts have generally been of an *un*critical kind. By this I mean that such studies support and adhere to the tenets associated with what I have termed a liberal ecological outlook – an outlook imbued by *anthropocentric* principles and practices. To recap, liberal ecology views environmental problems as symptoms of unchecked – but ultimately controllable – market forces. It is no surprise, then, that the solutions to environmental crime (and environmental harm more generally) have in the main been posed in terms of how best to a) modify (but not radically alter) industrial processes, b) modify (but not radically alter) environmental law, and c) modify (but not radically alter) the nature and limits of enforcement (see, for instance, del Frate and Norberry, 1993; Grabosky, 1994; Gunningham et al., 1995; McDowell, 1997; Grabosky and Gant 2000). A closer analysis of a relevant text will illustrate my concerns.

In a recent piece by the Deputy Commissioner of the Australian Federal Police (AFP), Davies (2002) offers a brief overview of the cost and scope of the illicit trade in wildlife, 'said to exceed five million birds, thirty thousand primates and fifteen million furs per year'. He continues, 'The economic value of this trade is estimated at US$1.5 billion and throughout the world over 600 species are threatened by th[e] trade [in wildlife]' (Davies, 2002, p. 20). These are, without doubt, statistics to be deeply troubled by. But equally troubling is the way in which enforcement agencies portray their activities along binary lines. Specifically, the limits of *real* environmental harm are given to equate to all those activities of an ecologically damaging Nature *as proscribed by law* (for example wildlife smuggling, illegal dumping of chemicals, and so on). For instance, Davies writes that 'Environmental criminals can include the highest level of corporations, organised crime, and as we are now well aware, terrorists' (2002, p. 21). Here, a definitive line is drawn between the 'inside' and 'outside' of environmental crime, and, more particularly, who counts as 'real' environmental offenders and who do not. On the inside are the illegal activities of individuals and corporations who/which are capable of being formally construed as environmental crime in a court of law (typically and most problematically a court severely limited in power and jurisdiction).[2] On the outside, though, are all those actors and activities which are, for all intents and purposes, untouchable. What these actors do (and do not do) may be intentional, may be harmful, and may lead to long term deleterious effects on ecosystems, but so long as such acts occupy a sphere beyond that dealt with by enforcement agencies, they do not, indeed cannot, constitute environmental crime.

This is a highly problematic state of affairs because one of the greatest perpetrators of ecological damage happens to be the (post)modern state (see Goff and Geis, 1993; Williams, 1996; Halsey 1997b). And yet the body of this offender will not – indeed cannot – make it onto Davies' (nor any other liberal ecological) list of environmental criminals due mainly to the structural constraints which attend a system geared toward exponential profit and commodification of earth. There is a serious problem, therefore, with the way in which enforcement bodies envision, speak about, and frame environmental harm.[3] The most dangerous of these is the

2 In a three year period spanning 1994–96 the Victorian Environment Protection Agency (the primary regulator of a southern Australian State composed of some 4.5 million people) prosecuted a total of 133 cases with a conviction rate of 38%. The most common penalty in this period was a fine (n=75) and the average amount imposed was $2750 (ranging from $40 for littering to $16,000 for breaching air pollution statutes) (see Environment Protection Authority, 1994, 1995, 1996, 1997). This situation continues to reflect national trends up to and including the end of 2002 (see prosecution data given in the annual reports of each Environment Protection Authority). The fact that so few people receive substantial fines or go to prison for environmental offences surely cannot be an indication that all is well with humanity and various bioregions (that is that the harms perpetrated against earth are somehow small, discrete, unintentional or the like). Equally, the fact that the most common type of environmental crime (from an international perspective) likely to result in a prison sentence is 'exceeding bag limits' for various fish species does not mean that the damage 'caused' by such offences is the most serious environmental problem which people the world over consciously or actively perpetuate. Rather, such a circumstance is, critically, an indication of what regulators 'choose' or, more accurately, have the capacity, to name and (where possible, enforce) as environmental crime. There are many important parallels here with the way in which formal definitions of violence are constructed in a manner to exclude much of what governments, corporations, police and armies do (see Box, 1983).

3 There is, of course, a substantial criminological literature (for example Tappan, 1947; Sutherland, 1949; Schwendinger and Schwendinger, 1975) dealing with what should fall within and beyond the criminological gaze. My own view is that criminology should not be constrained by a strictly delimited field of analysis. Indeed, the vitality of the discipline depends on its capacity to subject to critique events and processes which, when viewed through one lens or another, are apt to attract the label 'harm' or a closely associated term. Indeed, a key critical criminological task is to bring to light the factors which function to divide criminal from so-called normal, routine or acceptable practice. This, arguably, is what is so striking about environmental issues and their relation to the criminological purview: namely, that it is very difficult to rename and re-envision much of what we take to be pleasurable, profitable and progressive as one and the same as those events which contribute to the diminution of species and the toxic transformation of the biosphere.

belief that the factors which compel people to commit environmental crime are somehow logically separate from those factors and conditions which lead the state to permit environmental damage by other means and at different speeds and scales from moment to moment. Put another way, it is the height of naiveté to believe that capturing environmental criminals means arresting the alliances, personal habits and institutional routines that sanction a more generalised mode of environmental decay.

In addition to the above type of text there is, of course, a (small) body of criminological writings on environmental harm which is concerned to move beyond the problems harboured by liberal ecology. Indeed, several well known criminological and socio-legal journals have, in recent times, devoted whole issues to addressing themes such as, 'The Environment and Social Justice' (Goff and Geis, 1993), 'Environmental Victims' (Williams, 1996), 'For a Green Criminology' (Beirne, 1998), 'Interdisciplinary Perspectives on Environmental Law' (A-Khavari, England and Godden, 1999), 'Environmental Justice Policy' (Seis, 1999) and 'Globalisation and Environmental Harm' (Shank, 2002). In addition to these, several books have been published dealing with matters of ecological criminality (for example Edwards et al., 1996; Pearce and Tombs, 1998). Environmental criminological texts situated beyond liberal ecology fall into two broad ecophilosophical schools of thought – *biocentrism* (deep ecology) and *ecocentrism* (ecomarxism, ecofeminism and social ecology) (for a criminologically based outline of the basic principles behind each of these ecophilosophical schools, as well as that of anthropocentrism, see Halsey and White, 1998). Although the vast majority of this literature adopts a critically informed position on the structures and processes leading to environmental damage, there are a number of problems associated with such efforts which need, I think, to be brought to light. As a means of elucidating some of the problems associated with these ecophilosophical schools generally, I will examine the biocentrically informed work of Barnett (1999) and the ecocentrically based work of Benton (1998) as well as that of Lynch and Stretsky (2003).

The problem of biocentrism

Barnett's article, 'The Land Ethic and Environmental Crime', attempts to build an 'eco-critical' definition of, and means for dealing with, environmental offences based around the writings of Aldo Leopold – specifically, his 1947 work *A Sand County Almanac*.[4] Specifically, the category 'environmental crime' should be reorganised

4 The use of Leopold's work is in itself a problematic move since it does not sit easily along side the main tenets of eco-critical criminology (see Seis, 1993). One of the key claims of eco-critical criminology is that the human capacity to colonise and dominate most if not all parts of the biosphere *distinguishes* it from *all* other species. Leopold, on the other hand, was firmly of the view that humans are, as he puts it, merely 'plain members' of the biotic community. In short, it is probably not a wise decision to call upon a biocentric theorist to fill out the tenets of an eco-critical criminology since the latter is somewhat removed from the principle of biospheric egalitarianism (that is the belief in the moral equivalence and worth of

around Leopold's edict that, '[A] thing is right when it tends to preserve the integrity, stability and beauty of the biotic community. It is wrong when it tends otherwise' (quoted in Barnett, 1999, p. 162). The failure to base definitions of environmental crime around this principle has led, according to Barnett, to a sharp 'divergence between environmental harm in fact and environmental harm as conceived in law' (1999, p. 182). Further, Barnett explains that Leopold's work is not some romantic call for a 'return to nature' but is instead the result of 'good science'. As he writes, 'Leopold's observation of ecosystem dynamics led to *his scientific understanding of sustainability*. He considers the land ethic as science-based in that it aligned ethical demands with *objective need*' (1999, p. 182 emphasis added). Such an ethic – grounded as it is in science – has, according to Barnett, the capacity to radically transform social relations because 'land owners [would come] to recognise the realities of interdependency and sustainability and accept[ ] self imposed limits on their behaviour' (1999, p. 182). In addition to Leopold, the work of Edwin Sutherland is invoked by Barnett as a means of illustrating the power of group norms over law in influencing and changing behaviour – the idea being that people learn and internalise environmentally destructive rules and rationales and that they can therefore replace these with rules and rationales of an ecological kind.

From this brief summary it should be clear that there are a number of problems with Barnett's attempts to reframe matters of environmental harm within a biocentric framework. First, the urge to identify 'right' conduct with everything that tends toward 'integrity, stability and beauty' is a decidedly modernist not to mention dangerous idea. For one thing, it ignores the fact that ecosystems do *not* operate around steady-state principles. Instead, the so-called 'integrity' and 'stability' of 'the biotic community' fluctuates in accordance with forces often generated from those biotic communities themselves – storms, drought, fire, volcanic eruptions, and so forth. On a second and related count, it is questionable whether it is possible to logically speak of 'the biotic community' as something existing externally to the happenings of 'humanity'. Perhaps a more productive approach would be to say that there are numerous and heterogeneous interfaces between bodies and practices – some leading to monstrous crossbreeds (for example dioxin) and black holes (for example nuclear waste repositories) and some drawing lines of deterritorialisation (for example hemp based paper mills, nuclear free zones) (Deleuze and Guattari, 1996). Determining whether one is witnessing the former or the latter is an ongoing contestable project that cannot be brought to a halt by some casual and ontologically questionable reference to absolute beauty or integrity.

all species). This said, the point of Barnett's article is to establish a new relationship between (environmental) law and ethics. Indeed, he makes the general point that law necessarily stems from an ethics of one kind or another (1999, p. 166). This is, of course, a fair enough contention. However, it is also important to know that much law is predicated on *moral* not ethical principles (where morality denotes discursive practices of right and wrong whose form and limits are informed by religious or other transcendental narratives).

One might say, therefore, that the concepts of 'ecosystemic integrity', along with that of the 'beauty' of biotic environments, are anything but an objective means of positing a socio-environmental ethic(s). Indeed, what is most apparent is the way in which state departments co-opt the concept of ecosystemic integrity to justify present modes of harvesting and managing all manner of resources (fibres, grains, fruits, flesh, skins and so forth). The fact, for example, that clearfell logging and the concept of ecological integrity are made to stand as synonymous events in the eyes of most foresters should indicate that what matters in environmental conflict is not the 'harm' attached to a given state of affairs, so much as how various elements (bureaucratic, protest, and so on) bring about particular alignments between expert discourse and the cultural imaginary (see Luke, 1997). By taking the concept of beauty as timeless rather than discursively constructed, Barnett is unable to account for the fact that – to continue the example – forest administrators generally view a newly felled coupe as something of great beauty since it represents the opportunity for 'new' forest structures to emerge (where each stand of trees will be incessantly managed to display the same age, height and density). This, it should be recalled, is the bureaucrat's vision of a forest exhibiting unsurpassed levels of 'ecological integrity' and 'stability'. One might also draw attention to the way in which beauty has been used to oppress, injure and restrain not just bodies of Nature but the bodies of women as well (for example the practices of Chinese foot-binding, genital mutilation, and the like). This again shows that of critical importance in environmental matters is an awareness of how words and their associated (assembled) meanings evolve with respect to configurations of power and desire.

A third problem with Barnett's work is its uncritical adherence to the Western scientific method and its ability to know or recognise 'sustainability' in all its guises. Numerous studies have shown that science holds little capacity to name or capture the combination of forces which lead to environmental damage (see Beck, 1992; Lash et al., 1996). Moreover, where science believes it has adequately categorised Nature this has most often led not to benign practice but to a range of unforeseeable deleterious effects (for example failure of coupes to regenerate, sedimentation of fresh water streams, declining numbers of arboreal and ground dwelling mammals, and so on). In short, there is ample reason to be highly suspicious of any theory or ethic which tries to derive legitimacy on the basis of its scientificity. Biological science, just like criminology, is a discourse which, while leading to real effects, is constituted and sustained through all manner of rhetorical manoeuvres and assumptions about the limits of knowledge and the operation of power. For this reason alone, science needs always to be subject to critique not blind acceptance.[5]

A fourth and final problem associated with Barnett's work is his reluctance to think through the criminal justice oriented implications of defining environmental

5 This thought of course extends to the ecological trends cited at the outset of this discussion. That is, information contained in the World Resources text produces *truth claims* (by injecting a body of data into the body of particular social and political networks) and not *the* Truth about ecosystemic deterioration.

crime according to the tenets of the land ethic. As he admits, this approach will see a whole host of acts presently cast as 'environmental harm in fact' (that is harms which fall outside the boundaries drawn by law) come under the rubric of the juridical armature. This, I would suggest, is somewhat antithetical to the project(s) of critical criminology which, as I understand it, advocates for *less* not more state intervention in social, economic and ecological life. Moreover, criminologists have shown time and time again that criminalising a behaviour is a very poor way of reducing its occurrence. Admittedly, Barnett does invoke Sutherland's work as a means for suggesting that of ultimate importance in ecological matters is that ethics eventually must replace law/juridical coercion. But this does not go very far toward explaining how such an ethic might arise. Indeed, one might question whether it is in fact desirable for all persons to live by the tenets of one edict above all others. One could even say that such a plan harbours the potential for perpetuating a kind of (ecological) fascism. This is something that biocentrists do not seem to want to grasp – that there is strength in diversity of socio-ecological knowledges and practices and that the nature of Nature is not its capacity to foster an equality of relationships or some perfect symbiotic state, but its tendency toward disequilibrium and difference. Given such conditions, it is very hard to see how 'correct action' or 'best practice' could equate to rigidly adhering to the terrains and experiences mapped out by a single edict/principle. Profit, Christ, Progress, and Reason have all, at one time or another (and even collectively) been touted as *the* way to a perfected state of affairs. And all, of course, have led to untold violence for countless human and nonhuman worlds. How logical, therefore, is it to think that the 'new' idols of Integrity, Stability and Beauty will bring an end to such violence?

The problem of ecocentrism

Perhaps the key criminological statement to emerge around an ecocentric theme in recent times is by Ted Benton (a long time proponent of ecomarxism) entitled 'Rights and Justice on a Shared Planet: More Rights or New Relations'. This piece – appearing in what has become a key collection in the criminological literature on environmental harm – offers a sophisticated account of environmental protection based on an ecocentric conception of rights and obligations. It discusses and moves beyond both Peter Singer's utilitarian approach and Tom Regan's deontological (consequentialist) stance to the protection of species in order to chart a 'relational' ethical programme for combating human-induced environmental decay. Benton sums up his outlook as follows, 'The aim would be to generate harmonious, benevolent and co-operative spirals, as against destructive, competitive and antagonistic ones, through the establishment of new dominant patterns of interaction, experiences and spontaneous sentiments' (1998, p. 171). He continues,

> This alternative would be a many-sided project for social, economic and ecological transformation inspired by spontaneous moral sentiments which flow from anxiety and horror in the face of continuing human destruction of non-human nature, and by the

> egalitarian co-operative and popular democratic values inherited from earlier anarchist and socialist traditions, and now carried forward by the feminist, peace, green and other progressive social movements (1998, p. 171).

To be fair, Benton is quick to admit the utopian nature of his perspective. But such a recognition does not counteract other shortcomings harboured by his work. These have mainly to do with the problematic conception of human nature as well as the championing of a *universal* system of human and nonhuman rights. On the first count, the notion of human nature deployed by Benton is one which claims there is something that – after all is said and done – gives humanity an *essential* aspect. For Benton, this aspect waxes and wanes between the two poles of innate aggression/competition as against co-operation/reciprocity. The very fact that he acknowledges these *two* poles should dispel any possibility of a *fixed* human nature. To posit a human nature is to side with the view that humans are essentially and always x *not* y. But in his work, this tension is unresolved and it is this bipolar stance which leads Benton to call *both* for extensive state regulation *and* the maintenance of spaces/opportunities for 'spontaneous moral sentiments' which would somehow 'naturally' lead, as he terms them, to improved socio-ecological relations.

One could say that if there is a human nature it would exist always and absolutely or not at all. Here, Benton – as well as anthropocentric, biocentric and ecocentric theorists generally – runs up against a highly problematic view of the human subject. This problematic revolves around placing the seeds of ecological renewal *either* at the mercy of a benevolent and essentially co-operative subject waiting to be 'released' from systems/structures of antagonism and repression via sustained periods of mass reflection and rationally planned action, *or* such seeds are given over to the workings of an essentially malevolent and egoistic subject doomed to entrench structures of ecological collapse. In either case, there is a failure to develop a processual view of subjectivity – one which posits that human nature (just like Nature) is produced and reproduced through the *textual machines* which cut across the *assemblages*[6] (familial, pedagogical, political, leisure) each inhabits from one moment to the next. Criminologically, it is the work of Stuart Henry and Dragon Milovanovic (1996) that has come closest to outlining such a conception. I will say more on this shortly.

On the second count, problems also accompany Benton's appeal to a universal system of rights as the vehicle most capable of protecting human and nonhuman environments. Again, to be fair, Benton admits that 'rights may be little more than an empty formality, serving merely to legitimate persisting de facto inequalities' (1998, p. 162). However, he nonetheless goes on to place considerable faith in the 'inherent' emancipative powers common to movements and political creeds which draw/rely heavily upon appeals to universal rights (see Benton, 1998, p. 171). Indeed, the conclusion to his piece – which speaks of a time when 'Public regulation would be upholding and protecting what was already favoured and nurtured by every day experience of interaction with humans and other non-human

6 See Chapter 4 for a discussion of these terms.

beings and environments' – is laden with all the (problematic) rhetoric of modernity and its inability to resist positing foundations for measuring the moral aptitudes of the universal human subject (1998, p. 173). As Benton concludes, 'Above all, … a strongly institutionalised protection of universal civil liberties would still be required [in Eco-/Utopia?] to offset any tendency for new forms of oppression and exploitation to emerge, or for old ones to reassert themselves' (1998, p. 173).

This, of course, would present to many as a highly logical and prudent programme. However, I would argue that such a vision is imbued by the modernist dimensions and structures which have helped create and entrench anti-ecological networks across much of earth. For when, it might be asked, have institutions (which necessarily harbour an abstracted/reified account of 'the individual' and their circumstance(s)) ever been capable of upholding the *rights already extant* in international laws and treaties? Further, what kinds of narratives/voices would such institutions inadvertently marginalise or malign in the quest to uphold the 'Truth' of its socio-ecological vision? In short, and to draw on Foucault's sentiments in the foreword to *Anti-Oedipus*, how would such institutions learn to look for the micro fascist leanings inside each of its structures and programmes? There is, quite demonstrably, an urgent need for the emergence of a very different regulatory terrain – specifically, one which constantly puts asunder the concepts of 'Nature', 'sustainability', 'culture', 'economy' and 'humanity' which pervade its aspects. Contrast this against Benton's observation that in the future world governed by a 'relational' ethical outlook, 'Every imaginable form of human social life … will stand in need of regulation' (1998, p. 172). Here, the world conjured by Orwell in his *1984* seems perilously close – especially if by 'regulation' Benton means governance of human conduct by 'external powers' (this concept, it should be noted, is never clarified in his work).

Before offering some suggestions of how one might leave the shortcomings of green criminology behind, I want to offer a brief critique of one of the latest pieces to appear in the field. The relevant work here is entitled 'The Meaning of Green: Contrasting Criminological Perspectives' (Lynch and Stretsky, 2003)[7] and stands, I would argue, as one of the more thoughtful pieces to appear under the banner of green criminology.[8] The primary argument put by Lynch and Stretsky is that criminologists have a choice between two competing versions of what it is to be 'green' – the *corporate* perspective and the *environmental justice* view. The former defines environmental crime as events in contravention of the law and tends to disregard the impact of race, gender and power upon the formulation of such definitions (2003, pp. 229–30). The latter, on the other hand, defines 'a green

7 Despite stating that their aim is to 'highlight a human-centred orientation' for green criminology (Lynch and Stretsky, 2003, p. 218), I have included this text under ecocentrism because it a) seeks to move beyond crude market forces as solutions to environmental problems (placing it outside a liberal or anthropocentric framework) and b) views the human capacity for global ecological destruction as setting this species apart from all others (placing it outside a biocentric stance).

8 Lynch, it should be noted, was one of the first to raise the possibility of a green criminology (see Lynch, 1990).

crime [as] an act that 1) may or may not violate existing rules and environmental regulations; 2) has identifiable environmental damage outcomes; and 3) originated in human action' (Lynch and Stretsky, 2003, p. 227). Along with this definition goes the concern to analyse 'how forms of race, class and gender inequities affect the social construction of environmental laws' (2003, p. 228).

At first glance this sounds highly promising. However, there are a number of problems that need surveying. First, Lynch and Stretsky do not clarify their position regarding the role of the state and its relationship to strategies of environmental renewal. This is an absolutely critical issue because, as Stanley Cohen, reminds us, if more events are formally defined as crime the result will be a far wider array of acts (potentially) brought before authorities. The closest Lynch and Stretsky come to clearing up their position is their assertion that the green 'definition focuses attention on acts that, whether or not defined as illegal, *should nonetheless be considered criminal*' (2003, p. 229 emphasis added). If, on the one hand, they wish to argue – as they seem to do – that the capitalist state is the archetypal example of an institution suffering from chronic regulatory capture (see Paehlke and Torgerson, 1990), then they need to explain how such an institution could ever see its way clear to criminalise all those events which, to put it bluntly, make capitalism work. But if, on the other hand, the (future) role of the state is to remain largely unchanged, then (and this brings me to a second point of contention) Lynch and Stretsky need to advance a far more nuanced conception of (socio-cultural) power than they do. Here, it is boldly stated that 'Power … is the key issue that separates the[ ] opposing stances' of the corporate as against the environmental justice version of green criminology (2003, p. 230).

One of the great weaknesses of Lynch and Stretskys' piece is, I would submit, that they align themselves to a Marxist notion of power – a hydraulic rendering which says there are people/groups who possess power (in the manner of an object) and those who are devoid of it (for a critique, see Foucault, 1977, 1982). Indeed Lynch and Stretskys' text is imbued by all the traditional dichotomies which flow from such a conception (equality/inequality, powerful/powerless, corporations/citizens, First World/Third World, global/local, to name several).[9] The problem here is that such a view of power – and, specifically, the kind of stochastic modelling of the world it produces – ignores the *micropolitical* and *heterogeneous* practices, thoughts and routines which various persons/groups engage. It is, arguably, through the intra- and intersubjective modes (doing, thinking, ritualising) that the reproduction of the discursive frames used to justify, neutralise or normalise (environmental) harm occurs. Lynch and Stretsky are, in one sense, right to point out that the vast bulk of environmental damage stems from privileging 'the *economic sphere* over other

9 Perhaps the most striking (and damaging) binary in their work is that which attends the statement, '[Beyond all other definitions of environmental crime], [o]nly one viable option remains: the more radical environmental justice definition of green outlined [in our work]' (Lynch and Stretsky, 2003, p. 233). Here, a theoretical fascism has replaced any concern for open-ended exploration of socio-ecological possibilities.

social structures and issues' (Lynch and Stretsky, 2003, p. 231, emphasis added). But I want to suggest that structural economic power relies for its efficacy not simply on the relations between government, law and economy so much as on the *flows of pleasure* which invest the population at any one time. Not only is it profitable to be environmentally destructive (in the sense of mining, manufacturing cars, clearfelling forests), it *feels* good too (in the sense of purchasing a gold necklace, driving on the open road, looking at a table, chair, or house constructed from redwood, mahogany, mountain ash or the like). *Environmental damage is, in short, as much a corporeal (bodily/subjective) event as it is a corporate state practice* and Lynch and Stretsky do not address this situation.

A third criticism of Lynch and Stretskys' work concerns their invocation of a dialectical view of society (that is one that proclaims the existence of opposites (humanity/Nature) and that the resolution of opposites is possible and necessary). A green criminology, they argue, must strive for 'the elimination of social and economic inequalities' (2003, p. 229). Similar to that extolled by Barnett, Benton and others, this conception of the logics of social relations is of the modernist variety. It suggests that it is possible to invent a place and time where all humans can peacefully co-exist – and that universal goodwill toward one another will naturally be extended to nonhuman worlds as well. This, of course, is hubris.[10] To desire an end to 'social and economic inequality' may be politically correct, and may make certain people feel good about their regard for others, but it ignores the issue of how one judges (not to mention *who* would judge) where *difference* ends and inequality begins. The point here is that the judgements (laws, discourses, categories) which organise the earth and its inhabitants are viewed as sufficient to their task when they in fact harbour all manner of epistemological dilemmas – such as that concerning language and its (in)ability to adequately name or convey the meaning of events (ecological, cultural, and so on). Here, one runs the very real risk of marginalising that which gives the world its vitality. These are issues which Lynch and Stretsky neglect to address.

My fourth and final criticism relates to Lynch and Stretskys' deployment of the phrase 'environmental justice'. In this case they write as if they know – beyond any shadow of doubt – how to recognise this brand of justice (and, presumably, injustice) wherever and whenever it might occur. There is, in other words, an alignment to an Aristotelian view of justice (and thus of knowledge about the world). The classically Aristotelian question is of the form: What is x? Here, one either admits of essences and absolutes – that hiding behind appearances and surfaces (of each environmentally harmful event) lies the true or hidden meaning of things, or, one admits that 'truth', just like 'justice' or 'freedom' is discursively produced from moment to moment. Lynch and Stretsky fall foul of the first scenario – which is curious to say the least. For they correctly state that 'Crimes are constantly made and unmade through acts of social construction and deconstruction' (2003, p. 228). But, and this is critically

---

10 Derrida (1992, p. 28) once remarked, 'Nothing seems to me less outdated than the classical emancipatory ideal' (meaning that there can be no repressed or latent subjectivity waiting to be released to some ideal state).

important, they do not extend this same constructionist outlook to the concept of environmental justice. It is as if such justice is instinctual, universal, always already 'there', simply waiting to be pronounced. But this again is an absurd and dangerous position. What is called 'environmental justice' will be as susceptible to the forces of social, symbolic and rhetorical competition as those impacting the meaning(s) of environmental crime/harm. Justice, to be clear, is never pure or unadulterated. Instead, it arrives through the pronouncements of bodies who are themselves subject to a multitude of genealogical forces – forces which govern what it is logically possible to say about a given (criminal/harmful) event at any one point in time.

In search of an alternative terrain

In light of this critique, it is apparent that there are a number of problematic assumptions underpinning recent efforts by criminology to theorise environmental harm. These revolve mainly around: a) the general reluctance to put into critical relief the concept of environmental damage and the associated (but manifestly distinct) category of environmental crime; b) the inability to move beyond dialectical models of society and conflict resolution; c) the unwillingness to do away with modernist accounts of the relationship between 'words' and 'things'; and d) the incapacity to develop a nuanced account of human/environmental interaction. But given the ways criminology has envisioned Nature throughout its *his*tory these oversights are none-too-surprising. In highly schematic form, I would say that Nature – as deployed across two centuries of criminological thought from Beccaria to Lombroso, through to Becker and up to Henry and Milovanovic – functions in four main ways. First, in classical criminology Nature appears as the original or primordial sign – as that which can be read, deciphered, and mirrored by humanity in the laws it posits and the conceptions of the body it holds (rational, wilful, responsible, introspective). Here Nature presents as a *mimetic force* – it is something orderly, hierarchical, powerful and thus so should be the key institutions and principles characterising liberal democracy. Second, in positivist criminology, Nature presents as that which incites persons toward irrational and problematic conduct. Under this scenario, humanity loses the capacity for free and spontaneous action and is subject to the unpredictable conditions and trajectories that Nature summons forth *within* the human body. In a sense, Nature is cast here as a *dangerous and uncontrollable force*.

Third, in critical criminology (spanning social reactionist perspectives up to and including marxist and early feminist accounts of crime), Nature presents as the *external* factor which shapes and influences the capacity for benign or damaging conduct to materialise in a vast range of contexts (peer groups, families, schools, work places, neighbourhoods, states, and so on). In more detailed terms, Nature appears and disappears from the critical criminological scene in line with attempts to come to grips with the thresholds at which consciousness (the transcendental subject) and environment (enunciated not in terms of its ecological dimensions but in terms of *goods* (for example alcohol, drugs, guns), *services* (for example police, welfare, shelter, hospitals) and *external stimuli* (for example media, school curricula, peers, popular culture)) combine to produce scenarios of conflict rather than something other. Within critical criminology, Nature, it could be said, presents as the *recurring yet discursively absent other* – as the force which constitutes the objects of the criminological terrain[11] but which has been simultaneously made, until very recently, to occupy a location at the periphery of criminology's 'real' business.

Fourth, and finally, there marches the extension of critical criminology informed by a mixture of postmodernist and poststructuralist observations. Here, Nature has yet to be adequately theorised or discussed within criminology (but see Groombridge, 1998; Lane, 1998; Halsey, 1999). It is nonetheless important to draw attention to the kind of criminological work which resonates with what I have been advocating here. I mentioned earlier that Henry and Milovanovic (1996) are two seminal authors concerned to advance a criminological perspective which eschews modernist as well as (some kinds of) postmodernist constraints (see also Nelken, 1994; Young, 1996, 2004; Pavlich, 1999, 2000, 2001). Central to their work has been the formulation of a *constitutive* definition of crime – a definition that enables commentators to conceive of crime as having corporeal effects without having to rely upon notions of 'human nature' or the 'universal subject' nor upon linear conceptions of cause and effect. Although at times their articulation of such a definition seems imbued by an anthropocentric outlook,[12] and, further, although the very positing of a definition is in many senses a decidedly modernist trait (embodying the will to represent or contain events) – there remains, I believe, something useful in such an attempt. In specific terms, Henry and Milovanovic assert,

> Crimes [...] are nothing less than moments in the expression of power, such that those who are subjected to them are denied their own contribution to the encounter and often to future encounters, are denied their worth, are simultaneously reduced and repressed in one or several ways. Crime [...] is the power to deny others their ability to make a difference. It is the ultimate form of reification in which those subject to the power of another agency suffer the pain of being denied their own humanity, the power to make a difference... (1996, p. 116).

Clearly, it is necessary to view 'others' as having to include nonhuman as well as human bodies. It is also necessary to envisage 'the power to make a difference' as denoting the literally infinite array of colours, smells, sounds, as well as geological/botanical/hydrological flows and coagulations of particular regions which, if allowed to emerge, might meaningfully impact social, legal, political and aesthetic relations.

---

11 For example, police vehicles are linked to the production of magnesium and other metals as much as they are a means of transport or surveillance, and prisons – in so far as they require multiple resources for their construction and day to day operation – are as much a drain on the earth's ecology as they are places for incapacitation or rehabilitation.

12 For instance, at one point these authors remark, '[C]rime is the expression of some agency's energy to make a difference on others and it is the exclusion of those others who in the instant are rendered powerless to maintain or express their *humanity*' (Henry and Milovanovic, 1996, p. 116, emphasis added).

Here, the major strength of Henry and Milovanovics' work is that they are sensitive to the fluid nature of the concept 'harm' as well as to who or what is capable of being harmed from one moment (or politico-historical juncture) to the next. As they write, 'We need to define crime and its harm in terms of specific, but historically contingent, victim categories, but *to be aware of the emerging social constructions whose relations of power are relations of harm*' (1996, p. 119). In this sense the problem is not crime but the limits placed upon who and what can count as criminal subjects and/or criminal objects. More than this, *the problem is how to think beyond crime as a useful category of thought*.

A further strength of constitutive criminology is its understanding of the role of language in framing and producing harm – that words are, to greater or lesser degree, violent events,

> The call for universality in discourse (as in Habermas' call for a search for consensus in 'ideal speech situations') is a form of harm: it makes common that which is irregular, it homogenises the heterogeneous. As an alternative to the legalistic definition of crime, our postmodernist definition of crime focuses on harm inflicted *in all its guises* and would certainly include the 'violence of language' [...], particularly how the disenfranchised, disempowered, and marginalised have been denied expressive forms for their desires and yearnings ... (Henry and Milovanovic, 1996, p. 118).

What matters here is not the truth or falsity of Henry and Milovanovic's conception of crime so much as *how it might be put to work*. That is, what counts is the fact that such a definition may open up new discursive and *extra*-discursive pathways where other definitions have fallen short. As a means of teasing small-scale/local revolutions from overarching (seemingly fixed) situations or states of affairs, a definition of crime that puts the emphasis on inter-relatedness over and above segmentation would seem to be a good starting point. The utility of a definition of environmental crime will be the degree to which it elicits new types of existential territories, makes possible new modes of envisioning the human/earth nexus, invites a reconceptualisation of the relationship between speed and damage, and, following Spinoza, asks of bodies what each can *do* rather than what each *is* (that is what manner of becomings are sustained or curtailed by particular decisions to use or regulate earth).

Another sign of a good definition[13] of environmental crime would be its ability to chart *multiple ethical paths* and programmes without at the same time falling into a hyper-relativism. Following Nietzsche, it is crucial to consider the value of current values, which means, in effect, to consider which kind of body modernity has most often aligned itself with – the body of the herd, the same, and the representative?, or the body ceaselessly transforming, reaching, and creating 'beyond itself'? A crucial part of enacting a *transvaluation of all values* (Nietzsche, 1968) is to see

---

13 Of course, the plane of consistency knows nothing of definitions and perhaps, in an 'ideal' world, it would be best to be rid of them. But as a means of marking out the vicissitudes of various problems – indeed what counts *as* 'a problem' – definitions would seem to be an indispensable aspect of current states of affairs.

to it that one does not remain overtly and purely nihilistic – something which Henry and Milovanovic go to great lengths to reiterate.[14] Significantly, the process of de(con)struction[15] always already has an ethic or a trajectory residing within its parameters. The challenge is to discern the limits of the process of *re*construction, the limits of affirmation, the limits, in other words, of the new alignments between bodies and words that (might) emerge from critique. But just as it is important to be affirmative, it is equally important to be aware of the logic underpinning affirmation. For to chart a definition of crime or harm is to side with a *particular logic of accusation* (Pavlich, 2000). And to do this is to bring (back) into play at least some of the dualisms so common to the criminological terrain (harm/benign, cause/effect, culpability/incapacity, and so on). This in turn often leads to the appearance of bodies whose task it is to judge the moment when one side of the binary should divorce from the other. But in a constitutive world, it will be necessary to focus not on 'environment' versus 'jobs', 'protesters' versus 'administrators', 'crime' versus 'law', nor 'harm' versus 'integrity', but on the molarised structures which force particular assemblages of enunciation (such as courts, science, politics) to view these aspects as discrete points on a plane of reference rather than as becomings or intimations of the possible on the plane of consistency. And what of the role of commentary in a constitutive environment? Simply, *the task of the critic will be to draw attention to the possible by showing the contingent dimensions of the actual.*[16] More than this, the challenge becomes one of nurturing assemblages (academic and countless others) whose effect is to throw the transformative weight of the acategorical behind socio-ecological struggles. In an effort to put together such an assemblage, I turn in the next chapter to the work of Gilles Deleuze and Felix Guattari.

---

14 This is evident in their efforts to chart the distinction between a nihilist and an *affirmative* postmodern stance.

15 I am using this term in the Derridean sense. Pavlich (2001, p. 162) gives voice to this by observing, 'Deconstruction … is concerned with experiences that dissociate, open, welcome and include; it is not concerned with attempts to gather, entrench, defend or exclude by defining the present in absolute ways'.

16 In the words of one writer, each 'becomes the watch, the witness, who flags multiple shifting dangers that attach to social formations' (Pavlich, 2001, p. 163).

Chapter 3

Ecology and Machinic Thought: Deleuze/Guattari

> Not man as the king of creation, but rather as the being who is in intimate contact with the profound life of all forms or all types of beings, who is responsible for even the stars and animal life, and who ceaselessly plugs an organ-machine into an energy-machine, a tree into his body, a breast into his mouth, the sun into his asshole: the eternal custodian of the machines of the universe.
>
> Deleuze and Guattari, *Anti-Oedipus*, 1994, p. 4

The theme of this chapter is ecology and its relationship to machinic thought. As will become apparent, machinic thought opposes both modernist and structuralist accounts of environmental conflict (and therefore of subjectivity, power, knowledge, and desire).[1] It is a way of thinking-acting that regards as futile all political programmes aimed at the final resolution of the struggle between 'humans' and 'Nature', 'science' and 'opinion', or, in Nietzsche's terms, 'good' and 'evil'. Indeed, machinic thought holds such divisions to be not only ontologically problematic but socially, culturally and ecologically damaging. In plain terms, machinic thought is *post*structuralist in orientation. This means, primarily, that it harbours an inherent suspicion of any perspective or theory claiming necessary and/or immutable relations between signifier (for example forest block, rainforest) and signified (for example profit, conservation). As Deleuze and Guattari remark, 'Signs are not signs of a thing; they are signs of deterritorialization and reterritorialization, they mark a certain threshold crossed in the course of these movements ...' (1996, p. 67). In other words, signs – that which signifies and causes in us the urge to interpret or to ascribe meaning to particular phenomena – do not have lurking within them an essence or an eternal 'expressed'. If this were the case there could be *no* debate over the precise signifi(c)ance of such processes as global warming, habitat fragmentation, bleaching of coral reefs, falling numbers of the Spotted Quoll, and the like. Everything, or more accurately, *everysign* is open to interpretation,

> There is a simple general formula for the signifying regime of the sign (the signifying sign): every sign refers to another sign, and only to another sign, ad infinitum. That is why, at the limit, one can forgo the notion of the sign, for what is retained is not principally

---

1 For the classic account of structuralism, see Saussure, 1966. For applications in anthropology, psychoanalysis, and literary criticism, see, respectively, Levi-Strauss 1963; Lacan, 1968; Barthes, 1993.

> the sign's relation to a state of things it designates, or to an entity it signifies, but only the formal relation of sign to sign insofar as it defines a so-called signifying chain. The limitless of signifiance replaces the sign (Deleuze and Guattari, 1996, p. 112).

Whereas modernity attempted/attempts to locate an internally consistent relation between signifier and signified – one that would stand for all peoples for all time – poststructuralism tries to subvert such a programme. Indeed, 'The most fundamental difference between the structuralist and poststructuralist enterprises can be seen in the shift from the problematic of the subject to the deconstruction of the concept of *representation*' (Harari, 1979, p. 29, emphasis added). 'With representation,' writes Deleuze, 'concepts are like possibilities, but the subject of representation still determines the object as really conforming to the concept, as an *essence*. That is why representation as a whole is the element of knowledge which is realised by the recollection of the thought object and its recognition by a thinking subject' (1994, p. 191, emphasis added). Within a poststructuralist purview, representation stands as that which suspends *difference* – the difference immanent to persons, rivers, deserts, forests, invertebrates, music – in short, the difference immanent to life itself. And why is difference of such importance to poststructuralist thought? Because difference is that which serves to undermine the *model* – the model society, the model legal system, the model regulatory strategy, the model forest, the model crime, the model protester.[2] Accordingly, to represent the world (or a forest, or a forest protest) in an eternal or 'logical' fashion (whether this be through the auspices of God, science, or the propositional form) is to relegate thought to something little more than 'organized memories' (Deleuze and Guattari, 1996, p. 16).

Another key distinction to draw between structuralism and poststructuralism is that the former attempts to represent the world via the 'radical dismissal of the speaking subject' (Harari, 1979, p. 30). What subjects (that is 'persons', 'selves') say, do, and think in their day to day struggles is of importance for structuralism (and no less modernity) only because such struggles (can be made to) reflect 'larger' laws and processes. It is only by referring the desires, movements and anxieties of bodies back to some *Other* unifying force (mummy, signifier, god, state) that such phenomena can be 'fully' understood. By way of contrast, poststructuralism is highly sceptical of attempts to dissolve all semblance of subjectivity – especially through the positing of modernist structures (government, law, science, experts, family) which portend to know in advance precisely how and why bodies (will) think and behave. In specific terms, poststructuralism tries to explicate *both* the limits *and* possibilities of the subjectivities emerging from various representations of life – whether these manifest themselves through legislation, political manifestos, films, corporate slogans, protest banners, graffiti or whatever. Since it is intimately concerned with the forms, compositions, and effects of subjectivities – of what bodies can and cannot do – it becomes necessary to reject at the outset any notion that poststructuralism leads to

---

2 For further discussion of the concept 'difference' as the 'acategorical of thought', see Chapter 4.

extreme relativism, or worse, nihilism. In contradistinction to this oft laid charge, poststructuralism encourages merely the death of Man *not* subjectivity *per se*, or, more accurately, processes of subjectivation (that is the conscious manufacture of new existential territories). Having said this, it remains the case that '[t]he poststructuralist attitude is ... literally unthinkable without structuralism' – indeed 'it relies on structuralist premises in order, paradoxically, to show that structuralism has not fully pursued the implications of those premises' (Harari, 1979, p. 30).

There is now a considerable literature devoted to applying poststructuralist (as well as postmodernist) thought to environmental problems (see, for example, Cheney, 1989; Chawla, 1991; Hallman, 1991; Acampora, 1994; Bruner and Oelschlaeger, 1994; Litfin, 1994; Gare, 1995; Luke, 1995, 1997; Lash et al., 1996; Conley, 1997; Peace, 1997; Rutherford, 1997; Seddon, 1997; Virilio, 1997; Darier, 1999). But there is, somewhat incredibly, very little work examining the environmental and regulatory implications of two of the most important poststructuralist thinkers of the last three decades – Gilles Deleuze and Felix Guattari (but for notable exceptions, see Conley, 1997; Hayden, 1997; Halsey, 1999). This 'lack' of interest may simply be due to the fact that Deleuze, but less so, Guattari, spend very little time actually talking about environmental problems (at least in the orthodox sense). Or it may be due to the dense and frustratingly elusive nature of their work. Whatever the reason, a prime objective of this book is to demonstrate that Deleuze and Guattari are highly relevant to matters of environmental conflict and regulation – and specifically, in the present context, to matters of forest use and abuse in south eastern Australia.

Like Nietzsche, Deleuze and Guattari make thinking an inherently ethical project – meaning that when one thinks one is in fact never 'One' (a rational, independent subject) but a site always already infused by multiple forces and trajectories (or *machines*, see below),

> There are no individual statements, there never are. Every statement is the product of a machinic assemblage, in other words, of collective agents of enunciation (take 'collective agents' to mean not peoples or societies but multiplicities). The proper name (*nom propre*) does not designate an individual: it is on the contrary when the individual opens up to the multiplicities pervading him or he, at the outcome of the most severe operation of depersonalization, that he or she acquires his or her true proper name. The proper name is the instantaneous apprehension of a multiplicity. The proper name is the subject of a pure infinitive comprehended as such in a field of intensity (Deleuze and Guattari, 1996, p. 37).

There can be, therefore, no proper or authentic voice (of politicians, lawyers, loggers, protesters, and so on). Further to this, Deleuze and Guattari argue that the only 'true' form of thought is that which breaks with orthodox or traditional understandings of what it is to think. This orthodox understanding of thinking is termed by Deleuze the *image of thought* (and later in conjunction with Guattari the *strata*). The image of thought – the discursive structuring and limiting of what can be said and done – rigidly marks out the thresholds dividing self from other, inside from outside, the familiar from the unfamiliar, and, importantly, the ecologically significant from the ecologically expendable. On this basis, disengaging the image of thought – or 'the figure in which *doxa* is universalized by being elevated to the rational level' – becomes, for Deleuze and Guattari, the key to rewriting the world, and thereby its regulatory mechanisms, anew (Deleuze, 1994, p. 134). Put simply, as long as strategies for dealing with environmental conflict continue to unfold in the shadow cast by the image of thought or the strata, *nothing new will happen*. It is therefore necessary to discern if, how, and to what extent environmental regulation remains a prisoner of the familiar, of the recognisable, of the discursive – in short, of that which makes (common)sense. Typically such matters have invited little more than an explication of the processes contributing to 'regulatory capture' (Grabosky and Braithwaite, 1986; Gunningham et al., 1995; Howard, 2000). Under such a scenario, 'better' environmental regulation equates to transferring the structural power of those regulated (typically small and big business) to those responsible for administering and enforcing various laws. On other occasions business is encouraged to 'self-regulate' their interactions with Nature (Grabosky and Gant, 2000). Clearly, such approaches – along with numerous others (see Halsey, 1997a) – serve only to *mimic* rather than seriously impair the image of thought. This is chiefly because the political, industrial, juridical and social structures of Western democracies are allowed to remain intact despite considerable evidence showing these to be major *contributors* to environmental damage, or, more accurately, to its discursive limits (that is of what can 'rightfully' be said and done about such events) (Weisberg, 1971; Paehlke and Torgerson, 1990; Beck, 1992; Halsey, 1997b).

Deleuze writes, 'Thought is … filled with no more than an image of itself, one in which it recognizes itself the more it recognizes things: this is a finger, this is a table, [this is a forest, this is environmental harm] …' (1994, p. 138). To break with the image of thought (and indeed, one might say, the image of *Nature*), to get, in other words, beyond habit and the well-worn refrains of environmental regulatory institutions (and here such 'institutions' are taken to include human and nonhuman bodies with their various flows, speeds and intensities), one thing above all else is required – namely, the courage to invent and apply *new concepts* to socio-ecological problems. As philosophers (but also as people responding to social dilemmas in the fields of politics, psychoanalysis and elsewhere), Deleuze and Guattari are extremely adept at such inventions and applications. Indeed, it is their sustained capacity to contort and invent the world through conceptual phenomena that makes them integral to the current study. Whether it be the concept of *socius* or *assemblage* or that of the *plane of consistency* or the *fold*, there is something in their work (both independently and collectively) that provides the basis from which to think about environmental regulation, and in particular, environmental conflict, in very different terms than has hitherto been the case.

In general terms, the work of Deleuze and Guattari provides a means for keeping pace with the mobility of environmental problems by considering Nature and systems of environmental regulation as always already discursively produced and contested. They make no grand claims concerning 'solutions', or, as the present case demands, the precise conditions for long-term 'ecological sustainability'. Indeed terms such as these (that is 'solution', 'sustainability', 'programme', 'short-term', 'long-term') should be subjected to rigorous interrogation and perhaps ultimately effaced from the lexicon of environmental struggle. In a sense, it may be better to do to Society and Nature what Nietzsche did to God and man. The claims, therefore, made by Deleuze and Guattari – and, more importantly, those tendered by the present study – are decidedly modest. And they are modest insofar as no attempt can or will be made to uncover the general rules or structures of environmental conflict. Instead, this study focuses distinctly and exclusively on the activities impacting a geographically small (but in no sense insignificant) area in the southeast corner of Australia. As mentioned in the Introduction, the goal will be to map the combination of statements and practices that have marked this space over time and which, as a result, have made certain renderings of Nature and Man visible, thinkable and acceptable, and others marginal, nonsensical and dangerous. My contention in this book is that knowing how Society and Nature have been textually incorporated in times past is integral to knowing the limits and potentials of current environmental regulatory policies.

There remain, now, two interrelated tasks to be completed below. The first – foreign as it may seem – involves very briefly surveying the significance of thought of Friedrich Nietzsche. In many ways Nietzsche was the thinker who provided the bridge between the processual/machinic philosophies formulated in Greek thought (predominantly Ionian Cosmology) and the poststructuralist/postmodernist enterprises emanating from France during the 1960s and beyond with such figures as Lyotard, Foucault and Derrida. The second task will be to introduce some of the key aspects of Deleuze and Guattari's work.

Precedents to machinic thought

To think machinically is to view the world in terms of an incessant mutability or flux. Perhaps the first individual to articulate the machinic or processual nature of the world was Thales. His speculations (and subsequently those of Heraclitus, Homer, Anaximander and Cratylus) seriously undermined the deifying/Apollonian overtones of ancient Greek thought. Although Thales' work on the subject is thought never to have existed in chirographic form, it is commonly understood that he conceived *water*, rather than man or god, to be 'the reality of all things' (Nietzsche, 1994, p. 42). The interesting issue here is why would water be chosen to fulfil this role. Thales himself left no explanation (see Collingwood, 1960, pp. 30–2), but several reasons can be posited. First, and as Aristotle ventured, 'moisture is necessary for the nourishment of every organism' whereas Man has long posed as a threat to such organisms. Second, and again as Aristotle proffered, 'every animal's life begins in seminal fluid' making Man – from the very 'first' – the subject of a *flow* rather than a structure or teleology (Collingwood, 1960, p. 31). Third, water is active and transformative whereas Man is reactive and imitative. Fourth, water is always arriving or exiting whereas Man is characterised by a becoming-still. Fifth, water is composed of infinitely varied speeds whereas Man is something constant,

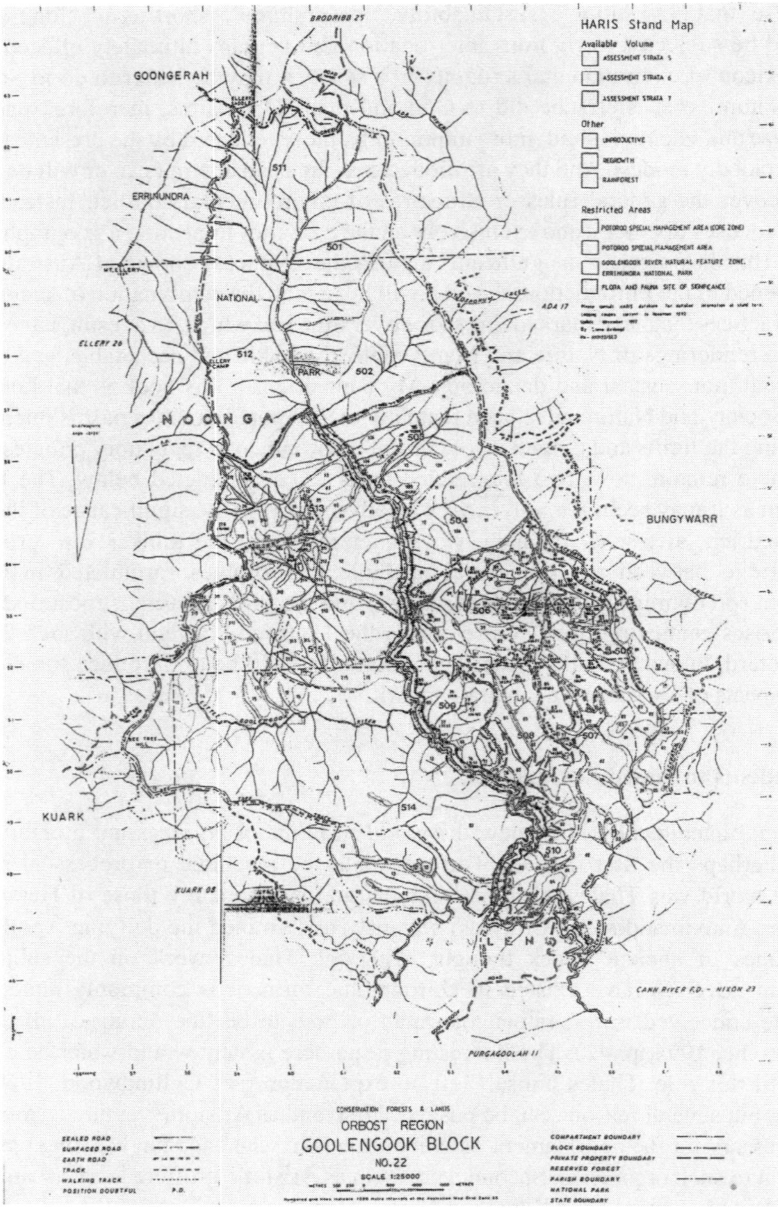

Figure 1 **Map displaying location and distribution of forest stands and compartments for Goolengook forest management block, 1992. Sourced from Department of Natural Resources and Environment, Orbost, Victoria © State of Victoria, Department of Conservation, Forests and Lands (1992)**

Figure 2 **Photograph of author standing on the track dividing the northeastern portion of Goolengook forest block from Ada block. The featured tree is most likely a Messmate (eucalyptus obliqua) and stands about 70 metres (220 feet) tall. Photography: Adam Biggs**

predictable and habitual. Finally, water – through processes such as evaporation and osmosis – makes a mockery of the reactive forces of containing, trapping, fixing and dominating. Man, on the other hand, revels in being the object of such forces – that is, reactive man desires to be folded, subjected, limited. In effect, water is chosen by Thales for its ability to proliferate a *philosophy of flows and becomings* instead of a metaphysics of structures and beings.

It was precisely this philosophy of fluxes and becomings (of decentred subjects (humans) and objects (world)) that proved too much for the ancients (and nearly all subsequent epochs) to bear. Why? Chiefly because a philosophy of flows – living one's life as a becoming-other – is both liberating *and* dangerous. *Liberating* in the sense that a philosophy of flows promotes a new-found lightness of the relation between culture and earth – a space where life can be affirmed as something joyful, active, creative and as existing in a realm 'beyond good and evil'. As Zarathustra remarks, 'And this is the great noontide; it is when man stands at the middle of his course between animal and Superman and celebrates his journey to the evening as his highest hope: for it is the journey to a new morning' (1969, p. 104). *Dangerous* in the sense that this freeing of active or Dionysian forces demands that each and every *body* becomes a commander of its own capacities and desires – that each invents what Nietzsche called a radical 'will to self-responsibility' (1990a, p. 102). The risks inherent within such a task (of becoming-legislator of one's own existence) are many. As Zarathustra declares,

> [C]ommanding is more difficult than obeying. And not only because the commander [active force] bears the burden of all who obey [reactive force], and that this burden can easily crush him. In commanding there appear[s] ... to be an experiment and a risk: and the living creature risks himself when he commands. Yes, even when he commands himself: then also must he make amends for his commanding. He must become judge and avenger and victim of his own law (Nietzsche, 1969, p. 137).

What is crushing here is the preponderance of Dionysian forces (flux, flow, change, chaos) over Apollonian forms (stasis, structure, sameness, order). Here, man is like a child who gets the toy (that is freedom from Idols/Ideals) he desires minus instructions for its safe or benign use. The question emerging here is: How does one impose form and predictability in world declared (by Ionion Cosmology at least) to be in a constant state of flux? Relatedly, by what authority does one begin to legislate where God, Reason, Logic and so forth have all been imploded? These are the questions which have for so long haunted modernity. Indeed they have functioned, as Bauman shows, as its essential aporia. 'The everlasting and exclusive coming-to-be, the impermanence of everything actual, which constantly acts and comes-to-be but never is, as Heraclitus teaches it, is a terrible, paralyzing thought. Its impact on men can most nearly be likened to the sensation during an earthquake when one loses one's familiar confidence in a firmly grounded earth' (Nietzsche, 1994, p. 54). This is where the journey of self-overcoming, of embracing the great noontide, of starting the perilous journey toward the overman (or toward what Deleuze and Guattari term a *body without organs*) proves too hard for the majority – and most certainly for all social and political *systems* (of modernity). At such a point, man recoils on 'ultimate man' instead of unleashing the *ubermensch* (Nietzsche, 1969, pp. 46–7). Man, in other words, continues to be a *slave* (of other people's drives) rather than a *master* (of 'his' own desires). And Nature continues to be something fixed, exterior, explicable, controllable.

The case of Nietzsche

In terms of those who have struggled to free the human subject – and indeed Nature – from the discourses spawned by the Enlightenment (that is discourses of right, rationality, consciousness, cause, effect), Nietzsche stands alone as the figure who never tired of proclaiming processuality as the defining (or in Deleuzean terms *immanent*) aspect of the cosmos. With a vigour and style like none before him, Nietzsche writes,

> And do you know what 'the world' is to me? ... This world: a monster of energy, without beginning, without end; a firm, iron magnitude of force that does not grow bigger or smaller, that does not expend itself but only transforms itself; ... enclosed by 'nothingness' as a boundary; ... not a space that might be 'empty' here or there, but rather as a force throughout, as a play of forces and waves of forces, at the same time one and many, increasing here and at the same time decreasing there; a sea of forces flowing and rushing together, eternally changing, eternally flooding back, with tremendous years of recurrence, with an ebb and a flood of its forms; out of the simplest forms striving toward the complex, out of the stillest, most rigid, coldest forms toward the hottest, most turbulent, most self-contradictory, and then again returning home to the simple out of this abundance, out of the play of contradictions back to the joy of concord, still affirming itself ... as a becoming that knows no satiety, no disgust, no weariness: this my *Dionysian* world of the eternally self-creating, the eternally self-destroying, this mystery world of the twofold voluptuous delight, my 'beyond good and evil,' without goal unless the joy of the circle is itself a goal; without will, unless a ring feels good will toward itself – do you want a name for this world? A *solution* for all its riddles? ... *This world is the will to power – and nothing besides!* And you yourselves are also this will to power – and nothing besides! (1968, §1067).

The objective in this remarkable passage is to destroy the bodies, images and representations (of thought) constructed by certain metaphysicians (Plato, Aristotle, Socrates, Kant, Rosseau) – bodies, images and representations which have long served to imprison or tame the *active* forces within human beings/Nature (see Hallam, 1991; Parkes, 1999). The concept 'will to power' was invented by Nietzsche because he felt it best reflected the world of which he was a part. This was a world where seasons, friends, conversations, diets, thoughts, kings, cities, diseases – in a word, *everything*, came to pass. The will to power is therefore immanently *anti-arborescent* in that it is opposed to foundations or original causes. Like Deleuze and Guattari's conception of *desire* (see below) it proliferates beyond itself, beyond its own image of the universe and the established 'order of things'. As Deleuze writes, '*The will to power is the element from which derive both the quantitative difference of related forces and the quality that devolves into each force in this relation*. The will to power here reveals its nature as the principle of the synthesis of forces. In this synthesis – which relates to time – forces pass through the same differences again or diversity is reproduced' (Deleuze, 1983, p. 50).

For Nietzsche, the production of differential forces could only be realised via an ongoing *pathos of distance* and a belief in the *transience of all things* (even of his own philosophy). In the first case, this meant upholding a pathos within and between *cultures*: 'No people could live without evaluating; but if it wishes to maintain itself it must not evaluate as its neighbor evaluates' (1969, p. 84); and within and between *institutions*: 'Liberal institutions cease to be liberal as soon as they are attained: subsequently there is nothing more thoroughly harmful to freedom than liberal institutions. One knows, indeed, *what* they bring about: they undermine the will to power, they are the levelling of mountain and valley exalted to a moral principle, they make small, cowardly and smug – it is the herd animal that triumphs with them every time. Liberalism: in plain words, *reduction to the herd animal*' (1990a, p. 102). In the second case, the production of difference meant believing in the *transience of scientific knowledge*, 'There are no facts, everything is in flux, incomprehensible, elusive; what is relatively most enduring is – our opinions' (1968, §604); the *transience of first principles*, 'It is *we* alone who have fabricated causes, succession, reciprocity, relativity, compulsion, number, law, freedom, motive, purpose; and when we falsely introduce this world of symbols into things and mingle it with them as though this symbol-world were an "in-itself", we once more behave as we have always behaved, namely *mythologically*' (1990b, p. 51); and the *transience of being*, '*cogito ergo sum*: that means: Something is believed therefore something is believed – a vicious circle. One would have to know what being is in order to get the *sum* from the *cogito*; one would also have to know what "knowing" is: one starts from the *belief* in logic – in the *ergo* before all else – and not uniquely from the position of fact!' (quoted in Kofman, 1991, p. 178).

But Nietzsche also insisted that if one was to fully comprehend those factors which contributed to the demise of difference (to the colonisation of earth as unbounded matter and energy) one had necessarily to be aware of the hypostatising and reifying effects of *language*, of the manner by which the intra- and intergenerational qualities of discourse (re)present certain ways of articulating bodies as natural and/or timeless. 'I shall reiterate a hundred times that "immediate certainty", like "absolute knowledge" and "thing in itself", contains a *contradictio in adjecto*: we really ought to get free from the seduction of words!' (1990b, p. 46). 'I fear we are not getting rid of God because we still believe in grammar' (1990a, p. 48). And again, 'The significance of language for the evolution of culture lies in this, that mankind set up in language a separate world beside the other world, a place it took to be so firmly set that, standing upon it, it could lift the rest of the world off its hinges and make itself master of it' (1991, p. 11). Nietzsche was one of the first to point out the violence attached to speaking and writing – or, to what amounts to the same thing, the violence of concepts, categories and names. In or around 1870, he observed,

> All the knowledge which is of assistance to us involves the *identification of things which are not the same*, of things which are only similar. In other words, such knowledge is essentially illogical.
>
> Only in this way do we obtain a concept. Then afterwards we behave as if the concept, e.g. the concept 'man', were something factual, whereas it is surely only something we have constructed through a process of ignoring all individual features. We presuppose that nature behaves in accordance with such a concept. But in this case first nature and then the concept are anthropomorphic. The *omitting* of what is individual provides us with the concept, and with this our knowledge begins: in *categorizing*, in the establishment of *classes*. But the essence of things does not correspond to this: it is a process of knowledge which does not touch upon the essence of things [...]
>
> We produce beings as the *bearers of properties* and abstractions as the causes of these properties. That a unity, e.g. a tree, appears to us to be a multiplicity of properties and relations is something doubly anthropomorphic: in the first place, this delimited unity, 'tree', does not exist; it is arbitrary to carve out a thing in this manner (according to the eye, according to the form). Furthermore, each relation is not the true, absolute relation, but is again anthropomorphically colored (Nietzsche, 1992, pp. 51–2).

It should come as no surprise that Nietzsche – before, even, the publication of such works as Wittgenstein's *Philosophical Investigations* – would comment on the limits of language. He was, after all, convenor of a course on Rhetoric at Basel University (taught, purportedly, to an audience of two). The fact that Nietzsche took seriously the epistemological and ethical issues at stake in the relation between word and world, means that he must stand at the forefront of any poststructuralist analysis of the discursive and textual (re)production of environmental conflict and its regulation.

Like any erudite thinker, Nietzsche knew better than most the danger(s) of ignoring his word. 'The time for petty politics is past: the very next century will bring with it the struggle for mastery over the whole earth – the *compulsion* to grand politics' (1990b, p. 138). One might also include here the compulsion to 'grand corporatism' and the commodification of the Other. 'For some time now, our whole European [read global] culture has been moving as toward a catastrophe, with tortured tension that is growing from decade to decade: restlessly, violently, headlong, like a river that wants to reach the end, that no longer reflects, that is afraid to reflect' (1968, §2). Does this not speak directly of the politics of denial currently practised in respect of ecological ruin? '[T]here will be wars such as there have never yet been on earth' (1979, p. 127). Wars over ozone, fresh water, oil, fishing stocks, biodiversity, salinity, uranium and so forth. 'No herdsman and one herd. Everyone wants the same thing, everyone is the same: whoever thinks otherwise goes voluntarily into the madhouse' (1969, p. 46). The marginalisation of the 'loony left', the hippies, the monkey-wrenchers, the new-agers, the full-time dissenters. From the present vantage point, it was as if Nietzsche was gazing into a crystal ball. The twentieth century indeed fostered a will to fascism (to a becoming-the-same, to a becoming-herd-conscious) across the surface of the earth. But this is a fascism not only rooted within those so-called 'evil' and 'barbaric' nations of Mussolini's

Italy, Hitler's Germany, Stalin's Russia, Deng's China or Castro's Cuba. Rather, it is a fascism which holds equal sway (under different guises and channels) in Bush's US, Blair's Britain, Howard's Australia, and elsewhere. In fact, difference (flow, process) is threatened whenever and wherever a will to a system predominates. For all systems are founded on – take root around – *arborescent* principles. And arborescence, according to Deleuze and Guattari, is antithetical to processuality, to a maintenance of the conditions for difference, to a fostering of forces which allow for the proliferation of active bodies and, of course, socio-ecological vitality.

Deleuze/Guattari

It is within the above context that the work of Deleuze and Guattari gains much of its significance. Like Nietzsche, Deleuze and Guattari are deeply troubled by the subjectivities holding sway in contemporary culture. And like Nietzsche they interpret the so-called 'lack' of a transcendental foundation or teleology as leading to *more*, not fewer, ethical decisions. Here, the unfolding of life becomes an immanently ethical process since it is always already tied to all manner of other bodies – social, legal, political, biological, geological, geographic, industrial, molecular, scientific, technological and so forth. All this in a world where there is and can be no intrinsic congruency between reality (world) and representation (signs) and no definitive or consistent ontological divide between subject (Man) and object (Nature). For present matters, then, the crucial question is this: On what authority – by what epistemological criteria – do we presently name particular kinds of bodies and force them to stand in multifarious (indeed some would say, *monstrous*) alignments? What is it, for example, that we do, when we make the body of the Slender Tree Fern stand alongside the body of a forest coupe plan? What kinds of becomings are either facilitated or cast aside in such scenarios?

These kinds of questions guide the tenor of analyses undertaken in ensuing chapters. They are questions which arise from a realisation that current methods of regulating environmental harm/conflict tend too often toward the preservation and legitimisation of the kinds of subjectivities (or existential territories) responsible for such conflict. They are also questions formulated in the knowledge that there can be no single solution to socio-ecological problems – that the destruction of the earth derives from a multiplicity of sources (hence the need for a schizoanalytic rather than purely structuralist or modernist accounts of socio-ecological ruin). Finally, they are questions that treat seriously the cultural (masculine, feminine, Indigenous), economic (material) and epistemological (philosophical) dimensions of human-induced environmental damage. There is no disputing the idea, in other words, that politico-social 'systems' founded on, for instance, the subjugation of women and men, exponential material growth, and/or a fervent disdain of philosophical inquiry, will eventually ruin the entropic limits of the earth (not to mention other planets/bodies – witness the geological and topographical surveys of mars and the moon). The objective now will be to offer a general overview of Deleuze and Guattari's thought. This will facilitate a better grasp of the methodology and lexicon discussed in Chapter 3 and beyond.

Schizoanalysis (thinking machinically)

As already explained, to think machinically is to invoke a processual conception of society and subjectivity (see Guattari, 1995, pp. 1–32),

> [The] idea of process is fundamental. It assumes that one has discarded the idea that one must absolutely master an object or a subject – and that [...] analytical research is given a dimension of finitude, singularity, existential delimitation, precariousness in relation to time and values ... [T]here are neither ends nor means; only processes; nothing but processes; processes auto-constructing life, auto-constructing the world, with mutant, unforeseen, unheard-of affects (1996, p. 277).

This is, quite clearly, a very different conception of social relations and 'self-hood' than that configured by modernity. Processes or machines bring an omnipresent volatility to the *concepts* (ways of thinking) and *subjectivities* (ways of existing) previously understood to be immutable, normal, and otherwise wholly sufficient to their task. The kinds of concepts of relevance to this study are those such as 'sustainable yield', 'geographic representation unit', 'forest perimeter', and 'old-growth'. The subjectivities at stake are those such as 'forester', 'conservationist', 'protester', and 'consumer'. Arguably, something highly unsettling happens to each of these once the idea of process has taken the place of structure (that is once the privileged position of the signifier has been undermined). For when, it may be asked, does a heathland 'end' and a forest 'begin'? At what point, precisely, does/should/can a forest be classified as 'negligibly disturbed' rather than 'old-growth'? How does/can one know that a forest is adequately represented or conserved? On what basis do we chart the distinction between the 'ecologically significant' and the 'ecologically insignificant'? Questions such as these have no definitive answers and yet modern environmental regulatory strategies have always given out the opposite impression – as if the aporia at work here were merely a fleeting itch to be scratched rather than an enduring ethical moment to be seriously contemplated.

One could also ask: How is it that consumers of, say, building products or copying paper, are conceived as inhabiting logically distinct worlds to that of a forest? Is it not possible that the divisions erected between 'everyday' consumers and so-called 'distant' forests are sustained by nothing other than rhetoric (that is the tropes of metonymy, synecdoche, metaphor, mimeses and so forth)? In other words, isn't it probable that, as Nietzsche would say, such divisions hold good only to the extent that Aristotle's law of contradiction is uncritically ascended to? – a law which dictates that 'we are unable to affirm and deny one and the same thing' such as that a consumer is always already immersed in urban *and* rural flows and that even the division between these flows is one which has more to with grammar than some enduring 'reality' (see Nietzsche, 1968, §516). Alternatively, one could pose the question: On what authority do we assert the forester body to be wholly divorced from that of the protester body? Might there not be, in other words, something of a 'minor protester' in the forest bureaucrat? Equally, might there not be something of a 'minor bureaucrat' in the forest protester? There is no good reason for thinking the hands which operate a chainsaw cannot or will not one day be those holding an anti-logging placard. But neither is there good reason for thinking the opposite. All that can be said is that 'reality' – the common ordering of uncommon events – assumes its forms according to the lines or machines which run through and across the plane of consistency (earth) from moment to moment. Mapping the lived and potential effects and affects of these lines is the task Deleuze and Guattari set themselves.

Deleuze and Guattari call their philosophy *schizoanalysis* (also termed throughout their work 'micropolitics', 'pragmatics', 'rhizomatics' and 'nomadology'). Schizoanalysis is intimately interested in the machines or lines which, on the one hand, divide the world into subjects and objects and make certain bodies knowable and recognisable, and, on the other, implode the division between subjects and objects and cause certain bodies to resist or complicate the roles and categories to which they have been assigned. Schizoanalysis is therefore concerned both with what gets captured *and* with what eludes categorisation – whether this be a crime, a certain section of forest, a form of protest, a kind of odour, or whatever. Under this scenario, the 'world' is no longer conceived (as is in Foucault's writings on panopticism) as some kind of unity or series of disciplinary regimes where nothing flees. Instead, the guiding thought is that 'Everything escapes, everything creates – never alone, but through an abstract machine that produces continuums of intensity, effects conjunctions of deterritorialization, and extracts expressions [that is statements, words, signs] and contents [that is bodies, representations, things]' (Deleuze and Guattari, 1996, p. 142). The social, in Deleuze's own terms, 'is something that never stops slipping away' (1995, p. 271). Such a view of socio-ecological relations, or of what Deleuze and Guattari term the *mechanosphere*, has, as shall be seen, the function of circumventing the aborescence of State philosophy (or Royal science) and its longing for permanent closure around such notions as 'subject', 'object', 'crime', 'environment', 'sustainability', 'rationality', 'cause' and 'effect'.

The notion that society is constantly 'slipping away' is an extremely important one. It suggests the greatest problem confronting 'humanity' and, more particularly, the numerous 'directors' of apparatuses of control (politicians, judges, police, army, CEOs, scientists, parents, teachers) is how to prevent the world from fleeing in all directions and not, as some would have it, how to incite change. 'It is wrongly said (in Marxism in particular) that a society is defined by its contradictions. That is true only on the larger scale of things. From the point of view of micropolitics, a society is defined by its lines of flight, which are molecular. There is always something that flows or flees, that escapes the binary organizations, the resonance apparatus, and the overcoding machine: things that are attributed to a "change in values," the youth, women, the mad, and so on' (Deleuze and Guattari, 1996, p. 216). In short, no one knows ahead of time what will happen.[3] This fleeing, this continual secretion of difference, will be brought to the fore in ensuing chapters when examining the repeated attempts to administer Nature or a particular 'forested' area. Such an administering equates to what Deleuze and Guattari term the organisation or 'machining' of the 'plane of consistency'.

Plane of consistency Schizoanalysis posits the operation of multiple abstract machines across what Deleuze and Guattari call the 'plane of consistency' – which is, in some sense, the equivalent to saying that Earth is coded and inscribed in multiple ways producing a certain alignment of bodies. The concept of machine will be elaborated in greater depth in Chapter 4. However, there are two points to note here. First, the function of machines is to break and redirect flows – flows of capital, wood, metal,

3 In Deleuze and Guattari's terms, a 'leak' may in fact become a 'rupture'. For example, the persistence of environmental conflict works on, eats away and brings about leakages in political notions of resource use (leading to the establishment of the Resource Assessment Commission). These leaks in the notion of resource use can and sometimes do effect leakages in the concept of economic rationalism (leading to the concept 'ecologically sustainable development'). Leakages in the notion of ecologically sustainable development on occasion produces leaks in the practices of industry (heralding the establishment of the National Pollution Inventory). Leakages here – in the form of publicly disseminated information about greenhouse gas emissions – could effect a rupture in the equation 'economic growth = ecosystemic health'. This in turn could lead to ruptures in the ethic driving consumer culture. Leakages in this notion may secrete new forms of subjectivity or 'singularised existential territories' freed from the constraints and neuroses produced by present configurations of the social machinery (Guattari, 1995). And then again, none or only one or two of these mutations may occur. Worse still, leaks may be met by a proliferation of molar blockages (for example waving of environmental impact statements for large firms, the approval of pollution permits, the subsidisation of the practice of clearing native vegetation, tougher penalties for protesters). In Deleuze and Guattari's terminology, the trace (*same*) may well prevail over the map (*diagram*). The liberating affects of smooth space may be forsaken for the 'security' of striated space (see 1996, plateau 14). The opportunity for a relative deterritorialisation of the ecologically injurious body may be passed over in favour of a reterritorialisation of the consumer driven subject. Incorporeal universes and asignifying regimes may cease to proliferate. The construction of a plane of consistency, which is in fact 'a plane of continuous variation' (1996, p. 511), may be blocked. All this depends largely on the nature of, and speed with which, the various apparatuses of capture are able to recode those bodies attempting to give force to a particular mode of becoming. For instance, a politician commenting on the inefficacy of carbon sinks as a means of reducing greenhouse gases (a becoming-active) might be recoded by a number of distinct apparatuses of capture (a becoming-reactive) such as political machines, industrial machines, constituent machines, media machines and so forth. In turn, the success of these apparatuses of capture will further depend on the extent to which each is able to lodge itself within a range of bodies distributed across the mechanosphere. In this case, those bodies would be politicians, heads of industry, voters and journalists. Another way of saying all this is that the capacity for a leak to become a rupture (to become-other, to open onto a line of flight, or in old parlance, to usher in 'radical' change) is dependent on the proximity of the different machinic assemblages (which are always already collective

genes, friendship, knowledge, work and so forth (see Deleuze and Guattari, 1994a, p. 36). Second, when Deleuze and Guattari talk about machines they are not talking about some 'inhuman' or purely mechanical device. Instead they are talking about the processes which give to the earth its discursive qualities and quantities (the effects levied by abstract machines of coding) and which, on occasion, implode the logic underpinning such qualities and quantities (the effects levied by abstract machines of absolute decoding). Without machines, then, there would be no such thing as Nature, Man, Woman, Species, Environmental Harm, Conflict, Forest, Spotted Quoll, and the like. Instead, and most significantly, there would pass the continual variation and return of the flow of unformed elements unmarked by anthropomorphisms or distinctions between words and things. This moment of 'pure intensities' is the plane of consistency and presents as an important concept for teasing out the effects of naming, dividing, and dichotomising the cosmos,

> The plane of consistency … is opposed to the plane of organization and development. Organization and development concern form and substance: at once the development of form and the formation of substance or a subject. But the plane of consistency knows nothing of substance and form: haecceities, which are inscribed on this plane, are precisely modes of individuation proceeding neither by form nor by the subject. The plane consists abstractly, but really, in relations of speed and slowness between unformed elements, and in compositions of corresponding intensive affects … Spinoza, Holderlin, Nietzsche are

---

assemblages of enunciation) to various abstract machines (Deleuze and Guattari, 1996, p. 504).

To take another example, the persistence of crime – in many ways the leak *par excellence* – has often been known to bring about leakages in juridical notions of specific and general deterrence (leading to decriminalisation). These leaks in the notion of deterrence can and sometimes do effect leakages in the concept of punishment (leading to decarceration or community service). Leakages in the concept of punishment on occasions lead to leaks in the procedures administered by the juridico-legal complex (for example Royal Inquiry into Aboriginal Deaths in Custody). Leaks or ruptures (two very different things) in the latter could effect leaks in the idea of the 'rule of law' (that the law is inherently discriminatory and selective). Leaks in the rule of law, may well effect (or give force to nascent) leaks and ruptures in (neo)classical notions of responsibility, rationality and legitimacy. Leakages in these notions may again secrete new forms of subjectivity. But it is equally likely that none of this will occur. Molar blockages in the form of 'three strikes and you're in', midnight curfews for troublesome youth, manufacture of new offence codes, and greater numbers of police may all ensue. Again, what happens will depend on the ability of the apparatuses of capture to recode bodies becoming-other. A judge commenting on the inefficacy of prison as a means of deterrence and rehabilitation (a becoming-active) might be recoded by a number of distinct apparatuses of capture (a becoming-reactive) such as government, the legal profession, the bench, academia, the media, public surveys, schools, families and so on. In turn, the success of these apparatuses of capture will further depend on the extent to which each is able to lodge itself within a range of bodies distributed across the mechanosphere. In this case, those bodies would be attorneys' general, lawyers, fellow judges, crimino-legal experts, journalists, statisticians, teachers, parents and so forth.

the surveyors of such a plane of consistency. Never unifications, never totalizations, but rather consistencies or consolidations (1996, p. 507).

From this passage it can be said that schizoanalysis is concerned to show the price paid for blocking/filling out the plane of consistency with particular kinds of bodies – forests, rivers, races, genders, economies, chronologies, legalities, policies. A sustained engagement with Deleuze and Guattari prompts the question: *At what social, cultural and ecological cost do – indeed can – we presently name, divide, and regulate the plane of consistency*? It should not in any way be supposed that the plane of consistency resides as some kind of lost panacea for current ills. For how could, in any case, something be considered 'lost' that is *always already there*? Rather, the plane of consistency (the plane of supermolecular Nature) is that which has the potential to radically problematise present ways of conceiving the society-economy-culture-Nature nexus. More than this, it causes each rendering of 'the real' (for example forest), 'the proper' (for example function), and 'the authentic' (for example custodian) to be put asunder. Through its concern to map both the ambiguity of bodies and the (traditionally molar) responses levied by particular agencies to such ambiguity, schizoanalysis stands as a technique for problematising and perhaps even disengaging the structures of modernity (or the image of (environmental) thought).[4] As Guattari remarks, 'Destiny is not inscribed in an infrastructure. Capitalist societies secrete a society, a subjectivity which is in no way natural, in no way necessary. One could very well do something else. What I refuse is the idea of an inevitable and necessary program' (Guattari, 1996a, p. 277). For Deleuze and Guattari, the structuring of what is necessary and what is inevitable – whether this be in relation to environmental conflict and its regulation or something other – occurs at the level of the 'socius'.

Socius The socius (also termed the 'mechanosphere') inscribes the plane of consistency with words (for example 'integrated harvesting', 'old-growth') and things ('loggers', 'trees'). It assembles the subject (the organism, the forester, the administrator) and the object (the organs, the forest, the management plan) and makes historically and politically specific relations seem timeless and immutable. The term 'socius' is indicative of the fact that social relations always already involve a contorting of individuality and a limiting of various bodies' potentials. 'The social machine or socius may be the body of the Earth, the body of the Despot, the body of Money ... The prime function incumbent upon the socius ... [is] ... to codify the flows of desire, to inscribe them, to record them, to see to it that no flow exists that is not properly dammed up, channeled, regulated' (Deleuze and Guattari, 1994a,

4 As a metamodel, schizoanalysis knows nothing of the model, of representation, of authenticity. 'What distinguishes metamodelization from modelization is the way it uses terms to develop possible openings onto the virtual and onto creative processuality' (Guattari, 1995, p. 31).

p. 33).[5] In this sense the socius functions only by producing and attaching itself to *bodies* (student, politician, judge, forest, environmental activist) and *statements* (end of term reports, maiden speeches, sentences, coupe plans, placards). Massumi (1992, p. 76), tracing the work of Deleuze and Guattari, writes,

> A society is a dissipative structure with its own determining tension between a limitative body without organs and a nonlimitative one. Together, in their interaction, they are called a 'socius' (the abstract machine of society). The nonlimitative body without organs of a socius is the sum total of its constituent supermolecular bodies, or individuals, from the point of view of their potential for 'free' or 'willful' action, in other words for the undetermined selection of singular states as a locally-globally correlated population. The limitative body without organs of a socius is a set of whole attractors proposed by a society for its individuals, the better to exploit their habit-forming potential.

The idea expressed here is thoroughly Nietzschean. Far from cultivating freedom and spontaneity, society and culture are structures which *tame* and *subdue* creative forces. Witness, for instance, the censoring of art, the marginalisation of subsistence living, the delineation and othering of *wild*erness, and the suppression of 'youthful' desires. The socius is the abstract machine *par excellence* since it extracts bodies of finitude and molarity (similarity) from a sea of infinitude and multiplicity (difference/plane of consistency). It is, in Massumi's terms, '... *the overall abstract machine* [which] brings the content formed by the machinic assemblage and the expression formed by the collective assemblage of enunciation into an asymptotic encounter ...' (Massumi, 1992, p. 27, emphasis added). What Massumi is saying here is that the socius brings together *words* (for example 'environmental crime', 'ecological sustainability') and *things* (for example faulty exhaust, regrowth forest) and makes them stand in an orderly and knowable (or 'asymptotic') fashion (for example 'this is pollution', 'this is good environmental management'). Money is an obvious example of an abstract machine feeding into and transforming the socius. But so too is the idea/stereotype/moralised construct Nature or the conceptions of

5 The socius is therefore anti-Spinozist and anti-Nietzschean. It does everything within its power to keep the question 'What is a body capable of?' (and responses such as becoming-subsistent) permanently to one side (see Spinoza, 1996, pp. 71–4). It has as its aim the subversion of Nietzsche's message that 'The body is a great intelligence, a multiplicity ...' and that this body has as its most fervent object a desire 'to create beyond itself' (Nietzsche, 1969, pp. 61–3). It is, in other terms, the role of the socius to bring together the molar machines (of agriculture, town planning, transport, health, water quality, law enforcement, work, leisure, and so on) and collective assemblages of enunciation (farming bodies, architectural and engineering bodies, transport bodies, medicinal bodies, regulatory bodies, prosecution bodies, employment and training bodies, tourism and sporting bodies) in order to ensure the arrangement, location, segmentation, coding and where necessary decoding and recoding of all the bodies (the (un)fed, the (un)housed, the (im)mobile, the (un)well, the (un)lawful, the (un)employed, the (un)productive) in a manner conducive to the reproduction of capital on ever increasing scales. Are not schools the most exquisite example of the socius assembling and contorting desire?

'nonhumanity' erected by government, law, science and so forth. And it is here that another of Deleuze and Guattari's concepts needs explicating. For whatever the machine, whatever its powers of extraction or coding, the socius continually contorts and assembles the flow of 'desire'.

Desire Desire is an incredibly important if complex notion. In very simple terms it is that which flows at different speeds and intensities across the plane of consistency. In contrast to authors such as Freud and Lacan, desire is held by Deleuze and Guattari to be 'a process of production without reference to any exterior agency, whether it be a lack that hollows it out or a pleasure that fills it' (Deleuze and Guattari, 1996, p. 154). Elaborating on this definition Guattari states that,

> [D]esire is everything that exists *before* the opposition between subject and object, *before* representation and production. It's everything whereby the world and affects constitute us outside of ourselves, in spite of ourselves. It's everything that overflows from us. That's why we define it as flow [*flux*]. Within this context we were led to forge a new notion in order to specify in what way this kind of desire is not some sort of undifferentiated magma, and thereby dangerous, suspicious, or incestuous. So we speak of machines, of 'desiring machines', in order to indicate that there is as yet no question here of 'structure', that is, of any subjective position, objective redundancy, or coordinates of reference. Machines arrange and connect flows. They do not recognize distinctions between persons, organs, material flows, and semiotic flows (Guattari, 1996, p. 205).

This, to my mind, is a beautiful passage for it expresses what so often passes as inexpressible in the context of environmental conflict and regulation. This inexpressible, this *a*categorical, is earth *minus* anthropomorphic inventions and interferences. *Earth without Machines*. Desire in one sense *is* this 'first' nature. But not 'first' in the sense of a chronological antecedent. And *not* the (molar) Nature which (molar) Man has constructed. Rather, this nature (or Earth without Machines) is that which gets inscribed (given form and function) by all manner of discursive and textual forces. It is critical to distinguish, therefore, 'molar Nature' (plane of organisation) as against 'molecular Nature' (plane of consistency) – just as it was important in the previous chapter to distinguish molar Man and Woman (the becoming-the-same of humanity) from molecular man and woman (the becoming-other of humanity). 'The [...] molar and the molecular are distinguished not by size, scale, or dimension but by the nature of the system of reference envisioned' (Deleuze and Guattari, 1996, p. 217). Thus, when Deleuze and Guattari write that 'Desire is always assembled; it is what the assemblage determines it to be' they are saying that molar Nature – the Nature that resides within and through official or popular discourse – emerges from the combination of particular kinds of captured bodies (political, legal, departmental, green) and well-rehearsed enunciations (laws, policies, codes of practice, slogans) (Deleuze and Guattari, 1996, p. 229). And when they write that '*There is only desire and the social and nothing else*' they mean there is only *flow* (molecular Nature) and the *machinic assemblages of enunciation* which extract and ascribe a particular order or (common)sense to such flow (Deleuze and Guattari, 1994a, p. 29). Orders such as: subspecies, species, family, genus; understorey, overstorey, canopy; ecological vegetation class, broad vegetation type, forest type. Commonsense scenarios such as: 'economic growth is essential for ecological sustainability'; 'Nature needs to be managed'; 'regrowth forest is a sign of healthy forest terrain'. And here we return to the concept of socius. For it is the socius which arrests desire or molecular Nature and puts it to work in a certain manner – moulding it (forest block) and sending it in one direction (contributor to GDP) instead of another (contributor to biodiversity). Hence the importance in Deleuze and Guattari's work of what they term the three *apparatuses of capture* – 'LAND (as opposed to territory), WORK (as opposed to activity) and MONEY (as opposed to exchange)' (1996, pp. 443–44). These are, in many ways, the three main abstract machines of coding scarring or running across the plane of consistency – each working to produce alignments of bodies conducive to the extension of capitalism. However, one should not assume that such apparatuses represent a complete blockage of desire – that molecular Nature is everywhere moralised.

Flow and multiplicity One of the key heuristic devices for Deleuze and Guattari is the notion of 'flow'. 'What is it,' asks Deleuze, 'that moves over the body of a society? It is always flows, and a person is always a cutting off of a flow. A person is always a point of departure for the production of a flow, a point of destination for the reception of a flow, a flow of any kind; or, better yet, an interception of many flows' (Deleuze, 1971). In *Anti-Oedipus* Deleuze and Guattari write, 'Amniotic fluid spilling out of the sac and kidney stones; flowing hair; a flow of spittle, a flow of sperm, shit, or urine that are produced by partial objects and constantly cut off by other partial objects, which in turn produce other flows, interrupted by other partial objects. Every "object" presupposes the continuity of a flow; every flow, the fragmentation of the object' (Deleuze and Guattari, 1994a, p. 6). And from *A Thousand Plateaus* it is asserted that 'The four principal flows that torment the representatives of the world economy, or of the axiomatic, are the flow of matter-energy, the flow of population, the flow of food, and the urban flow. The situation seems inextricable because the axiomatic never ceases to create all of these problems, while at the same time its axioms, even multiplied, deny it the means of resolving them (for example the circulation and distribution that would make it possible to feed the world)' (Deleuze and Guattari, 1996, p. 468).

What these passages point toward is a cosmos traversed by flux – by the ceaseless movement of unformed elements and intensities (that is the plane of consistency) made periodically into bodies of one kind or another. 'Societies', 'selves', 'knowledges', and 'forests' all occur only as particular kinds of discursive and textual arrangements of the otherwise unbounded and asignifi(c)ant flow of unformed elements and intensities. For instance, the scientific name '*Eucalyptus obliqua*' not only delineates a particular kind of botanical body for a specific field of knowledge so much as it forms part of a much wider effort to transform the 'chaos' and 'dangers' of the plane of consistency into knowable and quantifiable terms and images. It could be said, therefore, that modernity is the era marked by repeated attempts to perfect the kinds of bodies capable of dealing with such chaos (with *flux*) – the *body of science* conceived to combat the flow of unknown variables, the *body of law* designed to combat the flow of criminality and dissent, the *body of conservation* founded to combat the flows of biotic degradation, and so forth. As mentioned in the previous chapter, the attempt to plug up or seal off each of these and other flows has been anything but successful. In fact, efforts to 'contain' various flows has brought with it all manner of monstrous secretions (the containment of uranium secreting Chernobyl, the containment of crude oil secreting the Exxon Valdez, the containment of chlorofluorocarbons secreting increased skin cancers, the containment of Third World labour secreting tropical deforestation).[6]

For Deleuze and Guattari the disjunction in evidence here has largely to do with the fact that each body – each force erected to capture or contain a flow – is always already a site of instability. In other words, far from being homogeneous or sutured entities, bodies are a *multiplicity*. 'A multiplicity', write Deleuze and Guattari,

> is defined not by its elements, nor by a center of unification or comprehension. It is defined by the number of dimensions it has; it is not divisible, it cannot lose or gain a dimension *without changing its nature*. Since its variations and dimensions are immanent to it, *it amounts to the same thing to say that each multiplicity is already composed of heterogeneous terms in symbiosis, and that a multiplicity is continually transforming itself into a string of other multiplicities, according to its thresholds and doors* (1996, p. 249).

The idea that bodies are multiplicities applies as much to the so-called 'nonhuman' body of a spent nuclear fuel rod, or an electorate, or a forest, as it does to the 'human' body of a scientist, a politician or an environmental protester. What is most significant about multiplicities is that they never cease to pervade or break through the organised spaces borne by the Signifier – that 'despotic agency that substitutes itself for asignifying proper names and replaces multiplicities with the dismal unity of an object declared lost' (Deleuze and Guattari, 1996, p. 28). A good example of a 'despotic agency' or overcoded concept is the signifier 'environmental activist'. This phrase tends to conjure a particular kind of image or body – one that, for instance, has little or no respect for authority, is unclean, probably unemployed, and acts in their own rather than on behalf of the 'national interest'. At the same time, environmental activists are much more than the sum total of these things.

6 The ideas expressed here echo the distinction drawn by Virilio between the 'specific' and 'generalised' accident. In relation to the former he remarks, '[E]very time a technology is invented, take shipping for instance, an accident is invented together with it, in this case, the shipwreck, which is exactly contemporaneous with the invention of the shipwreck' (Virilio, 2000, p. 40). Virilio goes on to contend that with the application of the 'absolute velocity of electromagnetic waves' to certain bodies (such as nuclear reactors) we are now in the midst of technologies that allow for the occurrence of the integrated or generalised accident. As he comments, '[W]hen an event takes place somewhere today, the possibility arises that it might destroy everything' (Virilio, 2000, p. 40). In the final chapter of the present study, it will be argued that the division and organisation of forested terrains in East Gippsland are apt to produce the generalised accident of habitat loss/depletion of biodiversity.

Indeed, when written as a multiplicity this body begins to extrude all manner of other meanings and possibilities. The environmental activist body could also be the body of a concerned resident, a mother, a father, a child, a fully paid professional, a retiree, a student, a member of local Council, or whoever.[7] As Deleuze and Guattari assert, '... [A] rhizome or multiplicity never allows itself to be overcoded ...' since each of these is '... defined by the outside: by the abstract line, the line of flight or deterritorialization according to which they change in nature and connect with other multiplicities' (1996, p. 9).

In contrast to the structures erected by binary (or arborescent/modernist) thought, the concept of multiplicity 'ceases to have any relation to the One as subject or object, natural or spiritual reality, image and world. Multiplicities are rhizomatic, and expose arborescent pseudomultiplicities for what they are. There is no unity to serve as a pivot in the object or to divide the subject. There is not even the unity to abort in the object or "return" in the subject' (Deleuze and Guattari, 1996, p. 8). It is no longer possible, in other words, to posit the existence of essences (truth, good, evil, harm) or enduring entities (self, other, society, Nature) – although this is in no way to imply that these particular abstract machines have no significant or knowable effect(s). Instead, everything that can or ever could be conceived or spoken of (for example a forest, a crime, and so on) must now be considered a blockage on the plane of consistency and as a body waiting to flee the categories, codes and laws that produce them.[8] 'Nature' needs therefore to be viewed not in terms of some

---

7 Another example of the way the Signifier feeds into and sustains the image of thought can be found in the marxist configuration of the human body. Consider the humble arm, which, under marxism equates to little more than an appendage of labour power – an economic category. To schizoanalysis, this would indeed constitute a legitimate reading since there is, of course, ample evidence to demonstrate that arms function for certain durations as the means for economic production (lifting, turning, holding, pressing, pointing, signalling). But a machinic philosophy would contend that reducing arms to an economic category is an example of aborescent thought taking hold – of a language putting down its roots and settling doggedly on a given perspective in order to declare economics to be the end of the matter. And all this despite the fact that an arm can never be *just* an economic appendage. This could only occur if each body was forced to labour day and night in perpetuity which, of course, is a biological impossibility – something explicitly noted but not elaborated by Marx himself in *Das Capital*. Machinic thought, by way of contrast, conceives arms to be immersed in all kinds of processes – inscription (tattoos), display (body building), affection (hugging), support (headrest), battle (striking), subversion (writing) to name several. Further, arms (and indeed legs, heads, stomachs, hair) are conceived as machines which plug into an infinite number of other machines. For example, an arm-machine may form a barrier between the eye-machine and the sun-machine to create a vision-assemblage. And in so doing this simple action (deploying an arm as a shield) simultaneously brings about the redirection of certain *flows* (neurones) and *intensities* (light) which, at a particular *speed* (a few seconds), transforms a visually-impaired-assemblage into a visually-effective-assemblage.

8 Recognising multiplicities is to admit that *being is incapable of subsuming becoming*. Trees, for example, are a multiplicity (an excess) in that they open onto a plethora of other machinic assemblages (construction-machines, bird-machines, insect-machines, sun-

primordial or eternal entity occupying a space beyond or outside 'humanity', but as an *affect* produced continually along side – indeed through – the various machines (political, scientific, industrial) that spill forth various bodies, statements, and signifying regimes from one moment to the next.

In sum, the proliferation of multiplicities – the immanent deterritorialisation[9] or dissipation of bodies – enables machinic thought to replace the traditional pedagogical concern with *structures* (of the brain, family, society, economy, environment) with a preference for mapping the composition, direction, effects and *a*ffects of bodies and their alignments. One commentator has written that '[T]he brain is as much in the world as it is in the head' (Ansell-Pearson, 1999, p. 178). In keeping with the ideas presented above, one can add that (molar) Nature is as much in our heads as in the world. This is not to say that writing the world in its multiplicity leads automatically to chaos or disorder – to a random distribution of bodies and abstract machines with no way of unfolding an ethic. In fact, configuring an individual, or a group, or a corporation, or a forest as a multiplicity is an act which has very serious consequences for the socius. Why? Because 'the social' and 'the environmental' is a decidedly false (reactive) dichotomy. Two passages from Deleuze and Guattari affirm this point,

> [M]an and nature are not like two opposite terms confronting each other – not even in the sense of bipolar opposites within a relationship of causation, ideation, or expression (cause and effect, subject and object, etc.); rather, they are one and the same essential reality, the producer-product. Production as process overtakes all idealistic categories and constitutes a cycle whose relationship to desire is that of an immanent principle (1994, pp. 4–5).

A decade later – using slightly different terminology – they write,

---

machines, playhouse-machines, and so on). And these 'secondary' machines all deterritorialise and reterritorialise around other multiplicities (resident-machines, worm-machines, leaf-machines, seed-machines, nostalgia-machines) and infuse different kinds of flows (familial, invertebrate, cellular, granular, neuronal). Wood is also an excellent example of the immanence of becoming-other. Under the right conditions and left long enough wood becomes stone or coal. Coal eventually turns to diamond. Diamond, with the continued movement of tectonic plates returns to earth. Earth becomes nutriment for seeds. Seeds, with a little bit of luck, sunshine and rain become trees. Over time, trees decay and become wood. And wood becomes coal, or canoe, or plank, or shelter, or bridge, or roost, or status symbol (mahogany). A rhizome rather than the root. Proliferation in place of arborescence.

9 'Deterritorialisation' is a term deployed by Deleuze and Guattari to denote an 'uprooting of structure organized within a definite territory' (Guattari, 1988). The importance of deterritorialisation to machinic thought is borne out by Deleuze's remark that, 'A society, but also a collective assemblage, is defined first by its points of deterritorialization, its fluxes of deterritorialization' (Deleuze, 1987, p. 125). 'Immanent deterritorialization' means that every*body* – whether it be a flower, bird, forest, regulatory institution, or whatever – continually faces, intermingles with, draws energy from, or opens onto other bodies *which are themselves multiplicities*.

> [E]ach individual is an infinite multiplicity, and the whole of Nature is a multiplicity of perfectly individuated multiplicities. The plane of consistency of Nature is like an immense Abstract Machine, abstract yet real and individual; its pieces are the various assemblages and individuals, each of which groups together an infinity of particles entering into an infinity of more or less interconnected relations. There is therefore a unity to the plane of nature, which applies equally to the inanimate and the animate, the artificial and the natural (1996, p. 254).

What else is environmental conflict if not the visible and audible result of attempts to constitute various portions of earth as a unity in spite of it being a multiplicity? The task in the next chapter will be to outline the methodology and lexicon engaged to write such events.

Chapter 4

Event, Method, Lexicon

Everything that enters consciousness as 'unity' is already tremendously complex: we always have only a semblance of unity.

Nietzsche, *The Will to Power*, (1968) [1886–1887], §489

To Ms Tehan,

[...] Logging commenced in the heart of Goolengook forest block in early June 1997... Your department has ignored the ecological recommendations of the pre-logging survey, completed by botanists working for the DCNR [Department of Conservation and Natural Resources] which identified seven sites of significance and stated that this should be the minimum excluded from logging to preserve the biological integrity of this highly sensitive environment ... In conjunction with irreplaceable rainforest values, slender tree ferns and pristine water catchments, Goolengook contains at least five pairs of sooty owls making it the most highly concentrated region in Victoria. Owls and gliders require old growth trees with large hollows in which to rest and roost. Clearfelling destroys their habitat forever. Goolengook is also an important habitat for the tiger quoll, which has recently been listed as an endangered species. I am outraged that logging for an industry which is neither economically nor environmentally sustainable is valued as a higher priority by our current government than preserving Goolengook – a vital tourist area which can never be replaced.

Extracted from a leaflet headed 'Goolengook: Too Precious to Log', addressed to the Hon Marie Tehan, Minister for Conservation and the Environment, distributed for public signing by Friends of the Earth, circa July–September 1997

Dear Sir/Madam,

[...] Logging in the Goolengook forest block should be seen in the context of the East Gippsland region ... The disputed area of forest in Goolengook forest block totals approximately 800 ha. Coupes totaling an estimated area of 506 ha are scheduled for harvesting in this area over the four year period 1996–2000 ... Pre-logging flora and fauna surveys between 1983 and 1993 covered 36 of the 103 forest blocks in East Gippsland. The department draws heavily on data from these surveys and the expertise of its biologists for the planning of conservation and management strategies ... All the significant values identified by the report are protected in the Errinundra National Park, the Goolengook River Heritage River, the Special Protection Zone or by other conservation strategies established in the East Gippsland Forest Management Plan.

Extracted from an information sheet headed 'Timber Harvesting in the Goolengook Area', distributed by Forest Services Division, Department of Natural Resources and Environment, 13 October 1997

Event

Of what do these passages speak? Clearly, the first speaks of a space under siege, one whose so-called 'pristine' character is in the process of being irrevocably transformed. It speaks, in other words, of the *embattled* body of a forest and the species which dwell within it. The second passage, though, offers a very different rendering of the same space. It talks of a terrain whose aspects are well protected, a space whose constitution needs to be viewed in the context of the larger geographical and administrative unit of which it has been deemed a part. In short, the second passage speaks of and thereby produces the body of a *sufficiently protected* forest.

These passages are typical of the kind of polarisation that has held sway for many decades surrounding the logging of native forest in far eastern Victoria and Australia generally. Goolengook forest block is in many senses the latest and most visible version of such polarisation. As mentioned in the introduction to the book, it would be comparatively easy to write this conflict as being about the privileging of profits over ecology, or jobs over the environment, or in terms of 'greenies' versus loggers, or police versus 'feral' protesters, or indeed in any other manner that pits one 'side' or faction against another. However, the issues surrounding the management of Goolengook forest block extend far beyond such renderings. In subsequent chapters, an attempt will be made to depart from traditional ways of writing about forest conflict in order to suggest that Goolengook *as event* is not really about forests at all. Instead, the ensuing analysis will start with the notion that places like Goolengook *become* – they are always already invented, fabricated, without essence. This is not to say, however, that they are any less 'real'. Deleuze and Guattari remark, '[A] line of becoming has neither beginning nor end, departure nor arrival, origin nor destination' (1996, p. 293). My contention is that the process of 'becoming-known', 'becoming-forest' and, thereby, of 'becoming-contested', is intimately related to a multitude of historical events or textual machines. Accordingly, 'Goolengook' needs to be considered in accordance with the particular ways of enunciating, configuring, utilising and occupying the geopolitical terrain(s) of which it has formed a part over time. For the moment, 'event' or machine can be taken as that which interrupts or transforms a 'state of affairs' and yet nonetheless 'eludes its own actualization in everything that happens' (Deleuze and Guattari, 1994b, p. 156). By 'state of affairs', Deleuze and Guattari mean an 'actual system … or a domain of functions' which exist as 'a time between two instants, or as times between many instants' (1994b, p. 157). What the following chapters attempt to convey, therefore, is a 'history' or, better still, a micropolitics of the textual machines or processes of codification that have contributed to the invention of the space now commonly referred to as 'Goolengook' – a schizoanalytic of states of affairs or bodies and of the functions pertaining therein.

It is important to understand that such a history will not – indeed cannot – be that which seeks to locate an origin (that is the 'real' or 'authentic' Goolengook). As Deleuze and Guattari assert, 'All history does is to translate a coexistence of becomings into a succession' (1996, p. 430). In keeping with Deleuze's reading of Spinoza, it will be necessary to put aside the question of what the body of Goolengook *is* or is not (essence) in order to ask what the body of Goolengook can or cannot *do* (affect). In simple terms: Of what is Goolengook capable subsequent to the production of different texts and the (re)alignment of (its) body/bodies? In formulating a response to this question, my analysis focuses predominantly on matters of vision (ways of seeing Nature), naming (categories of Nature), speed (rates of transforming Nature), and affects (relations between 'natural' and 'artificial' bodies). The kind of 'history' at stake here will therefore be geared toward the production of Goolengook as a *multiplicity* not a unity – a 'history' that records Goolengook as something more than a timber production zone, conservation zone, or site of conflict. This, *ipso facto*, requires that Goolengook be written both as a site of ascribed functions (or what Deleuze and Guattari call a 'full body') *and* as a site for continual experimentation with the real (or a 'full body without organs'). In simpler terms, a schizoanalytic of Goolengook requires that it be interrogated in terms of its capacity to produce the same as well as its capacity for the production of *difference*.

The notion of difference – or, what amounts to the same thing, *the plane of consistency* – has been all but neglected in the context of theorising environmental regulation (for an explication of Deleuze's conception of difference, see May, 1997; Ansell-Pearson, 1999). This is, to say the least, a surprising state of affairs. For what, it may be asked, is environmental regulation if not the 'formal' imposition of categories over parts of the earth? And what is difference (*desire*, *haecceities*) if not the ensemble or flow of forces which evades or problematises such impositions and efforts to segment the world according to this or that unit of value? In an erudite review of Deleuze's *Difference and Repetition* Foucault remarks,

> The most tenacious subjection of difference is undoubtedly that maintained by categories. By showing the number of different ways in which being can express itself, by specifying its forms of attribution, by imposing in a certain way the distribution of existing things, categories create a condition where being maintains its undifferentiated repose at the highest level. Categories organize the play of affirmations and negations, establish the legitimacy of resemblances within representation, and guarantee the objectivity and operation of concepts. They suppress the anarchy of difference, divide differences into zones, delimit their rights, and prescribe their task of specification with respect to individual beings ... Difference can only be liberated through the invention of an acategorical thought (Foucault, 1980a, p. 186).

This passage succinctly captures a key contention guiding analyses throughout subsequent sections of this book – namely, that the categories which *organ*ise the earth are too often viewed as sufficient to their task when they in fact harbour all manner of epistemological dilemmas and rhetorical shifts. What will be illustrated is that the production of categories *always already* harbors an ethic linked to the production of a life (or lives) and/or a death (or deaths). For instance, configuring the concept 'forest' to mean 'an area...dominated by trees having usually a single stem and a mature or potentially mature stand height exceeding 5 metres' (Commonwealth of Australia, 1992) rather than, say, 20 metres, has serious consequences for biodiversity, employment, resource security, research and development, and so forth. Conceiving the production of categories as an immanently ethical project is to invoke what Guattari has termed a 'new aesthetic paradigm', a paradigm that 'has ethico-political implications because to speak of creation is to speak of the responsibility of the creative instance with regard to the thing created, inflection of the state of things, bifurcation beyond pre-established schemas … The genesis of enunciation is itself caught up in the movement of processual creation' (1995, p. 107). It is precisely because Goolengook forest block is part of an ongoing *assemblage of enunciation* (rather than a sutured discursive formation) that it can be shown to have significant implications for the way in which regulatory agencies write and rewrite the nuances of environmental regulation and conflict.

Harking back to the previous chapter, it is clear that the notion of process – as opposed to reality, structure or being – is crucial to explicating the multifarious dimensions of environmental conflict. Specifically, machinic thought allows 'history' to be viewed as *interruptive* rather than dynamic.[1] According to Deleuze and Guattari, 'the past' can never be completely expunged from 'the present', just as the present can never really be separated from a so-called 'future'. Instead,

> At the limit, there is a single phylogenetic lineage, a single machinic phylum, ideally continuous: the flow of matter-movement, the flow of matter in continuous variation, conveying singularities and traits of expression. This operative and expressive flow is as much artificial as natural: it is like a unity of human beings and Nature. But at the same time, it is not recognized in the here and now without dividing, differentiating (Deleuze and Guattari, 1996, p. 406).

By this reckoning, what creates 'a history' is the phylum of machines interrupting the flow of matter-energy/plane of consistency (that is the world as an infinite becoming-other). The task in the remainder of the book, therefore, will be broadly twofold. First, I will attempt to 'follow' the machinic phylum of Goolengook forest block in East Gippsland, Victoria – that is, to write the categories and arrangements of bodies that have contributed to the invention of this site over time.[2] Second, and more importantly, my aim will be to use this 'following' or mapping in a manner that leads to the reorganisation and perhaps even *dis*organisation of the body or bodies exhibited at 'Goolengook'. As Deleuze and Guattari insist, 'Writing has a double function: to translate everything into assemblages and to dismantle the assemblages' (Deleuze and Guattari, 1986, p. 47). There will be, in other words, a sustained effort to *re*invent, or better still re*map* 'Goolengook' in order to produce it as a site where

1 In conversation, Peter Rush, 22 May 1998.

2 'Following' should not be confused with 'reproducing' or tracing. As Deleuze and Guattari put it, '[O]ne never follows in order to reproduce ... Reproducing implies the permanence of a fixed point of view that is external to what is reproduced … One is obliged to follow when one is in search of the "singularities" of matter, or rather of a material, and not out to discover a form …' (1996, p. 372). See also the distinction drawn between a mapping and a tracing (Deleuze and Guattari, 1996, pp. 11–12).

the maximum number of speeds, trajectories and intensities can pass.[3] But prior to an engagement with the textual production(s) of Goolengook, there are four additional issues that need to be addressed, three of which have to do with methodology. Firstly it is necessary to know how best to name, for the purposes of analytical productivity, the space recently designated 'Goolengook forest block'. That is, how might one best refer to this space in a manner that doesn't evoke the politico-philosophical baggage of an overcoded category like 'forest block'? The second matter will involve clarifying the types of data used to (re)build the body/bodies of Goolengook. The third task will be to explicate the line dividing 'relevant' from 'peripheral' material. The fourth and final matter centres on articulating the key philosophical concepts that will hold particular salience throughout the remainder of the book.

Method

Naming

The process of naming is of central importance to this study. Names are machines which bring certain objects into view whilst displacing or pushing back the prominence of others. As Deleuze eloquently puts it, 'As soon as we "name" or "designate" something or someone, on the condition that this be done with the necessary precision and above all the necessary style, we "denounce" as well: we remove the name, or rather cause the multiplicity of the denominated to rise up under the name; we divide, we reflect the thing, we give, under the same name, many objects to see, just as seeing gives, in a glance, so much to speak about' (Deleuze, 1990, p. 284). In this light, naming brings forth the topography of the world – in the form of mountains, rivers, and forests, but also in the form of peoples, practices and knowledges. Up until now, the phrase 'Goolengook forest block' or 'Goolengook' has been used to denote the terrain for analysis. However, to speak firstly of 'Goolengook' (a location), and secondly of a 'forest block' (a function), is to pass over the numerous machines and mutations which have taken effect prior to the invocation of these terms. Arguably, a contributing factor to the conflict at 'Goolengook' is the continual reference to 'Goolengook' *as forest management block*. Configuring the area as a forest block is just one way of doing so. It could just as easily qualify as a space to graze cattle, a place for mineral exploration, a site of biological significance, a place to 'get away from it all', a water catchment, a national park, a quarry, a site of Indigenous significance and so forth. What is needed, therefore, is a way of talking about this area that doesn't embody or suggest a *permanently ascribed function*. This is necessary in order to distinguish 'Goolengook forest block' (as an overcoded territory) from the space it was prior to anthropomorphic inventions. Again, this

3 Deleuze and Guattari assert that 'Maps should be made of things, organic, ecological, and technological maps one can lay out on the plane of consistency [or site of incessant experimentation with the real]' (1996, p. 61). 'The map has to do with performance, whereas the tracing always involves an alleged competence' (1996, p. 13).

should not be mistaken as a search for an origin so much as an attempt to locate a limit – a limit where many things are possible in respect of a given area because certain stratifications have yet to occur. In the remainder of this book, I will invoke the use of the strikethrough[4] as a means of demonstrating that any site of environmental struggle exceeds the meanings associated with one particular term. ~~Goolengook~~ thus has the effect of dislodging this space from any preconceived notion of what it has been or might become. In fact, ~~Goolengook~~ sets in motion a presence-absence dynamic such that the naming of this space becomes an act of the utmost ethical weight. Like Nietzsche, Deleuze and Guattari demonstrate that the most subtle and insidious forms of violence are bound up with lexicon (see Lecercle, 2002). This, therefore, is the key task – to make mutable and unknowable that which previously presented as unified and plain, to turn a molarity into a multiplicity.

Building

How, then, should one go about building or assembling the body of ~~Goolengook~~? How, in other words, should the relevant flows, speeds, intensities and blockages of ~~Goolengook~~ be explicated? For reasons stated below, ~~Goolengook~~ will be given form(s) and function(s) by way of the body or bodies left in the wake of various *texts*. What joins bodies to the world and each other is not their biology or anatomy nor indeed the physical force of gravity. Rather, bodies exist and subsist by way of textual incorporation. In many instances, a text will adequately capture its subject (for example accountant, judge, teacher, politician, mother). But sometimes a text will stutter to the point where it is unable to articulate events (for example the accountant-becoming-junkie, the judge-becoming-homosexual, the teacher-becoming-paedophile, the politician-becoming-environmental activist, the mother-becoming-criminal). The relationship pertaining between texts and human bodies holds equally for so-called 'nonhuman' bodies as well. Here, texts (such as scientific reports) often give the appearance of knowing or capturing 'Nature' (for example mallee scrub, river, forest, protected species). But sometimes these too are imploded by certain events (for example the mallee scrub-becoming-salinised, the river-becoming-hydroelectric force, the forest-becoming-housing estate, the protected species-becoming-human quarry).

The texts examined in this study will be shown to levy a complex series of thresholds marking the arrival, movement and exclusion of bodies and practices

---

4 This borrows from Derrida's analytic that all words are always already under erasure (*sous rature*). Derrida, however, is concerned with originary presence. I'm not, and neither, more importantly, are Deleuze and Guattari. In the context of the present argument, therefore, the omnipresence of erasure functions as a machine of deterritorialisation. It helps bring forth the virtual from the actual in order that so-called forested, industrial or conservation areas lose their signfi(c)ance as forest, as logging zone, as ecological site. The strikethrough forces each and every body (word and interpreter) to reckon with multiplicities in place of unities. And this, in turn, is to commence a line of flight (however treacherous) toward a different kind of ethic(s). (Thanks to John Fitzgerald for assisting the author with this matter.)

across ~~Goolengook~~. The objective of invoking such texts will most certainly *not* be to elucidate a lost truth. It is, rather, to shatter the meanings usually ascribed to a particular kind of *event* – sometimes known as 'forest conflict'. More specifically, the aim will be to build a *chirographic machine* capable of increasing the velocity and trajectory of the *becoming-other* of ~~Goolengook~~ as event – a machine that will make no*thing* of ~~Goolengook~~ such that it becomes impossible to align its aspects or potentials to any one group or teleology over all others. This is, of course, a thoroughly poststructuralist way of proceeding. It is based on the idea that the bodies we refer to, rely on, breathe life into, and destroy, have – quite necessarily – a textual dimension. Everything signifies and is represented – forests, endangered species, heritage rivers, but also management plans, scientific data, and catchment boundaries. But precisely 'what' is signified or represented is, for poststructuralism, neither preexisting nor primary. Meaning, and therefore practice, is always invented, posited, imagined. Most significantly though, the meaning(s) or affect(s) of a given event may fall within *or* beyond discourse – the utterable, the knowable, the recognisable. This, of course, points toward the importance of distinguishing between a 'text' and a 'discursive formation',

> *Text* is here defined as something that differs from discourse, where discourse is understood as a signifying whole that tends to create a fixed, established and univocal link between the signifier and signified … In relation to the text, therefore, *discourse* moves asymptotically in the direction of what we traditionally call the Logos, and its meaning is most closely tied to the skills language displays as a system, or differential logic. Nietzsche [and one can unproblematically say Deleuze and Guattari], […] thinks of life as something extra-logical [and] through his style or text strives to exceed the limits of logical discourse, in order to enable the text, a meaning that is always constituted in a *said*, to be the *saying* of life, history, the body, to 'live', in both the rhetorical and philosophical sense … For the text goes beyond the limits of the said by referring to its other, which it does not entirely dominate, an area outside discourse that may be based on events or history, or drives, such that the appropriateness of the signifier for the signified becomes pluralized … The text belongs to an attempt on the part of philological and philosophical reading to rediscover […] just what type of plurality and unity the text installs, to what univocal and plural referent it refers, […] and on what model of plural unity the text works […] in order to help us to think and speak of life as a body and spirit (Blondel, 1991, pp. 22–3).

The importance of this passage is that it shows that texts can be used to map the virtual whereas discourses are concerned solely with knowing or reiterating the 'actual'. The key aspect of any text is, accordingly, not its 'truth', or its 'past', but *how it works* – how it might be plugged in to a chirographic machine capable in this case of producing ~~Goolengook~~ as a multiplicity rather than a unity. As Deleuze and Guattari remark, 'Reading a text is never a scholarly exercise in search of what is signified, still less a highly textual exercise in search of a signifier. Rather, it is a productive use of the literary machine, a montage of desiring machines, a schizoid exercise that extracts from the text its revolutionary force' (cited in Deleuze and Guattari, 1986, p. xxii).

Selecting

Given the above, it is important to know how to distinguish texts relevant to the production of ~~Goolengook~~ from those that are less so? At first glance, it might be assumed that the *only* texts with which this study should concern itself are those which actually mention the word 'Goolengook'? This, however, is a somewhat problematic stance for there are, as will be seen, many texts which speak precisely of the area in question using very different names and terms than that of 'Goolengook'. Should, therefore, the criteria for selection be 'geographical proximity'? That is, should the *only* texts examined be those which talk of things occurring within the physical boundaries of ~~Goolengook~~? Arguably not, for ~~Goolengook~~ has been made to occupy different geographical dimensions at different times, sometimes an Indigenous territory, at others a European administrative unit for the government of persons, property or 'natural resources'. Accordingly, should the texts examined be *only* those which speak of events that, although occurring beyond the immediate vicinity of ~~Goolengook~~, have nonetheless impacted this terrain in subtle ways? Again, arguably not, since this would mean forsaking those texts which speak *directly* of ~~Goolengook~~. How, then, should this methodological 'impasse' be resolved? Perhaps the answer here is to say that the texts chosen for examination will be those which meet *one or more* of the criteria just mentioned – that is, they should *either* a) mention the word 'Goolengook', b) talk of the territories presently embodied (either partially or generally) by ~~Goolengook~~, or c) discuss practices effecting the combination of bodies across ~~Goolengook~~ at any time. It is, of course, impossible to offer a complete textual reproduction of Goolengook/~~Goolengook~~. This is chiefly because ~~Goolengook~~ exists as much *between* and *beyond* texts (and discourse) as much as it resides within any of these – a point that may ultimately shed considerable light on the conflict arising over this terrain. Accordingly, the texts examined will be those emanating between August 21, 1770 (declaration of Captain James Cook configuring ~~Goolengook~~ as an outpost of the British Empire) and October 25, 2000 (an email sent to protest groups concerning the projected movements of police and protesters within ~~Goolengook~~).

(Re)presenting

It will become apparent over ensuing chapters that many of the texts invoked as part of this study have been relayed 'in full' and, where possible, in ways akin to their 'original' format. Some of these texts are quite lengthy and may, at times, present as somewhat cumbersome or tedious. It is appropriate, therefore, to briefly outline the reasoning underpinning the decision to relay texts in extended fashion rather than quoting or referring to parts thereof. Here, there are two points to be made. First, according to Deleuze and Guattari neither form nor content should hold sway over each other. Indeed, these writers do everything possible to collapse the distinction between the two altogether. At one level this means that form and content infuse one another – that content cannot be understood without reference to form, and conversely, form cannot be sufficiently understood without some recourse to the statements, objects and meanings which certain forms envelope or carry. Accordingly, the *way* documents are (re)presented at various moments is every bit as signifi(c)ant as their so-called content or 'message'. Meaning always already resides within form. Form, and everything associated with it – style, breadth, length, presentation – has social, and therefore political, salience. It should not be truncated by the (modern) urge toward brevity or the need to get to 'the heart of the matter' or 'the essence of things'. In sum, the emergence and decline of bodies has as much to do with the parameters governing texts as it does with the 'content' or meaning generated within such parameters.

Second, and following Deleuze's reading of Foucault, it is important to bring to light not just 'words' or 'phrases' so much as the *statements* which contribute to the construction of particular types of bodies,

> In effect the statement is to be associated not with the transmission of *particular* elements presupposed by it but with the shape of the *whole* curve to which they are related, and more generally with the rules governing the particular field in which they are distributed and reproduced (Deleuze, 1988, pp. 3–4, emphasis added).

In a sense, this study is concerned with the shape of the curve which traverses and combines key moments in the lexical folding (and unfolding) of 'Goolengook'. Arguably, the inclusion of a number of texts 'in their entirety' (as opposed to quoting their 'particular elements') will assist efforts to discern how this curve was given to occupy a particular trajectory and, more importantly, how this trajectory might be altered or interrupted. In Deleuzean terms, if one wishes to know the lines that mark a certain type of body, it is necessary to have a grasp of texts in terms of their molar, molecular and supermolecular dimensions. In a sense, to quote selectively from texts – to gloss over their format, their medium, their tone, their numerous inflections – is to bring forth a molar politics. For to quote in part is at least in some way to profess to an audience that one has found the essence of an idea or work and that everything else is or can be disregarded as chirographic 'noise' or 'clutter'. In this study, it will be largely up to the reader to decide where to draw a distinction between the two. The only caveat here is that,

> One must pursue the different series, travel along the different levels, and cross all thresholds; instead of simply displaying phenomena or statements in their vertical or horizontal dimensions, one must form a transversal or mobile diagonal line along which the archaeologist-archivist must move (Deleuze, 1988, p. 22).

In short, instead of moving logically and rationally from one arborescent structure to another (from one signified to the next), one must move schizoanalytically *within* and *across* texts to show how their long-held banality and innocence in fact harbours conditions of violence and sacrifice (to humans and nonhumans alike).

Lexicon

The previous chapter dealt in depth with some of the key concepts pervading the work of Deleuze and Guattari. It was argued, amongst other things, that these thinkers continue and radically transform the processual view of the cosmos initiated by Thales, Heraclitus, Nietzsche and others. The lexicon of Deleuze and Guattari should be somewhat familiar to this point. Over the next three chapters, though, it will be necessary to have an especially clear understanding of the following three concepts: 'machine', 'assemblage', and 'fold'.

Machine

Guattari (1995, p. 58) writes, 'From now on the machine will be conceived in opposition to structure, the latter being associated with a feeling of eternity and the former with an awareness of finitude, precariousness, destruction and death. Beneath the diversity of beings, no univocal ontological plinth is given, rather there is a plane of machinic interfaces'. Critically, and in contradistinction to structuralist and modernist arguments, there is no single unified subject that commands or sets in train any given machine (entailing that there can be no single cause nor solution to particular kinds of dilemmas). Instead, machines have a thoroughly social dimension to their aspect (everyone and no one is implicated). Poststructuralists argue that the world is best conceived in machinic or textual terms – as replete with formed and unformed things whose meaning is continually negotiated, posited, remade, solidified and put asunder by signs which are '*differential*, not referential' in their performance (Belsey, 2002, emphasis added). For Deleuze and Guattari, signs do not have lurking within them an essence or an eternal 'expressed'. If this were the case – and this is something which modernity is structurally bound to overlook – there could be *no* debate over the precise signifi(c)ance of such processes as global warming, habitat fragmentation, bleaching of coral reefs, falling numbers of the Spotted Quoll, and the like. In this study, texts (for example government reports, Acts of Parliament, cadastral plans, photographs, newspaper articles) will be written as *machines*,

> A machine may be defined as a *system of interruptions* or breaks (*coupures*). These breaks should in no way be considered as a separation from reality; rather, they operate along lines that vary according to whatever aspect of them we are considering. Every machine … is related to a continual material flow (*hyle*) that it cuts into (Deleuze and Guattari, 1994, p. 36).

At each stage of the study, it will be necessary to ascertain whether a text brings about a proliferation of different bodies or whether it elicits a production of the same. Broadly speaking, there are, according to Deleuze and Guattari, three types of machines – *machines of consistency* (or absolute decoding), *machines of stratification* (or (re)coding) and *machines of axiomisation* (or overcoding) (1996,

p. 514).[5] Each of these speaks to the production of a particular kind of body or bodies – *supermolecular* pertaining to the absolute or constant implosion of bodies (becoming-immanent), *molecular* pertaining to more supple and ambiguous bodies (becoming-other), and *molar* pertaining to fixed and rigid bodies (becoming-the-same). As a general rule, difference – as a means for denoting the *a*categorical of thought – decreases in intensity as one moves from the supermolecular to the molar, although this should in no way be taken to mean that difference 'vanishes' at the point where molarity takes hold. To the contrary, moralisation – the organisation of a body according to a single principle, form or function – assures the 'eternal return' of difference. What is most pertinent to ecological matters is the speed at which such difference recurs, and, subsequently, the manner by which it becomes (or not) an 'object' of discourse and various texts.

Another key aspect of machines is that they bring about a specific relationship between words (legislation, graffiti) and things (heritage river, old-growth forests). This means that texts *as machines* (for example the East Gippsland Forest Management Plan), impact on the production of concepts (for example General Management Zone) and practices (for example timber harvesting, sightseeing). What should become clear is that ~~Goolengook~~, in so far as it stands as an object of discourse, is the product of the comings and goings of numerous textual machines rather than universally accepted ideas or creeds. Not one machine but many machines, each having a mutating effect on the bodies they cut into and across. For example, marking or configuring (that is, *machining*) parts of ~~Goolengook~~ as ecologically significant helps produce it as ecologically expendable. Marking ~~Goolengook~~ as ecologically expendable helps produce it as a timber production zone. Marking ~~Goolengook~~ as a timber production zone contributes to its production as a site of environmental conflict. Marking ~~Goolengook~~ as a site of conflict helps produce it as an area of restricted access. And so on and so forth. Deleuze and Guattari remark, 'There is always something that flows or flees, that escapes the binary organizations, the resonance apparatus, and the overcoding machine' (1996, p. 216).

Assemblage (body)

Wherever there is an arrangement or ordering of practices and concepts within a defined territory there is, according to Deleuze and Guattari, the production of an assemblage or *body*. 'We will call an assemblage every constellation of singularities and traits deducted from the flow – selected, organized, stratified – in such a way as

5 It is important to note the distinction between an axiomatic and a code. An axiomatic 'maintains the energy of the flows in a bound state' (1994a, p. 246). Distinct from this, 'a code determines the respective qualities of the flows passing through the socius' (1994a, p. 247). The difference here has to do with thresholds – with the degree to which certain flows are prevented from entering or leaving a particular strata (or site of capture) and its assemblages (or bodies). There is a greater degree of elasticity in codes than with axiomatics. Capitalism – as a system for the exponential transformation of the Earth – can exclude some consumers (or flows of credit) from its wares (code) but it *must* have consumers (axiomatic).

to converge [...] artificially and naturally; an assemblage, in this sense, is a veritable invention' (1996, p. 406 emphases removed). For the purposes of this study the terms 'assemblage' and 'body' will be taken to mean one and the same thing. On such a count, a Deleuzean body has ' ... neither base nor superstructure, neither deep structure nor superficial structure ...' (1996, p. 90). Bodies, in other words, are impermanent but this certainly does not mean they are without effects. Instead, each body (the body of a water catchment, the body of a pastoral district, the body of a national park, the body of a forest) will be conceived as a zone of intensity occupying a space between two poles or 'vectors'. Deleuze and Guattari call these poles the *stratified vector* (or stratum) and *destratified vector* (or substratum). Between these vectors (that is throughout a body) there is a constant tension between states of *molarity* (reaction, becoming-the-same), *molecularity* (action, becoming-other) and *supermolecularity* (hyperaction, becoming-immanent). In other words, a body is a conglomeration of volatile forces effected by numerous machines at any one time, a site of rigidities, regularities and blockages (a *territory*), but also a site of experimentation, contingency and possible escapes (a *deterritorialisation*). Bodies, therefore, are always already of the order of micropolitical in(ter)ventions.

The relation between machines and bodies is of paramount importance for what follows. This is because '*Machines are always singular keys that open or close an assemblage [or body] ...*' (1996, p. 334, italics in original). It is important to make recourse to an ethic(s) of difference and (bio)diversity when ascribing a value to a particular machine and the bodies they invent, order or arrange. This means there is no apriori reason for writing the molar as 'bad' or reactive and the molecular or supermolecular as 'good' or active. What is important is that machines lead to the presence and absence of various bodies over time and that each of these have their own *flows* (of matter-energy), *speeds* (of decay and rejuvenation) and *intensities* (key thresholds of mutation). For Deleuze and Guattari the task is to make known the occasions or points where a body meets a limit – a *machinic threshold* – of one kind or another. At such points it becomes possible to speak of bodies in terms of sites which either facilitate or block the production of difference. This is why, in the present context, it will be necessary to ask what the body of ~~Goolengook~~ can *do* as it moves from one text to another (as opposed to asking what ~~Goolengook~~ *is*).

Fold

A 'fold' will be said to occur whenever a machine causes a body to relocate itself on, between, or outside the image of thought or *strata*, the latter being conceived by Deleuze and Guattari as 'acts of capture' or systems of organisation which maintain strict divisions between subjects and objects across defined territories (see Deleuze and Guattari, 1996, p. 40). In juridical terms, there is an administrative strata, an enforcement strata and a judicial strata which are effected by numerous machines each carving up the socius in distinct ways. In the analyses to follow, each carving – each new arrangement of bodies – will be treated as a *fold*. This will allow the world (and therefore ~~Goolengook~~) to be thought of as exhibiting continuities which are always already discontinuous and discontinuities which are always already continuous (as always entering new machinic relations or systems of coding, knowing, arranging, doing, enunciating) (see Halsey, 1999). Rajchman comments, '[T]he fold, which fills up the space, is at the same time what takes the space out from itself, bursting it open and smoothing it out …' (Rajchman, 1998, p. 34). As a way of clarifying matters, imagine a mobius strip looped around the edge of a picture frame so that half the area of the strip is within the frame and half extrudes beyond it. Imagine now a point on the upper most surface of the mobius strip that falls within the frame. Where is this point? Is it not *both* 'inside' the frame *and* on an exterior surface whose trajectory leads 'outside' the frame? 'Passing over the inside of the frame only sends us back to the outside of the strip', does it not? (Cache, 1995, p. 72). The relation between a 'knowable' point on the mobius strip and its position with respect to the frame approximates the relation between machines, bodies and folds. Accordingly, the *texts* examined in the following chapters can be viewed as contiguous with such knowable points on the mobius strip or BwO called ~~Goolengook~~.

Beyond stochastic renderings

It is considered that a change in lexicon (machine as opposed to reality, assemblage or body as against structure, fold as opposed to essence) will allow places like ~~Goolengook~~ to be thought of in ways that go beyond traditional dichotomies (humans/forest, ecologically significant/ecologically insignificant, jobs/environment). To forge new ecological alliances (or, as Guattari would say, *ecosophical* territories) requires that stochastic (that is, modernist) renderings of socio-environmental problems be abandoned. For to date, the modern socius – at costs largely unknown – has made of Nature an other, a pariah, an outside(r). And it has done this even and perhaps especially through its attempts to care for and responsibly manage 'Earth' or 'The Environment'. What should become clear over the course of the following chapters is that '[t]he outside is not a fixed limit but a moving matter animated by peristaltic movements, folds and foldings that together make up an inside: they are not something other than the outside, but precisely the inside *of* the outside' (Deleuze, 1988, pp. 96–7). This last fact clearly means there can be no 'essential' Goolengook/~~Goolengook~~. There are, however, numerous policies and machinic thresholds whose job it is to portend otherwise. To say there is no essential or enduring body of ~~Goolengook~~ is in no way to suggest it will be impossible to distinguish between practices and conditions which alter its speeds and intensities or deplete its (bio)diversity. Rather, to deny ~~Goolengook~~ all semblances of a transcendental or immutable status is not only ontologically consistent but, it is hoped, (micro)politically strategic. For such a strategy may prevent the various molar bodies (for example loggers, sightseers, miners, pastoralists, scientists, conservationists) which have long haunted ~~Goolengook~~ from invoking the rhetoric of an 'original' or 'authentic' past in support of their programmes. Authenticity is in fact always already of the order of the simulacrum. In place of authenticity, or, as it may be, of an originary forest, river, or lexicon, runs the ethical implications of textual machines and the bodies they extract and inscribe. To write the socio-ecological cost of these bodies with respect to ~~Goolengook~~ – that is the challenge.

PART B

Chapter 5

Becoming Known

Nature is acquainted with neither shape nor size; only to the knower do things appear to be large or small.

Nietzsche, *The Philosopher*, (1992) [1872], §123

The texts examined over the course of the next three chapters have been arranged chronologically. However, this should not be taken to mean that 'history' happens in linear fashion (see De Landa, 1997). Deleuze and Guattari write that '[E]verything operates through abstract-real machines which have names and dates' (1996, p. 146, parentheses removed). This means that the formation of bodies (a mineral body, a forest body, a recreational body) cannot be divorced from the enunciations (or process of naming) that brings them into being. Put differently, bodies cannot and should not be separated from the convergence of times and nomenclatures that divide and organise the plane of consistency into discrete zones of such and such proportions and uses. Adding to the methodological notes given in the previous chapter, the names and dates outlined below are derived from texts which speak both of *indexes* (that is the lines dividing one body or territory from another) and *intensities* (that is the types of forces able to occupy such bodies or territories). In simpler terms, indexes can be taken to concern the geographic or administrative units effecting ~~Goolengook~~ (for example pastoral district, water catchment), whilst intensities can be understood as having to do with the attributes deemed to fall within such units (for example cattle, riparian environment).

It is also important to understand that each text is both productive and produced, which is to say that machines are both constitutive and constituted. In the first instance texts *make* the world, but in a second instance their matter and form are always already the result of numerous machinic convergences. For example, a government gazettal notice proclaiming a water supply catchment produces machinic effects (carving the world into this or that unit and bringing about a new arrangement of bodies and practices) but is only made possible by countless other machines (political, geodetic, hydrological, botanical, geological, agricultural, pastoral, and so on) which have already executed their task, so to speak. Among my objectives below will be firstly to name each type of machine, and, secondly, to explicate the particular type of transformation that ~~Goolengook~~ undergoes as a result. Here, I acknowledge that ascribing a name to a machine is always already a political act insofar as machines do not come ready made with some kind of transcendental name (or function, or resulting series of effects). A 'conservation machine' could just as well be labelled an 'unemployment machine'. Similarly, a 'forestry machine' could, by some means, be called an 'ecosimplification machine'. This largely depends upon one's own site of enunciation and the politic or ethic that pervades a work. Following Deleuze and Guattari, I intend to name machines according to the primary or dominant flows they seek to interrupt or redirect. If a text speaks of the exploration of minerals, then the primary flow will be one of metal, and the machine will be that of a mining machine. If, on the other hand, a text speaks of assessing the distribution of flora and fauna, then the primary flows will be vegetation and flesh and the machine will most likely be a scientific machine. In selected instances, various texts, various machinic incisions, will be accompanied by a map of the body or bodies of ~~Goolengook~~. This will give a visual basis to the stratifications and sedimentations that have occurred across the site in question. With all this in mind I now turn to the texts themselves.

18,000 BCE: site of Aboriginal occupation

Prior to the landing of Captain James Cook at Possession Island in 1770, ~~Goolengook~~ was inhabited by the Aboriginal peoples of the Bidwell tribe. Clearly, there is no single text attesting to this situation. Instead, it could be said that such texts are embedded in the features located at and around ~~Goolengook~~. On this count it is the scar trees, the middens, the stone implements, the rock carvings and paintings, the burial grounds and so forth that function as sites of multiple textual performances. These are in no way 'exterior' to ~~Goolengook~~ (as Western documentation of its aspects is) but immanent to it. A micropolitics of this site could not possibly proceed without acknowledging the presence of and the role played by the first humans to occupy ~~Goolengook~~, regardless of the precise 'nature' or form of these texts. What is of significance here is that it is only very recently that such texts have been reclaimed as part of a strategy to highlight Indigenous occupation of ~~Goolengook~~ and surrounding regions. Aborigines are known to have occupied East Gippsland – the region of which ~~Goolengook~~ has been deemed a part – for at least 18,000 years (Department of Conservation and Natural Resources, 1993a, p. 4). The Bidwell people traversed the area around the headwaters of the Bemm River which adjoins the main river in ~~Goolengook~~. Probably in collaboration with bands such as the Kurnai and Ngarigo, the Bidwell gave a number of different names to the territory within and around ~~Goolengook~~. These names, which exist today as Parishes, are 'Goolengook', 'Noonga', 'Bungywarr', 'Goongerah' and 'Kuark'. Each of these had/has different tribal significance. It is generally accepted amongst the descendants of the Bidwell people that the territory of ~~Goolengook~~ (as opposed to the larger area later called ~~Goolengook~~ forest management block) was used as a place of banishment for those who broke tribal law. The remaining territories were used for hunting and ceremonial purposes. Aboriginal occupation of these areas came to a decidedly abrupt end as a result of Europeans moving into the East Gippsland region early in the eighteenth century. It has been estimated that there were between 15,000 and 50,000 Aborigines in East Gippsland in the early 1800s. However, contact with Europeans over subsequent decades brought 'conflict and attendant problems of disease and depressed birth rates … so that by 1877, the recorded Aboriginal population of the region had dropped to 213' (Australian Heritage Commission/Department of Natural Resources and Environment, 1996, p. 8).

1770: site within the British Empire

On August 21, 1770 Captain James Cook, at Possession Island off Cape York, 'formally claimed for his country all of eastern New Holland and named it New South Wales' (Ward, 1965, pp. 23–24). Here, the colonial machine interrupts the flow of (Indigenous) sovereignty in order to (re)discover a 'new' land. This seemingly simple act transformed ~~Goolengook~~ into an outpost of the British Empire. The scale at which the management and movement of bodies took place was transformed from tribal territory (several hundred square kilometres and ill-defined) to subcontinental (eastern third of Australia). A new way of envisioning the landscape was also brought to the fore insofar as Eurocentric visions were pitted against that of indigenous ways of seeing. The name 'New South Wales' was so chosen because 'The mildness of the climate of an Australian autumn, and the picturesque ruggedness of the coast, reminded Cook of familiar scenes in the southern part of Wales' (Cornish, 1975 [1880], p. 260).

1788: site within the waste lands of the Colony of New South Wales

On January 26, 1788, under the provisions of an Imperial Act, Captain Arthur Phillip raised the Union Jack at Port Jackson (Sydney) and took possession of all land 'from Cape York in the north in latitude 10° 37' south to South Cape in 43° 39' south and inland as far as the 135th degree of east longitude' on behalf of King George III (Auchmuty, 1976, p. 48). This area was equivalent to about the eastern third of the land mass of Australia – well over 100 million hectares.[1] New South Wales fell under English law and 'at [a] ceremony on February 7, this "already established fact" was proclaimed' (Shaw, 1976, p. 8). From the moment of Phillips' declaration, 'Australia' became Crown land of the Colony of New South Wales. Such land was 'under direct control of the Ministers of the Crown in London' and fell into two broad categories – land within proclaimed counties, and waste lands of the Crown (Historical Subcommittee of Centenary Celebrations Council, 1934, p. 124),

> The term 'waste lands' embraced all lands outside the limits of location, which simply meant beyond the boundaries of the proclaimed counties within which land could be sold or leased, at auction solely. These boundaries were known as the border, and therefore waste lands were beyond the border. The authorisation of occupation of these lands was in the hands of the Commissioners of Crown Lands, generally known by the abbreviated

1 '[T]he whole of the continent was declared British when Perth was settled in 1829' (Auchmuty, 1976, p. 48).

designation of C.C.L. (Historical Subcommittee of Centenary Celebrations Council, 1934, p. 124).

Since ~~Goolengook~~ fell well outside the boundaries of proclaimed counties it was deemed to fall under the term 'waste lands'. As a category, 'waste lands of the Crown' speaks of a new way of valuing or envisioning the world, one that would have been anathema to the indigenous inhabitants. It is a category that casts the land beyond counties as (use)less, without value, and without form. It is a category stemming from the invocation of the colonial machine whose task is to contain the flow of population resulting from European settlement as well as those of disease, money, labour, knowledge, food and so forth.[2] Political, juridical, social, industrial and scientific assemblages are constituted anew, each striving to control a whole host of new forces.

1836: site within the Pastoral District of Port Phillip

Around 1828, the Home Office in London issued a decree to Sydney Colonial Office to stem the spread of population beyond penal settlements. 'In 1829 … Governor Darling proclaimed nineteen Counties, beyond the boundaries of which settlement was strictly forbidden' (Dunlop and Pike, 1965, p. 82). Despite this measure, the influx of settlers into territories beyond Counties continued. This 'unchecked' occupation of land quickly led to the invocation of additional administrative boundaries. In 1836 an Act was passed by the New South Wales legislature to legalise the occupation of land beyond Counties for pastoral purposes. These lands, of course, were the aforementioned 'waste lands of the Crown'.[3] In conjunction with this legislation, the Sydney Colonial Office divided the colony of New South Wales into a series of Pastoral Districts and ascribed each district a Commissioner of Crown Lands (CCL). At such time ~~Goolengook~~ became a potential site for depasturing within the District of Port Phillip.[4] The way of envisioning the landscape was altered as

2 'Phillip was charged with the task of founding a colony which should become self-supporting within the shortest possible time. His detailed instruction from the British Government commanded him to secure himself and his people from attack by the natives [flows of resistance], to proceed to the cultivation of the land [flows of food], to use every proper degree of economy and to prepare stores of food and supplies for future cargoes of convicts [flows of labour]. He was expected to establish a penal colony too far from Britain for convicts to return [flows of geography], with as little expense as possible to the home government [flows of money]' (Dunlop and Pike, 1965, p. 31).

3 'The annual fee for a license to depasture was fixed at £10' (Historical Subcommittee of Centenary Celebrations Council, 1934, p. 124).

4 'In 1839 the Port Phillip District was proclaimed a dependency of New South Wales' (Dunlop and Pike, 1965, p. 84, see *Government Gazette* 22/5/1839). A census conducted in that year showed the population of Port Phillip District to be around 5000. The amount of land under cultivation at this time was a mere 200 acres (Turner, 1973, p. 304). By 1841, the population had climbed to 12 000 – 'of whom nearly one third were children'. One half of the

a result of the 1836 Act. Lands previously held to be 'waste lands' were ascribed a specific function – namely, cattle grazing. The administrative boundary used to manage persons associated with this and other activities was transformed from a sub-continental to district scale (although the district of Port Phillip was at this time roughly equivalent to the area later inscribed by the State of Victoria spanning some 22,740,400 hectares).

1847: site within unsettled districts

'[A]n Order in Council of [9 March] 1847 divided the pastoral lands of the Colony [of New South Wales] into three classes – settled, intermediate, and unsettled' (Dunlop and Pike, 1965, p. 93). The Order was published in the *New South Wales Government Gazette*, October 7, 1847. Due to its isolation from European settlements, ~~Goolengook~~ was ascribed the category of 'unsettled' – despite it still being occupied by members of the Bidwell people. ~~Goolengook~~ was now therefore part of the 'unsettled' districts within the larger District of Port Phillip of the Colony of New South Wales. Apart from the obligations imposed by the *Crown Land Sales Act* 1842 – that all Crown lands be subject to competitive bidding prior to occupation – there were no specific regulations governing the use of land within ~~Goolengook~~ at this time. However, both the scale and mode of envisioning the land at ~~Goolengook~~ had changed. 'Unsettled districts' was, necessarily, a smaller unit of administration than the District of Port Phillip as a whole. The unit of which ~~Goolengook~~ became a part was therefore of a more defined nature (however large this unit may have been). Further, the category 'unsettled districts', like that of 'waste lands of the crown', speaks to the issue of vision in that it construes the landscape in terms of a *lack* – as an 'empty' body that somehow would neither 'come to life' nor yield its 'true potential' until 'settled' (or rendered as a full or molar body with only one function).

1848–55: site of depasturing

The history of pastoral licences in the District of Port Phillip is concomitant with the history of the earliest European settlement in what would later become the State of Victoria.[5] Depasturing licenses gave the owners of cattle the right to occupy a specific

---

total population at this time existed within 'Melbourne and immediate suburbs' (Turner, 1973, p. 204).

5 'The first settlements in the [East Gippsland] region [or the most easterly portion of the Port Phillip District] were established in the 1840s, around Delegate and Dellicknora, and in the south eastern corner near Mallacoota, Genoa and Wangarabell. These were outlying stations of the southern New South Wales pastoral industry and were among the first white communities in Victoria. Leases for pastoral runs in this period were administered by the colonial Government of New South Wales' (Woodgate et al., 1994, p. 162). 'The first cattle were depastured in the forests of East Gippsland by graziers from southern New South Wales, driven into the region by a run of dry seasons in the 1830s and 1840s. They started a tradition

territory for the purpose of grazing their stock. As mentioned previously, ~~Goolengook~~ became an 'unsettled district' in 1847. This meant a lease over such land could run for a period of 14 years (as opposed to one and eight years within intermediate and settled districts respectively). Records at the Land and Survey Information Centre – a division of the Department of Natural Resources and Environment – show that from 1848 to 1863 a pastoral run known as 'Cann' existed in the vicinity of ~~Goolengook~~. Whilst the run was by no means permanently occupied, those who did occupy it would have been amongst the first Europeans to impact on ~~Goolengook~~ in a material sense.[6] For present purposes, the degree to which the run was actually occupied (as opposed to merely tendered for) is not of ultimate consequence. What is of interest though, is, firstly, the way the applications for the Cann Run describe (or envision) the territory around ~~Goolengook~~, and, secondly, the process of administration used to connect 'humans' (pastoralists) with certain parts of 'nature' (land). As will hopefully become clear, the decidedly vague descriptions of the land tendered for in these texts stands in stark contrast to later techniques of mapping, surveying and apportioning land for specific uses (although, as shall be seen, these 'modern' techniques carry their own set of problems). In short, these early texts illustrate the predominantly

---

in the region which continues today, where cattle are depastured in State forests and on unoccupied public land, usually by farmers in need of extra pasture' (Woodgate et al., 1994, p. 164).

6 The Public Records Office at Laverton has the Cann Run filed under 'Parish of Noonga, County of Croajingalong'. Whilst there is some doubt that this is an appropriate categorisation (insofar as the whole of the run probably did not fall within Noonga), there is evidence to suggest that the run did fall at least *partly* in this Parish and therefore in very close proximity to ~~Goolengook~~. A map of pastoral runs produced by the Department of Lands and Survey dated January 1863 has the Cann Run located about 24 miles north west of the Sydenham Inlet on a river now known as the Bemm. The accompanying note to the map cautions, 'This map is published in order to meet the present demand for information respecting runs. The boundaries are laid down approximately being generally the projection on paper of the gazetted descriptions. A correct map will be issued as soon as the runs are surveyed'. Notwithstanding this provision, the location of Cann on the 1863 map is well within the vicinity of ~~Goolengook~~. To this day there is a clearing known as 'Boulder Flat' just above the intersection of the Bemm, Combienbar and Errinundra Rivers – a point about 24 miles north east of the Sydenham Inlet. This area currently supports a few dozen head of cattle and lies less than 1 kilometre from the south eastern boundary of ~~Goolengook~~. My contention is that applicants for the Cann run were initially applying for land which was in fact located on the Bemm River not the Cann River (some 20 kilometres to the east). This situation probably pertained until 'official' publication of the location of the run in the *Victorian Government Gazette* of June 1860 – although this could also have stipulated an incorrect position. The inability to confirm the precise location of the Cann run stems from the administrative procedures at work during the formative days of the pastoral industry (that is the 1840s and 50s). At such time, the Commissioner's of Crown Lands in each District had to rely solely on the calculations of tenderers (that is prospective pastoralists) when charting the location and boundaries of new runs or properties. This was especially the case in the 'unsettled districts' where it took many months if not years for a run to be formally surveyed.

destratified nature of the site (lands) in question – they speak, in other words, of a space still to be named, marked, segmented, and controlled.

Microfiche reproductions of pastoral run tenders show that Cann was Run No. 207 – the details of which are located in Pastoral Run Papers 259 and 260. The name is variously spelt in these papers as 'Cann', 'Khan' and 'Kann' (Microfiche 259 Copy 3 (M259, 3)). The first application is dated 4 August 1848, and, excepting the handwriting too difficult to decipher, reads,

TENDER FOR A LEASE OF A NEW RUN OF CROWN LANDS.

INTERMEDIATE OR UNSETTLED DISTRICTS.

In accordance with the provisions contained in Her Majesty's Order in Council, published in the *New South Wales Government Gazette*, of the 7th October, 1847, and of the Regulations of 1st January, 1848, published in pursuance thereof,* [ ] **William Hibbard** of† **Pampula**[7] **nearest Post Town Eden** do hereby propose to take lease for‡ **14 years** years, of the Crown Lands known as **Cann** in the District of **Port Albert** ; which Lands are particularly described in the Schedule annexed to this Tender. And in consideration of such lease|| **I am** willing, and hereby offer to pay yearly in advance, the minimum rent of ten pounds, with two pounds ten shillings added, for every thousand sheep or their equivalent in cattle, above four thousand sheep or their equivalent, which the run shall, under the provisions of the said Order in Council, be estimated as capable of carrying, and also the additional sum or yearly rent in advance of **nil** for every thousand sheep or their equivalent as aforesaid, by way of premium for the said lease.

GIVEN under§ **my** hand this **first** day of **August** A.D., 18 **48**

¶ **William Hibbard**

[signature – probably of processing clerk]

TO THE HONORABLE
THE COLONIAL SECRETARY,
SYDNEY.

* "I," or "We," as the case may be; insert Christian and Surnames *at full length*.
† State usual place of residence, or nearest Post Town.

7 'Pampula' is located about 20 kilometres north of Eden in New South Wales and is now called Pambula.

‡ If the Land applied for be situated in an intermediate District, the duration of the Lease [must not] exceed eight years; if in an unsettled District, the term must not exceed fourteen years.
|| "I am," or "We are," as the case may be.
§ "My hand," or "our hands," as the case may be.
¶Signature of applicant or applicants.

The tender was sealed with the words 'Orders in Council – Port Phillip (Land)' (M259, 4). The relevant schedule to the application reads (M259, 5),

SCHEDULE REFERRED TO IN THE FOREGOING TENDER.

Commissioners District and General Locality	Name of Run	Estimated Number of Acres	Estimated Capability for Grazing		Description of the Lands by Reference to Leading Geographical Features, and Marked or Determined Boundary Lines
			Cattle	Sheep	
[ ] Commissioner [T]yers Port Albert[8] 30 miles from [Maneroo]	Cann	20,000	640	4000	Bounded by the mountain range beyond Maneroo to the north by a creek running from Maneroo on the west [and by] the sea coast to the south

(Signature of Applicant)

William Hibbard

The 'Description of Lands' supplied above clearly indicates the deterritorialised nature of the pastoral site in question, and therefore, of ~~Goolengook~~ as well. When something is deterritorialised it is without an ascribed structure or function – a site of pure intensities. Phrases like 'the mountain range', 'a creek', and 'the sea coast' attest to the *smooth* rather than striated nature of the land at stake. Smooth spaces are those occurring between two lines – mountain range/creek, or mountain range/sea coast. Striated spaces, on the other hand, are characterised by many lines between many *known* points (such as post offices, significant peaks, domestic or commercial dwellings) (see Deleuze and Guattari, 1996, pp. 474–500). What is in evidence in the schedule is the inability to name and capture a space due predominantly to its unknown

8 Here the applicant gives 'Port Albert' as the district of the run which in turn leads him to send his application to the Colonial Secretary's Office in Sydney. Instructions for applicants published in the *Port Phillip Government Gazette* of January 1848 required that 'The Tenders in the prescribed form are to be addressed to this Office [i.e. Sydney], if the land be situated in the Middle District [within what is now known as part of New South Wales], or to the office of His Honor the Superintendent at Melbourne, if situated in the Port Phillip District [within what is now called Victoria]' (Tenders for New Runs II.2. *Extract from notice dated Colonial Secretary's Office, 1st January, 1848*, M259, 11, published in *Port Phillip Government Gazette*, Number 3, Wednesday January 19, 1848). A note from the Colonial Secretary's office in Sydney (most likely written between August 1 and 6, 1848) reads, 'I am not in a position to report on this run – it being beyond my reach – The boundaries [to which] do not seem to be sufficiently [supplied]' (M259, 10). Another note most likely from the same office dated 7 August 1848 explains, 'This tender ought to have [been] addre[ss]ed to His Honor the Sup[erintenden]t of [Port] Phillip to whom it is forwarded accordingly' (M259, 12). A miscellaneous note relating to the progress of the application simply states, 'To furnish fuller description' (M259, 8).

proportions and features. This would certainly have had something to do with the fact that as of 1848 the vast majority of rivers, mountains, settlements, and roads in the District of Port Phillip generally (and the far east of the District in particular) had yet to be named, surveyed and depicted on standardised (government issue) maps. This made it very difficult for Crown land authorities to verify the boundaries and location of prospective runs.[9] In addition, it also left considerable scope for applicants to be sufficiently vague about the precise size and location of prospective runs (the larger the run the higher the annual fee) (see Historical Subcommittee of Centenary Celebrations Council, 1934, p. 125). In the mid-nineteenth century, therefore, it was largely the pastoralists themselves – not government officials – who initially 'mapped' the location of pastoral runs.[10]

The information given in the above schedule heralded the first occasion whereby an aspect of ~~Goolengook~~ was conceived in numerical terms – numbers of acres, numbers of sheep, numbers of cattle. Deleuze and Guattari write, '[T]he number has always served to gain mastery over matter, to control its variations and movements, in other words, to submit them to the spatiotemporal framework of the State … [N]umbers appear as soon as one distributes something in space, instead of dividing up space or distributing space itself' (1996, p. 389). In the present case, the process of enumeration is bound up with efforts to monitor one's stock, but it is also something else. More particularly, it is an expression of *carrying capacity* – a projection of the numbers of cattle the land at and around ~~Goolengook~~ is capable of sustaining

9 The records of the Cann Run are dotted by requests from officials for more information regarding the description of the terrain and location. In response to a request for a 'fuller description', the aforementioned applicant – William Hibbard – on an unspecified date, completed and submitted another schedule to the Port Phillip authority. This schedule was of the same format as the one previously completed, except that the left hand column was now headed 'Name of Applicant' instead of 'Commissioner's District and General Locality'. Hibbard filled out the schedule with the same details as displayed on his initial application. There was only one notable difference – at the conclusion of his description he included the words '[3]0 miles from Maneroo' (M259, 9). 'Maneroo' at this time was a pastoral district located immediately above the eastern most portion of the District of Port Phillip. It is now known as 'Manaro'. Evidently, the authorities were not satisfied with Hibbard's effort. A note dated 5 February 1849 and signed by Robert Hoddle (charged with the task of surveying the city of Melbourne) reports that, 'This application is not in a position to be entertained' (M259, 7). Finally, a 'Mr Hayden' was granted the Cann Run some time between 1849 and 1856. Unfortunately, the details of the application are not amongst the records of the Cann papers and can therefore be presumed lost or destroyed.

10 Confirmation of this comes from Section 13 of Her Majesty's Order in Council dated 9 March 1847 published in the *Port Phillip Government Gazette*, Number 3, Wednesday 19 January, 1848. It reads, 'If any individual be desirous to acquire a new run of land which has never been occupied before, he shall be at liberty to send in a sealed tender, at such time and place, and in such form, as may be appointed by the Governor, or Officer administering the Government of the said Colony, for receiving tenders of new runs, and shall set forth in his tender a clear description of the run for which he applies and of the boundaries of the same …' (M259, 11).

from one year to the next. Here, it is the administrative law machine (in the form of tenders and schedules) that creates the pastoral body, a body whose function is to conduct flows of flesh (meat), skin (leather), and hair (wool) within a certain territory. It could be said that these flows represented nothing new, that Indigenous peoples were just as reliant on the qualities of flesh, skin and hair for their survival. But the pastoral machine ushered in a different set of intensities, ones that had to do with *how* bodies moved from place to place. A deterritorialisation of the foot and the earth occurs here – the padded paw becomes cloven whilst the soil becomes compacted. In this sense, cattle (meaning, in fact, cows, sheep, horses, mules) form a machinic phylum with the bulldozer, the truck, and the four wheel drive in so far as they all constitute new (and some might say damaging or monstrous) ways of moving across the earth, across ~~Goolengook~~.

1851: site within the Pastoral District of Gippsland, Colony of Victoria

On 1 of July 1851, the District of Port Phillip 'was, under the provisions of an Imperial Act of 5 August 1850, entitled "An Act for the Better Government of Her Majesty's Australian Colonies," separated from New South Wales, and constituted into a self-governing colony under the name of Victoria …'. In the same year 'the Governor and Legislative Council of New South Wales passed the Victorian Electoral Act … which provided that a Legislative Council be constituted for Victoria'. The Electoral Act of 1851 'also divided Victoria into sixteen electoral districts'. District number eight was deemed the 'Pastoral District of Gippsland', the boundaries of which apply to this day (*Victoria Year Book 1907–8*, p. 42). At this time ~~Goolengook~~ was transformed by the political machine into a location within the Pastoral District of Gippsland of the Colony of Victoria. The way of envisioning the land at ~~Goolengook~~ remained unchanged to the extent that it was still considered to be 'pastoral territory'. However, the administrative unit of which it was a part was reduced twelve-fold from 24 million hectares to about two million hectares.

1855: site within the sovereign state of Victoria

On November 23, 1855 an Act was passed to constitute Victoria as a fully self-governing state. All governmental ties to New South Wales ceased at this time. This was the moment where the movement and creation of bodies (rivers, forests, agricultural lands) at and around ~~Goolengook~~ became a solely a matter of State concern. It would be well over a century before a government other than that of the Victorian Parliament played a direct role in the formation of policies (particularly forest policy) effecting this site.

1856–60: site of depasturing

On July 25, 1856, John Stevenson from the NSW town of Bombala (about 65 kilometres west of Eden), applied for the lease of the Cann Run (M259, 13 and 14).[11] He marked up the schedule to his application as follows (M259, 15),

SCHEDULE REFERRED TO IN THE FOREGOING TENDER.

Commissioners District and General Locality	Name of Run	Estimated Number of Acres	Estimated Capability for Grazing		Description of the Lands by Reference to Leading Geographical Features, and Marked or Determined Boundary Lines
			Cattle	Sheep	
Gippsland River Cann about 18 miles from the 90 Mile Beach 20 from Delegate Hill & 28 from Wangrabill	Cann	6000	300		There is only a flat on the whole of the land now applied for the same being surrounded by dense Scrub.

(Signature of Applicant)

John Stevenson[12]

The description of the land at and around ~~Goolengook~~ relayed here is remarkable for its mode of envisioning. The area described as 'dense scrub' would much later be deemed to be amongst the most diverse animal and plant communities in Australia, containing some of the tallest and most diverse forests in the southern hemisphere. But with the term 'dense scrub' comes a homogenisation of multiple terrains – a production of the same at the expense of the production of difference. In the first case, 'dense' is a word that speaks to the immalleability of bodies – a body beyond instruction, a body of enduring and impenetrable qualities (at least to Europeans). On the other hand, 'scrub' is a term that helps to cement the process of homogenisation. It conjures images of a 'sub-standard' vegetation – one that is low in height and floristically similar throughout. It is, therefore, the mode of envisioning – and not just the mode of production – that brings forth the pastoral assemblage with its cattle, campfires, sheds, gates, tracks, stock persons and so forth. A land enunciated as 'dense scrub' is politically far more suited to depasture than one enunciated as an 'undisturbed catchment' or as exhibiting 'warm temperate rainforest'.

On December 7, 1857 John Alexander Junior applied for the run. He filled out the schedule thus (M259, 22),

---

11 Stevenson was the first person to be granted a depasturing licence in what is now East Gippsland. This was issued on November 16, 1839 for a run at Wangarabell in the far eastern corner of the region (Wakefield, Royal Society pp. 18 and 22). Wangarabell was the place of residence given by Stevenson on his application for the Cann run.

12 A note from October 7, 1856 concerning Stevenson's application reads, 'A Mr Hayden is in occupation of a Run called "Cann" – I presume it is the same as herein tendered for (?) Has Mr Hayden paid his license fee?' (M259, 19). Stevenson was unsuccessful in his application because the run was already tendered to Hayden.

SCHEDULE REFERRED TO IN THE FOREGOING TENDER.

Commissioners District and General Locality	Name of Run	Estimated Number of Acres	Estimated Capability for Grazing		Description of the Lands by Reference to Leading Geographical Features, and Marked or Determined Boundary Lines
			Cattle	Sheep	
Gippsland	Kann or Cann	18,000	200		Bounded by Cann River on one side and Bush Country unoccupied on the other side[13]

(Signature of Applicant)

John Alexander Junior

The boundaries stipulated here do not so much enclose a space as supply a territory with latitudinal limits. The pastoral body produce thereby is one without a topography, without depths and heights, and without rivers, forests, fauna and so forth – a territory without a body.

On June 9, 1859 John O Shea applied for the Cann Run (M259, 27). His application (M259, 29), in the form of a letter, ran as follows,

83 Swanston Street,
Melbourne June 8. 1859

To
The Chief Commissioner of Crown Lands, Victoria

Sir,

I beg to apply for the undermentioned country called the 'Canns' Station which was formerly occupied by Mr Hayden, but which has been vacant for some time. In the event of this Station being granted to me, I beg to request that the pre-emptive right will be re-allowed with the run.

Cann Station is on the Bemm River which empties itself into Sydenham Inlet in Eastern Gipps Land. The Eastern boundary is the range of hills which divide the Waters of the Tamboon and Bemm Rivers, the Southern boundary is a line running parallel with the Coast from which it is distant sixteen miles, this line being the Northern boundary of the Sydenham Station lately applied for by Mr Th[om]as. The Western boundary is the line of hills on the West of the Bemm, which bound the Watershed of that river, the Northern boundary are the Mountains dividing the sources of the Bemm from those of the Delegate and Dorimity rivers. The run is estimated to carry five hundred head of cattle.

I have the honor to be sir, Your obedient Servant,

John O'Shea, [ ] Solicitor[14]

---

13 A note from May 1858, signed by Commissioner Charles J Tyers states, 'All boundaries of proposed runs should be described and bearings and distance from some known point given' (M259, 26).

14 In terms of the records in the Cann file, this is by far the most 'comprehensive' description of the location and dimensions of the run. It dictates that the run was situated

This passage again points to the destratified nature of the site at hand. The Bemm River is stipulated by O'Shea to reach as far north as the mountain range dividing it from the Delegate River whereas today the Bemm is shown to fall a considerable distance to the south. Its northern aspect is now known as the Errinundra River. The Dorimity River – shown on the aforementioned map of East Gippsland from 1847 – was later to become the Bendoc River. On June 20, 1859, the Crown Lands office recorded the following observation concerning O'Shea's application,

> The land applied for does not appear to comprise any [known] lease or license. Mr John Stevenson applied for it in 1856 but it was then believed to be in the occupation of Mr Hayden who appears to have now for some time abandoned it. The public interest does not require the [reservation] of any portion. The description given appears to indicate correctly the land applied for (M259, 30).[15]

---

on the Bemm River and *not*, as the name would suggest, the Cann River (which is about 20 kilometres to the east). It also specifies that the southern edge of the run was the boundary formed by the Sydenham Run – later called the Bemm run. From several distinct sources such as the map of pastoral runs produced by the Department of Lands and Survey in 1863, the map of pastoral holdings from 1835–51 published by the Crown Lands Department of Victoria in 1932, and a map of pastoral holdings by Spreadborough and Anderson from 1983, it is clear that the Sydenham Run (at one time known as the Bemm Run) extended as far north as the township of Club Terrace. Club Terrace is just under 6 kilometres from the south eastern boundary of ~~Goolengook~~.

15 From Twofold Bay near Eden in NSW, John Alexander [Junior] wrote a letter to the Commission dated July 20, 1859 inquiring whether his application of February had 'been attended to' (M259, 31). Alexander wrote a further letter concerning the same matter on December 20, 1859 (M259, 32). A note from the Commissioner of Crown Lands office dated January 19, 1860, reads 'Mr Alexander's descriptions of the boundaries of the run applied for being insufficient, he was requested by [ ] Com[missioner] Tyers to furnish a more accurate description – date May/58' (M259, 33). On 27 January 1860 the Crown Lands required one of its staff to 'Inform Mr Alexander that the descriptions of the Boundaries of the Run applied for being insufficient – he was requested by the Crown to forward a more accurate one – letter dated May/58. If another description is furnished The Board of Land & Works will be applied to for authority to invite Tender forthwith' (M259, 32). Some time between April 1 and 14, 1860 John Alexander visited the Crown Lands Office at Palmerston 'to furnish personally some explanations referring to the boundaries of the [Cann] run' and to 'serve[ ] his application' (M259, 35). The official recorded Alexander's description thus (M259, 36),

> Situated about 30 miles South of Genoa. Commencing at a point on the East Bank of the Kann River twenty miles from the sea coast in a direct north & south line. Bounded on the South by a line running East two (2) miles. On the East by a line running North four (4) miles on the North by a line running West about two (2) miles to the Kann River and on the West by that River to the commencing point. Estimated area 5000 acres. Grazing capabilities 200 cattle.
>
> This application does not comprise any land under lease or license. The description given appears to correctly indicate the land applied for. The public interests do not require the reservation of any portion.
>
> [relevant signatures]
>
> applied for by Mr John Stevenson in 1856 Mr John O'Shea 20/6/59 Mr John Alexander 14/10/59.

These remarks are significant because they cast the land at and around ~~Goolengook~~ as being beyond the realm of 'public interest' – meaning that as of 1859 *none* of this space was envisioned as fulfilling (even potentially fulfilling) significant social, industrial, scientific or cultural functions. This may seem a banal point. However, when this way of envisioning or valuing the territory around ~~Goolengook~~ is contrasted against future textual renderings, it will help to provide a concrete illustration of the fluidity of 'words' and 'things', and thus of the changing relation between 'humans' and 'nature' as well.[16]

The interesting aspect of this passage is that it attests to the ambiguity of the exact location of the Cann run. John O'Shea's letter of June 9, 1859 specified the location of the run as being on the Bemm River to which the department responded, 'The description given appears to indicate correctly the land applied for' (M259, 30).

16 On May 23, 1860 the Commissioner of Crown Lands wrote, 'Several applications having been made for License for an abandoned Run known as Kann or Cann – in Gipps Land – I beg to recommend that tenders be invited' (M259, 34). The *Victorian Government Gazette* of June 8, 1860 (p. 1304) advertised the tender for the Cann run as follows,

> Crown Lands Office (Occupation Branch)
> Melbourne 8th June, 1860
>
> Tenders will be received until the 10th day of July next, for the Occupation for Depasturing purposes only, to the end of the current year, of the New Runs described hereunder. Tenders to be sealed and endorsed, "Tenders for New Runs". The Government will not necessarily accept the highest or any tender. Further particulars at this office.
>
> DESCRIPTION OF RUNS
>
> *No.* 1
>
> [...]
>
> *No.* 2
>
> Situated about thirty miles south-west of Genoa. Commencing at a point on the east bank of the Kann River, twenty miles from the sea coast, in a direct north and south line; bounded on the south by a line running east two miles; on the east by a line running north four miles; on the north by a line running west about two miles to the Kann River; and on the west by that river to the commencing point.
>
> *Estimated area.* – 5000 acres.
>
> *Grazing capabilities.* – 200 cattle.
>
> James Service,
> Commissioner of Crown Lands and Survey.

The description of the run provided here matches that given by John Alexander two months earlier at the Crown Lands Office at Palmerston. The only other mention of the position of the Cann Run in Pastoral Run Paper 259 is in the context of a tender application dated July 28, 1860 by a Mr William Dickson who offered 'the Sum of £15 Fifteen Pounds [ ] for the New Run Cann. Situated on the River Cann' (M259, 52). Remaining details of the Cann Run are located in Microfiche 260 (17 pages in total). These contain the bids from 11 different applicants for the years 1861–63. Each of these was a reply to the notice placed in the *Government Gazette* of June 1860. In the main, each applicant describes the location in accordance with this notice. The one exception to this appears in the final application for the

1865: site of potential reservation of timber

Part III of *The Amending Land Act* 1865 is headed 'Leases and Licenses for other than Agricultural or Pastoral Purposes'. Section 41 concerns 'Timber reserves' and reads,

> The Governor in Council may make and proclaim reserves for the preservation and growth of timber and may from time to time alter and revoke any such proclamation and the Board of Land and Works may issue licenses to cut timber upon such reserve or of any part thereof on such terms and conditions and subject to the payment of such license fee as shall from time to time be approved of by the Governor in Council and be set forth in such license.

In the context of Victoria, this was the first time power had been installed in the Governor to reserve areas for the supply of timber. Here, the proximity of 'exterior' speeds and intensities becomes more immediate as ~~Goolengook~~ is reconfigured as a potential site from which to yield flows of wood.[17]

1869: site of prevalent timber

In line with a request by the State Forests Board, Arthur Everett, using data 'from the Record Maps in the Office of the Surveyor General, and other authentic sources' produced a map entitled 'Victoria: Distribution of Forest Trees'. This text is dated January 15, 1869 and is, from all accounts, the earliest (European) cartographic record of the distribution of flora across Victoria. Colour coded, the map shows ~~Goolengook~~ to consist of two kinds of 'forest trees' – namely, 'Stringy Bark' and 'Messmate'. At one level this is a highly molar rendering of ~~Goolengook~~. But when compared to the description of the same territory given in the pastoral run papers it is apparent that the body of ~~Goolengook~~ is assigned a less rigid (if binary) aspect. It is no longer 'dense scrub' or 'bush land' but the site of two particular species of tree, the notes for which read,

---

run dated February 6, 1863. John Alexander Junior (who first tendered for the run in 1857) tendered £40 per annum. He describes the Cann Run as 'situate in North Gipps Land with a frontage to "Kann" River of 4 miles N & E. 16 miles from Ninety Mile Beach, about [ ] forty miles N.E. from the Snowy River, consisting of [dense] Scrubby Land and capable of containing from 100 to 200 head Cattle …' (M260, 17). A note written by an official of the Department of Crown Lands and Survey dated some time on or after February 23, 1863 reads 'Gazette Boundaries required'. This suggests either that the applicant must use the gazetted description, or perhaps that the gazetted boundaries are incorrect and in need of review. Either way, the ambiguity surrounding the location of the territory remains. A note written on February 21, 1863 indicates that even though the run was 'submitted to public tender' it was 'not taken up' during these years.

17 'In 1867 nearly 116,000 acres were declared State Forests and timber reserves' (Moulds, 1991, p. 14). ~~Goolengook~~, however, was not amongst this area.

> Eucalyptus nervosa *and* Eucalyptus fissilis, *Messmate, two of the species so called.*
>
> Euclayptus obliqua, *the Stringy Bark tree, is in vast masses, constituting, on the barren ranges in nearly all parts of our colonial territory, the prevalent timber.*

In these notes ~~Goolengook~~, or at least a part thereof, is (re)configured as a site of 'prevalent timber'. It is a space whose becomings have been coded or stratified according to a single capacity: the potential to satisfy commercial and domestic needs. The exploitation of ~~Goolengook~~ for its timber did not take place on a sustained and uniform scale until over a century after the publication of this text. Nonetheless, the text stands as an important moment on the machinic phylum of becoming forest, if only because it heralded the first occasion whereby the 'whole' of ~~Goolengook~~ was written or depicted in terms of forest trees.

1871: site within the County of Croajingolong

On February 24, 1871, the County of Croajingolong was proclaimed (*Victorian Government Gazette*, 1871, p. 334). The County took its name from the Krauatungalung tribe that once traversed East Gippsland (the Bidwell people were (and remain) one band of this larger tribe). Of slightly different spelling, the word 'Krowathunkooloong' described an Aboriginal from the Snowy River region who possessed what was called 'kooloot' – a power to know things which others did not. Such men 'could decide who had committed an offence and his *kooloot* enabled him to take life secretly' (Pepper and De Araugo, 1985, p. 5). Croajingolong was mapped to include all land in Victoria east of the Snowy River. The proclamation of the County relied on the completion of the geodetic boundary known as the Black-Allan line. It was this (molar) line which divided Croajingolong from New South Wales. In the main, this survey line was marked out to prevent disputes over the rights to certain goldfields. But it was to have another, more telling effect. It would come to signify a distinct break in the way vegetation – and indeed all flora, fauna and geographical features in Croajingolong – would be managed. No longer was ~~Goolengook~~ part of the lands traversing south eastern Australia. Instead, it, and the vegetation up to and along the New South Wales border, could now lawfully be managed as if the rest of Australia had vanished. Whole clusters of distinct classificatory regimes could now be applied to lands that were, for all intents and purposes, part of the same material flow as that in existence 'over the border'. This division of administration was to have a very real effect on the composition and continuity of land in south eastern Australia generally and Croajinoglong in particular. The geodetic machine made (and continues to make) possible new sets of scales (state rather than national, regional instead of state, county in place of regional, parish in place of county) and new series of speeds (faster and more calculated movement of bodies within ever smaller units of management) across a given portion of the earth. ~~Goolengook~~ here becomes part of a County which is only one third the size (that is around 800,000 hectares) of the District of which it had been a part – the District of Gippsland.

Counties become a means for the tabulation of a multitude of variables within a proscribed territory – wool clipped and baled, wheat harvested, cattle slaughtered, hides tanned, butter churned, metals extracted, land selected, dwellings and fences erected, direction and length of rivers, quality of soils, projected position of roads and railway lines, and so forth. It could be said, therefore, that the proclamation of the County of Croajingolong heralded a new scale for the mapping of various bodies. It would take just over a decade for ~~Goolengook~~ to be subject to such mapping, a mapping that would ascribe it geodetic co-ordinates.

1872: site of depasturing

On 8 January 1872 two pastoralists from Bendoc named Hamilton Reed and John Lock[18] wrote to the District Surveyors Office in Bairnsdale to 'Request a renewal of License for a section of 640 acres under the 47th Sec[tion of the Land Act 1869], situated in Gunagrah' (M414, 3).[19] On March 27, 1872 the District Surveyor at Bairnsdale (a Mr A. Black, responsible during the years 1869–72 for completing the survey of the NSW/Victorian border by marking the western section of the straight line from Cape Howe to the River Murray) noted that, 'The land in question does not interfere with any Run now up to auction and so far as I am aware does not interfere with any existing run. The attached tracing shows approximately the outline of the new Run I would recommend' (M414, 10). The tracing mentioned here has been reproduced as Pastoral Run Plan 700. The hand-written note accompanying the map reads,

18 Woodgate et al. (1994, p. 166) have Reed and Lock as East Gippland Pioneers who were the first to be issued a mining claim in 1855 in East Gippsland at Bendoc.

19 This was a request for 'renewal' because the land had been occupied by the applicants since 1868. The pastoral run papers for this earlier application were not in the records at the Land and Survey Information Centre. A comment by an official dated January 16, 1872 in respect of this application reads, 'The renewal of this license may interfere with the new runs about to be exposed to public auction on the boundary between Victoria and N.S.Wales' (M414, 3). However, the application was approved by the Board of Land and Works on January 20, 1872 and was then subject to further scrutiny by the District Surveyors Office at Bairnsdale (M414, 3). A note dated March 12, 1872 reads 'Referred to the District Surveyor at Bairnsdale to report if the land in question interferes with any runs now up to auction[,] if not to forward a plan of the land as a new run' (M414, 5). Like that of 'Cann', the name 'Goongerah' has been spelt several ways in these papers including 'Goonegrah' and 'Gunagrah'. It is an aboriginal word, most likely of the Bidwell people, meaning 'egg rock' on account of the huge round boulders occurring at the summit of Mt Ellery. Government maps presently denote it as 'Goongerah', the township of which now lies at the intersection of Brodribb River and Goongerah Creek (about 10 kilometres north-west of ~~Goolengook~~).

D.S.O. Bairnsdale 28/3/72

A large proportion of this country is worthless, the only part good for anything being the valley of the Goongerah Creek in the vicinity of Messrs Reid and Lock's homestead. The grazing capability is therefore small in proportion to the area and I consider £20 a fair rent though the number of cattle the place will keep alive may exceed 100.

A Black
D.S.

This passage is an excellent example of the fluidity of vision – of the situation whereby the optic is formed through the operation of machines which are spatially and temporally distinct (scale machines, speed machines, scientific machines). The area referred to here as 'worthless' would one day become the site of one of Victoria's premier national parks, containing large stands of old-growth forests and many rare and threatened species such as the Spotted Quoll, Sooty Owl, Long-Footed Potoroo and the Slender Tree Fern. In June of 1872, the tender for the Goonegrah Run was published in the *Victorian Government Gazette*. It read,

NEW AND FORFEITED RUNS FOR SALE

In pursuance of the 67th section of The Land Act 1869, it is hereby notified that a public auction will be holden at Two o'clock p.m. on Tuesday, 18th June 1872, at the Auction Rooms of Messrs. Gemmell, Tuckett, and Co., Collins street west, Melbourne, for the sale of the undermentioned new and forfeited runs for the period specified.

The highest bid by way of premium will be accepted, and must be paid at the time of sale.

Special conditions will be anounced at the time of sale.

J.M. GRANT,
President of the Board of Land and Works.
Land and Survey Office,
Melbourne, 15th May 1872.

[…]

Lot 5. Name of run, Goonegrah; estimated area, 50,000 acres; annual rent £20; district of Gippsland North; period of occupation, to 31st December 1880. All the unalienated and unlicensed Crown lands within the following boundaries: Commencing at the trigonometrical station on Mount Ellery (Goonegrah); thence by a line bearing West about 4 miles to the Goonegrah Creek thence by a line bearing North 45° west about three and a half miles to the summit of the range forming the watershed between Goonegrah Creek and the Yalmy or Rodgers' Creek (also known as the Broadbent River); thence northerly and easterly by the range forming the western watershed of the Goonegrah Creek to its source; thence easterly and southerly by the ranges forming the eastern watershed of said creek to the point of commencement.

Mount Ellery – surveyed and (re)named only about a year before this notice appeared – is about 1.5 kilometres from the north western boundary of ~~Goolengook~~. The land at and around ~~Goolengook~~ is referred to as 'unalienated and unlicensed Crown land', an 'empty' land without form or function that is about to be 'filled' with new kinds of intensities. Indeed, the pastoralists and stockmen and women associated with the Goonegrah Run would have been amongst the first Europeans to venture across ~~Goolengook~~, their primary objective being the successful mustering of their cattle in order to take them to market. There is little doubt that cattle roamed the ridges of ~~Goolengook~~ and continued to flow in and out of its territories over the course of many decades. Jack Green, a local of the area, reports that he rode through ~~Goolengook~~ on horseback in the 1920s and saw cattle grazing on its ridges.[20] The western boundary of ~~Goolengook~~ – 'Green's Road' – was named after Jack's father Bill who cut the track around 1910 for the purposes of moving cattle from one pasture to another (this track was later used as a means to access the forests of the Errinundra Plateau in the 1960s for timber). Jack also recalls that graziers would light small fires in an attempt to encourage new growth for depasturing. The intended aim would be to burn a small area – usually about four hectares. But often these fires burnt far more than the area intended. It is now generally accepted that fires associated with the pastoral industry impacted markedly on the structure and composition of what would later be referred to as 'the forests of East Gippsland',

> Stock was grazed in the forests around settlements, and experience had shown that cattle would thrive on the regeneration of grass, herbs and shrubs following a fire. Two to three years after burning, palatable feed became scarce. Another section of the forest would then be fired because the accumulation of at least five years forest litter was necessary before burning could be repeated successfully on any area…
>
> It was inevitable that systematic burning was used to promote the growth of forage. Although cattlemen wanted a localised fire which limited the far ranging of stock, the timing of the burn was difficult, and instead of a low intensity fire burning under climate controls late in the season, forest fires often ranged out of control.
>
> The chaotic structure of forest stands of the foothills and mountain slopes is a result of repeated burning of the forests in the past. There are few areas with no evidence of past fires [in East Gippsland], and many which have been swept by fires recurrent and intense (McKinty, 1969, pp. 131–32).

A field naturalist who explored the valley of the main river running through ~~Goolengook~~ in 1888/89, recorded that fires had recently passed through the lower stretches of the area at that time (see below). Some of these fires would certainly have been caused by lightning strikes but many would have been the result of grazier induced burnings that spread over large areas. In this sense, fire is a force that creates a phylum of impacts. It leaves a series of traces which demonstrate, in a

20 In conversation, March 18, 1999.

most concrete sense, that past actions (like depasture burns) are part of a flow, not a discrete structure.[21]

1876: site of remnant 'wild people'

In 1876 a missionary named John Bulmer – who devoted his life to converting Aborigines around Lake Tyres and elsewhere in Victoria to the Christian faith – published a brief account of the emergence of the 'last' of the so-called 'scrub-dwellers' of East Gippsland. His recollection was recorded in the *Church of England Mission to the Aborigines, Annual Reports* (located in the La Trobe Collection, State Library of Victoria, Melbourne). He wrote as follows,

> The past year has been a remarkable one. Quite unexpectedly the last remnants of the wandring tribes of Aborigines from beyond the mountains made their appearance. We have often heard in days gone by from our blacks of those 'warical' tribes far away who would some day come down upon them and do them much harm. So great was the fear, that mothers frightened their children by telling them of those wild people … The expressed fear was needless, for the 'waricals' did not appear, and we naturally concluded that they had passed away like many other tribes in different localities of the colony. At last we learnt that there were some left, and they did come, in a most deplorable condition, but in a friendly way … (quoted in Pepper and De Araugo, 1985, p. 150).

This is an incredible text – if only due to it being one of just a handful which speak specifically of ~~Goolengook~~ and its Indigenous inhabitants. But it is remarkable on other counts as well. First, it is a text permeated by a particular *teleology* concerning the 'proper' relation that should pertain between Europeans, Indigenous persons, and landscape. What I mean here is that the text considers the emergence of the Bidwell peoples as not only 'desirable' but as *inevitable* as well. Inevitable in the sense that the goal of human (European) history has always been to overcome or free 'man' from the ravages of nature – to rise above chaos and put an everlasting divide between civilisation (society) and the so-called 'barbarous realm' (nature, primitivism, savagery). Bulmer speaks of the Bidwell peoples as if it is the most 'natural' thing in the world for them to leave their 'wild' ways and give themselves over to a 'better', more 'productive' existence – an existence where Christianity looms large and where the prospect of saving souls is paramount.

Secondly, Bulmer's words invoke all manner of hierarchies and dichotomies such that the very idea of Aboriginality emerges as a problematic or deferred term (see Davies, 1994, pp. 254–59). Through his words (and all the complex codings and orderings they entail) Bulmer literally carves an 'Other' out of the face of the earth.

---

21 One other interesting point to emerge from these pastoral run papers is a reference in a letter by Reed and Lock dated February 26, 1872 to 'the Parish of Gunagrah' (M414, 7). This confirms that 'Goongerah' as a Parish was in existence and known to people of the Gipps Land district very early in 1872. More will be said about the significance of Parishes later in the context of administering the movement of bodies.

This Other is, of course, the Indigenous body. One commentator has spoken of this carving (machining) in the following way,

> When European colonialists and explorers encountered native peoples for the first time there arose a need to reconcile preconceived expectations with actual observations. The indigenous people of the new and recently colonised world became the 'ethnographic Other'. Through the process of colonialism and exploration the Other came to be defined through a series of binary oppositions. These dichotomies, manifested in descriptions of the Other in terms like noble savages, cannibals and natural slaves, distinguished the Europeans as superior and indigenous cultures as inferior and weak. The Other was also perfidious, treacherous and untrustworthy; capable of being childlike and deserving of paternal care but also able to behave with utter contempt for European authority. This unpredictability was perceived partly as the result of their state of savagery and immaturity which stood in stark contrast to the sophistication of the civilised Europeans (Russell, 1998, p. 51).

Constituting the 'Other' means, *ipso facto*, constituting a 'Self' as well. Here, this Self is the Anglo-European subject. Through a series of rhetorical shifts (involving the invocation of dichotomies such as those just mentioned), this historically *limited* subject somehow manages to create itself as a universal and transcendent force. This, of course, has tremendous implications for the Other (that is, for those occupying the distant 'outside' or problematic 'margins' of society). In the present case, it means that Europeans can look upon those emerging from the mountains as 'late-comers' (as the *remnant* or *anterior body*). The binary counterpart of late-comer must surely be the *expeditious* or *timely body*. Since all things flow from civilisation, Bulmer is able to conjure for himself (and for all Europeans) a philosophical and geographical monopoly over what is and what is not 'timely'. This is why so many have no difficulty conceiving a culture some 40,000 years old as anterior to that which has existed for only a little over two centuries.

A third and related point arising out of Bulmer's words has to do with how they leave the body of ~~Goolengook~~. Here one might ask: What kind of space emerges in the wake of the exodus of the Bidwell – that 'wild' and 'warical tribe[ ]'? Arguably, ~~Goolengook~~ emerges as a space marked by a becoming-vacant – a 'primitive' space largely unoccupied and unknown to Europeans. But at the same time we need to recognise that this 'vacancy', this 'ambiguity', in fact *increases* the probability of ~~Goolengook~~ being transformed by multiple machines. There is no escape from machinic incisions. There are merely pauses, breaks and further reterritorialisations and deterritorialisations. One could say, therefore, that with the exodus in 1876 of the Bidwell people, the apparent 'emptiness' of ~~Goolengook~~ simultaneously transformed it into a space replete with all kinds of (monstrous/molar) possibilities.[22]

22 It is interesting to note that in the same year Bulmer recorded his observations, the State of Victoria was taking its first steps toward regulating 'forests'. On December 22, 1876, as 'construed as part of "*The Land Act* 1869"' (S.1), the Victorian Parliament passed the *State Forests Act* 1876. This was 'An Act to provide for the Care Management and Control of State Forests Timber Reserves and other Crown Lands and for other purposes'. Although

1885: site of alleged payable gold-field

On 6 July 1885, John Grimes Peers – a surveyor for the Department of Mines and Water Supply – wrote a brief report about the discovery of gold at Black Watch Creek. This Creek occurs within the south eastern part of ~~Goolengook~~ and runs immediately west of what is now called Blackwatch Track. Peers' notes appeared in *Reports of the Mining Registrars for the Quarter Ended 30th June, 1885*, Appendix B, pages 70 and 71. Although decidedly brief, it is a remarkable text because it was most likely the first time an area within ~~Goolengook~~ had been written up in 'official' or 'formal' terms.

---

decidedly brief, it was, as mentioned, the first piece of legislation to deal *specifically* with the management of Victorian forests. Section 2 of the Act established Local Forest Boards who were charged with 'the management and control of such reserves for the preservation and growth of timber … and shall have power from time to time to grant to any applicant a license to enter upon the said reserves or other portions of Crown lands upon payment to such Board of such fees …'. Section 3 allowed for the appointment of 'a sufficient number of fit and proper persons to be called foresters … [who] may conduct all prosecutions or proceedings against persons who offend within the said reserves or other portions of Crown lands against any of the provisions of the Act No. CCCLX. [that is *The Land Act* 1869]'. Section 4 of the State Forests Act made it illegal for unauthorised persons to remove anything from such forests,

> [I]f any person shall be found on any Crown lands whatever or on any such reserve or other portion of Crown lands as aforesaid having in his possession any live or dead timber gravel stone limestone salt guano shell sand loam brick earth or bark he shall for the purposes of this Act and the Act No. CCCLX. be deemed to have cut dug taken away stripped or removed the same from Crown lands, and it shall lie on such person to prove that he did not so do or that he had authority so to do.

This passage heralded the first significant occasion where forests were segmented according to their capacity to provide a range of different 'resources' beyond that of timber. It also stood as the first time the State actively took possession of the different features of such Crown lands and subjected the use of them to legal procedures. Section 5 made it illegal for anyone to damage any built structure (for example a 'fence', 'gate', 'wall' or 'stile') on 'any Crown lands' and stipulated a maximum fine of 'ten pounds' for doing so.

Previous to the State Forests Act of 1876, the earliest formal controls over the cutting of timber in Victoria (or, as it was known at the time, the Port Phillip District) date back to 1839. These controls had little effect and were later amended in 1852,

> The Victorian Government *Gazette* of 14 July 1852 referred to then existing licensing procedures of 1839 for cutting timber on Crown Lands, and proceeded to amend them. Every applicant for a timber cutting license had to be 'supported by the recommendation of at least two respectable persons' and the Crown Lands Commission could 'exercise a full discretion in giving or withholding the licenses according to the merits of each case' (Moulds, 1991, p. 13).

The forests of primary concern here were those which lay within or just beyond the settled and intermediate districts of established and expanding townships. Accordingly, it was the forests of northern and central Victoria that were first logged in an effort to fuel the activities

REPORT ON THE ALLEGED DISCOVERY OF A PAYABLE GOLD-FIELD AT BLACKWATCH CREEK.

Mining Surveyor's Office,
Bairnsdale, July 6th, 1885.

SIR,

In compliance with your instructions of the 24th ultime, I have the honour to inform you that I have visited and inspected the new 'rush' at Black Watch Creek, and beg to enclose a tracing showing, approximately, the position of the same. Reports of new 'finds' and the growing excitement of the public seemed to demand that accurate information should be supplied to the department at once, and accordingly, on the 25th ultime, I started for the new workings. Numbers of men from all parts of the colony were passed on the way

---

associated with the gold rushes of the mid-nineteenth century, and to assist the construction of dwellings and infrastructures at and around the burgeoning 'city' of Melbourne. In practical terms though, the timber licensing system of 1852 – like that of 1839 – did little to stem the tide of forest destruction that had been taking place for in excess of two decades in these forests. A key clause to the licensing procedures ran,

> [T]he preceding regulation does not apply to the lesse in settled districts, who is at liberty to cut any timber growing thereon for domestic uses, firewood, fencing or other convenience for the enjoyment of the land, but not for sale or barter (quoted in Moulds 1991, p. 13).

The effect of this clause was to expose large areas of forested Crown Lands to indiscriminate cutting. The forests of (East) Gippsland, however, fared far better than most if not all other areas of Victoria. Timber from these forests were mainly being used for the construction of small dwellings associated with the influx of pastoralists into the area. McKinty (1969, p. 131) contends that the first pit-sawing of timber from the forests of East Gippsland probably took place at Bendoc in 1852. This timber was most likely used in the construction of mining shafts and dwellings during the gold rush era. Presently, the town of Bendoc lies approximately 6km south of the Victoria/New South Wales border and about 25km north of ~~Goolengook~~. Those taking timber from forests around Bendoc at this time would have been amongst the first to have fallen under the requirements of the new timber licensing system – few as these requirements may have been. As Woodgate et al. (1994, p. 173) comment,

> Timber splitters worked relatively unhindered in [East Gippsland] forests in this early period. For the payment of a licence fee to a local official or police constable, their splitting and halving operations went unsupervised, and few restrictions were placed on species, size or quantity... Sawmills could be erected on Crown land for the payment of an annual license fee, but no limit was placed on the quantities of logs obtained and the fee was not related to the volume extracted. This was changed in 1893 when royalty rates for red gum sawlogs were restructured from an 'area' to a 'volume' system. The new system was gradually extended to all sawlogs and other forest products by 1905 [...].

In light of this, one could say that as of 1852, ~~Goolengook~~ – although a considerable distance away from the activities associated with gold mining and timber cutting – nonetheless was transformed into a potential site for the extraction of timber for commercial and/or domestic use.

– some of whom had sold household furniture, & c., to provide tools and outfit for the journey.

The first part of the journey to Orbost, Snowy River, was performed by buggy, via Cunninghame, thence on horseback to the alleged gold-field. After leaving the Snowy River settlement, the track passes through very good agricultural land situated between Brodribb River and Black Watch Creek; the country is steep, but consists of good chocolate soil (similar in character to that of South Gippsland), heavily timbered with mountain ash, with dense undergrowth in places, at present comparatively inaccessible, but good roads may be made. The road is fairly good, but there is no food for horses nor accommodation of any kind.

The Black Watch Creek is situated about ten miles in a south-easterly direction from Mount Ellery. The workings (now almost abandoned) extend about three miles along the course of the creek. The sinking is easy, being chiefly through loam (depth about 3½ to 5 feet), but contains little or no gold. On my arrival only 35 out of 100 men remained; 30 of these I interviewed. Many stated the result of their labours had been *nil*. Some had obtained a 'colour,' *but no one had made wages*. Not more than two ounces of gold has been found on the creek; and of this 1½ ounces was obtained by the prospectors after about three months' labour. This small quantity of gold, however, proves the country to be auriferous; but in my opinion, payable gold is not likely to be discovered in this part. In this opinion I am supported by experts in prospecting whom I met on my visit, and who have been engaged in the locality for the last twelve months.

One of these (W. Dennecker) I employed as a guide. He took me through some country nearer the coast, which presented a more promising appearance as regards the existence of gold. I think this country is worthy of a more thorough trial than it has yet received, but no man should go who is not prepared to find himself in food and tools for say five or six months at least. Tools and stores are procurable at Orbost.

On my return I met parties of men from Tasmania, Sandhurst, St Arnaud, & c., on their way to the 'new rush,' but, on hearing my report, they turned back; others, waiting my report, went no further, seemingly very pleased to escape a long and expensive journey with a disappointment at the end.

It is difficult to discover the origin of these misleading reports. In this case no blame appears to attach to the prospectors; their modest report of 'colours' travelled a long distance, and at each succeeding store or hotel grew into grains, pennyweights, and ounces. Newspaper paragraphs did the rest, and very great losses were thereby inflicted on men who were ill able to bear them.

I have. &c.,

JOHN GRIMES PEERS,
Mining Surveyor.

C.W. Langtree, Esq.,
Secretary for Mines, &c.

The Secretary for Mines and Water Supply found the issues raised in this report to be of sufficient magnitude to mention them in the summary attached to the volume of the *Mining Registrars Reports* in which Peers' passage appeared. Next to the sub-heading, 'New Discoveries', he wrote,

> Towards the end of the quarter an alleged discovery of payable gold at Black Watch Creek (Snowy River district) caused a 'rush' to the locality, which would probably have attained large proportions, and entailed a good deal of hardship and suffering on the adventurers, were it not for the early publication of an official report describing the real character of the discovery. This report will be found in Appendix B, and a perusal of it should have the effect of making miners more cautious about crediting the wild rumours that get afloat from time to time respecting the existence of new El Dorados in distant and not easily accessible regions (1885, p. 8).

There are a number of important points to make about these passages. Firstly, they harbour a certain way of envisioning the territory at ~~Goolengook~~. No longer is the area merely one of 'dense scrub'. Instead it is 'heavily timbered' with 'good chocolate soil'. Moreover it is ascribed a general gradient – namely, 'steep'. On a second count, they speak of the difficulties of travelling to ~~Goolengook~~ (a 'distant and not easily accessible region[ ]') and to the lack of European settlement in the area ('no accommodation of any kind'). Thirdly, the texts speak of the speeds and slownesses that need to be invoked in order to successfully negotiate the terrain and sustain one's existence at ~~Goolengook~~ – 'food and tools for ... five or six months' (whereas today one can travel from Black Watch Creek to the nearest store in less than an hour). Fourthly, they allude to the *unknown* or *possible* potentials and intensities of the region – 'this country is worthy of a more thorough trial than it has yet received'. Fifth, Peers' text speaks directly to the relation between words and things, or as Deleuze and Guattari might say, between expressions and contents. Expressions – in the form of rules, commands, statements – insert themselves into the contents (or bodies) of a particular assemblage in order to 'anticipate them or move them back, slow them down or speed them up, separate them or combine them, delimit them in a different way' (1996, p. 86). The text in question is a collection of statements which effects particular flows and impacts on the movement of certain bodies. It fuelled the deterritorialisation of the alluvial mining assemblage at Black Watch Creek – an assemblage which territorialised around a particular flow – that of alluvial gold. It also interrupted and redirected the flow of miners on their way to Black Watch Creek – 'on hearing my report, they turned back; others, waiting my report, went no further'. The sixth and perhaps most important point to be derived from Peers' text is that it marks the first occasion whereby aspects of ~~Goolengook~~ are enunciated in terms of *volume* – as yielding so many ounces of gold. As a unit of measurement, 'volume' produces ~~Goolengook~~ quantitatively. A certain molarisation occurs here as ~~Goolengook~~ is ascribed a solitary function over and above all other capacities or possible affects.

In addition to all this, Peers' text illustrates Deleuze's idea that a break with or discontinuity in one flow (that is a territorialisation on the banks of Black Watch

Creek) is really only a moment on the way to interrupting or impacting on other kinds of flows – to 'some country nearer the coast, which present[s] a more promising appearance as regards the existence of gold'. It is never, therefore, a case of 'erasing' or 'defeating' an assemblage. Instead, the task is one of incessantly striving for an alteration of the speeds, scales and durations with which each assemblage effects the flow of matter-energy.[23]

1887: site of unknown qualities

In 1887, 'a naturalist [named Edwin Merrall] explored along the recently cut mining track' from Orbost to Bendoc (O'Bryan, 1983, p. 37). The details of his journey were 'Read at the Ninth Ordinary General Meeting of the Royal Geographical Society of Australasia, 9th August, 1887', and soon after published as 'An Unknown Portion of Victoria' in *Transactions and Proceedings of the Royal Geographical Society of Australasia (Victorian Branch)*, Part 1, Vol. 5, March 1888, pp. 9–13. The opening passages of Merrall's presentation ran,

> A glance at the map of Victoria shows Croajingolong to be one of the largest of our counties. It will also be observed that the space comprising the interior is almost a blank; that is to say – unknown.
>
> Many years ago [1869–71] Professor Ellery's geodetic party operated within the county, fixing its chief mountain peaks, and it is from their work, such bald plotting as we have of the area was taken; since that time it has received but scant attention.
>
> There was, however, reason to believe the area to be auriferous; and with this supposition in view it occurred to the Mining Department – about three years ago – to let a little light into this dark country, by cutting a track running in a north easterly direction from Orbost (Merrall 1888, p. 9, italics removed).

By road, Orbost (proclaimed a township in April 1885) is about 50 kilometres from the southern aspect of ~~Goolengook~~. Merrall described the route of the track from Orbost to Bendoc as follows,

23 The discovery of gold at Black Watch Creek would have interrupted something more than flows of metal. In addition there would have been changes made to the surrounding flows of vegetation and water. Trees would have been felled to facilitate the construction of mines, temporary shelters on the banks of the creek, and for fuel for cooking. A Victorian Parliamentary report from 1874 headed 'Waste of Timber under Present System' confirms the use of surrounding forests for mining activities indicating that, 'It is the usual practice of licensees to take only the prime parts of the trees they fell, leaving large quantities of timber to go to waste, and rendering the forest liable to injury from extensive conflagrations, owing to the [e]ncumbrance of the ground by so much felled and abandoned wood. The waste is more than usually noticeable in forests near important goldfields, in which immense numbers of young trees are cut for mining purposes' (Victoria, 1874, p. 21).

> At about twenty miles from [Orbost, along the Old Bonang Highway], the track crosses the Broadribb River [now 'Brodribb'] … After crossing the Broadribb, the mining track ascends [along what is now called Sardine Creek Road], and traverses for some miles, high ranges; its next descent [along what is now called Cattleyard Track] being upon the St Patrick's River, thirteen miles from the Broadribb crossing … The St Patrick's River runs north and the mining track, continuing a straight course for a few miles [along what is now recognised as Bee Tree Track] crosses the Goolengook [River] running south … A couple of miles further on, is the Black Watch creek … and at a distance of three miles from the Black Watch, this track enters the Yerungunderah valley [now known as the Errinundra valley] … At the head of the valley the mining track breasts the coast range … [O]n th[e] ascent the vegetation becomes extremely dense culminating at the summit in a sassafras jungle, a sort of tableland [now called the Errinundra Plateau] … From its southern fringe the tableland, although somewhat broken by shallow gullies, slowly ascends for about four miles when the crest of the range represented by Mount Goonmurk is crossed and the country slopes away gradually northward. This slope, from Goonmurk down the Delegate River and into Bendoc, is an extensive area suitable for settlement, much of it indeed being of first-class quality, the great drawback however being its long severe winter (Merrall, 1888, pp. 9–13, emphases removed, for trajectory of track. Additional information concerning present day names and locations adapted from O'Bryan, 1983, p. 36).

This is a good example of a machine (the industrial-exploratory machine) helping to constitute several distinct assemblages (and not just those concerned with the distribution of minerals). In the first instance, the desire to explore for minerals brings about track-cutting assemblages. But in a second instance, these assemblages open onto or make possible other kinds of arrangements (*agencements*) as well. Merrall's presence on this track heralds the appearance of a naturalist assemblage – one that is concerned with something other than auriferous occurrences or alluvial flows. His notes are remarkable for many reasons not the least of which is that they stand, in all likelihood, as the first European text to mention the word 'Goolengook'. Indeed, until Merrall explored the area, ~~Goolengook~~ River was literally *unknown* to Europeans. Those who worked Black Watch Creek in 1885 may well have crossed it, but there is no evidence to suggest any of these were aware of its aboriginal name, its size, or its ecological importance. Merrall writes,

> This Goolengook is an interesting little river heading apparently from Mount Ellery, and is entirely unexplored. To use a mining phrase it cuts across the strata and for this and certain other indications *is likely to be auriferous*.[24]
>
> The track cutters of this north-easterly mining track, supposed it to be the Yerungunderah. [Quite a mistake however as that river is five miles north.] I obtained its name 'Goolengook' from an aboriginal, the last remnant of the Bidwell tribe, who formerly roamed over this territory. A couple of miles further on, is the Black Watch creek, the site of that wretched

---

24 The 'interesting little river' stumbled on here would become the subject of a Supreme Court hearing late in 1998.

> little *fiasco*, known as the 'Black Watch rush'. Last June, the Mining Department projected a track from here, northward, to reach Bendoc … (Merrall, 1888, pp. 10–11).

As of 1887 ~~Goolengook~~ River – the main river located within ~~Goolengook~~ – was merely 'an interesting little river' that was 'entirely unexplored', although the aboriginal inhabitants (once) knew it intimately. In a sense, ~~Goolengook~~ River was something like a body without organs – a force yet to be organised, classified and contained by 'modern' methods of assessment (annual stream flow, turbidity rating, biochemical oxygen demand) and categorisation (river, stream, estuary, creek). To Merrall, it is likely that ~~Goolengook~~ River would have presented itself as a *haecceity*, as a moment or event that transcends all references to subjects and objects (self, forest, water, rock) – hence the need to inquire as to its name. At the time of Merrall's 'discovery', the most up to date map of Croajingolong was from 1876 (drawn up by the Department of Crown Lands), and it did not depict any portion of ~~Goolengook~~ River. Merrall's text provides a concrete illustration of the way in which machines, by interrupting various flows, bring about new combinations of forces or bodies. Specifically, the exploration/mining machine works upon the flows of vegetation and water and in so doing literally assembles (arranges) the body of a naturalist and the body of a river (and the body of the Errinundra Plateau more generally). Eventually, when reterritorialising on the city of Melbourne, the academic machine and the writing assemblage take hold. The writing assemblage dissipates however with the invocation of yet another machine – that of commercial publishing which involves the juxtaposition of new kinds of bodies (the body of a text and the body of a consumer/audience). It is here – by way of Merrall's text (a textual machine) – that part of the world (namely, ~~Goolengook~~) is deterritorialised and subsequently reconfigured as a place of something more than merely 'auriferous qualities'. In addition, ~~Goolengook~~ becomes part of a larger region that is itself 'unknown', a region of infinite becomings (~~Goolengook~~ potential). Of the territory occurring westward of Errinundra valley (which includes ~~Goolengook~~) Merrall remarked,

> This chain of mountains extends from Mount Ellery eastward, and although about thirty miles in length and considerably over three thousand feet in height, the map of Croajingolong knoweth it not (1888, p. 11 emphases removed).

> Near the base of Mount Ellery, fern tree flats of rich black soil are to found. [I] crossed this patch of splendid land, under the disadvantage of a pouring rain; and cannot consequently speak with accuracy as to its extent. This however will probably be the first intimation the public will have of its existence (1888, p. 10 emphases removed).

Of the St. Patrick falls to the west of ~~Goolengook~~ Merrall writes, 'It is impossible by description to convey an idea of the beauty of this scene … The number of people who have as yet seen these falls may be counted upon one's fingers' (1888, p. 10). Speaking about his experience of emerging from a camp located just west of the northern aspect of ~~Goolengook~~ (a point later to fall within the Southern extension of Errinundra National Park), Merrall writes,

A Native Crystal Palace. – We were high up the range and during the night it snowed. The next morning our surroundings were singular, but beautiful. The fronds of the giant fern trees which covered the mountain side so thickly had intercepted the falling snow and thereby roofed us in, so that we marched along through a crystal palace of ten thousand arches nor was Alladin's jewelled fruit absent from this fairy scene, for from every twig and leaf the beams of the rising sun flashed upon myriads of tiny icicles whose rainbow tints flickered around us (1888, p. 12).

In contrast to this 'Eden' of light and snow, Merrall also talks of the lands further north of this camp as being shrouded in darkness,

In the High Lands. – ... It was all shade up there, and trees around the camp of the Department's track cutters were felled to let a little sun in. A thunder storm every twenty-four hours appeared to be the normal atmospheric condition when the lightning tears through the forest in terrible beauty and its accompanying thunder rolls and reverberates grandly among the mountain peaks and valleys. Dense mists occasionally enveloped the tableland when every leaf distilled drops of water so that to a man beneath the canvass it appeared as if a heavy shower of rain were falling (1888, p. 12).

Merrall's text also contains a passage relating to what is now called Boulder Flat or 'Burtons' – the land originally tendered for as part of the Cann Pastoral Run. He comments that the valley of which it forms a part – the Errinundra – is 'a large area of splendid grazing country [with] the flats being admirably adapted for agriculture. The land is however heavily timbered and scrubbed' (1888, p. 11 emphases removed). Specifically of Boulder Flat he writes,

A Happy Valley. – The Yerungunderah valley is admirably sheltered, and when the writer entered it in mid winter it was nearly knee deep in luxuriant green grass. Who *would have imagined that a fine little station like this of thirty thousand acres should have existed unoccupied and unknown in Victoria?* (The first grazing license for this oasis was only issued during the present year.) (1888, p. 11).

So what does Merrall's text 'do' to the body of ~~Goolengook~~? I think it serves to decode it. The text speaks about ~~Goolengook~~ and its surrounding regions in multiple ways pointing to the diversity – not the similarity – of what pertains. To be sure, it is an auriferous region and one that, according to Merrall, 'will doubtless be occupied within a few years' (1888, p. 13). However, it is equally for him 'a sassafras jungle', a place of 'terrible beauty', a land of 'brilliant blossoms', of 'gnarled and twisted trunks', of 'matted wire grass', of 'giant eucalyptus gums', of a 'great coast range', and of 'luxuriant green grass'. The final passage of Merrall's report runs,

The Beauties of Nature. – The tourist seeking health and the beauties of nature can here meet with her in her wildest and most romantic form. The botanist might fairly revel in the boundless extent of floral wealth spread out before him, and the geologist also find much of deep interest. Standing as I now do in the valley of the Yerungunderah I am aware that no human habitation exists within a radius of thirty miles, nevertheless there is no sense of solitude for the valley has a population of its own. Flocks of duck descend upon the

> river and from its waters the piscator can readily fill his basket with the delicate blackfish throughout the entire year. Gorgeous king parrots and the pretty satin birds banquet upon the jungle fruits. The stirring note of the lyrebird can be heard at all times whilst at night the unmelodious howl of the dingo arouses the torpid echoes. The Alpine wilds of Croajingolong are beautiful in the extreme, and under a wise administration of land laws, I look forward to a grand future for the unknown county (1888, p. 13).

The effect of Merrall's text is to leave ~~Goolengook~~ as a multiplicity – as a site *without* a body. For to produce a body is to organise forces into a finite domain of forms and functions. And to limit form and function is to advocate a becoming the same over and above a becoming immanent. It is the molecularity, the decision *not* to impose a molar identity on ~~Goolengook~~, that stands as the significant aspect of Merrall's text.

1889: site of botanical exploration

The edition of *Victorian Naturalist* dated May–June 1889 carries an essay entitled 'Trip to Croajingolong' by Professor Baldwin Spencer and Charles French. Like Merrall's publication, this work included a map of the relevant area. And again, like Merrall's and Peers' text, Spencer's speaks of the time and method involved in reaching the territory in question. On the morning of December 28, 1888, Spencer and four other naturalists departed Melbourne with the intention of exploring the botanical aspects of Croajingolong. Travelling by steam-train to Sale, by horse and coach to the La Trobe River, then by steamship down the La Trobe River to Paynesville, and finally by a second steamship across Lake King toward Lake's Entrance, they reached the Entrance well after 9pm. They had travelled approximately 300 kilometres (the same trip today would take about 3 hours by car). Lacking suitable transportation Spencer's team stayed two nights at Lake's Entrance and departed by horse and coach at 7am on December 30 for Orbost. They arrived later that day. The remoteness of the area is illustrated by Spencer's reference to the fact that the boundary line dividing Croajingolong from New South Wales had only been marked out by geodetic surveying teams in 1870. A key instrument in the formation of States for minimising disputes over territory was (and is) the deployment of geodetic surveying teams. Once land is surveyed, it then becomes possible to claim control over the bodies (biological, mineral, esturine) distributed within discrete boundaries. As mentioned earlier, Deleuze and Guattari use the term *striated space* to describe the territory that results from this process of demarcation – a territory where things have been counted, measured and named, in order that they it may one day be occupied and controlled. Spencer's remarks on arriving at Orbost emulate this idea,

> The township at present consists of one main street, with indications of one or two others, and gives promise of rising to importance in future years, when the now wild district of Croajingolong shall have become settled, and its valleys and mountain-sides brought under cultivation (1889, p. 5).

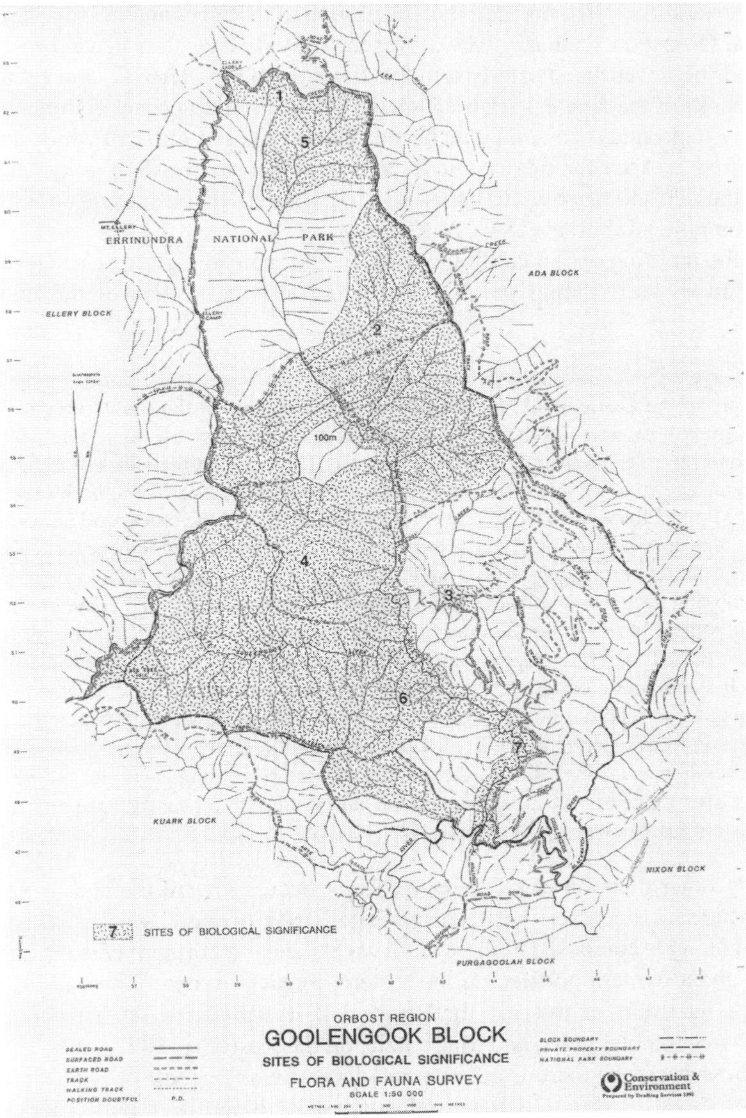

Figure 3 Map displaying sites of biological significance within Goolengook forest management block, 1991. Extracted from Lobert, B.O., Gillespie, G.R., Lunt, I.D., Peacock, R.J. and Robinson, D. (1991) Ecological Survey Report no 35 Flora and Fauna of the Goolengook Forest Block, East Gippsland, Victoria, East Melbourne: Department of Conservation and Environment © State of Victoria, Department of Conservation, Forests and Lands (1992)

With the addition of a guide and three pack-horses, Spencer and his four colleagues departed Orbost on 1 January 1889. Over the next six days they headed east toward the Brodribb River then north-east in the direction of ~~Goolengook~~, and set up camp on the banks of the Arte River on 7 January. Of the terrain Spencer comments, 'Acre after acre of ground is covered with beautiful coral and star ferns, of which one never grows tired … After the ridge comes a creek with dense growth of gully vegetation, and on the rich soil large white-gums growing, then another ridge and another creek, and so on mile after mile' (1889, p. 13).

On the morning of January 8 the team caught their first glimpse of ~~Goolengook~~ River and its surrounding terrain. Spencer recalls this aspect of the journey as follows,

> We leave the uncomfortable camp without regret and again strike north, till we descend sharply to the Goolengook, by the side of which is a small flat, now overgrown with a rank growth of grass. In the valley the soil is rich, and there are some fine white gums. Beyond the river, in the angle between the Goolengook and the Black Watch Creeks, is a high ridge running down from the north, separating the two rivers, both of which rise near Mount Ellery. In half a mile we ascend 400 feet from the creek, and here stop to put up a tent, in which to store our provisions, as we intend to come near this spot on our return journey. From our tent we have a fine view of the country away to the north. We are looking up the valley of the Goolengook. On each side the hills come down into the broad valley, blocking up the northern end of which is Mount Ellery with its two main peaks, one of which is made prominent by being crowned with a large mass of granite which stands out clearly against the sky. Save for this single block of granite, there is nothing to be seen but one vast extent of forest, looking down upon which the tree-tops appear to form a perfectly flat field. Up the hill on which we stand the track winds, with the pack-horses in single file. In the middle distance everything is purple, and beyond this range after range of blue hills falls into the valley, until, in the far distance, the large mass of Mount Ellery closes in the scene (1889, p. 14).

The only other mention of ~~Goolengook~~ River occurs toward the end of Spencer's essay where he discusses the 'General Topography of the District'. He notes that Croajingolong is composed of three main watersheds – a northern portion, an eastern portion and a western portion. Of the eastern, Spencer writes, 'There are two chief streams – the Cann, on the east; the Bemm with its tributaries, the Errinundra, Ada, Black Watch, Goolengook, and Mackenzie, on the west…' (1889, p. 32).

In these passages there is again a recoding of ~~Goolengook~~. It is now 'one vast extent of forest', exhibiting 'range after range of blue hills', within the 'eastern watershed'. There is a very specific mode of envisioning occurring here, one that talks of different resolutions and the proximity of 'viewer' and 'viewed'. The 'single block of granite' Spencer mentions is, from another vantage point, actually many different rocks, all of unique size, weight, colour and so forth. Similarly, the 'perfectly flat field' becomes an undulating and diverse territory to those occupying it – a place of multiple crevices, valleys, streams, lichens, temperatures, fauna, flora, gradients. The phrase 'there is nothing to be seen', therefore, is one that necessarily speaks more about the (com)position of that which *gazes* than that gazed upon.

In addition to those concerning ~~Goolengook~~ River there is an important passage which mentions the area between this river and Black Watch Creek,

> Just beyond our tent Bruce's [track] is joined by the Miner's track coming in from the west. Still rising we reach a height of 1,100 feet, and cross to the southern side of the ridge, where the country has recently been fired, and descend 600 feet very abruptly, in a zigzag course, to the Black Watch Creek. Only a very few years ago gold was discovered in the creek and a 'rush' took place. It was soon over, however, and now nothing remains but a few dangerous holes hidden by scrub, a broken-down bark hut, and a rudimentary letter-box on a tree. A mile's scramble through jungle and scrub brings us to a curious little geological formation, first discovered by Crawford [a member of Spencer's team], and not yet described; in fact, no one has seen it besides the few miners who took part in the Black Watch 'rush'. On the east side of the creek, lying directly on the silurian sandstones and slates of which the steep hills are formed, is a little cliff, at most 200 feet long by 60 feet high, with a roughly semicircular face turned towards the creek, and on its top a flat platform covered with grass and *Senecio lautus*. The main mass of the cliff is formed of limestone, above which comes a layer of very moist, black-coloured soil, some 10 feet deep, though this does not appear to extend to the face of the cliff, and above the soil layers of moss, upon which lime has been deposited, so that they now form a crisp surface. At the present time water drips over the cliff face, upon which stalactites are formed as evaporation of the trickling water goes on. Where the lime has come from is difficult to say; but it must be dissolved by the water at a spot some considerable distance away, as there is no limestone in the neighbourhood, nor does there seem to be any other formation similar to this in the district (1889, pp. 14–15).

Here, Spencer talks of the remains left by the mining assemblage. The sink-holes, previously a means of obtaining gold (and wealth), now become hazardous bodies to be negotiated by Spencer and his party. The letter-box, once a site for the reterritorialisation of news, is now just 'rudimentary', a sundry item, hubris. The 'broken down bark hut', at one time a vital component of the mining assemblage, is now derelict. What is important here is that all these 'things' are as much a part of the lexical folding of ~~Goolengook~~ as any discussion of its so-called 'natural attributes'. Such remnants allow for the invocation of a *social heritage* machine (a machine concomitant with the *becoming-active of decay*). The presence of stalactites, on the other hand, attests to the geological time-scales operating within ~~Goolengook~~. Like the remnants of the mining assemblage, this rock formation provides a basis from which to invoke another kind of machine – one of geological heritage.

There is one other set of remarks from Spencer's text which holds relevance here. These concern efforts to locate 'the higher forms of life' in Croajingolong (1889, p. 32),

> Of the higher forms of life there was, as we were led to believe before leaving Orbost, a remarkable dearth. Kangaroos, wombats, platypus, bandicoots, phalangers, and oppossums were the only mammals seen during the whole journey, and these, save the phalangers, were exceedingly few in number, and we went whole days without catching sight of one. This is, of course, partly to be accounted for by the density of the scrub, into which, in

> most parts, it was simply useless to penetrate, as progress would be, perhaps, at the rate of a few yards per minute (1889, pp. 32–33).

Spencer touches here on the phenomena of *density*. It is clear that ~~Goolengook~~ and surrounding territories are places of considerable mystery to the extent that they *resist* penetration ('a few yards per minute'). Put another way, the penetration of ~~Goolengook~~ requires a particular speed and intensity of movement of bodies. It is only 'impenetrable' to those bodies which do not engage the right kind of becoming. A becoming-dingo or becoming-bandicoot would certainly lessen the so-called density of ~~Goolengook~~. Prior to the European occupation and use of ~~Goolengook~~, notions of 'fast' and 'slow' would have been nonsensical. Such terms mean something only when placed amongst a specific schema – namely, that of 'point, line, point'. In a concrete sense, the mining track cut from Orbost to Bendoc in 1884 (which Peers, Merrall and Spencer all travelled along) was the force that ruptured the *non*-relation between time, movement and bodies that had pertained at and around ~~Goolengook~~ for millions of years. In Deleuzean terms, this (molar) track provided and still provides the basis from which to initiate a multitude of deterritorialisations across ~~Goolengook~~. Road-making is therefore an ethical event as much as it is a technical feat.[25]

1888–91: site of geodetic survey

During the late nineteenth century and into the early part of the twentieth the Department of Lands and Survey (now a division of the Department of Natural Resources and Environment called Land Victoria) was the government body responsible for managing the terrestrial areas of Victoria. The Department's main charter was to impose a network of lines and boundaries across the State – to bring a grid-like character to so called 'empty', 'unknown' or 'derelict spaces'.[26] Geodetic

---

25 The western portion of the southern boundary of Goolengook forest managment block is that of Miner's track – that is, that cut by the Department of Mines in 1884.

26 In 1860 Victoria's first Land Act – known colloquially as Nicholson's Land Act – came into effect. The Government's primary concern here was to 'open[ ] the land for agricultural rather than pastoral production' (O'Bryan, 1983, p. 23). Crown land in Victoria – including that traversing ~~Goolengook~~ – could 'be selected after survey and payment at 1 pound per acre, but no one could select more than 640 acres per year' (O'Bryan, 1983, p. 23). Nicholson's Land Act was repealed in 1862 by the Duffy Land Act, again in 1865 and 1869 by Grant's Land Acts, and once more in 1884. The purpose of each of these Acts was/is to make provisions for the reservation and alienation of Crown Lands. What is important about each of these acts is that they were concomitant with a need to survey or 'know' the land and its potential uses. Surveying was one such means of coming to know a territory and the trajectories of bodies moving through them. 'It appears that from this period, encouraged by the provisions of the 1884 Act and subsequent amendments, large scale settlement spread into the timbered and hilly regions. The Act did however preclude selection of certain areas of Crown Land, for example, auriferous lands, swamp land, and land reserved for State forests,

survey teams helped to divide Victoria into a series of Counties and Parishes (the latter being the smaller unit of the two) so that by the turn of the century the State was made up of 36 Counties and in excess of 2000 Parishes. Parish plans, along with the hand-written notes of those responsible for surveying Parish boundaries, further contribute to the textual folding of ~~Goolengook~~.

Plan 44E/8248 (area traversing ~~Goolengook~~ River/Black Watch Creek)

Plan 44E/8248 is headed 'Tracks Rivers and Creeks, County of Croajingolong', bears the signature of the District Surveyor, and is dated 23 April 1888. The text displays portions of the ~~Goolengook~~ and Bemm Rivers as well as Black Watch Creek (the south eastern portion of ~~Goolengook~~). The area south of ~~Goolengook~~ River and north of Miner's Track is said to exhibit 'Gum, Stringybark, Peppermint, Box, Lightwood, Hazel, Mountain Ash, Musk, Kanaka & Wattle' on 'Fair Hill Slopes'. The area between ~~Goolengook~~ River and Black Watch Creek just north of Miners Track is given to contain 'Gum, Stringybark, Box, Peppermint, Bastard Mahogany & Wattle' on 'High Rangy Back Country' of 'Fair Soil'. This area extends east of the site of the Black Watch rush (some '43 miles' from Orbost). Further to the north, and east of Black Watch Creek, the land is described as 'High Rangy Back Country' with 'Fair Soil' but 'Rocky in Places'. The trees here are said to be those of 'Gum, Stringybark, Lightwood, Box, Peppermint & Wattle'. ~~Goolengook~~ River has been mapped for a distance of about two miles north and one mile south of Miner's Track. Miner's Track itself has been marked up at one mile intervals. Finally, a number of trees have been used as points from which to survey the trajectory of the track.

This plan is an excellent example of a text that contributes to the invention of a landscape – a territory in the process of being ascribed organs of one kind or another. Water, *the* flow par excellence, has always been of chief concern to the State – where it flows, when it flows, how it flows. It is water that is crucial to the survival of *all* bodies. It is of no surprise therefore that the main features shown on the plan in question are the trajectories of the ~~Goolengook~~ River, Bemm River and Black Watch Creek as well as numerous 'small creeks'. Previously I mentioned that the mining track brought about a deterritorialisation and recoding of certain bodies. ~~Goolengook~~ River is one such body. On the plan, ~~Goolengook~~ River becomes that which 'begins' and 'ends' between surveyed or *known* points. Only outside of these co-ordinates, outside of this gridding, does it become a more supple, molecular body, one indicative of a flow rather than an organisation. Plan 44E/8248 therefore illustrates the becoming molar of ~~Goolengook~~ River – a marking out of a body *separate to* rather than an extension of surrounding bodies (such as the body of a Stringy Bark, the body of Mt. Ellery, the body of Bemm River).

---

timber, or water supply purposes. The Act also made provision for the cutting of timber and for timber reserves denuded of timber to be made available for selection (O'Bryan, 1983, p. 36).

There is another very important feature exhibited on this plan having to do with the charting of distances and trajectories across ~~Goolengook~~. Through the imposition of one-mile intervals ~~Goolengook~~ becomes a navigable body that can be enunciated in terms of its relation to a series of already known points (that is Orbost, Bendoc, Mt. Ellery).[27] The construction of a single path that leads from one town to another (Orbost to Bendoc) brings with it a new way of envisioning the territory between points. Bodies can now be enunciated according to their *relative degree of separation from urbanity*. The phrase 'high rangy *back* country', for instance, makes sense only if one accepts the notion that the town (and not the earth) is the *fore*ground (the town as 'anti-back country'). Deleuze and Guattari write, 'It is not the country that progressively creates the town but the town that creates the country' (1996, p. 429). As a sedentary body, it is the town that brings about a relation with the earth (with ~~Goolengook~~) that is peristaltic rather than fluid. ~~Goolengook~~/Earth can now be conceived in terms of its proximity to civilisation or to the 'foreground'. In other words, the body/bodies of ~~Goolengook~~ must literally be made to 'come to the fore'(ground), whether this be on account of a capacity to produce timber, or minerals, or meat, cereals, knowledge, pleasure or whatever. 'The town … represents a threshold of deterritorialisation, because whatever the material involved, it must be deterritorialised enough to enter the network, to submit to the polarisation, to follow the circuit of urban and road recoding' (Deleuze and Guattari, 1996, p. 432). ~~Goolengook~~ here becomes part of circuit or gridding of functions and movements rather than a flow. Surveying is therefore a political act precisely because it allows for the controlled or, better still, *prescribed* movement of bodies across the earth. One path, one trajectory, one speed – a path that encourages the movement of bodies through a territory rather than a deterritorialisation of bodies through multiple movements.[28]

Plans 1890–91/608 and 609 (area traversing ~~Goolengook~~ River/Black Watch Creek)

The plans headed 'Copy of Field Notes of Surveys, Parish of Bungywarr, Co[unty] [of] Croajingolong' date from 1890–91 and are, in effect, diagrams of the same area exhibited on plan 44E/8248 with three major differences – they are three years hence, they display the position and dimensions of projected roads, and they depict parish boundaries. In the Parish of Noonga around the headwaters of Blackwatch

27 Bendoc was first surveyed in 1871 whilst Orbost was proclaimed a township in April 1885.

28 The cadastral plan dated June 9, 1891 entitled 'Road Survey and Parish Boundary Lines, Parishes of Noonga, Bungywarr, Cobon and Goongerah', marks out the dimensions of a track called Whitelaw's Mining Track (named after A.D.L. Whitelaw the geological surveyor responsible for cutting the track around 1887). This track 'begins' at the intersection of Black Watch Creek and Miner's Track and continues north to the township of Bonang. Part of Whitelaw's track was to later function as the north west boundary of ~~Goolengook~~ (Ada Divide Track) whilst the part that falls within ~~Goolengook~~ was renamed Houstens Track.

Creek, the text reads 'Good Scrub Land, Chocolate and Black Soil, Gum, Messmate and dense Jungle'. The south west corner of the Parish of Bungywarr (straddling Blackwatch Creek) is described as exhibiting 'Steep Ranges, Fair Grazing Land, Blue Gum, Messmate and St[ringy] Bark'. The border of the two Parishes is marked by the phrases 'steep gully' and 'very steep'. A number of trees have been used as trig points (or 'reference trees') from which to survey the boundaries of the Parishes (for example 'R.T. Gum' and 'R.T. Messmate'). Elsewhere, the words 'Blue Gum on Line marked PBT' designates the point where Bungywarr meets the Parish of ~~Goolengook~~. 'BT' stands for 'Blazed Tree' – a tree whose bark and sapwood was removed on the side skirting the Parish boundary. In this case, the 'P' may well have meant 'Partially' – yielding 'Partially Blazed Tree'.[29] The same Plan also displays a section of 'Two Chain Road' (Whitelaw's Track) which leads north 'to Bonang'. Just east of this track the terrain is marked by the words 'very steep', 'gully' and 'water'.

This text speaks of the techniques used to assemble the navigable or knowable body of a Parish and, therefore, of ~~Goolengook~~. Far from being viewed as a source of fuel or fibre, trees are construed as bodies on which to inscribe permanent co-ordinates. Here the geodetic machine has a mutating effect on ~~Goolengook~~ producing it as a site for depasturing ('fair grazing country'), a site for agricultural production ('chocolate and black soil') and as an impenetrable body ('dense Jungle') all at once. Nonetheless this same machine also has a stratifying effect as it segments ~~Goolengook~~ via a series of molar lines which apply to the present day (Parish boundaries, Mount Ellery datum, and so on).

In concert, cadastral plans provide the basis from which to organise the movement and composition of 'natural' and 'built' objects within defined territories. For a burgeoning State, this is an important task (see Seddon, 1997, pp. 150–52). The creation of a centralised register of territorial boundaries – many times smaller than counties – allows for greater control over who and what can occupy a given area,

> One of the fundamental tasks of the State is to striate the space over which it reigns, or to utilise smooth spaces as a means of communication in the service of striated space. It is a vital concern of every State not only to vanquish nomadism but to control migrations and, more generally, to establish a zone of rights over an entire 'exterior', over all of the flows traversing the ecumenon. If it can help it, the State does not dissociate itself from a process of capture of flows of all kinds, populations, commodities or commerce, money or capital, and so on There is still a need for fixed paths in well-defined directions, which restrict speed, regulate circulation, relativise movement, and measure in detail the relative movements of subjects and objects (Deleuze and Guattari, 1996, pp. 385–86).

The latin root of 'cadastral' is *cadastra* meaning 'to cut up' or 'segment'. This is very close to the concept of a machine. Machines, it will be recalled, interrupt or cut into various flows. In this sense, cadastral plans are textual machines which display the

29 In conversation with Bill Black, Land Victoria, 8th Floor, 456 Lonsdale Street, Melbourne, March 15, 1999.

precise divisions (cuts, *coupres*) between flows (for example pastoral, agricultural, urban, hydrological). For Deleuze and Guattari the primary function of the State is to constrain the flow and distribution of bodies across land, sea, air and water scapes – to organise, in other words, spaces as geopolitical terrains. The word 'State' derives from *stat* meaning 'not moving' or 'immutable'. 'Everything changes with State societies: it is often said that the territorial principle becomes dominant. One could also speak of deterritorialisation, since the earth becomes an object, instead of being an active material element in combination with lineage' (1996, p. 388). Geodetic survey teams initiate a series of deterritorialisations (that is displacement of indigenous peoples and nomadic ways of life) and reterritorialisations (that is influx of pastoralists and agriculturalists and a sedentary existence) across the earth, and in this instance across Croajingolong. As mentioned earlier in the chapter, the lands within the parishes of ~~Goolengook~~, Noonga and Goongerah, once played a significant role in the lives of the Bidwell people. However, there is no trace of the indigenous significance of these areas on cadastral plans. This is because geodetic survey teams – like mining assemblages – produce ~~Goolengook~~ in a quantitative fashion (as so many distances, lines and degrees). Under such a scenario, ~~Goolengook~~ is not a place of indigenous, geomorphological, hydrological nor even botanical importance. Rather, it is a thing to be measured, marked and segmented – a territory where everything is counted and delineated in order that it may eventually be occupied by 'new' (that is, European) forces. In Foucault's parlance, this is an instrument of biopolitics at work – of a centralised organ of power learning to manage and regulate the affairs of bodies occupying diverse and distant portions of the Earth. In Nietzschean terms, it is a strategy aimed at sublimating or containing multiple wills to power. In Deleuze and Guattari's view, it is a process of capture, an appropriation or molarisation of bodies which attempts to arrest desire or becomings molecular.

Chapter 6

Becoming Forest

From the turn of the twentieth century, the trajectory which characterised ~~Goolengook~~ assumed something of a molarised form. It was not that everything was set in place or ordered ahead of time so much as the events which occurred here curtailed the range of envisionings and intensities that might otherwise have informed this space. To put it simply, the period spanning 1908–1972 saw ~~Goolengook~~ slowly but surely enunciated as a timbered body to the exclusion of all other capacities and potentials. To be sure, other ways of encoding ~~Goolengook~~ were indeed proposed by various sectors. However, those responsible for managing ~~Goolengook~~ ultimately viewed its aspects as awaiting (industrial) transformation.

1908 (March): site of protected forest

In accordance with the *Forests Act* 1907, the State forests of Victoria (as delineated on maps produced under the *State Forests Act* 1876 and the *Land Act* 1890) were divided into two categories – *reserved forest* and *protected forest*. Reserved forest comprised all permanent forest and timber reserves on Crown land.[1] Protected forest was made up of 'all unoccupied Crown land proclaimed as a protected forest pursuant to th[e] [Forests] Act' (Section 4). Since 1788, all or portions of ~~Goolengook~~ had remained under the broad category 'unoccupied Crown land'. On Wednesday 4 March 1908 the *Victorian Government Gazette* declared all land in this category to be protected forest. The relevant section reads,

> PROCLAMATION OF A PROTECTED FOREST
>
> WHEREAS by section 29 of the *Forests Act* 1907, it is enacted that the Minister of Lands may at any time proclaim any unoccupied Crown land to be a protected forest, and may at any time alter or revoke any such proclamation: Now, therefore, I, John Emanuel Mackey, Minister of Lands, do hereby proclaim all unoccupied Crown lands in the State of Victoria, except such portions as are in course of being dealt with under the provisions of the Land Acts, to be a protected forest.

1 'Permanent forest' could 'be excised only by Act of Parliament or for specific public purposes or by exchange for private or unoccupied Crown land'. 'Timber reserves', on the other hand, could 'be alienated only by a resolution of both Houses of Parliament or by exchange as [previously related]' (Ferguson, 1957, p. 9).

> Given under my hand, at Melbourne, this second day of March, in the year of our Lord One thousand nine hundred and eight.
>
> J.E. Mackey,
> Minister of Lands.

This notice, this text, is a machine of *axiomisation*. All of ~~Goolengook~~ is brought under the single, non-differentiating category of 'protected forest'. 'Protected forest' should not be taken to mean 'protected from intensive industrial use'. In fact, precisely the opposite was/is so. The word protection is used here to indicate what might be termed 'administrative sovereignty'. Protected forest thus indicated forest whose produce was solely controlled by the State Forests Department rather than the Lands Department (which controlled all other aspects of the land where such forest occurs). Prior to the advent of this text there were no forests at ~~Goolengook~~. There was 'dense scrub'. There was 'bush country'. There was a land 'heavily timbered'. There were 'forest trees'. And there were 'Stringybarks', 'Messmate' and 'Gums'. But there was *no* 'forest'. *This gazettal literally assembles and distributes the body of a forest across* ~~Goolengook~~. It assigns ~~Goolengook~~ a molar category, a single identity. The 1907 Act also defined for the first time the terms 'timber' and 'tree',

> 'Timber' includes fallen trees felled trees and all wood whether sawn split hewn or other wise fashioned; and
>
> 'Tree' or 'trees' included trees shrubs bushes seedlings saplings and reshoots whether alive or dead (S.4)

What happens to ~~Goolengook~~ must now occur through the aborescent principles upon which the body of a protected forest is founded. It was the State Forests Department that took direct control over all forest produce in protected forest in Victoria and therefore at ~~Goolengook~~.[2] The 1907 Act gave two definitions of 'forest produce'

2 The *Forests Act* 1907 commenced its '[ ] operation on 1 January 1908 [ ] and, in February 1908, a State Forests Department under a Minister of Forests came into being, constituted as provided by Section 5 of the Act' (Carron, 1985, p. 183). Prior to the Act becoming law, 'practically no attempt was made to survey or assess the forest resources of the State. The task of surveying and demarcating forest boundaries, and of introducing plans of work in the management of forest reserves, was imposed on the Forests Department by this Act' (Forests Commission of Victoria, 1928, p. 44). From the passing of the first Forests Act in 1876 up until that of 1907, control of Victoria's forests was handed back and forth between three Departments – the Department of Agriculture, the Lands Department, and the Mines Department. Each of these were branches of the much larger Lands and Survey Department (Forests Commission of Victoria, 1928, p. 41). The 'dual control' by the Lands Department of forest and land matters provoked many problems for early forest management. As Woodgate et al. (1994, p. 172) write, 'For most of the nineteenth century in Victoria any person holding tenure over Crown land, including a Miner's Right, pastoral run, selection purchase lease or a license to split or mill timber, could cut down trees virtually unhindered and unsupervised. Forests in proximity to settlements were subjected to the greatest devastation'. The series of

– one for produce extracted from reserved forest and one for produce emanating from protected forest,

> 'Forest produce' where used in reference to or in connexion with or as to anything in any reserved forest includes the following things namely: Stone gravel limestone limesalt sand

---

Land Acts in operation up to this time (and beyond) facilitated the development of Crown land by alienating land from the Crown and selling it as private property, and/or by leasing it to those willing to clear it for pastoral or agricultural purposes. In the latter stages of the nineteenth century and into the early stages of the twentieth large tracts of forest were removed or burnt without regard for the associated economic and environmental losses. In 1901 a Royal Commission into Victoria's forests found that 'The forest laws of the country are inadequate [...] They have ... been allowed to lie fallow, and have sometimes even been superseded by contradictory and mischievous circulars and reports' (in Forests Commission of Victoria, 1928, p. 42). A passage from the *Victorian Year Book* of 1902 echoes these concerns. It reads,

> The area of forest reserves is becoming so curtailed year after year by alienation, that it will not be possible to continue to grant licenses for timber cutting, except under the most stringent conditions, and then only to a limited extent.
>
> A greater danger than even the saw-mill industry is that which has been brought about in the past by the entrance of splitters upon the reserves. These men cut down the trees in ruthless fashion, and were altogether regardless of any precautions that might have been taken, and heedless of any safeguards that might have been effective in saving the forests ... Large areas of valuable timber are destroyed or damaged by the spread of extensive fires in the hot season. Many of these are unquestionably due to the carelessness of settlers in clearing their land, and of timber-getters in leaving their camp fires unextinguished (*Victorian Year Book*, 1902, p. 258).

In this context, the *Forests Act* 1907 was significant for two reasons. First, it 'remov[ed] ... the forest reserves from the direct control of the Lands Department [allowing] a more or less stable policy of administration [to be] formulated' (Forest Commission of Victoria, 1928, p. 42). Section 15 (1) states,

> As soon as the Department is constituted then notwithstanding anything contained in the Land Acts –
>
> (*a*) it shall not be lawful for the Governor in Council by virtue of the said Acts at any time to increase or diminish the area of State forest reserve or timber reserve or to grant a lease or license of or in respect of any Crown land within any reserved forest...

Section 5(1) establishes a separate department responsible for overseeing forestry related matters,

> A Department of the Public Service shall be constituted and shall be called the State Forests Department having under the direction of the Minister of Forests such powers authorities and duties as are provided for by this Act.

Section 8 details the 'Business of Forests Department',

> The Department shall subject to this Act have the exclusive control and management of
>
> (a) All matters of forest policy;

> loam brick earth trees timber firewood sawdust plants grass creepers fibres leaves blossom flowers ferns fruit seeds roots bark gum kinos resin sap charcoal honey or beeswax but does not include any gold or silver or metal or mineral.
>
> 'Forest produce' where used in reference to or in connexion with or as to anything in any protected forest means trees timber charcoal and bark (S.4).

(b) The granting issuing and enforcing of all leases licenses permits or authorities under this Act;
(c) The collection and recovery of all rents fees royalties charges and revenues under this Act whether in respect of leases licenses permits or authorities granted before or after the commencement of this Act;
(d) The planting or thinning of forests and the making laying out and maintaining of plantations and nurseries and the distribution of trees therefrom; and
(e) The administration generally of this Act.

Sections 16 and 17 provided that all areas of permanent forest reserves and timber reserves be subject to leases and licenses issued under the Act (mining licenses excepted). Section 24 dealt with the leasing of land in reserved forest for various purposes including sawmilling. It reads,

> Subject to such covenants terms and conditions and to the payment of such rent royalties or fees as may be prescribed the Governor in Council may grant to any person for any term not exceeding seven years a lease of any Crown land within any reserved forest –
>
> (*a*) of any area for the grazing of cattle;
> (*b*) of any area not exceeding One thousand acres for sawmilling purposes; or
> (*c*) for any purpose and area for which a lease may be granted under Division 8 of Part 1. of the *Land Act* 1901.

A second significant aspect of the 1907 Act was that it provided 'for the dedication of permanently reserved forest and provision for further dedications [and] for the control of forest produce on unoccupied crown land' (Carron, 1985, p. 183). Unoccupied land included ~~Goolengook~~.

Sections 34 and 35 dealt with fire prevention and made it illegal for any unauthorised person 'during the months of November December January February or March within any reserved forest or within one hundred yards of the boundary thereof' to light a fire (S.34). Section 35 gave the Conservator of Forests the power to order the occupier of 'any land within fifty yards of the boundary of any reserved forest' to burn or remove 'within fourteen days any dead wood branches of trees leaves or other refuse on any such land within fifty yards of the forest boundary'. This was a very significant moment in the environmental history of the Victorian landscape. For the first time there was a proactive policy aimed at controlling the effects of fire on forested terrains. However, one major problem with fire suppression in eucalypt forests is that fire is an integral part of the reproductive process of such forest. There is a complex relationship between temperature and the thresholds that need to be surpassed in order for eucalypts to drop their seeds.

Section 41 (1) gave forest officers the power to stipulate the position of tracks for the removal of forest produce. Sections 41 (2) and (3) gave forest officers and police the power to seize any forest produce suspected of being obtained in a manner contrary to the Act. Section 47 listed the offences created by the Act – the maximum penalties for which included one year of imprisonment and/or a fifty pound fine.

Here the body of ~~Goolengook~~ is rendered as something very different to that produced by the texts of Merrall, Spencer and others. It is no longer 'A Native Crystal Palace', nor a 'range of blue hills', nor a place of 'auriferous qualities'. Instead it is a body constituted *only* of 'trees', 'timber', 'charcoal', and 'bark'. ~~Goolengook~~ River, indeed all water at ~~Goolengook~~, has vanished, as has its 'dingoes', 'bandicoots', 'dense mists', 'jungle fruits', and 'tiny icicles'.

Section 25 sets out the types of licences that may be granted to those wishing to use Crown land in reserved and protected forest areas,

> Subject to such covenants terms and conditions and to the payment of such rent fees royalties or charges as may be prescribed the Governor in Council or any person authorised by him in that behalf may grant to any person for any term not exceeding one year –
>
> (*a*) a license of any Crown land within any reserved forest –
>
> (i) of any area for the grazing of cattle; or
> (ii) to occupy a special area not exceeding six hundred and forty acres for the exclusive cutting of timber;
> (iii) to thin out and remove trees;
> (iv) to cut dig and take away any specified forest produce;
> (v) to occupy for residence an area not exceeding one acre;
> (vi) for any of the purposes for which a license may be granted under Division 8 of Part 1. of the *Land Act* 1901 as amended by the *Land Act* 1904 and the *Land Act* 1905 or under sections nine to sixteen of the last mentioned Act; or
> (vii) for any other purpose whatsoever relating to or connected with a State forest or forest produce; or
>
> (*b*) a license to enter upon any protected forest to cut dig and take away forest produce.

It would take until 1975 for a licence to be issued for the 'cutting', 'digging', and 'taking away' of forest produce from ~~Goolengook~~.

Section 29 (3) dealt with the control of forest produce from protected forest,

> All forest produce in protected forest shall, subject to any leases or licenses of any land therein granted under any Act relating to Crown lands, be under the control and management of the Department. In every other respect all Crown land within a protected forest shall be subject to the control of the Minister of Lands in accordance with the Lands Acts.

Section 30 (1) made it an offence to,

> [F]ell girdle ringbark injure destroy or remove any growing tree or any timber in any protected forest without a permit in writing from the Minister of Forests or from some forest officer duly authorised by the said Minister to give such permits.

However, section 30 (2) allowed that,

> Nothing in this section shall prohibit any person in authorised occupation under lease or licence under the Land Acts of any area of protected forest from using in accordance with his lease or licence any timber which may be necessary for fencing such area or for domestic use of such person and the members of his household.

Section 33 stipulated that,

> No regulation shall under this Act be made with regard to any protected forest except as to the growth preservation protection or distribution cutting or removal of forest produce.

The components of the Forests Act 1907 outlined here constitute a defining moment on the machinic phylum of becoming forest. The vegetation at ~~Goolengook~~ now has a juridical as opposed to rhetorical foundation ('dense scrub', and so on). This is not to say that the juridical production of ~~Goolengook~~ *as forest* brought about an immediate exploitation of its forest produce. Indeed, in contrast to the reserved and protected forests occurring closer to Melbourne such as the Central Highlands and the Otways, such forests within the County of Croajingolong (and by default those at ~~Goolengook~~) remained predominantly free from commercial and domestic exploitation. This was the case despite the *Forests Act* 1907 handing the State Forests Department the authority to exploit both reserved and protected forest for various purposes. A passage from the *Victorian Year Book* of 1907–8 confirms the 'geographical limits' of such exploitation,

> Of the State forest domain, some 3,000,000 acres are situated on the slopes of the high mountain ranges, and their protection is essential for the maintenance of stream and springs; *over half a million acres are situated in the extreme Eastern part of the State, but, owing to difficulties of transport, are not at present accessible for practical working*; half a million acres in the central district, which have been cut over, are closed for the protection of the young timber; while in the remaining area, over 600,000 acres, timber cutting is carried on in various parts. The bulk of the forest revenue is, however, derived from a total of 100,000 acres, the trees being felled on the selection system of treatment; while for the supply of mine-props and fuel, large blocks are allotted and worked as coppice, or coppice under standards, thinnings only, light or severe as the circumstances require, being taken out in some districts.
>
> The license system is now abolished in the greater part of Victoria, and strict control enforced over the operation of timber-getters (*Victorian Year Book 1907–8*, p. 610 emphases added).

As of 1907 there were 119 licensed sawmills throughout Victoria producing 55,873,500 super feet per year of sawn timber valued at £181,590 (*Victorian Year Book 1907–8*; p. 711).[3] The forests located within Croajingolong were likely to have

3 One superfoot true is the equivalent of 0.0023 cubic metres (one cubic metre approximates one tonne).

yielded around 1.5 million super feet or 3450 cubic metres at this time.[4] Only one sawmill was operating in the County during this period – this being a mill at Orbost which supplied wood for the construction of domestic dwellings.[5] On this basis, the State forests of Croajingolong were, as of 1907, producing under 3% of the sawn hardwood timber in Victoria. This figure remained constant as of 1946 where such forests were used to produce 'less than five million [superfeet] per year' or 3% of the State's total hardwood output of around 160 million superfeet (McKinty 1969, p. 134). However, by 1969, these same forests – which had since 1770 remained predominantly free from intensive and sustained commercial exploitation – would be producing 25% or 107 million super feet per annum (about 250,000 cubic metres) of Victoria's total output of hardwood timber of around 428 million super feet (1 million cubic metres) (McKinty 1969, pp. 135–36, my conversions).

1917: site exterior to chief saw-milling localities

Nearly half a century after the production of the first map showing the distribution of flora in Victoria, the State Forests Department published a map showing the location of 'Forest Reserves', 'Towns', 'Chief Saw-Milling Localities', 'Bee Farming Districts' and 'Oil Areas' (that is, eucalyptus oil). Of 16 saw-milling localities, the operations at 'Tambo' were positioned closest to ~~Goolengook~~ – which, at this time, was at least 50 miles (80 kilometres) east of such activities. In the years prior to 1917, this distance would present as an insurmountable obstacle to those wishing to access 'nature' in the far east of Victoria. But with the completion of the railway from Melbourne to Orbost in 1916, notions of time and proximity took on radically new meanings. In other words, although ~~Goolengook~~ was cartographically configured as 'exterior' to the dominant saw-milling localities of the time, this 'exteriority' of ~~Goolengook~~ (its existence 'beyond' or 'outside' the limits of industrial activity) is actually no kind of exteriority at all. It is, rather, a folding – a fold that illustrates that the exterior (just like the interior) is always in the process of becoming-other. Here, after Deleuze and Guattari, the inside and the outside are not two opposing points on a continuum but expressions of a will to power or a molar desire to encode, striate, and mark off portions of the earth. No matter how 'precise' or 'ingenious' the instruments of cartography, the earth will never know anything of beginnings and ends, interiors and exteriors, heights and depths, or forests and rivers. What will be known, however, is something of the cost associated with inscribing the socius at various speeds and intensities over time.

---

4 The first forests to be permanently reserved in Croajingolong under the *Forests Act* 1907 were those in the Parishes of Bendoc, Noorinbee, Dellicknora, Nerran, Orbost, Wulgulmerang, Enano, Tambo, Colquhoun and Tildesley. The forests in this dedication covered 369,665 acres (McKinty, 1969, p. 129).

5 In conversation, Moray Douglas, 26 May 1999.

1921: site within the Orbost Forest District

Although the dedication of permanent forest reserves under the *Forests Act* 1907 was an important step toward securing a long-term forest resource, the Act fell short of establishing a body responsible for the day to day management and ongoing dedication of forest reserves. Whilst debating the passage of the Forest Bill of 1918, a member of the Victorian Legislative Assembly commented,

> Our forests have been neglected by Governments of this country. Honourable members can protest, but their protests have very little weight. As an ex-Minister has said, Parliament is becoming merely a registering machine … We know that the forests have been denuded, and we know that many rich forest areas were thrown open for selection. In that case they are either used for the timber or for grazing, and if they are used for grazing, the timber has to go. In cases where people think there is an ample supply of timber they will find that they are generally mistaken. The private individual has exploited nearly all our timber areas (Victoria, Parliamentary Debates, Session 1918, p. 3123).

In December 1918, the *Forests Act* 1907 was replaced by '…a much more comprehensive Forests Act' – that of 1918.[6] 'Under it, a Forests Commission of three came into being on 1 October 1919 … The Act provided for the establishment of a Forestry Fund of a fixed sum of £40,000 per year, together with half of any gross revenue over £80,000, for the improvement and reforestation of the state forests. It also authorised the Commission to recruit, employ and manage its staff' (Carron, 1985, pp. 183–84). The funding mentioned here was crucial in that it enabled the surveying and demarcation of forest reserves to be executed on a continuous basis. 'The broad outlines of the Commission's policy may be classed under three heads, viz.: 1. The conservation, development, and utilisation of the indigenous forests, based on sound forestry principles. 2. The establishment of adequate plantations of exotic softwoods. 3. The prosecution of essential research and experimental work' (Forests Commission of Victoria, 1928, p. 46). Here, the management of forests enters the domain of science and therefore of a particular kind of *logic* or way of knowing/deciphering the world (that is, 'nature'). This scientific method was of the form 'if x then y'. A tree cut in a particular manner could now be said to produce such and such a quantity of merchantable timber. Equally, a stand of trees harvested in one manner over another could now be said to result in varying qualities of regrowth. Forests are here subjected to increasingly technical means of physical transformation and become, more so than at any previous time, an object of (Western) knowledge and tabulation (concerning rates of growth, type and durability of timber yielded,

6 In addition to providing stability of management and resources, the *Forests Act* 1918 holds further significance in that it forms the basis of the *Forests Act* 1958. It is this last Act that presently governs the use of State forest in Victoria. At the time of writing, the 1958 Act was being rewritten. A key function of the new Act will be will be to provide a legislative framework more congruent with the classifications and thresholds of forest use in Victoria (in conversation with Norma Marshall, 18 March 1999, and Tony Bartlett, 24 March 1999, Department of Natural Resources and Environment, Nicholson Street Office).

relative ability to withstand wildfire, and so on). It was the desire for this kind of information that brought with it a new set of administrative units or boundaries within which survey work would take place. Accordingly, in 1921, ~~Goolengook~~ became part of the Orbost Forest District.[7] *The Handbook of Forestry* published initially in 1928 and subsequently in updated form in 1957 by the Forests Commission remarks, 'The forest district is the territorial unit of administrative control, headquarters being located usually in a central town where banking and other facilities are available' (Ferguson, 1957, p. 32). Perhaps as testimony to its relative inaccessibility, it would take just over half a century for the forests at ~~Goolengook~~ to be intensively exploited for their timber (flows of wood fibre).

1924–25: site of potential conservation

In the *Victorian Year Book* of 1924–25 J.W. Audas of the National Herbarium in Melbourne describes the forests of 'East Gippsland' under the larger heading 'Flora of Victoria',

> In Eastern Gippsland the influence of sub-tropical conditions is prolonged along the Pacific Slope, the eastern aspect, the protection of the coastal range, and probably the warm East Australian Ocean Current conducing to the extension in range of many plants ordinarily found in warmer latitudes … [There] is great exuberance in growth and the presence in moist sheltered valleys with a southern aspect of jungle flora of much interest as so far removed from its usual range (*Victorian Year Book*, 1924–25, p. 22).

Immediately following this is a section headed 'Forest Destruction', which runs,

> The Gippsland and Cape Otway districts have been famous for the extraordinary beauty of their fern gullies, and their extensive forests formerly containing, as in Gippsland in the Mountain Ash (*Eucalyptus regnans*), probably the highest trees in the world. Unfortunately, right from the first occupation of the forest country, much of which should have been rigorously reserved from encroachment and destruction has resulted in complete denudation of valuable forest areas, and ruthless destruction of the trees by fire and axe, so that the character of the country has been completely altered, new climatic conditions created, and the soil exposed to the action of atmospheric agencies causing rapid deterioration and irreparable diminution of our timber resources. Despite

---

7 Orbost was one of '[t]hree forest districts … set up in East Gippsland' at this time. Nowa Nowa [was located] directly west whilst Cann River district spanned the east (Woodgate et al., 1994, p. 173). These districts remain in place today. It should also be noted that an F.G. Gerraty held the position of District Forester, Orbost between 1 April 1920 to 9 August 1923 (Handwritten page within the historical records of the Forests Commission of Victoria held at the Public Records Office, Laverton, Victoria). Drawing on a variety of sources, one can, however, infer that the precise boundaries of Orbost District were not in place at the time he took up his appointment. I have therefore designated the year in which the District was marked out as 1921 not, as may be expected, 1920. Woodgate et al. (1994) seem to have arrived at the same conclusion.

> many warnings during the last 70 years as to the result of such an unwise policy, and notwithstanding the disastrous results shown from pursuing similar destruction in other countries, the forestry problem, of such outstanding importance to the State, has in the past received little if any attention. It is only now, when the most valuable areas have been devastated and the absolute necessity of conservation, selection, and protection of the depleted areas still existing has been tardily recognised through the increasing shortage in the world's timber supplies, that more vigorous action has been taken by the State and an effort made to cultivate a forest conscience in the people. Afforestation and reafforestation should be wisely, widely, and unremittingly carried on throughout the State.

The final section is headed 'Reservations and Sanctuaries'. In part it reads,

> Such being the case it is a wise provision and a duty of the State, in accordance with the long-neglected policy of preservation of forest areas for national purposes, to set apart suitable areas in which, as far as possible, our distinctive flora and fauna also can be preserved under natural conditions of growth ... [S]uch reservations should ... include comparatively large areas in Eastern Gippsland, the Mallee, the Grampians, the Otway district, and Yarra watershed respectively, each with typical flora of its own ... (*Victorian Year Book*, 1924–25, p. 24).

What is significant here is that these passages elaborate on the concerns raised in the Year Book of 1907–8 concerning dwindling forest resources around the main townships of Victoria. Specifically, Audas alerts the reader to two main issues. Firstly, he points to the fact that East Gippsland holds considerable – and perhaps the last – areas of predominantly unlogged forests which could, under sensible management regimes, be utilised to offset the dwindling supplies from the Otways and other areas. But secondly, he also formally recommends, most likely for the first time, that large areas of East Gippsland forest be placed in conservation reserves. It is perhaps understandable that such comments should have come around this time. One of the major hindrances to the development and intensive exploitation of East Gippsland's forests was the lack of infrastructure and technologies available to convey logs to regional and urban centres (particularly that of Melbourne). In 1916 the railway line from Melbourne to Orbost was completed which, theoretically at least, made possible the transportation of wood resources over large distances. It was the arrival of the locomotive that helped spawn not just a new mode of movement but a new way of looking at 'nature' as well. The locomotive belongs to the same machinic phylum as the mule, pack-horse, and stage-coach (the iron wheel as deterritorialised hoof, the cylindrical steam furnace as deterritorialised heart, the iron gauged line as deterritorialised dirt track). As the human body moved at ever greater speeds (via the technics of the railway/steam engine) the European eye was able to witness, and ascribe a new importance to, previously 'invisible' natures or terrains (forests of Croajingolong). Audas' comments are machinic statements precisely to the extent that they seek to interrupt the process of (aesthetic/material) deterritorialisation initiated by the locomotive. On the other hand, there was an 'underside' associated with moving at increased speed – namely that the uniqueness and differences between bodies were, more often than not, lost to the phenomena of blurred vision. Paul

Virilio (1997) remarks that a multi-coloured wheel presents as gray when spinning rapidly. It would take until 1988 for ~~Goolengook~~ to be envisioned and named for its differences (as a conservation zone). But this, as shall be shown, was as much a part of a molar politics as those texts that produce ~~Goolengook~~ solely as a timber production zone.

1928 (June): site lacking commercial value

On June 1, 1928, the Forests Commission of Victoria issued a map 'Showing Reserved Forests under Forests Acts, and distribution of principal species of tree size and commercial value'. The map was a feature of the '3rd Empire Forestry Conference, Australia and New Zealand, 1928' and used numbers spanning from 1 to 115 to designate economically significant tree species across Victoria. Significantly, ~~Goolengook~~ was neither a reserved forest nor of commercial value at such time and was therefore implicitly coded as value*less*. Around 10 kilometres to the west of ~~Goolengook~~ on the Brodribb River (and at an equivalent elevation) there is a listing of tree species for the Nerrang forest reserve covering some 35,600 acres (around 20,000 hectares). Twelve species of commercial value are shown to exist here – Yellow Stringybark, Red Ironbark, White Stringybark, Silvertop, Red Box, Black Wattle, Blackwood, Kanooka, Common Peppermint, Red Stringybark, Mountain Grey Gum and Musk. Compared to 1869 – when only 11 species of tree were denoted by the State Forest Board for the whole of Victoria (and only six at best for the whole of East Gippsland) – this list indicates a substantial change in the degree to which forests were 'known' by 1928. In the wider Orbost Forest District, there were now 19 species of tree identified as having commercial value. Still, three of the tree species that were to become of immense commercial value in the decades ahead (especially following the Second World War) were, according to this text, nowhere to be found as of 1928. The species in question are Mountain Ash (*E.regnans*), Alpine Ash (*E.delegatensis*) and Shining Gum (*E.nitens*). Even with commercial pressures coming to the fore, these three species somehow remained invisible to foresters and cartographers at the time of the 1928 conference. Perhaps this was due to their high inland elevation and subsequent distance from saw mills. Or perhaps there were so few of each species in East Gippsland that they were difficult nay impossible to locate. Whatever the case, Mountain Ash (the tallest flowering plant on earth growing to in excess of 90 m), Alpine Ash and Shining Gum (of comparable height) would, some five decades later, feature as the key species at stake in forest conflict at ~~Goolengook~~ and across Errinundra Plateau more generally.

It would be entirely remiss to think that the text of 1928 merely 'missed' certain species. Rather, the classification and demarcation of forest species and their locations is a *process* that has its own epistemological dimensions and problems. At first glance, the production of a map showing species of forest of commercial value appears an uncomplicated affair. But on closer inspection the attribution of *value* (whether it be economic, ecological or otherwise) functions as an extractive and destructive force insofar as it sets up all sorts of dichotomies (commercial/non-commercial, useful/defective, accessible/inaccessible, common/rare). These in turn help to sustain the idea that 'nature' is actually little more than a regime of signs waiting for a hermeneutician to 'correctly' and 'definitively' decode various attributes into their constitutent parts (taxa/genus/species, overmature/mature/regrowth, high elevation/foothill/low elevation). At the heart of the matter here is the tension between *bodies without organs* and *bodies of representation*. The (in)capacity to (mis)represent the earth underpins the ability to regulate and sustain ecosystems. Following Descartes, the classical episteme had a way of representing things as though there were an intrinsic and omnipresent relation between certain 'words' and certain 'things'. Foucault, in what surely stands as one of the most brilliant studies of this relation, remarks,

> Things touch against the banks of discourse because they appear in the hollow space of representation. It is not therefore at the moment when one gives up calculation that one finally begins to observe. We must not see the constitution of natural history, with the empirical climate in which it develops, as an experiment forcing entry, willy nilly, into a knowledge that was keeping watch on the truth of nature elsewhere; natural history – and this is why it appeared at precisely this moment – is the space opened up in representation by an analysis which is anticipating the possibility of naming; it is the possibility of *seeing* what one will be able to *say*, but what one could not say subsequently, or see at a distance, if things and words, distinct from one another, did not, from the very first, communicate in a representation (Foucault, 1997, p. 13).

The documentation of forest species and their commercial value is as much a part of natural history as is the recording, say, of the movement or morphology of animals. Indeed, in the context of the early decades of the twentieth century, it could be said that the attributing of economic value to particular trees was a decidedly more 'natural' or 'normal' event than trying to ascertain their hydrological or biological importance (that is their so-called 'natural' value). Representation expunges all semblances of difference, of the acategorical, of the asignifi(c)ant. To measure or document the earth in terms of its flora is, of course, just one of a multitude of ways of seeing nature. And to enunciate flora in terms of economically dominant tree species is one of many ways of speaking nature. But when particular ways of seeing and saying leave the plane of consistency and lodge themselves on a plane of reference, a plane where all things are mapped out in 'concrete' and 'scientific' terms, there marches the human – all too human – proclivity to trace the earth according to the limits of established discourse rather than invent it anew in keeping with the flow of desire.

Interlude

From the late 1920s to 1958 (the year of the inception of the current Forests Act) several events occurred (beyond the completion of the Melboure/Orbost railway) that were to have a marked impact on the rate and type of exploitation that was to occur across certain aspects of East Gippsland and thereby ~~Goolengook~~ during subsequent decades. In the present context, the three most important of these events were/are: 1) the Victorian bushfires of January 1939; 2) the arrival of the chainsaw, articulated trailer, and dozer in Croajingolong mid-century; and 3) the post-war housing and construction boom of the late 1940s and beyond. With one notable exception, documents concerning these events have proven extremely difficult – indeed impossible – to locate. Accordingly, I have chosen merely to briefly draw attention to these events and to put to one side the matter of their (lack of) textual incorporation.

1. 1939 fires

Subsequent to salvaging operations, the bushfires which raged for a week in January 1939 over most of Victoria, destroyed approximately 570,000,000 superfeet (1.3 million tonnes) of timber in East Central and Northern Victoria (Moulds, 1991, p. 84 and p. 87).[8] The area of forest lands destroyed was equivalent in size to the whole of East Gippsland (over 1.2 million hectares or 2% of Victoria). At the time the fires struck, the loss of timber was well in excess of ten years' supply of the State's sawn timber needs.[9] The Royal Commission's report into the fires began,

> And so it was that, when millions of acres of the forest were invaded by bushfires which were almost State-wide, there happened, because of great loss of life and property, *the most disastrous forest calamity the State of Victoria has known* ... Seventy-one lives were lost. Sixty-nine mills were burned. Millions of acres of fine forest, of almost incalculable value, were destroyed or badly damaged. Townships were obliterated in a few minutes ... The speed of the fires was appalling. They leaped from mountain peak to mountain peak, or far out into the lower country, lighting the forests six or seven miles in advance of the main fires ... for mile upon mile the former forest monarchs were laid in confusion, burnt, torn from the earth, and piled one upon another as matches strewn by a giant hand (adapted from the Introduction of the Forest Fires 1939 Royal Commission, quoted in *Forests and Man* 1978, p. 8, emphases added).

Somewhat significantly, the primary cause of the 1939 fires was determined to be the much smaller (but numerous) fires lit by graziers, miners and settlers. Due to a series of intervening factors (that is wind, temperature, accumulation of dry debris/fuel on forest floor, lack of fire management regimes) these so-called 'contained' spot-fires spread across the State. The particular impact of the fires on Victoria's forest resources came to light in a document of the Forests Commission dated August 1943 entitled 'Summary of Evidence presented before the Rural Reconstruction Commission of the Ministry of Post-War Reconstruction'. Here, heads of all Forests Commissions (or their equivalent) throughout Australia were required to respond

8 The Forests Commission put the losses at 'over a thousand million superfeet' or 2.2 million tonnes.

9 A small proportion of the forests of East Gippsland were burnt by these fires. Records indicate that around 100 hectares of ~~Goolengook~~ was engulfed (Department of Conservation and Natural Resources, 1993b, pp. 166–70).

to a lengthy series of questions concerning the nature, direction and role of forestry subsequent to the war. In relation to Victoria, post-war reconstruction also meant post-fire reconstruction. The second part of Question 2 went straight to this issue asking, 'Has the war (*or any other circumstance*) affected the prospective annual volume which should be obtained after the war?' (Forests Commission of Victoria, 1943, p. 5 emphases added). The reply ran as follows,

> Two factors have seriously affected the prospective yield from Victorian forests during the next 40–50 years, viz. fires and war. It is impossible to gauge accurately the true result of the operation of these factors, but they are so far-reaching as to necessitate a considerable degree of reorientation of Victorian forest policy, particularly with reference to management of the high quality stands of the mountain forest areas ... The most serious consideration, however, is the destruction of and damage to extensive areas of regrowth of all ages. Complete artificial replacement of such stands over many thousands of acres, and intensive silvicultural rehabilitation of the balance, is urgently necessary. A small proportion of the older age classes has been utilised for the production of case timber and pulpwood, but its potential value as the raw material for future milling is now entirely lost. Instead, it now constitutes a fire problem (Forests Commission of Victoria, 1943, pp. 6–7).

Clearly, the fires of 1939 were a major catalyst leading to the establishment of timber related infrastructures in East Gippsland (logging roads, forestry offices, demarcation of logging units, timber resource inventories, relocation of forestry expertise). As Carron (1985, pp. 190–91) writes, '[B]ecause the resource of the mountain forests within 100–200 km of Melbourne had been so badly affected by the 1939 fires, it was clear that ... large [log] conversion centres would have to be located closer to the forests of central and east Gippsland and that an extensive roading program would be necessary to tap this new resource'. Question 3 posed by the Rural Reconstruction Commission was telling in this regard, 'In your State are there any forest areas which, although at present are neither being exploited nor available for exploitation, would be worth exploiting for timber supplies in the event of a shortage? If so, please give reasons for this state of affairs and the steps which would be necessary before such utilisation could begin' (Forests Commission of Victoria, 1943, p. 8). After a brief reply outlining the need to further exploit the remaining stands of Alpine Ash scattered across the mountainous areas of the State, the reply focuses on 'the eastern parts of the State' as a site of additional 'sawmilling species',

> Besides the[ ] reserves of high quality timber [i.e. Alpine Ash and Mountain Ash], there are available vast areas of Stringybark and similar types of forest, *particularly in the eastern parts of the State*, which are capable of yielding very substantial quantities of timber, and with the prospective shortage of first-class material more intensive exploitation of this class of forest for sawn timber is inevitable. Although mature, the trees are generally of smaller size than are the recognised sawmilling mountain species, but there is no reason why this smaller dimensional material cannot be more extensively used for many high grade purposes with modern methods of fabrication. These timbers have the advantages of

> greater durability and strength than timbers of the Ash type. In any case, these forests must be drawn upon to supply the large quantities of scantling timber required in connection with war industries as well as for the building programme in the post-war period (p. 9, italics added).

Here the 1939 fires can be taken to induce a deterritorialisation of the concept 'sawmilling species' (Ash dominated forests) and a subsequent reterritorialisation of the concept of 'smaller dimensional material' (Stringybark forests). This latter included the 'Gum' and 'Messmate' forests earmarked on cadastral plans some five decades earlier as well as other eucalypt species like Cuttail and Silvertop. As was the case with the texts previously outlined, there is here a new mode of envisioning the landscape, or, more specifically, (economically) valuing certain of its aspects – a deterritorialisation of the scopic regimes attached to non-mountain forest types. But whilst it is indeed true that the fires of 1939 precipitated a massive industrial reterritorialisation on the terrains of East Gippsland, the form and intensity of the reterritorialisations of the forestry assemblage over this region would be dependent on a particular set of technological 'advances' (chainsaw, dozer, articulated trailer) and a particular mode of desiring (post-war housing boom).

2. Chainsaw, dozer, articulated trailer

The portable chainsaw was invented in 1927 and can be taken to form part of the machinic phylum of the *metal blade* (sword, sickle, axe, bow saw). When the fixed (static) blade was displaced (deterritorialised) by the *revolving* blade (the band-saw) in the late nineteenth century, the mechanics of cutting (into the flow of matter-energy) was radically transformed. Specifically, the band-saw allowed for a quickening of the saw milling process, whilst the production of the hand-held chainsaw allowed for an exponential increase in the rate at which trees could be felled. The seemingly simple transition from a rotating saw that had to be fixed to the workshop floor (that is, the bandsaw), to one that could be carried to any part of the earth by almost any person (that is, the chain saw), dramatically altered the speed and scale of tree felling. Indeed, it was this *reterritorialisation of the blade* in the form of the chainsaw that led (initially in the United States) to a completely new method of tree felling called clearfell logging (or 'clearfelling') (see Frawley, 1993). This technique was first introduced into the forests of Croajinglong in the early 1950s and set up a new relation between 'man' and 'nature' – a new juxtaposition of bodies. The flow of vegetation (but also flows of water, nutrients, in/vertebrates) could now be transformed with greater intensity than had hitherto been possible. A tree that previously took hours to fell could instead be felled in a matter of minutes. But speed was not the only important variable here. Rather, the scale at which logging was to take place was also of paramount importance. But scale would be transformed by something other than the chainsaw alone. Here, the bulldozer and articulated trailer stand as equally salient components in the transformation and invention of forests at and around ~~Goolengook~~.

Friction, and by extension, traction, occurs at the interstice of bodies and their respective rates of movement. World War One brought with it a new kind of warfare to the extent it was based around new techniques of mobility. It was the State's desire for minimal friction (and thereby maximum traction) during the course of the war that helped bring the development of the footed wheel (better known today as the caterpillar track) to the fore. The 'footed wheel' was invented by R.L. Edgeworth in 1770, eventually leading to the development of the 'jointed track' in 1801. This track was put to practical use in 1886 with the advent of the combustion engine. It was the jointed track and the internal combustion engine that together defined the movement of both the tank, and, subsequently, the caterpillar bulldozer.[10] The jointed track can be seen as a deterritorialisation of the circle (wheel) in favour of the elipse (multiple steel plates coupled around several strategically aligned wheels). In the latter there is a completely new way of moving across the earth, and, more specifically, of interrupting certain flows (vegetation, water, soil). According to McRae (1976, p. 68), the bulldozer found its way into East Gippsland during the late 1940s (the shovel dozer was not developed until 1944). At such time there was a freeing up of the relation between the construction of roads (for logging and related purposes) and the gradients of the earth. Indeed the definitions of 'steep', 'impenetrable', and 'inaccessible' all underwent something of a transformation with the advent of the dozer. Where road construction was previously possible only on angles less than 15° the dozer increased this to around 45°. Moreover, *dozers built roads not tracks*, and they were able to build such roads at a comparably fast rate. The track cut from Orbost to Bendoc in 1884 by axe over the course of two years, could be re-cut and widened by dozer in a matter of months. Of course, it was not simply that the dozer built roads faster, nor even better. Of greater import was the fact that dozers built the body of a *readily accessible forest* as well. They changed the scale and rate at which forests could be opened up for logging. Trees once considered 'uneconomic' to harvest on account of their (lack of) proximity to sawmills, could now be incorporated into yearly logging schedules. Dozers (the deterritorialised wheel in the form of the jointed track) markedly decreased the distance and travelling time between logging units and processing yards. One might even say that dozers created a kind of monstrous smooth space between the bandsaw and the tree(s) (of once 'impenetrable' forests). They helped convert 'dense' terrains into immanently traversable spaces. But there was one other factor that was crucial to the overall increase in the speed at which activities were to take place in the forests of Australia generally and those of ~~Goolengook~~ (Croajingolong) specifically – namely, the articulated trailer.

The articulated vehicle was developed in Europe some time during the 1950s. Two components known as the 'oscillation ring' and the 'articulation joint' brought about a (molecular) revolution in the way humans (predominantly of the Western ilk) moved across earth. More accurately, these inventions facilitated an exponential

10 The first track-type tractor was produced in the US in 1904. Rubber pneumatic tyres did not appear on tractors until 1932.

increase in the volume of materials that could be shifted from one place to another at any one time (minerals, timber, foodstuffs, and so on). The advent of mechanical articulation resulted, for the first time, in the deployment of the term 'semi-trailer', a vehicle whose cab and engine was housed in an entirely separable casing to that of its trailer or 'load'. Like the dozer this vehicle had far greater traction than the truck or lorry. 'Articulation' meant that all wheels could remain in contact with the earth even on the most uneven of surfaces/territories. In addition, the new juxtaposition of cab and trailer meant that bends of 45° could be successfully negotiated. The articulated vehicle contributed to the transformation of the terrains associated with the logging industry. More trees could be logged, not only because of a change in harvesting technology (chainsaw), but because there now existed the opportunity to transport such logs to the sawmills (and later woodchip mills) at a much faster rate. This was important because logs left lying on the forest floor can become damp (or water-logged) and damaged over a relatively short period of time. An articulated vehicle could carry up to ten times the volume of material capable of being hauled by a non-articulated vehicle. This carrying capacity – along with the increased speed at which these vehicles moved – effected the *scale* at which activities such as logging and road-building could take place. More logging units could be tended more often. Indeed, the articulated vehicle even helped to lengthen the 'logging season' from around eight months of the year to ten. Articulated vehicles could negotiate roads once rendered impassable by high rainfall and snow during the winter months. Here, there is – quite remarkably – a deterritorialisation of the seasons through the advent of the oscillation ring and articulated joint. When placed amongst the machinic assemblage formed by the chainsaw and dozer, the three factors outlined above all worked to remove or at the very least, significantly lessen, the 'obstacles' (for example density of vegetation, impossible gradients, muddy or non-negotiable tracks) lying between logging units ('nature') and log processing centres ('civilisation', Orbost, Bendoc, Club Terrace).

3. Post-war housing and construction boom

Beyond that of fire, the chainsaw, the dozer and the articulated trailer, *war* was the major factor contributing to the new mode of envisioning Croajingolong from 1940. The demand for timber both during and subsequent to the Second World War brought with it a more intensive and deliberate transition into the forests of East Gippsland.[11] One might say that it was the combination of social and 'natural' events rather than any crude programme of 'economic greed' that provoked this transition. Evidence

11 Of course, as Woodgate et al. (1994, pp. 173–75) note, timber had been cut in the region from the time of the arrival of the pastoralists and gold miners in the 1850s and 60s, then by those building the Sale to Orbost railway line in the early 1900s and subsequently by the 'sleeper and beam hewing' industry in the 1920s, 30s and 40s for markets in Melbourne. However, compared to the rest of Victoria, the forests of East Gippsland – especially those at higher elevations – had remained largely unlogged.

presented to the Post-War Reconstruction Commission illustrated that the war made 'the normal development of the [Forests] Commission's programme of works over the State as a whole … impossible' (1943, p. 7). The Forests Commissioner further submitted,

> Presupposing that no great further deterioration takes place in the position regarding labour, equipment and transport, the effects of timber shortage must become increasingly serious for both war and post-war needs unless, in anticipation of future demands, *untapped resources of sawmilling timber can be opened up for exploitation* (1943, p. 7, emphases added).

At the time this comment was made the forests of Croajingolong had only been sporadically and selectively logged. The problem therefore was that whilst the population of Victoria demanded/required an increase in the production of forest products, there was, by 1945, only about 30% of the forests of Victoria extant at the time of the first permanent European settlement at Portland in 1834. It can accurately be said that the forests of East Gippsland never looked so commercially important nor economically viable. But nor had forests ever so squarely faced the speeds and scales of transformation spawned in the wake of the Second World War. The textual incorporation and (re)production of ~~Goolengook~~ increased significantly increased from around 1958. As shall become clear, many of these texts have as their task the production of ~~Goolengook~~ as timber production zone. But equally there are those which attempt to fill the body of ~~Goolengook~~ with other features and functions. What matters is the degree to which ~~Goolengook~~ is invested with the capacity to become something other than it 'is' or is named to be. For from the mid-twentieth century, the western gaze tried vehemently to divide ~~Goolengook~~ into its constituent parts and to permanently classify its features for all time and for all places. A text of major importance in this regard was the *Forests Act* 1958.

1959: site of forest produce

The *Forests Act* 1958 was assented to on September 30, 1958 and came into operation on 1 April 1959 (see *Government Gazette* March 18, 1959). Like its predecessors, this was 'An Act to consolidate the Law for the Management and Protection of State Forests'. The categorisation of State forest remained identical to that previously outlined. However, the definition of forest produce was expanded for both 'reserved forest' and 'protected forest',

> **'[F]orest produce'** where used in reference to or in connection with or as to anything in any reserved forest includes the following things namely: Stone gravel limestone lime salt sand loam caly brick earth trees timber branchwood firewood chips sawdust plants grass creepers fibres leaves blossom flowers ferns grass-trees fruit seeds roots bark bulbs galls gum kino resin sap charcoal honey or beeswax or oil distilled from any species of eucalyptus or from any other tree or plant but does not include any gold or silver or metal or mineral (S.3(1)).

> **'[F]orest produce'** where used in reference to or in connection with or as to anything in any protected forest means trees timber branchwood firewood chips sawdust plants leaves blossom flowers ferns grass-trees roots bark gum kino resin charcoal honey or beeswax or oil distilled from any species of eucalyptus or from any other tree or plant (S.3(1)).

The latter definition differs considerably from that given in 1907 ('trees', 'timber', 'charcoal', 'bark'). There is, in other words, a further contribution or folding in the discursive production of ~~Goolengook~~ (and indeed all protected forest generally) by way of the 1958 Act. ~~Goolengook~~ is no longer composed solely of Stringybarks but also of 'firewood', 'flowers', 'resin', 'honey', and so on. One might even say that the 'structure' of ~~Goolengook~~ is enunciated at an entirely different resolution here – a deterritorialisation of the genus *eucalyptus* in favour of those bodies which surround, abut, or thrive because of such a genus. And yet at another level, a completely molar politics takes hold of ~~Goolengook~~. Activities once deemed a part of the flow of (modern) life (like collecting firewood, picking flowers, making honey, extracting eucalytus oil) are now deemed illegal. A series of blockages have been erected. A molar NO holds sway. This is hardly surprising since the State never ceases striving to obtain control over all the forces within its domain. Indeed, it is constantly carving out new domains within which to exercise control, within which to chart its key oppositional or 'outside' forces (the poacher, the trespasser, the vandal) – the transgressor, in other words, of 'rational' and 'necessary' regulations. But why code protected forest in this manner? Why this need to enunciate ~~Goolengook~~ in such specific terms? Why, in other words, was it necessary to ascribe ~~Goolengook~~ a plethora of minor bodies at this moment? Very simply, because aspects of ~~Goolengook~~ are, as of 1959, on the verge of undergoing a radical and some might say *monstrous* deterritorialisation wrought by the industrial machine. However, in order for such a deterritorialisation to take place, and, more importantly, in order for it to take place over and over again (to draw a plane of repetition, or a becoming the same), there must first be *a marking out and securing of territories*. The transition in the mode of envisioning ~~Goolengook~~ ('unoccupied bush country' to 'protected forest') brought with it an increasingly precise enunciation of its aspects (of earth). There is an important, if often neglected, relation between the limiting of (human) actions (better still, desires) and the discursive production of minutiae (resin, flowers, bark). For when the State protects (that is axiomises) the flow of wood fibre ('timber', 'tree', 'charcoal', and 'bark'), only to then proceed to code all manner of other flows associated with this 'primary' flow, it points to three kinds of political possibilities – a molar politics, a molecular politics, or a supermolecular politics. In the first, the earth is ascribed one use and one use only, in the second it is ascribed many possibilities but these are nonetheless subverted to a unitary/arborescent function, whilst in the third there is a rupturing of molar identities and the utilisation/occupation of the earth as plane of immanence rather than a plane of reference. In the years following 1959, ~~Goolengook~~ would straddle the terrains marked out by the first two brands of politics.

1960 (April): site of permanently reserved forest (stage 1)

Section 45 of the *Forests Act* 1958 (No. 6254) allows for the 'Future dedication of additional land for forest or timber reserves'. It states,

> (1) The Governor in Council may on the recommendation of the Minister of Forests and the Minister of Lands at any time by order published in the *Government Gazette* dedicate either as a permanent forest or as a timber reserve any area of Crown land including an area which has been theretofore a timber reserve. Any such area which has been a timber reserve shall after being so dedicated be a permanent forest and not a timber reserve.
>
> (2) Without prejudice to the powers contained in the last preceding sub-section the Governor in Council may subject to this Act upon the joint recommendation of the responsible Ministers of the Crown for the time being administering the Department of Forests, Crown Lands and Survey, Water Supply and Mines and after the publication of notice of intention to dedicate the same as provided in the next succeeding sub-section [which requires the publication of dedications in four consecutive issues of the *Government Gazette* and 'two consecutive issues of some newspaper circulating in the neighborhood wherein such land is situate'] dedicate as permanent forests all or any of the areas of unoccupied mountainous Crown lands forming the upper water sheds of permanent streams within Victoria.

The notice of dedication of the first permanent forests at ~~Goolengook~~ reads,

> EXCHANGE OF FOREST AREAS FOR CROWN LANDS
>
> *At the Executive Council Chamber, Melbourne, the twelfth day of April, 1960.*
>
> PRESENT:
> His Excellency the Governor of Victoria.
> Mr Bloomfield Mr Turnball
>
> In pursuance of the provisions of Section 49 of the *Forests Act* 1958, No. 6254, His Excellency, the Governor of the State of Victoria, by and with the advice of the Executive Council, doth hereby order that the areas of Reserved Forest situated in the Parishes of Brockie, Konardin, Mournpoul, Clarkesdale, …described in the accompanying Exicision Schedule No. 128 and comprising 45,595 acres more or less, be excised from the Forests Reserves and that the areas of unoccupied Crown lands in the Parishes of Dellicknora, Goongerah, Errinundra, Cobon, …and described in the accompanying Dedication Schedule No. 160 and comprising 48,388 acres more or less, be dedicated as Permanent Forest in exchange in lieu thereof.
>
> Such excisions and dedications to take effect on the fourteenth day after the publication of this order in the *Government Gazette*.
>
> […]

The Dedication Schedule (*Victorian Government Gazette*, 1960, p. 1234) relevant to ~~Goolengook~~ runs,

> DEDICATION SCHEDULE NO. 160.
>
> Forty-eight thousand three hundred and eighty-eight acres, more or less, of unoccupied Crown lands, comprising the areas tabulated hereunder and shown by diagonal-hatched lines in diagrams numbered 797 to 806 inclusive on the accompanying plan A 59 /2760
>
> 28.3.60.

Diagram No.	**Correspondence No.**		**Parish**	**Plan No.**	**County**	**Area in Acres more or less**
	Lands	**Forests**				
797	H025739	56/1353	Dellicknora, Goongerah, Errinundra, Cobon	161	Croajingolong	46,500

Those forests permanently reserved in the Parish of Goongerah form the northern portion of ~~Goolengook~~. This was the first area within ~~Goolengook~~ to be designated as part of the permanent forest estate, the rest remaining as protected forest under the *Forests Act* 1958. Ironically, the area permanently reserved within ~~Goolengook~~ in 1960 for timber production was never subjected to intensive logging. Instead it would form, subsequent to proclamation in 1988, part of the southern portion of Errinundra National Park. What is remarkable about these texts is their capacity to hypostatise the ontological status of certain portions of the earth. It is as if the phrase 'permanent forest' brings with it an iron-clad guarantee that such terrain will forever remain forest. But one might inquire as to the precise meaning of the term 'permanent'. For on closer inspection, 'permanent' does not in fact indicate a will to preserve forests in their same state in perpetuity. Rather 'permanent forest' is actually a truncated or coded way of denoting those 'highly productive' areas to be continually and repeatedly used for forest related activities – including clearfell logging. It is also a shorthand way of signifying land that cannot be turned over to agricultural pursuits. Thus, the term 'permanently' is an important rhetorical device which gives the appearance of perpetuity and continuity of flows, speeds and intensities (of flora and fauna), when it actually allows for vast areas of such 'permanent' forest to be razed to the ground.

1972: site of forest management block

On 21 December 1972 Orbost Forest District was divided into a series of forest management blocks (FMBs). This was a highly pivotal moment in the lexical/material folding of ~~Goolengook~~. The key text here is a memo from the Chief of Forestry Division presently located in file number 72/1007 of historical records of the Forests Commission of Victoria. It reads,

63/1841
21st December, 72
ICW/MB 7041

DIVISION OF FOREST MANAGEMENT

Mr. J. B. Johnston,
District Forester,
ORBOST, 3888

Subdivision of Orbost District into Management Blocks

The subdivision as shown on the attached map has been approved. It is expected that this subdivision will be used as a basis for referencing the location of forest resources and operations in your district.

The boundaries of logging units approved by the Commission to define licensed logging areas for sawmillers must, however, continue to be recognised. In correspondence with the Division of Economics and Marketing a cross reference between logging units and blocks should be provided so that the location of operations in regard to area rights is clear.

Blocks are intended to be relatively permanent units. If alterations are proposed a report via your Divisional Forester will be required giving reasons. The approval of this Division will be necessary before any alterations are made.

Additional copies of the attached map can be provided on request to the Draughting Section.

R.J.Grose,
Chief of Division

Enc. 6 copies of map for the Orbost District.

Copies forwarded for the information of: –

Mr. E.K. Gidley, Divisional Forester, Bairnsdale (enc. 1 map)
Mr. G. Griffin, Chief, Division of Economics and Marketing (enc. 1 map).

As is evident, the concept of a FMB was to be a permanent part of forest administration from this time forward. It would, in other words, become the (molar) referent from which all other enunciations concerning coupe locations, logging techniques, logging quotas, timber assessments, and so forth would emanate. ~~Goolengook~~ was at such time ascribed the name 'Goolengook' (after the main river traversing it), the forest district number '130', and the block number '22'. The boundaries of blocks were drawn up according to established roads and significant topographical features such as rivers and mountain ridges. ~~Goolengook~~ block took its shape and form from the intersections of four tracks: 'Greens Road' to the west, 'Bee Tree Track' to the south, 'Ada Divide Track' (see Figures 1 and 2 on pp. 62–63) on its north-eastern aspect, and 'Blackwatch Track' along its south-eastern portion. Block 130/22 or 'Goolengook' was marked out as covering 9166 hectares or 81 square kilometres (18 kilometres from its northern to southern most point, and around 10 kilometres from its western to eastern most point). In all, the Orbost district was carved into 38 blocks each around 10,000 hectares.

The *raison d'être* behind the advent of FMBs had as much to do with aesthetics as it did administrative efficiency (although the former helped to sustain the latter). A number of employees working in the Orbost District around the time the blocks were established claim that the idea came from New South Wales where the forest resource had recently been segmented into a number of discrete units and supplied a series of names. The New South Wales body responsible for forestry matters found that naming a forest enabled the public to more closely scrutinise the efforts expended on rejuvenating logged forests. Naming brought a certain order or method to what may otherwise have been interpreted as a largely haphazard set of production techniques (the so-called 'slash and burn' approach). The naming of blocks focused the eye (of the would-be dissenter) on the activities associated with a specific forested terrain as opposed to land (Croajingolong) in general. The advent of blocks allowed, in Deleuze and Guattari's terms, a *plane of reference* to emerge from a plane of consistency or infinite variation, a plane where things are ordered according to molar refrains ('timber production', 'sustainable yield', and so on). According to Deleuze and Guattari, a plane of reference requires that everything is known, so to speak, 'ahead of time'. It is a plane built on 'a renunciation of the infinite' where bodies are given a spine and made to move in one direction only (1994b, p. 124). It is a plane of 'independent variables' (segmented elements), 'partial observers' (masquerading as omniscient beings), 'functions' (determinate conditions limiting what can and can't happen in any one space at any one time) and 'states of affairs' (or 'supposedly closed systems') (Deleuze and Guattari, 1994b, pp. 132–33). Smaller units of analysis (block rather than district) meant that similar, but dispersed/geographically distinct, activities could be positioned, or better still, envisioned (perceived by the public) as part of an ordered plane (the plane of forest blocks occupied by a specific logic and by particular speeds of transformation). The term 'block' here assumes an extremely important role to the extent that it signifies that what is at stake 'within' its dimensions is not some living, vital conglomeration of complex forces so much as points that can be known, used and extracted from a knowable (quasi-geometrical) object. Indeed, the deployment of the word 'block' rather than 'ecosystem' (mechanosphere) helps to maintain a certain incorporeal or discursive effacement of the diverse topographical and biological features of this space. Since words are always already recodings or collapsings of various genealogies, the phrase 'Goolengook Forest Management Block' or 130/22, helps to render opaque the multiple histories that once unfurled across this space. A note concerning the status of 'resource information' for ~~Goolengook~~ block speaks to this idea,

> (a) East Gippsland Timber Co Pty Ltd (24,000 m^3)
>
> Allocated areas in Goolengook (Greens Rd) and Purgagoolah blocks. Travelling times to Goolengook block 1¼ hours, Purgagoolah block 1 hour. Poor resource information for both blocks so extensive walking required for resource and access. Great pressure to use Purgagoolah block for winter logging. Normally cut about 12,000 m^3.
>
> (b) Henderson Bros and Bell Pty Ltd (9,000 m^3)
>
> Allocated areas in Goolengook block (1¼ hours travelling) and Cabbage Tree (1 hour travelling). Some basic resource information available for both blocks but walking still required to check resource and locate access routes. Pressure to log in the Cabbage Tree block in the winter. Total allocation normally cut.
>
> (c) Broons Timbers Pty Ltd (12,000 m^3)
>
> Allocated areas in Goolengook block (1½ hours travelling) and Cabbage Tree (1 hour travelling). Some basic resource information available for both blocks but walking still required to check the resource and locate access routes. Strong pressure for winter logging in the Cabbage Tree block. Total allocation normally cut (file 73/1007, Appendix B, Analysis of Current Individual Supervisory Workload – Orbost Based Supervisors).

These seemingly banal passages betray a number of important points. First, they indicate that ~~Goolengook~~ – nearly one hundred years after Edwin Merrall's travels through its regions – remains to a very large extent *unknown* (at least in terms of the kinds of timbers and proportion of sawlogs its terrains are likely to yield). Secondly, the passages speak of the speeds of which ~~Goolengook~~ has become a part. Orbost has indeed become the point from which a series of molar lines may be drawn from it to various logging areas. Speed and time are no longer measured in terms of the rates of movement that pertain between the multiplicity of organisms which occupy ~~Goolengook~~, but in terms of how long it takes to travel from a designated centre (Orbost/civilisation) to a peripheral location (~~Goolengook~~/nature). Where this journey was once calculated according to the speeds associated with walking and pack-horses (several days), it is now computed in terms of the automobile (less than two hours). There is, in other words, a substantial *compression of time* between the town (urbanity) and its surrounding regions (~~Goolengook~~/forest blocks).

On a third count, the notes bring into view the specific technique used to gather data/information about ~~Goolengook~~. There is a method of knowing employed here that is somehow quite out of step with the 'progress' made in accessing places like ~~Goolengook~~. Put another way, there is a decided incongruency between the techniques used to move across the earth and those engaged in an effort to know it. It is as if Europeans (that is foresters) arrived too fast at ~~Goolengook~~ ('Poor resource information for [Goolengook] block[ ] so extensive walking required for resource and access'). Indeed, although areas along Greens Road within ~~Goolengook~~ block had been 'allocated' in late 1972, logging did not begin in this vicinity until December of 1978. Prior to this, the first act of clearfell logging within ~~Goolengook~~

took place in April 1976. Both these dates indicate a period where it was necessary to first 'know' ~~Goolengook~~ (in terms of its varying species types, gradients, rainfall, growth rates, likely regeneration techniques, possible access points) before it could be corporeally transformed. The key means of acquiring such knowledge at this time was by foot (due to ~~Goolengook~~'s density) and eye (due to the ill-economy of aerial photography). In any case, the eye looking down from above had first to learn what it was gazing upon (Shining Gum, Messmate, Slender Tree Fern, Sassafras, and so on). Timber assessment proceeds via a process of extrapolation, which is to say that they operate by means of synecdoche – by using knowledge of the *particular* (which is always already a multiplicity of forces, molecules, speeds) to build up and portray a picture of the *universal*. One could go so far as to say that the conflict over ~~Goolengook~~ in recent times is intimately related to the way in which certain discourses (or collective assemblages of enunciation) configure both the particular and the universal in respect of 'forested' terrains and the flows or bodies deemed 'absent' and 'present' therein. Modern discourses of forest management predominantly fail to see that the universal/particular distinction is a false, indeed highly dangerous, dichotomy – not to mention a decidedly bad method for coming to 'know nature'. At the heart of this matter lies, once more, the relationship between scales, speeds, and visions, and the way these combine to alter the production of difference and (bio)diversity.

In sum, from the beginning of 1973 forest administrators found themselves with a new rhetorical device – that of the plane of forest blocks. This plane has since been taken to be a natural, timeless, and indelible part of the landscape, a mode of organisation/categorisation that knows no origin and favours no particular political, cultural, economic or social plan. In Deleuzean terms, the phrase 'Goolengook forest management block' at such time came to function as an *overcoding machine*, as an order-word which cast(s) a dark shadow over all attempts to speak or think this space differently. Such, at least, was the situation for well over two decades.

Chapter 7

Becoming Contested

> Nature must be thought of as the principle of the diverse and its production. But a principle of the production of the diverse makes sense only if it does not assemble its own elements into a whole.
>
> Deleuze, *The Logic of Sense*, 1990, p. 266

The title of this chapter should not be taken to mean that ~~Goolengook~~ passed as uncontested prior to 1977. Nothing could be further from the truth. Like the happenings explicated in previous chapters, there are no immutable lines dividing the events which took place after 1977 from those that preceded it. There are, however, substantial alterations in the *frequency* of texts which incorporate ~~Goolengook~~ as its object from this time. In fact, one could say that conceiving ~~Goolengook~~ as a forest management block spurred its production as something beyond the confines of this category. Suddenly, ~~Goolengook~~ was something worthy of the Western gaze – worthy, that is, of intense contestation.

1977 (March): site of uncommitted land

In March 1977, the Land Conservation Council (LCC) delivered to the Minister for Conservation its report detailing final recommendations for the use of land in East Gippsland. This was the first report of its kind undertaken for the area and at the time of its completion the Land Conservation Council was in its seventh year, having been 'established by the *Land Conservation Act* 1970' (Land Conservation Council, 1977, p. 5). In its recommendations, the Land Conservation Council designated part of ~~Goolengook~~ to be 'uncommitted land',

> Land classed as uncommitted includes:
>
> - areas that, although not needed to satisfy any known demand, are retained to meet future demands as yet undefined
> - land known to have a high capability to satisfy one or more particular demands, but not at present committed to any one use, as foreseeable requirements can readily be met from other areas
> - areas on which further study is required to determine the capability of the land to satisfy particular present or future demands.
>
> Uncommitted land is to be securely retained as public land, although changes in its status may be required if these are recommended following a review by this Council. It may be

> used to satisfy present needs, provided this does not cause changes that would be difficult to reverse (Land Conservation Council, 1977, p. 59).

The report also stipulated that uncommitted land 'be Crown land withheld from sale and protected forest under the provisions of the *Forests Act* 1958' (Land Conservation Council, 1977, p. 59). There are ten such areas of land recommended by the report. Collectively, these lands span 203,000 hectares or 22% of land in the study area. The Land Conservation Council recommended that 'subject to certain conditions, harvesting operations … be permitted on uncommitted land (R1) – except as specified in recommendations R1 (c) (i) dealing with the ~~Goolengook~~ River area and recommendation R1 (c) (ii) dealing with the Gelantipy Plateau-Bowen Range area' (Land Conservation Council, 1977, p. 25). Section R1 (c) (i) reads,

> (i) Goolengook River (2,900 hectares)
>
> The council recommends that … the whole of the land in this category be withheld from logging or new roading until 1985, when it is expected that the use of this area will be reviewed. The area contains appreciable quantities of mature timber and also has high nature conservation values. It contains examples of shining gum, brown barrel, alpine ash, and messmate-gum open forest, and montane and lowland closed forest (Land Conservation Council, 1977, p. 60).

The area mentioned here straddles the Parishes of Goongerah and Noonga around the headwaters of ~~Goolengook~~ River. As 'uncommitted land', the Land Conservation Council preserves and produces a part of ~~Goolengook~~ as a body without organs – a body predominantly free from typical dichotomies/segmentations invoked by environmental regulatory agencies when talking about particular spaces and their uses (biologically significant area/biologically insignificant area, production zone/conservation zone, natural resource/waste). But in another way, the Land Conservation Council deploys a line of molarity – a line centred around a highly anthropocentric rendering of the term 'commitment'. For in what sense is it correct to speak of a 10,000 year old ecosystem (with its countless flows and becoming-other, its intricate recyclings of nutrients and debris) as 'uncommitted'? Here, what looks like an instance of ~~Goolengook~~ being written in terms of its acategorical aspects, is in fact an example of a modern account of prospective (use) value.

The remainder of ~~Goolengook~~ was ascribed the land use code 'E1'. This meant Council recommended it be used for 'hardwood production'. The relevant part of the text reads,

> **Recommendations**
>
> That the area of approximately 433,000 hectares shown on Map 1 be used:
>
> (a) primarily to produce hardwood timber in a manner having due regard for landscape values as seen from the main roads

that

(b) major secondary uses be to:

(i) provide opportunities for open-space recreation and education
(ii) conserve native plants and animals, and provide opportunities for the development of wildlife conservation techniques in consultation with Fisheries and Wildlife Division [...]
(iii) produce honey, forage, gravel, sand, and other forest produce as defined in the *Forests Act* 1958

(c) water production values be recognised

(d) particular values including those listed below be protected by means of reserves under section 50 of the *Forests Act* 1958, or by management prescriptions prepared (in the case of fauna) in consultation with the Fisheries and Wildlife Division

(i) particular attention should be given to the conservation of the following native animals – greater glider, yellow-bellied glider, tiger cat, potoroo, platypus, eastern water-dragon, sooty owl, and powerful owl

[...]

and that it remain or become reserved forest under the provisions of the *Forests Act* 1958, and be managed by the Forests Commission.

It is essential to note that the primary concern with the management of forests within E1 is with prospective *landscape values* – particularly 'as seen from ... main roads'. This is an interesting rhetorical shift, one that supplants concerns over the biological integrity of a region to its *aesthetic appeal*. Clearly, the political preoccupation with aesthetics echoes that underpinning the formation of forest blocks (see above). Aesthetics would, from this time on, come to play an increasingly significant role in forest conflict. Indeed, it could be said that a very large part of the conservation movement's attempts to raise awareness of forestry issues would come to rely as much on the *circulation of images* (predominantly of clearfelled areas and 'cute' or 'cuddly' endangered species) as it would on the circulation of scientific data or 'facts'. The same, of course, could be said of political and departmental assemblages which would seek to satiate public concern over clearfell logging by juxtaposing images of 'man' and his struggle in 'distant' and 'dangerous' areas to reproduce his own existence (via employment in the forestry sector) against those of the Spotted Tiger Quoll, the Sooty Owl, and the Slender Tree Fern. Of course, 'facts' (concerning such issues as effects of logging, species decline, water quality, biodiversity, levels of employment) would still play a major role in forest conflict. But without the publication of a new kind of text – one that relied for its affect on optical (the visual) rather than chirographic (written) factors – forest conflict would have taken on entirely different dimensions. Indeed, one could say that laws and regulations of forest production were shaped as much, if not more, by aesthetic machines than scientific machines from this point on. The production of forest aesthetics would reach something of a zenith in the closing years of the twentieth century. This would be a time when the textual reproduction of East Gippsland's forests would be delivered with 'unquestionable precision and accuracy' and with a seemingly limitless ability to definitively capture the colours, elevations and regional topographies of the earth. The technology that would allow a 'true' knowledge of forests to emerge would, of course, be the convergence of satellite imaging and computer enhancement.

1977: site of Stringybark forests

Some time in 1977 – most likely in the wake of the Land Conservation Council report mentioned above – the Draughting Section of the Victorian Forests Commission issued a map entitled 'Forests of Victoria'. Like all texts, this map is a key example of the relationship between *resolution* and *bodies* (or of the categories used to envision territories as against the things that such categories bring into and out of focus). In this instance, the forests of Victoria are deemed to occupy six distinct categories: 'Mountain' (subdivided into 'sub-alpine woodland and grasslands', 'alpine ash', and 'mountain ash and shining gum forests'); 'Stringybark'; 'Ironbark'; 'Red Gum'; 'Mallee'; and 'Plantations'. In this text ~~Goolengook~~ is rewritten as a terrain covered solely by 'Stringybarks' – the forest type which, according to the map, happens to occupy the greatest area of all forest types said to exist throughout Victoria. One of the most important things to be gleaned from the map is the use of particular colours to represent different forest types. Significantly, 'Stringybarks' are denoted by the presence of what might be described as an orange-brown wash. This wash conjures many associated images. However, one of the most pertinent is that of a barren and sterile region. In sharp contrast, three different shades of green are used to denote the rarest forest type on the map – namely, 'Mountain Forests'. Green is a colour that conjures substantially different kinds of images than orange-brown. In most instances, green stands for all that is healthy, lush, vibrant and alive. Orange-brown, on the other hand, tends to convey ideas of ill-health, banality, decay, and even perhaps death. Since Mountain Forests are represented as comparatively rare, this inadvertently amounts to configuring ~~Goolengook~~ – and the majority of Victoria's forests – as mediocre and therefore expendable (exploitable). Like the label 'forest block', the categorisation of ~~Goolengook~~ as simply exhibiting one kind of tree (that is Stringybarks) further contributes to the incorporeal effacement of the diversity of its terrain.

1981: site of invisibilities

There were three separately authored publications released in 1981 concerned with the nature and distribution of vegetation in East Gippsland. One of these, by A.C. Beauglehole, said of East Gippsland that 'It is by far the most species-rich (1432 Native vascular species) area for any region of comparative size in Victoria' (p iii). This text brings many things into view, but not that of ~~Goolengook~~. This is particularly significant in light of the fact that ~~Goolengook~~ would later be found to possess one fifth of all vascular plants in the East Gippsland area. The absence of ~~Goolengook~~ from this text illustrates the importance of the mode of envisioning or the methods deployed which bring portions of the earth into and out of focus. The fact that this publication and two separate texts within the same year looking at the same region were to draw substantially *different* conclusions about what is 'biologically significant' demonstrates that the meaning of this phrase – and its corollaries like 'rare', 'special', 'exceptional', 'vital' – are machinically produced and contested, not transcendentally given.

1981: site of botanical significance

Early in 1981, a report entitled *Sites of Botanical Significance in East Gippsland* was prepared for the Environmental Studies Division of the Ministry for Conservation. The report was authored by three employees (Forbes, Gullan and Walsh) of the National Herbarium, Victoria. Its main objectives were twofold,

> 1. To identify and describe the major vegetation types of the study area, both floristically and structurally, and give some indication of their abundance and distribution.
>
> 2. To comment on the quality of the vegetation throughout the study area, define sites of particular botanical significance and discuss factors which may cause a deterioration in vegetation quality (1981, p. 1a).

The method of survey involved the overlay of a series of rectangles measuring five minutes latitude and five minutes longitude across the entire study area, which included *both* East Gippsland and the Gippsland Lake Catchment. Across all rectangles, 1312 quadrats – each equating to about 1000 square metres (100 x 10) – were randomly plotted (see below for my comments concerning the 'actual' size of each quadrat). Four quadrats or 'sample sites' were then assigned to each rectangle. East Gippsland was ascribed 590 quadrats. There are two significant aspects to this report – the first relates to *terminology*, the second to *method.*

Terminology

The authors reported that 'Within each quadrat every vascular plant species was identified and assigned a *cover-abundance value* (Braun-Blanquet scale) corresponding to a *visual estimate* of its *performance* in the quadrat' (1981, 1b emphases added). It is interesting to note here the kind of lexicon deployed to describe the features of the plants within each quadrat. 'Cover-abundance value' suggests that the worth of any given plant species can be judged against the degree to which it spatially dominates (or not) an area. The dichotomies this classification unit produces, are, to say the least, somewhat dangerous. Wherever Europeans have spoken of an 'abundance' – whether this be of minerals, of forests, of animals, of fishes, of fresh waters – there has been the corresponding tendency to plunder and pillage. Accordingly, to write abundance – to visually estimate the frequency of populations – is perhaps an inherently ill-fated task. Why? Because 'abundance' automatically implies, does it not, a concrete knowledge of *under*abundance, which in turn implies a knowledge of the mean, the norm, the average, in short, of some primeval state that readily communicates the way things 'should be'. *'Abundant' can never mean anything more than an apparent or fabricated excess*. How then, it might be asked, is it possible to calculate the *performance* of this excess? For wouldn't the categorisation of a 'performance' depend for its lucidity on the ability to know something of the average, the commonplace, or the mean? In any case, do plants and animals actually perform? Moreover, could they ever do so in a manner that is knowable to others (that is scientists)? There is, I would suggest, a twofold aspect to 'abundance'. On the one hand, where abundance is 'lacking', it is a term that feeds into discourses of conservation. On the other, where abundance 'abounds', it is a term that satiates discourses of industrial consumption. Either way, the world is still written and lived stochastically – why else would we wish to know about abundance if not to mark out the thresholds at which we think it proper to *either* deplete or preserve? In the final chapter, I will suggest a way of thinking beyond such divisions.

Method

It is important also to know the proportion of terrain in East Gippsland actually *physically* examined/sensed by the scientists – that is, the terrain assessed 'in person' 'out in the field' as opposed to the terrain built from extrapolation involving past studies. The first thing to realise is the quite catastrophic printing error that exists under the heading '1.1 Sources of and Methods for Collecting Information' (1981, 1b). Here, each quadrat is said to be 'about 1000 metres squared' and, as mentioned above, that '[w]ithin each quadrat every vascular plant species was identified …'. This would mean each quadrat was 1km long by 1km wide. Were this actually to have been the case, it would have meant that Forbes, Gullan and Walsh (along with just 15 assistant field workers) managed to personally walk and examine *all* such plants in an area totalling 590 km^2 (or 24 kilometres x 24 kilometres) in a one-year period. This figure is equal to 59,000 hectares or around 4% of East Gippsland's total area. Even if this vastly exaggerated figure could be shown to be accurate, there would still have been 96% of East Gippsland that would *not* have been directly assessed. But what happens when the error is corrected? The authors themselves say that 'floristic information was collected along [a trap line commonly about 100 meters long] and approximately 5 meters to each side' (1981: 1b). They then go on to say that each quadrat totalled '1000 meters squared' instead of the correct size of *1000 square metres* (that is length of trap line (100 metres) multiplied by the average width of the variation from this line – which is, as they say, 10 metres (or 2 x '5 meters each side')). This scenario yields a very different picture of the terrain actually covered by the researchers. Each of the 590 quadrats in fact measures just 1000 square metres – a quadrat area *1000 times less* than that given in the report. This means the total area actually assessed through detailed fieldwork was just *59* hectares – an area 22,000 times *smaller* than the total area of East Gippsland. In the year it took to assess the vascular plants in this 59 hectare area the logging industry would, at this time, have clearfelled around 12,000 hectares of native forest. Put another way, the quantity and type of vegetation it took 18 scientists working full time for one year to gather information on, was removed through prescribed logging regimes in less than two days.

The point here is one concerning the means by which we come to know (or not) Nature. For, without doubt, these (and other) scientists are engaging in the most elaborate of *rhetorical exercises*. Specifically, the methodology employed is one that rises and falls solely around the efficacy of the rhetorical devices of *mimesis* and *synecdoche*. To what extent can science mimic or comprehensively reflect the world (~~Goolengook~~). To what degree, can, in fact, the part (of a forest) be said to stand for the whole? These questions haunt each and every effort of conservation and 'sustainable' resource use. And they are questions subverted or marginalised by *both* 'sides' of the forest conflict divide. Each, it could be said, has an interest in showing the universal applicability of their calculations and predictions. But what, it might be asked, is it that we miss or exclude in the haste to build up a general picture or overriding trend of a given animal, river, forest or Indigenous group? What slips through the cracks left by the (problematic) resolutions imposed by specific methodologies? In Deleuzean terms, what kinds of problems are secreted by the abstract machines whose task it is to fold or invent the perfect or sustainable forest body? I will attempt to address these and other questions later on in this chapter when examining the positioning of conservation zones (such as geographic representation units (GRUs) and national parks) and resource inventories (old-growth forest, negligibly disturbed, regrowth). For now, I simply want to summarise the way the present report configured ~~Goolengook~~.

As a result of Forbes, Gullan and Walsh's work, the northern third of ~~Goolengook~~ was deemed part of 'Major Site of (Botanical) Significance, No. 15' known as 'Errinundra Plateau' (1981, pp. 188–95). The authors state that 'The site takes in the upper catchments of the Queensborough, Cann, Errinundra, Gool[e]ngook, Brodribb, Bonang and Delegate Rivers' (1981, p. 190). What is truly significant here was that well over two thirds of ~~Goolengook~~ was, by default, categorised as something *less* than botanically significant. Of the 590 quadrats studied within East Gippsland for the report, only 2 fell 'within' ~~Goolengook~~. In effect this meant that just 2000 square metres of ~~Goolengook~~ was actively surveyed. Given that ~~Goolengook~~ had, by this time, been designated as encompassing 90 million square metres (around 9000 hectares), this puts the proportion of ~~Goolengook~~ actually physically examined during the course of the report at just one square metre for every 45,000 square metres of its 'total' terrain. Put differently, the area that remained 'unassessed' within ~~Goolengook~~ was 45,000 times larger than that from which recommendations of what was 'botanically significant' within ~~Goolengook~~ were derived.

1981: site of global zoological significance

Following the release of the above report, Norris and Mansergh issued a report for the Ministry for Conservation, Victoria, entitled, 'Sites of Zoological Significance in East Gippsland'. It outlined 'Twenty six sites of significance for the indigenous terrestrial vertebrate species of East Gippsland' (Norris and Mansergh, 1981, p. 3), and ascribed these sites one of six ratings – 'global significance', 'international significance', 'national significance', 'state significance', 'regional significance', or 'local or scientific interest'. Under this scenario, a small area in the north eastern portion of ~~Goolengook~~ fell within 'Block B: Errinundra', a site of state significance. But in addition to forming a small part of this block, the whole of ~~Goolengook~~ was deemed to provide part of the corridor of vegetation necessary to sustain the species between Block B and a block further south known as 'Block B: Bellbird'. Block B was given the status of 'global significance' due to it providing the territory for the 'only recent capture of the Long-Footed Potoroo' (Norris and Mansergh, 1981, p. 24). More accurately, ~~Goolengook~~ – along with designated land outside its borders – was deemed as providing the 'minimum estimate of what is "safe" for the protection of [the Long-footed Potoroo, Blue Mountains Tree Frog, Jervis Bay Tree Frog and associated species]' (Norris and Mansergh, 1981, p. 26),

> An area of minimum size should include the catchments of McKenzie River and tributaries, Bellbird Creek, Falls Creek, Cabbage Tree Creek and Dyer Creek, Goolengook River and west side of the Combienbar River (West Branch) south to the Princes Highway or 37°40'S latitude, whichever is southernmost … (Norris and Mansergh, 1981, p. 26).

In combination, the area described here was called 'Errinundra-Bellbird' and was ascribed global significance – one of only two sites deemed as such in the study. The effect of this scientific machine was to produce ~~Goolengook~~ as both a catchment in its own right, but as an *interstitial* territory as well.

1982: site for supply of 'defective material'

The *Export Control Act* 1982 is one of the few Acts that gives the Commonwealth some kind of control over what happens to forests located in Australian States and Territories. In the present context, this text was extremely important in the folding of ~~Goolengook~~. Its significance had to do with the preponderance of claims concerning the 'cause and effect' of native forest destruction. The Export Control Act allowed, for the first time, woodchips sourced from Australian native forests to be sold overseas. Typically, these woodchips have been sent to Japan and Taiwan and turned into copying paper. This paper is then imported back into Australia at a price of around $1000 per tonne (more than one hundred times the price obtained for the initial chips). In view of the fact that only around 15% of the volume of wood extracted from native forests each year ends up as sawlogs, it is logical to conclude that areas such as ~~Goolengook~~ would be used in some kind of woodchipping regime.

A common refrain of the conservation movement – both prior to and following the operation of the Act – had been that the logging of native forest is 'woodchip driven' not 'sawlog driven' and that the Export Control Act would only exacerbate this fact. In the years preceding the Act only a very small fraction of the total amount of 'waste' material accumulated through logging regimes in any one year was woodchipped. This was/is mainly because of the comparatively low domestic demand for woodchips in Australia. The concern from this time on was that overseas markets would begin to dictate the volume of forest logged in any one year, since the more sawlogs or 'non-defective' (that is straight) trees removed from native forests would automatically bring a nine-fold increase in the amount of 'defective' trees felled (and thus a corresponding increase in the volume of woodchips, and a windfall for the federal government in export dollars). In fact, this line of thought was to become a salient factor in forest protests of the 1980s and 1990s. However, a point that is often overlooked is that logging methods did not change with the introduction of the Act. Clearfelling was used in East Gippsland as early as around 1950 – three decades before the Export Control Act. In this intervening time, the amount of 'defective' trees or 'waste' produced per hectare from native forests would have been roughly equivalent to that produced by clearfelling post-1982. No matter which decade one is concerned with, clearfelling removes 90% of trees from each area. So waste had already long been a part of forest operations.

However, there is a concerning dimension to the advent of the Export Control Act. This concern centres on the relation between legislated sawlog volumes (presently set at 174,000 cubic metres/tonnes for East Gippsland), the size of the area needed to meet this threshold, and the waste or excess volume of wood accrued in search of good timber/sawlogs. Theoretically, the forest industry has the legal right to log as many areas as is necessary each year to meet the sustainable yield target for sawlogs. The only constraint here is that it must not log more than three adjoining coupes in any three-year period. What this means is that the forest industry can spread its search for sawlogs over a very large area – even where trees suitable for sawlogs are known to be in comparatively low numbers. Where this is the case, defective trees or those suitable for woodchipping will be in comparatively large numbers. The forest industry – loggers, contractors, hauliers, and so on – have to pay royalties to the State government for each sawlog tree taken from native forests. Conversely, these same groups pay nothing for sourcing defective or woodchip trees and indeed are paid by the government to do so. In addition, the system of log-grading – where logs lying on the forest floor after felling are marked up as being of a particular quality or grade – is largely free from strict regulatory enforcement. It is comparatively easy to downgrade a sawlog to a pulplog (from, say, C grade to D grade). With all these factors converging – and with international outlets for woodchips made possible by the Export Control Act – the fear has been, and remains, that logging contractors and departmental officials will target areas or coupes with a high proportion of 'defective' trees (which are actually amongst the most important from an ecological perspective) in order to gain the profits associated with woodchipping and avoid the costs associated with extracting sawlogs. It is the discursive slippage from *volume of sawlogs* to *area logged* that stands as the crucial transformation wrought by this text. From 1982, ~~Goolengook~~ became a potential area for the increased supply of defective material.

1982 (March): site of permanently reserved forest (stage 2)

As mentioned at Text 3, Section 42 of the *Forests Act* 1958 outlines the notion of 'reserved forests'. In terms of ~~Goolengook~~ FMB, a further transformation from protected forest to permanently reserved forest took place in 1982. Page 706 of the *Victorian Government Gazette* dated 10 March displays thirteen Dedication Schedules. The opening part of the dedication reads as follows,

> *Forests Act* 1958
> DEDICATION OF AREAS OF CROWN LAND AS RESERVED FOREST
> At the Executive Council Chamber, Melbourne, the second day of March, 1982
>
> PRESENT:
>
> His Excellency the Governor of Victoria
> Mr Houghton Mr Maclellan
> Mr Kennett
>
> In pursuance of the provisions of the Forests Act 1958, His Excellency the Governor of the State of Victoria, by and with the advice of the Executive Council thereof, doth hereby order that the areas of Crown land described in Dedication Schedule Nos. 241, 243, 246, 247, 248, 249, 250, 251, 252, 253, 254, 255 and 256 hereunder be dedicated as reserved forest.

Three of these Schedules relate to the area traversed by ~~Goolengook~~. These run,

> [...]
>
> DEDICATION SCHEDULE NO. 246
>
> 58,000 hectares more or less of Crown land in the Parishes of Bidwell, Bonang, Bullamark, Deddick, Goongerah, Moonkan, Tingaringy, Wat Wat and Yalmy as shown hatched on plan No. Vic. F.C. 16 lodged in the Central Plan Office.
>
> [...]
>
> DEDICATION SCHEDULE NO. 248
>
> 22,475 hectares more or less of Crown land in the Parishes of Bendock, Bidwell, Cooaggalah, Dellicknora, Kuark, Murrungowar, Noonga, Purgagoolah and Tonghi as shown hatched on plan No. Vic. F.C. 18 lodged in the Central Plan Office.

[...]

DEDICATION SCHEDULE NO. 249

51,000 hectares more or less of Crown land in the Parishes of Bungywarr, Cobon, Combienbar, Coopracambra, Goolengook, Noonga, Noorinbee, Nungal, Purgagoolah, Weeragua and Winyar as shown hatched on plan No. Vic. F.C. 16 lodged in the Central Plan Office.

The dedication concludes with the following words 'And the Honourable Thomas Leslie Austin, Her Majesty's Minister of Forests for the State of Victoria, shall give the necessary directions herein accordingly'. Excepting that classified as 'uncommitted land', all of ~~Goolengook~~ became reserved forest to be managed primarily for timber from this time on.

1983: site of institutionalised conflict

In 1982/3, a series of protests were held in the tall forests of the Errinundra Plateau. These led, amongst other things, to the establishment of a body known as the Cutting Areas Review Committee and, eventually, to the inception of Errinundra National Park in 1988 (see below). The impact of protests at this time is illustrated by the following passage emanating from the Timber Industry Strategy – a special report from the Victorian Auditor-General's Office in 1993. This reads, 'The Committee, established in 1983, was considered necessary to prevent any forest planning and management decisions by the Department [of Conservation and Natural Resources] which could result in a repetition of the Errinundra Plateau conservation campaign. Timber harvesting was halted in that area following extensive public protests regarding the loss of old-growth forest and rainforest. The area was eventually accepted for its conservation values and proclaimed a National Park in July 1988' (Auditor-General of Victoria, 1993, p. 88). The Committee gave various stakeholders the opportunity to object to the location of proposed coupe plans/harvesting schedules across Victoria. However, the effect of this was not to end conflict but to give it an institutionalised form. In the years following the inception of the Committee the Auditor-General determined that '[O]f 1,653 coupes planned since 1990–91, 531 were objected to by one or more members of the Committee. Around 70% of these coupes were located in the Tambo and *East Gippsland* Forest Management Areas' (1993, p. 88, emphases added). As a result of this Committee – which operated for a decade only – ~~Goolengook~~ became a site subject to formal review.

1986: site within East Gippsland forest management area

As a result of the Victorian Timber Industry Strategy of 1986, Victoria was divided into 15 forest management areas (FMAs). East Gippsland was one such FMA. It was remarked to 'contain[ ] Victoria's second largest resource of hardwood sawlogs' and given to supply over one fifth (250,000 cubic metres) of D+ grade sawlogs produced from Victoria's forests each year (Department of Conservation and Natural Resources, 1993a, p. 126). The plan articulates that 'The total area of the East Gippsland FMA is 1,217,000 hectares (5% of Victoria), made up of 159,000 hectares of private property and 1,058,000 hectares of public land …' (Department of Conservation and Natural Resources, 1993a, p. 1). The FMA was (and is) designed to take in the whole of the County of Croajingolong and all land occurring between the Snowy River and 'the main ridge of the Great Dividing Range, the Timbarra River, and various forest roads and tracks' extending from Lakes Entrance in the South to the beginning of the Murray River on the NSW/Victorian border (Department of Conservation and Natural Resources, 1993a, p. 1). ~~Goolengook~~, as a forest block of about 9000 hectares, constitutes just under 1% of land in the FMA.

1986 (July): site within the Bemm River Water Supply Catchment

Pages 2948 and 2489 of the *Government Gazette* of 30 July 1986 carried the following proclamation,

> *Soil Conservation and Land Utilisation Act* 1958
> *Land Conservation Act* 1970
> **BEMM RIVER WATER SUPPLY CATCHMENT**
>
> **PROCLAMATION**
>
> By His Excellency the Governor of the State of Victoria and its Dependencies in the Commonwealth of Australia. &c., &c., &c.
>
> I, the Governor of the State of Victoria in the Commonwealth of Australia, by and with the advice of the Executive Council of the said State and having considered a recommendation of the Land Conservation Council in pursuance of the provisions contained in section 5 (1) (*b*) of the *Land Conservation Act* 1970 (No. 8008), do by this Proclamation define the water supply catchment area to be known as the Bemm River Water Supply Catchment, in pursuance of the provisions contained in section 22 (1) of the *Soil Conservation and Land Utilisation Act* 1958 (No. 6372).
>
> The area proclaimed is the catchment to take an offtake pump controlled by the Orbost Water Board on the Bemm River adjacent to Crown allotment 64, section A, Parish of Bemm.
>
> The use of land within this catchment is subject to specification by notice or by determination made by the Soil Conservation Authority, acting under the provisions of section 22 (2) and section 23 (1) (*a*) (*b*) and (*c*) of the *Soil Conservation and Land Utilisation Act* 1958, as amended.
>
> The area described is indicated in Plan No. s-1420, the original of which is lodged at the office of the Soil Conservation Authority, 378 Cotham road, Kew, 3101.

[...]

Given under my Hand and the Seal of the State of Victoria aforesaid, at Melbourne, this twenty-second day of July in the year of our Lord One thousand nine hundred and eighty-six and in the thirty-fifth year of the reign of Her Majesty Queen Elizabeth the Second, Queen of Australia.

(L.S.) J. DAVIS McCAUGHEY
By His Excellency's command
FRANK WILKES
Acting Minister for Planning and Environment

GOD SAVE THE QUEEN!

All of ~~Goolengook~~ was contained within this proclaimed catchment. And yet the effect on timber operations was minimal to say the least. The *Forest Act* 1958, as mentioned previously, gave substantial overriding powers to those in forest management. This meant that the hydrological aspects of ~~Goolengook~~ were continually subordinated to its botanical dimensions – more specifically, to its capacity to yield wood for the construction industry. Those working for Water Catchment Boards found it very difficult, if not impossible, to obtain permission to carry out water quality assessments in areas where logging was taking place (for example near ~~Goolengook~~ River, Blackwatch Creek). Typically, water catchment officers are called in to State forest areas only 'when damage [from logging operations] happens'. However, such officers 'don't get a say in what activities take place' in such forests (in conversation, Robert Allen, 18 March 1999). Indeed there is real concern 'at being locked out of [the] State Rivers' which course through public forests.[1]

1986 (December): site of multiple use

In December 1986 the Land Conservation Council again made its recommendations on land use in the East Gippsland study region. And, once again, its decisions had direct implications for ~~Goolengook~~. Due to the significance of its recommendations, there is a need to quote at length here. In the section devoted to the creation of Errinundra National Park the Land Conservation Council commented,

> Errinundra Plateau and its surrounding country together form an area of international botanical significance. This area also supports some rare and interesting fauna as well as having outstanding scenic, landscape, and recreational values. Its botanical significance lies in the unique forests around the Goonmirk Rocks, the mixed forests on the Gunmark Range, the large stands of cool temperate rainforests on the plateau and escarpments, and the extensive stands of mature shining gum and brown barrel, which reach their maximum development here. Brown barrel is found nowhere else in Victoria other than in East Gippsland and both species are poorly represented in existing reserves. Available

1 In conversation, Simon Robertson, 12 March 1999.

> evidence suggests that the plateau might have functioned as a refuge for flora and fauna during past climatic changes, and it therefore has high biogeographical significance.
>
> The council is proposing establishment of a national park that incorporates the major elements of this unique area. The proposed park is centred on the existing Errinundra and Delegate River Flora Reserves and the Mount Ellery Scenic Reserve along with the adjoining headwaters of the Goolengook River. These features are linked by the headwaters of the Brodribb River. Three major components, the plateau proper, the southern fall, and the northern fall are all represented in the park (Land Conservation Council, 1986, p. 22).

Under the heading 'Catchments' the report reads,

> The headwaters of the Brodribb and Goolengook Rivers differ from those of the East Errinundra in that they are developed on granitic parent material. Furthermore, the Goolengook River, with its steep headwaters but relatively broad flat valley tract provides a valuable undisturbed example of a stream type that has been cleared for agriculture elsewhere (Land Conservation Council, 1986, p. 22).

Of 'Vegetation' the Land Conservation Council noted that,

> Overstorey eucalypts in the 'mixed forest' stands often display a multi-aged structure, implying that wildfires, when they have occurred, have not been severe enough to kill the mature eucalypts. Riparian occurrences of cool temperate rainforest are well developed along many of the streams in the proposed park, on both the southern and northern falls of the plateau. In the Goolengook River headwaters a transition from cool temperate rainforest to warm temperate rainforest occurs. The biogeographical significance of the area is further enhanced by the fact that populations of *Podocarpus* and *Tasmania spp.* may be distinct species and therefore endemic to the plateau (Land Conservation Council, 1986, p. 23).

Under 'Recreation' the Land Conservation Council determined that,

> Spectacular views can be obtained from the summit of Mount Ellery, while Ocean View Lookout in the head waters of the Goolengook River provides excellent views of this undisturbed catchment and forested ranges all the way to the coast (Land Conservation Council, 1986, p. 23).

In effect, there were four Land Conservation Council recommendations that had direct implications for ~~Goolengook~~. These were recommendations A8 concerning the creation of Errinundra National Park, E1 concerning hardwood production, E15 relating to the conservation of rainforest areas, and I6 concerning the establishment of a 'Natural Features Zone' along ~~Goolengook~~ River.

Regarding A8 the report reads,

> **Recommendation**
>
> **A8**
>
> That the area of 16,700 hectares, shown on Map A, be used to:
>
> (a) provide opportunities for recreation and education associated with the enjoyment and understanding of natural environments
> (b) conserve and protect natural ecosystems
> (c) supply water and protect catchments and streams
>
> that
>
> (i) logging not be permitted
> (ii) hunting and use of firearms not be permitted
> (iii) grazing not be permitted
> (iv) the environs of the Errinundra road, Greens road and Gunmark road, where they abut the park, be preserved
>
> and that the area be included in a schedule to the *National Parks Act* 1975 and be managed by the Department of Conservation, Forests and Lands (Land Conservation Council, 1986, p. 24).

Section E is headed 'State forest and timber production'. Recommendation E1 stipulates,

> That the area of 542,000 hectares, shown on Map A, be used to in accordance with the principles outlined above [concerning such matters as 'Soil conservation and catchment protection', 'Recreation and landscape', 'Nature conservation', and 'Historic sites'] to:
>
> (a) supply water and protect catchment and streams.
> (b) produce hardwood timber
> (c) conserve native plants and animals, and provide opportunities for the development of wildlife conservation techniques
> (d) provide opportunities for open space recreation (including hunting) and education
> (e) produce honey, forage, gravel, sand, road-making materials and other forest products.
> (f) provide opportunities for mineral exploration and mining, subject to the principles and guidelines outlined in Chapter P, Mineral and stone production.
>
> and that it become State forest, and be managed by the Department of Conservation, Forests and Lands.
>
> Note:
> This recommendation covers land previously recommended for hardwood production and uncommitted land, with the exception of areas for which other recommendations have been made in this review (Land Conservation Council, 1986, p. 61).

Under the same section, recommendation E15 stipulates,

That the areas indicated generally on Map A be used to conserve rainforest

that

(a) each area be protected by a buffer, the width of which should be delineated taking into account the factors outlined earlier
(b) when logging operations are conducted in the adjoining forests, no tree is to be fallen into the rainforest or buffer
(c) passive recreation such as nature study be permitted
(d) logging and grazing not be permitted
(e) all plans for new roads or road improvement works for those sections falling within rainforest should be submitted to the authority managing the rainforest for approval

and that they be permanently protected according to a procedure to be established by the Council in a future investigation of rainforest.

Notes:
1. At the scale of mapping used, the boundaries to the areas cannot be accurately defined nor are all the areas of rainforest indicated.
2. Further areas of rainforest may be identified in the future and this recommendation should also apply to these areas (Land Conservation Council, 1986, p. 63).

Section I is headed 'Rivers and streams'. Of relevance to ~~Goolengook~~ is the sub-section 'Natural features zones'. The rationale for these is that 'While it is not practical to create parks along each of the study area's major streams, Council considers the importance of these streamside areas warrants the adoption of management practices that have as their major aim the protection of these areas' special natural features, particularly as some of these streams provide an important link between the proposed parks in the mountainous regions of the study area and the Croajingolong National Park along the coast' (Land Conservation Council, 1986, p. 75),

Recommendation

I6

That, for those sections of streams indicated on Map A by cross-hatching, primary aims of management be:

(a) the protection of natural and scenic values
(b) the provision of recreational facilities and interpretative aids where this does not conflict with (a) above

that

(c) timber harvesting and gravel extraction not be permitted
(d) any new roading be constructed only where essential for the purposes of management protection, and transport of timber and be designed to minimise effects on scenic and nature conservation values.

> and that management be the responsibility of the authority managing the adjacent public land (Land Conservation Council, 1986, p. 76).
>
> Notes:
> 1. Portions of some streams designated as Natural Features Zones also include areas for the protection of rainforest. Management in these portions should give priority to the protection of rainforest, but should recognise that they also contain a valuable recreational and scenic resource.
> 2. The hatching on the map should not be taken as delineating exact boundaries to the natural features zones [...] Where necessary the width of the zone would increase up to 300 metres to incorporate the visual corridor and the environmental sequence.

Excepting its recommendations made a decade earlier, these passages represented the most comprehensive pronouncements on aspects of ~~Goolengook~~ to date. At first glance, the diversity of ~~Goolengook~~ looks to be secured – rainforest values are catered for, the headwaters of ~~Goolengook~~ River have been earmarked for placement 'in the park', and a Natural Features Zone will be established. Moreover, timber production is to be carried out alongside a range of other activities (supply of water, conservation of native plants and animals, recreational activities, production of honey, gravel, and road-making materials, as well as mineral exploration). But on closer inspection, it is apparent that the emphasis on environmental values (even within timber production zones) is infused by a logic (or image of thought) that entrenches, rather than alleviates, environmental degradation. What is in evidence here is the *realignment of terrains* at the expense of a radical *readjustment of forestry practices*. It is as if the prospective proclamation of Errinundra National Park compensates for any ecological problems likely to occur beyond such an area. But by what criteria does one distinguish the value of terrains which lie just beyond the boundary of a national park from those that lie just a few metres 'inside' it? Only by violently imposing an arbitrary line between that deemed sacred and that designated profane. Accordingly, the effect of the Land Conservation Council's recommendations is to map the anthropomorphic limits of ecological significance and to contain such limits within a finite series of domains (that is national parks). Here, the earth is made to exhibit its 'truly' significant areas and, by default, those that are in some sense expendable (or, at least, able to be subjected to entirely different management regimes). In Deleuze and Guattari's terms, the Land Conservation Council – in deeming certain areas as worthy of permanent conservation status – has set in train a series of molar refrains. In subsequent years, these refrains will be revisited by *both* loggers ('you've already got the best timbers locked up, what else do you want?') *and* conservationists ('our parks need expanding'). There are very important rhetorical devices embedded in such debates – primarily involving the tropes of metalepsis and synecdoche. These will be explicated in the context of examining the East Gippsland Forest Management Plan.

1988 (May): site of national park

In line with the recommendations of the Land Conservation Council, the *National Parks (Amendment) Act* 1988 was assented to on May 17, 1988. The purpose of this Act was 'to establish national parks in East Gippsland' (s. 1). Each new park constituted an Amendment of Schedule Two of the *National Parks Act* 1975 (the principal Act). Section 5 (g) of the Amending Act is relevant to ~~Goolengook~~ and reads,

> *Part 36 – Errinundra National Park*
>
> All those pieces or parcels of land containing 251 km^2 more or less, situate in the Parishes of Bendock, Errinundra, Goongerah and Noonga, being the land delineated and bordered red or green, excepting from them the roads shown as excluded in a plan prepared by the Surveyor-General lodged in the Central Plan Office of the Department of Property and Services and numbered NP 92.

The area of land given national park status across ~~Goolengook~~ was approximately 1648 hectares (roughly one seventh of its 'total' area). Here, modern bureaucracy formally acknowledged the significance of those aspects first noted by Merrall, Spencer and others a century earlier. But such an acknowledgement also entailed something other – something dangerous, something ominous. Specifically, the southern most portion of the national park levied a molar incision across ~~Goolengook~~ as a body without organs. It brought the problematic dichotomy of ecologically significant/insignificant to the fore. This is not to say that ~~Goolengook~~ could ever remain, or had remained, free from coding and striation. Rather it is to suggest that the declaration of ~~Goolengook~~ as part national park/part multiple use area brings with it as many problems as it solves. The plotting of the southern boundary of the national park is an event that well illustrates the shortcomings of attempts to name and dissect nature – especially in binary fashion. For all intents and purposes, there is little to differentiate the aesthetic brilliance or ecological importance of the terrain immediately north and south of the park boundary across ~~Goolengook~~. To be sure, the aim in the southern extension of the park was to provide adequate protection for the headwaters of the heritage listed ~~Goolengook~~ River. But in doing this, administrators inadvertently earmarked the remainder of ~~Goolengook~~ as less than significant, as common, as *lack*. National Parks may be beautiful. They may be much needed. But they are also mechanisms for discursively producing surrounding terrains as less than sufficient to their task *as forest*, *as river*, *as geological formation*, and so forth. In short, along with national parks comes the discourse of the proper and the true and the concomitant discourses of the deficient and the expendable.[2]

---

2 The great danger in believing that long-term ecosystemic well-being can be procured by turning places of 'high' ecological significance into protected geopolitical territories (that is flora and fauna reserves, national parks, wilderness zones), is that such a strategy has the potential to result in a fragmented series of 'environmental gems' situated amongst 'second-rate' land, water and sea scapes. Victoria (which covers 22,740,000 hectares and

1989 (May): site subject to code of forest practices

The Victorian *Code of Forest Practices for Timber Production* was the first code of its kind to operate in respect of the management of Australian forests. It applied both to forests on public and private land and outlined prescriptions under the three main headings of 'Establishing and Tending Timber Stands', 'Timber Harvesting', and 'Roading for Timber Production'. Coupes were to be a maximum of 40 hectares with no more than three adjacent coupes to be harvested over three years. Streamside reserves of 'at least 20 metres' were to be retained around permanent streams, springs,

---

has a population of around 4.5 million people) is a good example of a state that has adopted a programme of what I would term '*dis*located ecology'. Such an ecology signifies a mode of environmentalism that preserves areas in rural or 'remote' locations at the expense of the ecology of urban or so-called 'central' locations. I think there are sound ecological reasons for collapsing the distinction between 'remote' and 'central' areas such as the fact that the ecology of cities does not improve simply because there is clean air, clean water, good soils and sizeable areas of flora and fauna locked away in some distant location. Socio-ecological well-being is about the *proximity* and *continuity* of biodiversity not just the fact that 'it' exists somewhere 'out there'.

In 1970, Victoria's national parks, conservation reserves and 'other reserves' covered 3.5% of the state or 795,900 hectares. In 1997 this figure had increased to 4,297,860 hectares or 18.9% of the state's gross area (Land Conservation Council, 1997, pp. 11–13). Over the last three decades there has been, in other words, a six-fold increase in the area devoted to conservation. So 'successful' has this preservation programme been that Victoria called itself 'The Garden State' for much of the 1990s and prided itself on possessing a 'world-class system of parks and nature reserves'. And yet this same 'clean and green' State displays a capital city (that is, Melbourne) and satellite cities (for example, Geelong) with (frequently) poor air quality, main rivers full of toxins and built environments strewn with non-biodegradable debris. The disjunction is, I believe, of high cultural, political and environmental significance.

A garden, literally speaking, is 'a section of ground given over to the cultivation of *useful* or *ornamental* plants' (Bernard, 1989, emphases added). It is a delimited and continuously manicured piece of earth – earth minus its 'unpredictable' forces. Even in their role as spaces for 'spiritual renewal' or private territories where one goes to 'get away from it all', gardens retain a routinised and striated dimension (a place of measured, controlled, bounded and managed speeds and forces). I would contend that there are many similarities between gardens and formal preservation zones and that, further, this is ground for serious ecological concern. For the sake of continuity, consider the State of Victoria. Since around 1997, Victoria's entire collection of national parks, conservation reserves, wilderness zones and other such areas have been brought under the control of a body called 'Parks Victoria'. The accompanying TV and newspaper advertisements during this transition have been quite interesting. One newspaper advertisement displayed a picture of a forest in the Dandenong Ranges National Park about 40 kilometres from Melbourne. The caption at the bottom of the page read 'This might look like an untouched forest, but it's been carefully handled for over 100 years'. Here, 'nature' is configured as something that must be 'looked after' – as a body whose *wildness* cannot be allowed to proliferate. Forest fires must be 'controlled'. Undergrowth must be 'cut 'back'. Fallen logs must be 'removed'. The message is that 'nature' must be manicured before 'humans' can experience what 'it' has to 'offer'.

swampy ground and 'bodies of standing water' (Department of Conservation, Forests and Lands, 1989, p. 15). This reduced to five metres around temporary streams. The Code stipulated that harvesting operations be 'excluded from slopes greater that 30° ...' (Department of Conservation, Forests and Lands, 1989, p. 16). Wildlife corridors 'at least 40 metres wide' are to be retained between coupes and surrounding forest to 'provide for the movement of wildlife and for sufficient diverse habitat to maintain resident wildlife populations' (Department of Conservation, Forests and Lands, 1989, p. 17). These corridors are to be 100 metres or more where riparian environments are concerned. With regard to rainforest, the Code stipulated a minimum buffer of 20 metres around such vegetation (Department of Conservation, Forests and Lands, 1989, p. 17). No figure was given for the retention of habitat trees or trees with hollows that provide nesting sites for various animals. The Code merely stipulated the retention of 'as many habitat trees as practical' (Department of Conservation, Forests and Lands, 1989, p. 17). In addition to the 'protection' of water and wildlife

---

Another advertisement during this period informed the people of Victoria that Parks Victoria presides over a 'parks system'. This is somewhat troublesome because it implies that there are discrete parts within this 'system' and that the job – indeed the *duty* of humans working in and for this system – is to master, control and improve on each part so the overall system survives. I think this goes against basic ecological knowledge which says that even the smallest ecosystems are fluid and dynamic (that is ill-defined) – that ecosystems form links with and are interdependent on other ecosystems in ways that even the best science does not fully understand. Put differently, ecosystems do not cease at park boundaries – they impact on and are influenced by the kinds of activities and organisation of spaces beyond their prescribed limits. Old-growth eucalypt forests such as those exhibited across the southern part of the Errinundra National Park continue to be under threat even though they are 'within' a legislated protection zone. It may indeed be politically and legally accurate to say that logging which occurs up against the boundaries of national parks occurs 'outside' such parks. But ecologically speaking this is problematic. *Only in a grammatical sense is it possible to say that an action is 'outside' the ecosystem inscribed by preservation zone boundaries* – especially when the ecosystem is a combination of damp and wet sclerophyll forest whose mix of tree species continue well beyond such boundaries. In other words, the clean air, water and soils produced by old-growth ecosystems do not confine themselves to politically designated borders and limits. Nevertheless, government institutions like Parks Victoria sees itself presiding over a unity (a bounded entity) not a multiplicity (an ensemble of *rhizomatic* or fleeing forces).

The most interesting juxtaposition of words and images in the Parks Victoria advertising campaign occurred on TV. One of these commercials displayed a lengthy series of images of mist-shrouded forests and rivers and their respective sounds (running water, flapping bird's wings and so on). It also showed the kinds of fauna someone might see in Victoria's preservation zones – fauna whose remaining strongholds often occur *not* in the 'parks system' but in intensive forestry, grazing and mining zones. The same commercial also audibly and textually related a list of 'experts' who worked for and in the parks system – ornithologists, botanists, zoologists and so on. This has recourse to the ways in which 'nature' is configured as something *knowable* – but knowable only to those who formally study it and modify it so that it can be *re*presented to those (that is Park visitors) who wish to gaze at 'it'. Toward the end of the commercial a voice told the audience that 'Victoria's parks are not this beautiful

the Code also outlined basic procedures for such activities as road making, choice and servicing of machinery at logging sites, wet weather restrictions, and so forth. None of the prescriptions put forward in the Code were legally enforceable. In a sense, the prescriptions gave the processes which contribute to the fragmentation and simplification of forest habitat a more respectable basis.

1990: site for the realisation of sustainable yields

The *Forests (Timber Harvesting) Act* 1990 had two purposes: namely, '(a) to relate permitted hardwood sawlog production from State forests to the sustainable yield of those forests; and (b) to provide for public safety in relation to the taking of forest produce' (Section 1). This Act charted the volume of sawlogs to be supplied during the 15-year period commencing from July 1, 1991. It also required the

---

by accident, *they need to be managed*'. I can't think of many things more disappointing than visiting a forest or river that human beings have 'improved', 'tamed' or 'managed'. (There's also something very wrong with an environmental protection advertisement which encourages people or *consumers* to drive hundreds of kilometres to experience clean air and a decent array of flora and fauna.) Declaring that 'parks need to be managed' is akin to saying that 'nature cannot be left to its own devices' – more dubiously, that 'nature needs humans to intervene to make it (re)presentable to those who *use* it'. 'Parks-are-for-*people*' philosophies *strengthen* the managerial approach to preservation and reinforce the division between 'humans' and 'nature'. Arguably, preservation zones only need 'managing' because they are dotted with the kinds of infrastructures that people have become accustomed to 'outside' these spaces. Kiosks, toilets, power lines, lawns, roads and so on all need repairing or upgrading – especially where the surrounding 'nature' threatens to interfere with their ascribed functions.

If the challenge of political-ecology is something other than to create – as one commentator has termed them – a series of contrived 'wilderness prisons', then I think there are reasons to seriously question the long-term viability and effects of nature preservation strategies (Birch, 1990). Firstly, such strategies perpetuate the idea that 'nature' is something *independent from* everyday land, water and air scapes (that nature is an 'other', a 'freakish occurrence', or an 'exception' to most people's lives – which in one sense it is). Secondly, there is a need to look critically at nature preservation because such zones generally encourage people to interact with 'nature' in quite routinised and restricted ways (see Halsey, 1999). Thirdly, I believe there is a need to examine current modes of nature preservation because they have become, ironically, something of a weapon for industrial sectors. That is, many sectors point to preserved areas as evidence of the fact that 'nature' is 'doing well' or has been 'adequately taken care of'. From here, arguments proceed on the basis that if 'nature' has been 'properly catered for' there is nothing wrong with the government of the day allocating 'a' forest or 'a' stretch of water to industry. Indeed such arguments are often couched in very egalitarian terms – governments have done something for 'nature' so now they *must* do something for the 'real' generators of wealth. Again, this perpetuates the division between 'humans' and 'nature' in that it implies that ecology and wealth creation are logically distinct. Fourthly and finally, many recent government decisions have blurred the distinction between places of preservation and places of (intensive) industry (for example in Shark Bay world heritage area in Western Australia).

relevant Minister to review sustainable yield calculations at least once every five years. Section 5 outlined the sustainable yields for each FMA across Victoria. East Gippsland's quota was set at 174,000 cubic metres per year of A, B, and C grade logs. 'Sustainable yield is the achievement and maintenance in perpetuity of a certain level of periodic outputs of the products and services of forests without impairment of the productivity of the land' (Victorian Government, 1986, p. 33, emphases removed). This legislation required that ~~Goolengook~~ – and all other high yielding forests – 'play their part' in meeting supply quotas *irrespective of demand* for sawlogs. What the forestry industry is permitted to take it will take, even if it means accumulating vast stockpiles of sawn timber (and woodchips) that no one wants.

1991 (March): site of cyanide anomalies

On 21 September 1990 an exploration licence (EL 2145) was granted to the mining company CRA to explore the area denoted simply as 'Jungle Hill'. Following renewal, this licence would extend over a three year period. The exploration area encompassed some 264.5 square kilometres of land in Croajingolong and took in the southern portion of 839. Three progress reports were produced detailing exploration data.

CRAE Report No. 17360 summarised operations for the period ending 20 March 1991. The introduction remarks, 'Most of the area is hilly and dominated by state forest. Some of the alluvial flats form farmland. The title area is well accessible by forest tracks from the Princess Highway' (p. 5). In subsection 4.2 marked 'Previous work', mention is made of the Boulder Mine operations of the late 1890s at the headwaters of Bola Creek. However, no reference is made to the fact that Blackwatch Creek was mined for gold in 1885. Gold was found to occur at a concentration of 107 parts per billion (ppb) in the catchment of Bola Creek. The samples here were taken about three kilometres east of the headwaters of Bola Creek which run up to the border of 839. Maps attached to the report depict 839 as part of the 'Jungle Hill EL 2145 Locality Plan' (Vv6339), and as a site for 'Drainage Geochemical Sampling' (map Vv6340). Appendix 1 displays the 'Regional Reconnaissance Drainage Geochemical Sample Ledgers', which, in simple terms, indicates what metals were found at which locations within the exploration zone. Sheet 35808 records sample number 2176 627 as taken from Blackwatch Creek at Easting 666400, Northing 5849800, in the south east portion of 839. The hand-written description reads,

> Blackwatch Creek with catchment 6 km^2. Ck. 3.5 m wide, slow flow. Float sandstone, siltstone. Good sample site.

The ledger shows that the sample taken from Blackwatch Creek contained 1.65 parts per billion of Au (or gold). The relative concentrations of seven additional metals were also noted which included (Zn) zinc, (Pb) lead and (Cu) copper. A sample site from a tributary of Blackwatch Creek was also taken (sample number 2176626, Easting 666200, Northing 5849700). This was found to contain 0.65 parts per billion of gold. These were evidently of some interest to CRA. The final sentence of the report reads, 'It is recommended that only the cyanide leach anomalies in Bola and adjacent creeks be followed up in the coming field season' (p. 8). The adjacent creeks spoken of here were Blackwatch Creek and Shady Creek. Here, ~~Goolengook~~ is further striated due, in the main, to the perceived value of its geological stratifications. It is no longer simply flows of fibre which interest the industrial machine. Instead, the flow of (precious) metals takes on a significance not seen since 1885.

1991 (April): site of national park extension

The *National Parks (Miscellaneous Amendments) Act* 1991, assented to and commencing on April 9, extended the areas within a number of national parks. Errinundra was one of these and the area affected fell within ~~Goolengook~~. Section 5 of the Act dealt with the necessary Amendments to the principal Act. Part 5 dealt with the area within ~~Goolengook~~,

> In part 36 of Schedule Two to the Principal Act –
> (a) for '251 km^2' substitute '256 km^2'; and
> (b) for 'NP 92' substitute 'N.P. 92/1'.

The area added here was one of National Estate Forest and totalled approximately 500 hectares within the north eastern portion of ~~Goolengook~~. Again, the conservation machine levies a twofold effect. On the one hand, it conserves, it locks things away, it brings forth a different way of managing landscapes. But on the other hand, it charts an arbitrary (though no less real) line between the ecological 'rare' and the ecologically 'common'. The problem is that such divisions are premised on the belief that grammar can get to the essence of things (that is can articulate what a terrain 'really' is) when in fact it merely constructs the world in terms of its own limits. The 'rare' only has meaning in relation to the 'common' just as the common only retains its descriptive force in relation to what is rare. What, then, would become of rarity where the common itself had been depleted? Would one then be compelled to divide the rare in terms of its commonplaces and singularities (converting the sacred into the profane)? As of the closing decade of the twentieth century, the textual incorporation of ~~Goolengook~~ points precisely to the arrival of this state of affairs.

1991 (June): site of hydrological conservation

Following on from its work in 1986, the Land Conservation Council handed down its report entitled *Rivers and Streams, Special Investigation: Final Recommendations* in June of 1991. This investigation was in keeping with a 1987 Order in Council to '… carry out an investigation of the scenic, recreational, cultural and ecological values of rivers and streams in Victoria, and to make recommendations on the use of these rivers and how their identified values can best be protected' (Land Conservation Council, 1991, p. 1). As well as making a series of recommendations on 'Essentially natural catchments', 'Representative Rivers' and the like, the Land Conservation Council recommended that 17 areas across Victoria be given the status of 'Heritage River Corridor'. 'A8' connoted the corridor of most relevance to ~~Goolengook~~ and was given the name 'Bemm, Goolengook, Arte, and Errinundra Heritage Rivers Corridor' (Land Conservation Council, 1991, p. 31). Various aspects of ~~Goolengook~~ were articulated in the following way,

> The steep headwaters of the Goolengook River, developed on granitic parent material, open to a relatively broad flat valley tract, providing a valuable undisturbed example of a stream type that has been cleared for agriculture elsewhere in East Gippsland [...]
>
> [The] corridors [of this heritage river area] contain the best rainforest continuum in the State, with a near-continuous occurrence of cool temperate and warm temperate rainforest from 122 m elevation to close to sea level [...]
>
> Between 400 and 800 m elevation, elements of cool temperate and warm temperate rainforest intergrade [i.e. overlap], and occurrences are found on the Goolengook, Errinundra, and the Arte Rivers. In such areas southern sassafras, black oliveberry, and lillypilly are co-dominant overstorey trees. Such intergrades are rare in Victoria. Normally, although these two communities may be close together, substantial differences in elevation separate them (Land Conservation Council, 1991, pp. 57–8).

In addition to being subject to the general conservation recommendations (see Land Conservation Council, 1991, pp. 32–3), Council recommended the following in respect of the area enveloping ~~Goolengook~~,

> **Recommendation**
>
> A8 – Bemm River and its tributaries, Goolengook, Arte, and Errinundra Rivers
>
> That the 148 km river including the Bemm River and sections of its tributaries shown on Map A8 be used in accordance with general recommendations A1–A17 (a) to (l) above
>
> that
>
> (m) (i) the corridor be retained free from impoundment, artificial barriers or structures that impede the passage of in-stream fauna
>
> (ii) any new diversions of water only be permitted if their volumes, timing, and offtake do not significantly impair native fish habitat conditions, adversely affect rainforest and its continuity, or reduce scenic landscape value
>
> that
>
> (n) the following significant values be protected
>
> (i) rainforest values

(ii) long-footed potoroo habitat [...]

(iii) Australian grayling habitat, by retaining free passage for migration, and maintaining water quality, flow, and in-stream habitat conditions

(iv) native fish diversity in the lower reaches of the Sydenham Inlet

(v) Sydenham Inlet, an estuary of geomorphological significance

(o) other recreation activities continue where permitted in accordance with land status

and that the corridor be managed by the Department of Conservation and Environment, in conjunction with the East Gippsland Rivers Management Board in relation to waterway management.

Notes:
1. Recent instances of reduced river water quality as a result of turbidity following rain have been reported. The causes should be identified and remedial action taken.

[...] (Land Conservation Council, 1991, p. 60).

Whilst such recommendations may appear unproblematic they, just like calculations of sustainable yield or the establishment of logging roads, contribute to the production of ~~Goolengook~~ as a full body (that is as a body in the process of becoming organised or striated). Just like economic assessments, environmental assessments divide ~~Goolengook~~ in binary fashion. They fragment it. They name it. They categorise it. They attempt to articulate its 'special' or 'significant' elements as against its 'Other' features. The problem here is not so much with the naming as with the bodies and practices which emerge subsequent to this process. In addition, the problem has to do with the kinds of knowledges which underpin the manufacture and inception of particular thresholds – thresholds designed to keep certain bodies from mixing with other bodies. For instance, from the southern boundary of the Errinundra National Park to the entrance to the Sydenham Inlet there is to be a Natural Features Zone which prohibits, amongst other things, timber production in areas 100 metres either side of the ~~Goolengook~~ and Bemm Rivers. This means in effect that clearfelling can (and does) take place within 100 metres of such rivers. The question is, what are the long-term effects of aligning heritage river zones and clearfelled areas in such a manner? What kind of knowledge portends to *know* the answer to this question? The same could be asked in respect of the recommended 20–40 metre buffer zones which must be left around rainforest during timber harvesting. Is it reasonable to say that a rainforest ends where rainforest species cease – or is rainforest more than the sum of its parts?

Another important aspect of the Land Conservation Council's recommendations has to do with marking out the boundaries of 'Essentially Natural Catchments'. The definition of such a catchment 'is one with no urbanisation, clearing, intensive agriculture, grazing, timber harvesting, plantations, mining, extractive industries, water storages, water diversions, river engineering works, or roads parallel and immediately adjacent to streams' (Land Conservation Council, 1991, p. 93). In total, 45 catchments were identified across Victoria spanning some 154,020 hectares. The majority of such territory occurred in national parks (134,400 hectares) with the remainder occurring partially or wholly in State forests (Land Conservation Council, 1991, pp. 95–6). No aspect of ~~Goolengook~~ fell within such a catchment, the 'closest' being the Brodribb River Head Waters Catchment contained within Errinundra National Park. This meant that activities such as timber harvesting, clearing of native vegetation, mining, domestic stock grazing – essentially all the things prohibited in 'Essentially Natural Catchments' – could continue to occur across the body of ~~Goolengook~~. At such a time, 86% (7664 hectares) of ~~Goolengook~~ forest block was unlogged. There were only a few logging roads in its southernmost portions. No major mining activity had occurred within its boundaries. And although cattle had once grazed across the block, this activity was not taken to vitiate the concept of an essentially natural catchment. In such a light, and knowing that the topographical features which provided for the perimeter of ~~Goolengook~~ block were also those that made the block a catchment 'in its own right', it is perplexing that the Land Conservation Council did not deem *any* of this area (and therefore ~~Goolengook~~) as satisfying the criteria for an essentially natural catchment. What this shows is that the value of an area has very little to do with its intrinsic or enduring aspects and much more to with how various bodies envisage different terrains.

1991 (November): site of biological significance

In 1982 the Victorian government announced a new policy in relation to the harvesting of timber from public and state forests. This policy required that flora and fauna surveys be conducted for all logging blocks in Victoria's 15 FMAs that had had less than 50% of their potential sawlog volume removed. ~~Goolengook~~ block was one such block subject to a pre-logging flora and fauna survey. Field work at this block was conducted on 44 days between February and March of 1988 and 1989 (eight years prior to the forest blockade at ~~Goolengook~~ in November 1996). At this time, 7018 hectares (70% of the block) was classified as State forest and was the gross area available for timber production and harvesting (this includes the 1212 hectares logged from 1975 to 1986). The only areas not available for harvesting were those within the northern portion of the block inside Errinundra National Park and those excluded by prescriptions within the Code of Forest Practices. The five scientists in charge of surveying the block made their assessments and recommendations in light of conservation thresholds of plant and animal species occurring across Victoria at the time of the report. In short, although the report was later deemed by the Department of Natural Resources and Environment as 'site specific', it was in fact written with a more holistic view of forest protection and production in Victoria, and in some cases, Australia.

Ecological Survey Report no 35 Flora and Fauna of the Goolengook Forest Block, East Gippsland, Victoria was completed and distributed for public comment in November of 1991 and totalled 156 pages. Several maps were included which depicted the sites of biological significance, rainforest distribution and sample areas. Eight interrelated communities of forest were identified across ~~Goolengook~~ – community being defined as 'A collection of one or more sub-communities with floristic and environmental affinities' (Lobert et al., 1991, p. 10). Each of these communities were found to have extremely diverse subcommunities whose boundaries or divisions were arbitrarily established for the purposes of the report. The authors did not view one forest community as ending and another beginning at discrete points. Indeed one of the rarest and most biologically significant forests concerned not one but two communities which occur together in the Western portion of the forest block. This type of forest was termed 'cool-warm temperate rainforest overlap' and is considered very rare in Victoria and Australia. In addition to these rainforest communities, the report identified three other forest communities of high biological significance (Wet Sclerophyll, Montane Forest, and Lowland Sclerophyll Forest) (Lobert et al., 1991, p. 36). When combined with the Damp Sclerophyll and rainforest sites, the forests of ~~Goolengook~~ were found to support 328 species of vascular plants, 34 species of mammal, 77 species of bird, eight species of amphibian and 15 species of reptile. The report further determined that 4% of plant species, 53% of mammals, 14% of bird species, 12% of amphibian species and 20% of reptile species from the ~~Goolengook~~ site were under threat in the national context.

Throughout the report an emphasis was placed on the fact that ~~Goolengook~~ block forms a part of the undulations and geological formations of the Errinundra Plateau. The features of this plateau (such as its composition and variety of forests and forest dwelling species) are a product of complex ecosystemic processes and geological time-scales. Recommendations regarding the protection of portions of ~~Goolengook~~ were made with this latter time-scale in mind. The report specifically recommended against any kind of logging in those areas deemed sites of significance and especially against logging regimes based around 40–80 year rotations that would quash any possibility of the long-term floristic and structural diversity of old-growth forests being able to recover (Lobert et al., 1991, p. 108). Put another way, the pre-logging survey advised that the speeds common to the evolution of rainforest and other old-growth communities (concerning species maturation and declination, water retention and dispersion, soil movement and accumulation, carbon intake and conversion) be maintained.

Ultimately, the survey recommended that seven sites of biological significance be exempt from intensive human disturbance such as clearfell logging (see Figure 3 on p. 127).[3] The preamble to the detail of these sites reads,

3 Initially the scientists requested that the entire forest management block be declared the southern extension of Errinundra National Park. This, however, did not eventuate.

> The protection of these Sites should ensure that the full biological diversity of the Goolengook Forest Block is maintained … such a representative series of Sites will not only incorporate (and protect) known values, but is also likely to play an important role in the protection of little-understood and/or incompletely surveyed values (e.g. rare species of vascular plants and vertebrates, and all species of non-vascular plants and invertebrates) (Lobert et al., 1991, p. 108).

In relation to the largest of the biological sites of significance (Site 4, 2654 hectares) the report stated that it,

> ... contains many biologically significant values which, together, combine to make this area comparable to any site in East Gippsland, if not south eastern Australia. This site ... has been rated as a Site of National Significance for rainforest values ... It offers the best opportunity in Victoria for the protection of Cool Temperate Rainforest, Warm Temperate Rainforest and overlap forest, in three adjacent and intact catchments (Lobert et al., 1991, p. 113).

In total the seven sites covered 5022 hectares (56%) of ~~Goolengook~~ block. Approximately 4070 hectares of land within these sites fell within State forest, whilst 952 hectares fell within the Errinundra National Park. In effect the survey recommended that nearly two thirds (58%) of all State forest in ~~Goolengook~~ be formally conserved. This would have left 1750 hectares available for immediate timber harvesting (the actual area harvested would have been reduced as a result of calculating the gross and net productive areas within the block) and another 1200 hectares available subsequent to the successful regeneration of those areas that had already been logged in the block. Had the recommendations of the report been adopted in full, 68% (6220 hectares) of ~~Goolengook~~ block would have been formally protected. One of the most important statements made in the report dealt with the topography of the block and the location of the block's boundaries,

> The topographical characteristics of the Block, comprised almost exclusively of the Goolengook River catchment above its confluence with Blackwatch Ck., and the high ridges, saddles and steep slopes that delineate it, create an ideal land management unit: processes occurring within the Block are likely to affect large parts of the Block (where circumstances suit), while outside it are likely to remain peripheral in their influence. Thus, relative to surrounding areas, the Block is likely to function very much as a unit. That the Block has remained largely undisturbed (excepting logging in the south-east), i.e. few roads and a patchy recent fire history, has resulted in the maintenance of a high level of biological integrity. Although the maintenance of a high level of biological integrity within a functional biogeographic unit is a desirable conservation aim in many catchments, it is not always possible or practical. That it is possible and practical here is of particular importance, given the variety and nature of the significant biological values present (Lobert et al., 1991, p. 109).

This passage again speaks of the unique character of Goolengook block. As a relatively undisturbed catchment of particular dimensions and undulations it is also a space very much suited to conservation on its own terms (although there are many dangers[4] associated with this binary course of action – 'here exists the most important features, there the most expendable'). The publication of the East Gippsland FMP four years later would go against this line of thinking such that *none* of the sites of significance within State forest were offered legislated protection. It would take until April 1998 for any of the sites to be legally reserved from activities such as mining or timber harvesting.

1992: site of heritage river

Following the recommendations of the Land Conservation Council, the *Heritage Rivers Act* 1992 was assented to on June 16. Its purpose was,

> … to make provision for Victorian heritage rivers by providing for the protection of public land in particular parts of rivers and river catchment areas in Victoria which have significant nature conservation, recreation, scenic or cultural heritage attributes and to make related amendments to other Acts.

Schedule 1 describes the various areas declared to be Heritage River Areas. ~~Goolengook~~ River, the main river within ~~Goolengook~~, was one of these and was deemed, as previously mentioned, part of the 'Bemm, Goolengook, Arte and Errinundra Rivers Heritage Area'. This area covered 'All those pieces of land along the Bemm, Goolengook, Arte, and Errinundra Rivers and Errinundra River (East Branch) shown bordered in blue on the plan lodged in the Central Plan Office and numbered LEGL/91-10' (Schedule 1, Part 8). The width of the heritage river corridor along ~~Goolengook~~ River was to be 200 metres from the right and left banks. This extended from the headwaters of the river (located in the north of ~~Goolengook~~) to its intersection with the Bemm River and then south to the Sydenham Inlet. Section 4 provided that 'This Act binds the Crown, not only in right of the State of Victoria, but also, so far as the legislative power of the Parliament permits, the Crown in all its other capacities'. Section 8 part 9 dealt with subordinate legislation. It reads,

> Sections 5, 6 and 6A of the Subordinate Legislation Act 1962 apply to and in respect of a management plan made under this section, and any amendment or revocation of such plan, as if the plan, amendment or revocation were a statutory rule within the meaning of that Act, notice of which had been published in the Government Gazette on the day on which the Minister approved the plan, amendment or revocation.

In late 1997 the issue of what constituted subordinate legislation, along with that of the correct width of the heritage river corridor along the ~~Goolengook~~ River, would become a matters of legal debate in both the Magistrates, District and Supreme Court of Victoria. The creation of the heritage river corridor gave a legal basis for the enforceable exclusion of certain activities from the designated area. Section 10 (5) reads, 'Timber harvesting is not to be carried out in any heritage river area specified

4 See note 1 above.

in Column 4 of Schedule 3'. The Bemm, ~~Goolengook~~, Arte and Errinundra River Heritage Area is listed as such in Schedule 3.

1992 (October): site of acid dyke sampling

CRAE Report No. 18385 was produced for the period of operations ending September 20, 1992. A passage concerning follow up work on the samples from Blackwatch Creek reads, 'Mineralised float showing pyrite in Blackwatch Creek (plan Vv6340) was traced to acid dykes (see G.W. Patterson's report in Appendix I). Its highest Au value returned was only 10 ppb (see ledgers reports in Appendices II and III) …' (p. 2). Sheet 71454 displays the results of the rock samples taken from Blackwatch Creek. Patterson's report dated December 17, 1991 – in addition to detailing work on the Bola, Blackwatch and Shady Creek catchments – examined the regions of exposed rock along ~~Goolengook~~ Road. His attention was drawn to this road by Fons Vandenberg who had recently completed the Bendoc 1:100,000 Geological mapsheet. This mapsheet highlighted the Combienbar Fault which traverses the intersection of the Bemm, Errinundra and Combienbar Rivers, a point about three kilometres to the east of the southern portion of ~~Goolengook~~. The construction of logging roads in 839 has led to 'dykes [being] well exposed in road cuttings on Goolengook Road' (Patterson, Memorandum, December 17, 1991). On January 30 samples from these dykes were submitted for analysis for traces of gold. Kratochvil – the author of CRAE Report No. 18385 – later noted that '[N]o significant gold or base metals mineralisation was detected' from these samples (p. 2). Sheet No. 71458 displays the results of the sampling of materials taken from dykes along ~~Goolengook~~ Road. The main recommendation of this second report was that 'the area of 36 km^2 comprising the Crabhole Creek Prospect … be retained and the remaining 228.5 km^2 of the EL area be relinquished' (p. 2). This latter area included those exploration zones within ~~Goolengook~~.

1993 (June 7): site of hardwood forest resources

Resource Assessment Report No. 93/01 is entitled *Hardwood Timber Resources in the East Gippsland Forest Management Area: Areas and Volumes Report* (1993b). As the title suggests, it gives details of timber resources for all FMBs in the EG FMA. ~~Goolengook~~ block is ascribed the code 17122 ('171' denoting Orbost District, '22' the number of the block within the area). This is an extremely important text. It is one of the very few public documents which detail the age of the forest resource, the extent of logging that has taken place in the EG FMA, and the time at which such logging took place. Information is given under the following headings: Compartment Number and Stand; LCC study area recommendations; Forest Type; Age Class/ Origin; Stand Area; Productive Area (Gross and Net); Utilisation (history, category, class); Standing Volume (Sawlog C+ net, Sawlog Roundwood D+ Gross); Potential Yield (m^3/hectares, at age); and Date of Entry (Source of Data). ~~Goolengook~~ is written

Figure 4 **Photograph of block 839, Goolengook, compartment 513, stand 10, post-logging operations, April 1999. Still held to be sacred by descendants of the Bidwell tribe, the rock was blown apart by forestry workers in order to make room for a logging road. This road would enable access to timber located just below the southern boundary of the Errinundra National Park and immediately east of the heritage listed Goolengook River. In this photo, the said river flows parallel to the logging road approximately 400 metres from the rock debris. For a sense of scale, note the figure sitting on top of the rock abutting the track. Photography: Mark Halsey**

as displaying 15 compartments ranging in size from 287 hectares to 1726 hectares (see Figure 1 on p. 62). These compartments are divided into 181 stands from one hectare up to 1092 hectares. A total of 47 stands (a quarter of all compartments) covering 1212 hectares (yielding approximately 22,603 cubic metres of C+ sawlogs) are shown as having been logged (that is clearfelled) since 1976. Excepting these stands and those effected by wildfire (603 hectares), all remaining stands have been given the status of 'OM' (overmature) and assigned the number '1' (indicating 'no previous sawlog harvesting'). These overmature areas are 'stands where total growth increment is equal to mortality' (Department of Conservation and Natural Resources, 1993, p. 25). Since mature forests are usually those of 80 years or more, overmature forests would, by this reckoning, be in the vicinity of at least 150 years of age and possibly as much as 300 years. As of 1993 this meant that the area of overmature forest across ~~Goolengook~~ was around 7431 hectares (this figure increases if one presumes that at least a proportion of the 603 hectares affected by wildfire was left in a condition conducive to being ascribed the status of overmature). The figures and categories mentioned in this text are extremely significant. The reason for this is that the unfolding of *events over the next four years would see the area of overmature (and probably old-growth) forest reduced by half to just 3484 hectares – and this would occur without a single tree being felled.*

Focusing once again on the 1993 report, the net productive area – the area that can actually be harvested once logging prescriptions and forest within permanent conservation areas (that is Errinundra National Park) are accounted for – is recorded as 6365 hectares. In terms of sawlog volumes, Errinundra National Park (compartments 501, 502, 511 and 512) is given to contain 103,902 cubic metres of C+ grade sawlogs (that is logs capable of contributing to the EG FMA sustainable yield of 174,000 cubic metres and which, in practice, are suitable for use in the housing/construction industry). The State forest within ~~Goolengook~~ block is estimated to hold 96,109 cubic metres of such logs. Even if this amount were harvested in one operation, this would only provide enough timber to meet just over half the annual sustainable yield for the EG FMA. The total amount of D+ logs and roundwood (that is logs given over to woodchipping for pulp and paper) is 857,110 cubic metres. For comparative purposes, this is equivalent to about one sixth (n = six million tonnes) of the woodchips exported from native forests to Japan and Taiwan each year. Aside from this statistical information, the text reveals something else about ~~Goolengook~~ block and thereby the body of ~~Goolengook~~. Specifically, it displays the year(s) in which data was first collected regarding volume and age of timber in this block. The majority of information was entered into the HARIS database during 1992 based on data sourced from the years 1984 (ten stands), 1986 (two stands), 1987 (19 stands) and 1992 (150 stands). Clearly, the bulk of information about ~~Goolengook~~ block is of very recent origin with over 80% of stands being mapped in 1992 for their capacities to yield high volumes of timber.[5] But what is crucial here is not so much

5 There is evidence that timber assessments were carried out across ~~Goolengook~~ as far back as the 1960s (see Department of Conservation and Natural Resources, 1993a, Map 15).

the time when data was collected or sourced but the *methods* engaged to do so. The text denotes four distinct ways of collecting data about timber values,

> 1=**Intensive inventory**. Data have been derived from accurately mapping the forest using aerial photographs and measuring sample plots within the photo-interpreted strata.
>
> 2=**Reconnaissance inventory**. This usually involves stand mapping using aerial photographs but the level of field checking is less intensive and the number of inventory plots is much lower that for source code 1.
>
> 3=**Reconnaissance**. This involves only broad stand mapping with little or no field checking. Yields are usually estimated from utilization experience in neighboring forest of similar type and quality or based on the ocular estimates of logging supervisors. Inventory plots are not used for the calculation of volume.
>
> 4=**Desk study**. These data are an estimate based on experience and study of aerial photographs. There are no detailed maps or inventory plots available (Department of Conservation and Natural Resources, 1993b, pp. 28–9).

On this basis, the number of stands and their associated methods of assessment within ~~Goolengook~~ block are as follows: Code 1 = 0 stands; Code 2 = 31 stands; Code 3 = 45 stands; and Code 4 = 105 stands. The remarkable aspect here is that the majority of the body of ~~Goolengook~~ has been produced in the most vicarious manner possible. There is, in other words, a serious crisis of proximity between those who profess to know an object (that is resource managers) and the object of knowledge (that is trees). Equally problematic is the invocation of mimetic processes at method 3 used to derive one forest's attributes on the basis of those possessed by a 'neighbouring' forest. Nature never copies (itself). To call on Nietzsche, the only thing similar is the relative propensity of each observer to equate things which are in fact dissimilar – in both their composition and their location in space and time. One could say that the process of timber assessment is one which looks to carve out a uniformity of bodies where there could only reign difference. *Timber assessment as a mimetics par excellence*. Here, it is never a matter of simply knowing a forest resource. Rather, there is the process of violently abstracting and promoting a single potential (for wood products) above all other capacities.

1993 (June): site of uneconomic mineralisation

CRA report No. 18950 is the Final Report on the Jungle Hill Exploration Licence. It is dated June 1993 and offers an overall assessment of both the area previously relinquished and that retained for further exploration. The final sentence, 'From the reassessment of exploration results it is concluded that the mineralisation is uneconomic. As there is no potential for significant zones of economic mineralisation within the title area it is recommended that the EL area be relinquished' (p. 2).

1994: site of old-growth forest and ecological vegetation classes

In March of 1994 a much anticipated report entitled *A Study of the Old-Growth Forests of East Gippsland* was released. It was the first major study of old-growth forests in Victoria and was funded in part by the Commonwealth. The study had two major charters. First, to define and map the extent of ecological vegetation classes (or EVCs) in the EG FMA, and secondly, from this basis, to define and map the extent of old-growth forest in the FMA. 'Ecological Vegetation Class' was a concept developed in order to 'better' classify plant communities across large areas and was an adjunct to the broader category of 'forest type'. EVCs 'consist of one or a number of floristic communities that exist under a common regime of ecological processes within a particular environment at a regional, state or continental scale' (Woodgate et al., 1994, p. 39). By this definition the study distinguished 44 EVCs across the EG FMA. Nine of these EVCs were deemed to occur within ~~Goolengook~~, these being EVC 16 (Lowland forest, 126.207 hectares), EVC 18 (Riparian forest, 79.5162 hectares), EVC 21 (Shrubby Dry forest, 1080.55 hectares), EVC 29 (Damp forest, 2514.03 hectares), EVC 30 (Wet forest, 4598.3 hectares), EVC 31 (Cool Temperate rainforest, 166.779 hectares), EVC 32 (Warm Temperate rainforest, 318.918 hectares), EVC 38 (Montane Damp forest, 3.3969 hectares), and EVC 39 (Montane Wet forest, 33.7671 hectares).[6] In the year prior to the completion of this text, ~~Goolengook~~ was composed of just three forest types: mountain mixed species, scrub, and closed forest (cool or warm temperate rainforest). This recategorisation was not without consequences. Although functioning at a higher resolution, the category EVC in no sense brought Nature more precisely into focus. This concept, just like others before it, still involved pushing aspects of ~~Goolengook~~ into the background (structure, age) and bringing others to the fore (floristics). Even so, 'EVC' was to become the primary category used to map the location and extent of vegetation across the EG FMA from this time.

In addition to classifying the FMA into various EVCs, the study also developed a series of categories to denote the age and disturbance history of the vegetation within each EVC. Each would have major implications for conservation and intensive resource use. The categories developed in this regard were,

1. Undisturbed
2n. Negligible 'natural' disturbance
2u. Negligible 'unnatural' disturbance
3n. Significant 'natural' disturbance
3u. Significant 'unnatural' disturbance
3. Significant disturbance, type unknown
 Unknown disturbance recorded, level unknown (adapted from Woodgate et al., 1994, p. 70).

Undisturbed forest was given as,

6 Figures supplied by Jason Catlin, Arthur Rhylah Institute, Victoria.

> [a]reas with no recorded disturbance history … even though some environmental weed species may be present and wildfires have almost certainly occurred at some time in the past.

This category of forest was comparatively rare across the EG FMA totalling just 32,584 hectares (or 3% of the landed area). Only a very small fraction of ~~Goolengook~~ was deemed to fall under this category (less than 1%).

The definition of 'negligible disturbance' was given as,

> a disturbance for which there is an authentic record and which is unlikely to have altered the structure (growth stage ratios or crown cover projection) or the usual floristic composition of species for that ecological vegetation class; or if a disturbance did occur in the past the effect is no longer significant (Woodgate et al., 1994, p. 69).

This category of forest was divided in two sub-categories encompassing 'negligible *natural* disturbance' as against 'negligible *un*natural disturbance'. The former denotes areas where wildfire had occurred within an EVC but had only affected the understorey of the forest – that is, 'no growth stage or canopy damage was evident' (Woodgate et al., 1994, p. 70). The latter denotes areas where human-induced activities such as logging, clearing for agriculture, fuel reduction burning, or grazing had occurred but which resulted in only minor or 'non-existent' damage to the forest canopy.

The final category of importance here was that of 'significant disturbance' defined as,

> a disturbance which is likely to have altered the growth stage ratios, crown cover projection and the usual floristic composition of that vegetation class and which is detectable at the time of survey, or is indicated in an existing and authentic record (Woodgate et al., 1994, p. 71).

Again, this category took two major forms – unnatural and natural. 'Significant unnatural disturbance' was deemed to have taken place where a wildfire had significantly damaged the growth stage or canopy of a forest. 'Significant natural disturbance' was said to have occurred where such damage was due to either '[c]learfell logging, selective logging, agricultural clearing, grazing, mining or pathogens' (Woodgate et al., 1994, p. 70). Written records of such events were needed in order for such disturbances to be taken as 'authentic' or accurate. Under this definition, forest that had been clearfelled would be categorised as having being exposed to a significant unnatural disturbance).

For foresters and conservationists alike, the critical issue to be discerned in light of the above was how the disturbance history associated with each EVC overlapped with, or related to, the category 'old-growth forest'. This last type of forest had, after all, been steadily touted by green groups as the forest most critical to the long-term maintenance of biodiversity. In fact, the guiding thought throughout and subsequent to the 1980s was that the successful mapping of the location and extent of old-growth forest across East Gippsland (and indeed Victoria and Australia generally) would help put an end to disputes over forested terrains. Saving the remaining 'remnants' of old-growth forest from the chainsaw – from clearfelling regimes – was believed to be the equivalent of securing the future of forests at large. For it was *this* kind of forest *and no other* that held the highest aesthetic, archaeological and scientific/biological significance. But as shall become apparent, the focus on old-growth forest to the exclusion of other categories was to develop into a major tactical error in the fight to preserve East Gippland's biodiversity.

Noting the numerous definitions of old-growth forest that had been used throughout Australia, and the fact that such forests had been variously referred to as 'overmature', 'senescing', and 'ecologically mature' (Woodgate et al., 1994, p. 60), the authors of the 1994 report decided on the following definition of old-growth forest,

> Old-growth forest is forest which contains significant amounts of its oldest growth stage in the upper stratum – usually senescing trees – and has been subjected to any disturbance, the effect of which is now negligible (Woodgate et al., 1994, p. 64).

To understand this definition it is necessary to understand what is meant by 'upper stratum', 'crown' and 'significant amounts'. The phrase 'upper stratum' refers to the upper-most portion of a forest stand or collection of trees. 'Crown' or 'crown cover' 'is the percentage of the site (or stand of forest) covered by the vertical projection of the periphery of the tree crowns in the upper stratum …' (Woodgate et al., 1994, p. 64). Crowns were deemed by the study to be either 'dominant', 'co-dominant' or 'subdominant' with each of these signalling a crown cover of '>50%, 30–50% and 11–50% respectively' (Woodgate et al., 1994, p. 64). As trees reach their oldest growth stage their crowns or upper most branches begin to die. The phrase 'significant amounts of its oldest growth stage in the upper stratum' therefore refers to forest stands which, when mapped or viewed from above, exhibit dead or dying crowns in the percentages just outlined. The study also stipulated that, as a proportion of the overall crown cover, the presence of more than 10% regrowth would disqualify a given area of EVC being deemed 'old-growth'. In other words, if the area under scrutiny was 1000 hectares of EVC 21 (Shrubby Dry Forest), and 200 hectares of this was newly forming forest, it would not receive old-growth status.

Subsequent to the invocation of the above definitions and thresholds, ~~Goolengook~~ again underwent a substantial discursive alteration. From 1994, it was designated as exhibiting 3484 hectares of old-growth forest, 4216 hectares of forest of negligible natural disturbance, and 1212 hectares of significantly disturbed forest (in this case, regrowth from clearfell logging). Under this scenario, ~~Goolengook~~ contained 1.6% of all old-growth forest and about 2% of all negligibly disturbed (natural and unnatural) forest in the FMA.

As hinted at above, the significance of these thresholds and this definition of old-growth forest for conservation and other management initiatives in East Gippsland cannot be overestimated. In effect, the definition proffered by Woodgate et al. brought the variable of *age* – as opposed to disturbance history – to the fore in mapping old-growth ecosystems. This was to have remarkable implications for those areas that could be subject to activities such as timber harvesting. The Comprehensive, Adequate and Representative (CAR) reserve system of conservation initiated by the Federal government in July 1995 had stipulated a 'sliding scale' of conservation thresholds for all EVCs and old-growth forest on public land throughout Australia (see *National Forest Conservation Reserves, Commonwealth Proposed Criteria: A Position Paper*, July 1995, p. 2). In the Victorian context, therefore, the definition of forest(s) had probably never been so pivotal as they were at the time of the Woodgate study.

1995 (July): site of Commonwealth intervention

Following the release of the *National Forest Policy Statement* in 1992, the Commonwealth government took a number of steps toward mitigating forest conflict. One such step was the design and publication of broad benchmarks for forest conservation across all States and Territories. This resulted, in July of 1995, with the publication of text by the Joint ANZECC-MCFFA National Forest Policy Statement Implementation Sub-committee (JANIS, 1995). The three main thresholds articulated by the Commonwealth were formulated around the three principles of *comprehensiveness*, *adequacy* and *representativeness*. This system became known as the CAR system of forest management/conservation. The three thresholds were given as follows,

> (i) a broad benchmark of 15% of the pre-1750 distribution of each forest community to be protected within the reserve system;
>
> (ii) retention in reserves of at least 60% of existing old growth, increasing up to 100% (where practicable) for rare old growth; and
>
> (iii) protection of 90%, or more wherever practicable, of areas of high quality wilderness that exceeds minimum size thresholds (Forests Taskforce, 1995: Executive Summary, section 8).

It should be noted that the JANIS sub-committee recommended that 10% (as opposed to 15%) of pre-1750 forest distribution be reserved. For the purposes of Victorian policy, the larger of the two figures was (eventually) chosen as that which should be adhered to. The CAR system would later be used as a means of forming a series of Regional Forest Agreements (RFAs) between the States and the Commonwealth. The signing of such agreements was necessary before logging could continue in places put aside by the States in an effort to meet Commonwealth conservation benchmarks (such places were given the name 'Deferred Forest Areas' (DFAs)). As a result of the Commonwealth's initiatives, ~~Goolengook~~ became part of the East Gippsland DFA. More specifically, part of ~~Goolengook~~ was ascribed the status of 'Special Protection Zone'. This zone – and others like it across the FMA – was earmarked as exhibiting characteristics capable of contributing to the satisfaction of Commonwealth conservation thresholds. If retained, timber harvesting would be excluded from such zones.

1995 (December): site of multiple forest management

In December of 1995, ten years after the release of the Victorian Timber Industry Strategy, the East Gippsland Forest Management Plan (FMP) came into effect. The conditions and terms of the Plan are to apply until 2006 'unless a substantial change of circumstances (such as a major wildfire) warrants a review before then (Department of Conservation and Natural Resources, 1995, p. 1). 'The Plan … draws heavily on the extensive biological data available for East Gippsland from pre-logging flora and fauna surveys, the timber resource information in HARIS, the survey of old-growth forest values, and the assessment of national estate values …' (Department of Conservation and Natural Resources, 1995, p. 3). One of the major features of the Plan was the rezoning of State forest into three distinct areas,

- The **Special Protection Zone (SPZ)** [which] will be managed for conservation, and timber harvesting will be excluded. It forms a network designed to complement conservation reserves.

- The **Special Management Zone (SMZ)** [which] will be managed to conserve specific features, while catering for timber production under certain conditions.

- The **General Management Zone (GMZ)** [which] will be managed for a range of uses, but timber production will have a high priority (Department of Conservation and Natural Resources, 1995, p. 8).

This text invoked the number 839 to refer to ~~Goolengook~~. Appendix B of the Plan gives an annotated version of the zoning scheme for each block in the FMA by block name and site number. 'Goolengook 839' reads as follows,

Forest Block & site no.	Zone	Area (hectares)	Attributes
839/01	SPZ	1222	Long-footed Potoroo; Sooty Owl; rich bird site; OG (Wet Forest and Damp Forest); *Cyathea cunninghamii*; part RFSOS (72 Little Goolengook – national); includes part SOS 4
839/02	SPZ	44	Linear reserve (Goolengook River tributary); *Cyathea cunninghamii*; *Cyathea X marcescens* (3 records); RFSOS (73 Upper Goolengook – State); includes part SOS 2
839/03	SMS	20	*Cyathea cunninghamii*; *Cyathea X marcescens*; part RFSOS (73 Upper Goolengook – State); includes part SOS 2
839/04	SMZ	615	Powerful Owl; Sooty Owl; rich bird site; includes most of SOS 6
839/05	SPZ	44	Lowland Sclerophyll Forest (northern edge of range); includes part SOS 4
839/06	SPZ	96	Linear reserve; RFSOS (72 Little Goolengook River – national); includes part SOS 3
839/07	SPZ	259	Heritage River (Goolengook River upstream of Arte River) – 100 m buffers both sides
839/08	SPZ	67	Linear reserve; *Cyathea cunninghamii*; includes part SOS 2; Freddy Ck; no roading through linear reserve.

In terms of differentiating the activities which could occur within them, these zones, when combined with the General Management Zones, represented the highest level of segmentation to date. Once again, the body of ~~Goolengook~~ was transformed. Of the 4070 hectares of biological sites of significance in State forest recommended for protection, 2367 hectares (58%) were so protected (although none of these were given legal reservation status until 1998). Given the fact that portions of SMZ 839/04 could be harvested for timber under certain conditions, the Plan converted around 2000 hectares of State forest recommended for protection in 1991 into part of the GMZ. These segmentations, like all previous segmentations of ~~Goolengook~~, have real concrete effects on what can take place at any given moment. The best illustration of this occurred with the designation of 100-metre buffer zones at 839/07. This seemingly simple event was to have remarkable implications for the way the area would be viewed in future times (more on this below, see especially, critique under the heading 'site subject to Supreme Court decision').

Like all texts, the EG FMP is in large part a product of the stratifications emanating from other textual machines. As previously stated, the Commonwealth's CAR system presents as an important text in this regard (JANIS, 1995). Indeed it could be said that the thresholds contained within the CAR system functioned (and continue to function) as an abstract machine of overcoding. It is a text which brought, firstly, a massive deterritorialisation of bodies (that is an implosion of present conservation units and proportions), and secondly, an equally extensive *re*territorialisation (that is a new alignment of industrial zones and conservation zones). In more specific terms, the CAR system required all States and Territories to conserve each EVC (or their equivalent) according to a sliding scale based on rarity and/or disturbance history. In the EG FMP, details of this scale were given for EVCs generally and for the old-growth component of each EVC specifically. In relation to the former it was decided that,

> The following proportion of each EVC will be included in the SPZ and conservation reserves:
>
> - 30% of EVCs that occupy more than 1% of the FMA (approximately 10,000 hectares).
> - Between 30 and 90% of EVCs that occupy between 0.1% (approximately 1000 hectares) and 1% of the FMA, depending on the extent of the particular EVC.
> - 90% of EVCs that occupy less than 0.1% of the FMA.
>
> Selection of areas to meet these targets will be guided by the following principles,
>
> - Where feasible, approximately 1000 hectares of the larger EVCs should be protected in each geographic representation unit.

- Chosen areas should be practical management units, normally not less that 100 hectares, and defined by natural boundaries such as stream or ridge lines, or management boundaries such as roads.
- [...] (Department of Conservation and Natural Resources, 1995, p. 14).

The implications of these thresholds for biodiversity are substantial. In terms of the four most 'common' EVCs in the EG FMA – Lowland Forest (245,107 hectares), Damp Forest (238,293 hectares), Shrubby Dry Forest (209,978 hectares) and Wet Forest (90,287 hectares) – their level of formal protection was set at 39%, 44%, 53% and 46% respectively. In other words, these four 'common' EVCs spanned 75% of the total EVC coverage in the EG FMA and yet only around 45% of their gross area was protected. This is chiefly because when viewed at the FMA level they constitute far more than 1% of its area. There are very serious issues here to do with the relationship between notions of 'rarity' and the *scale* used to judge such a notion. Clearly, the EVC of Damp Forest is relatively common across the EG FMA. But in terms of the area enveloped by the state of Victoria, such forest is comparatively rare. Nationally, it is rarer still. Internationally, it is on the verge of being permanently exhausted. What is common, therefore, is, firstly, the habit of conceiving 'nature' in terms of discrete units, and, secondly, of writing these units as exhibiting an absolute – as opposed to an always already *relative* – abundance. Ecologically speaking, bodies believed to be common are always already part of an infinite dissembling of flows, speeds and intensities.

In terms of old-growth forest, the Commonwealth required that a minimum of 60% of such forest in each EVC be permanently conserved. This percentage increased to 100% for those EVCs with minimal remnants of old-growth. As a result of the determinations made by the Woodgate report, 26 of the 44 EVCs across the EG FMA were deemed to exhibit old-growth forest. Within the total EG FMA there were 5 EVCs whose old-growth characteristics were given full protection due to their comparatively small range and distribution. The remainder of old-growth forests (spread across 21 EVCs) were given a minimum of 60% protection. It is here that the categories of 'forest histories' developed by Woodgate et al. (1994) come to the fore. The EG FMP relied very heavily on such categories since they left open the possibility of accessing East Gippsland's ancient forests for timber and pulp. The absolutely critical distinction drawn in the Woodgate text was that dividing 'old-growth' forest from 'negligibly disturbed' forest. As mentioned above, for a forest to qualify as 'old growth' it must have 'significant amounts of its oldest growth stage in the upper stratum' (Woodgate et al., 1994, p. 64). The crucial question, though, is this: What does 'significant' mean? The answer to this question is – curiously enough – not stated alongside the actual definition of old growth, but is instead buried in the main text of the report. The relevant passage reads,

> It is considered that the senescing growth stage becomes a significant influence on the ecological process of the [forest] stand (for example growth of younger trees, development of hollows, nutrient cycling) when present in at least subdominant crown

> cover proportions, that is, approximately half the area of dominant or co-dominant growth stage(s) (Woodgate et al., 1994, p. 61).

With the possible exception of the introduction of the chainsaw and the articulated trailer, this threshold presents as one of the most important moments in the history/histories of the forests of East Gippsland. What this threshold meant, in effect, was that forests which exhibited little or no serious disturbance history (and may well have trees up to 150 years of age) but which at the same time did not – on account of their 'younger' age – exhibit a predominantly senescing or dying crown, would be exempt from inclusion in the category 'old growth'. And why was the exclusion of such forest so important to forest administrators? Answer: Because the Commonwealth required that a minimum of 60% of old-growth forest in each EVC be permanently excluded from logging and indeed any other intensive industrial style activities. As a result of the Woodgate text, over a quarter of the FMA was assigned the status of negligibly disturbed forest when – but for the sake of crown chronology – it could just as easily have been brought under the rubric of old-growth. The final figures (derived directly from Woodgate et al., 1994) for the distribution of forests across the EG FMA are as follows,

Old Growth Forest	224,657 hectares
Negligibly Disturbed	285,404 hectares
Other	541,039 hectares
Total	1,051,100 hectares

Adhering to the Commonwealth's requirements meant that at least 60% of the 224,657 hectares of old-growth forest needed to be reserved from logging. This puts the figure somewhere in the vicinity of 130,000 hectares (and indeed the figure presently reserved is slightly higher than this). However, if the forest identified as negligibly disturbed were categorised as old-growth (for such forest would, with the passage of time, develop *all* of the old-growth characteristics identified by Woodgate) this would result in a very different equation. Specifically, it would mean that at least 60% of 510,061 hectares (as opposed to 60% of 224,657 hectares) would need to be permanently reserved from logging. This would put the relevant figure somewhere in excess of 300,000 hectares – a marked and exponential increase on that which currently pertains. But this did not occur. And the chief reason it did not occur was/is that crown chronology and appearance were given privileged status over and above disturbance history. More critically, the present (the actual) was privileged over the future or the *yet-to-come* (the virtual). Another way of saying this is that the only thing separating negligibly disturbed forest from old-growth forest is *the passage of time*. The Woodgate report and the EG FMP literally called a halt to a particular kind of becoming: namely, a *becoming-old-growth*. The effect of this interruption upon aspects of ~~Goolengook~~ was dramatic to say the least. In essence, the lexical division between old-growth and negligibly disturbed forest meant that the 7500 hectares of overmature forest that existed within ~~Goolengook~~ just two years previously was discursively effaced to just 3000 hectares. This effacement and those like it across the FMA would enable forest administrators to declare that the majority of timbers extracted from places like ~~Goolengook~~ were something other than old-growth. What better way to quell conflict over the clearfelling of ancient forests than to invent a system of categorisation that calls them by another name? On this basis, the EG FMP needs to be regarded as a text that governs access to 'nature' via a series of carefully planned discursive manoeuvres and rhetorical devices.

The division between old-growth and negligibly disturbed had implications not just for ~~Goolengook~~ but for the region of which it formed a part – the EG FMA. Accordingly, another critical aspect associated with the EG FMP was the inception of 'Representative Conservation' and, more particularly, the marking out of areas known as *geographic representation units* (GRUs). The 'official' purpose of these units was to ensure that 'representative' samples of forest/vegetation were left intact within ascribed zones. Such units were, and indeed 'are based on similar land form, geology, vegetation and climate. Their boundaries generally follow topographic features such as streams and ridges, and also conform to those of forest management blocks, or compartments where blocks are subdivided' (Department of Conservation and Natural Resources, 1995, p. 13). In all, 'Eleven […] [GRUs] have […] been identified that reflect the scale of landscape change across East Gippsland' (Department of Conservation and Natural Resources, 1995, p. 13).

The name given to the unit of which ~~Goolengook~~ formed a part was 'Brodribb Foothills', also known as GRU 6. In statistical terms this unit contained 18% (40,230 hectares) of all old-growth forest and 26% (74,515 hectares) of all negligibly disturbed forest in the FMA. It also contained 25% (58,665 hectares) and 35% (31,560 hectares) of, respectively, all Damp and Wet forest in the FMA. These last figures are significant because the timbers from such forests are the most highly sought after. The trees are typically much taller than 40 metres and they yield a higher proportion of usable timber per log than logs extracted from other ecological vegetation classes (for example Shrubby Dry Forest). One of the major problems, of course, is that Damp and Wet forests are also some of the most biologically diverse and aesthetically appealing forests in Victoria (not to mention the world over). An important effect of introducing GRUs was that debates about conservation and resource use could be conducted at a completely new level than had previously been the case. What mattered now was not simply the proportion of forest conserved in each unit (or indeed in each forest block). Instead what now mattered was the *total conservation threshold* yielded by the combination of all eleven units. Indeed, the introduction of the GRU as a so-called management unit also heralded at one and the same time its irrelevance to issues of resource management. For all intents and purposes, it was (and is) as if each GRU never existed. Indeed, the FMP states,

> Specific representation targets were not established at the GRU scale because the distribution of certain EVCs in some units comprises scattered, fragmented or disturbed stands that do not lend themselves to creation of practical or meaningful components of the SPZ. Moreover, some EVCs were well represented in national parks in immediately adjacent units (Department of Conservation and Natural Resources, 1995, p. 15).

Given this state of affairs, and as of December 1995, the most important unit for forest management and conservation was no longer the block, the compartment, the stand, or the coupe. Instead it was the much larger unit of the FMA. For well over a century, the units for forest management had been getting smaller and smaller. But now, at the conclusion of 1995, an entirely different direction was assumed – a direction that would, ironically, allow vast areas of forest to be logged within each GRU on the proviso that the remaining forest scattered across the FMA conformed to the thresholds of EVC conservation set by the Commonwealth. In this sense, the importance of GRUs to the conservation and management of East Gippsland's forests is thoroughly undermined.

The absence of specific thresholds within each GRU meant, amongst other things, that a considerably small proportion of each EVC could be preserved in one GRU so long as other units brought the total conservation level to the targets articulated by the Commonwealth government. This meant, for instance, that only 52% (n=19,330 hectares) of old growth forest within GRU 6 was formally protected from logging (that is is within national parks or special protection zones). Such a figure is well short of the Commonwealth threshold of 60%. But in the context of the EG FMP, such shortfalls are viewed as 'unproblematic'. And why? Because the EVCs exhibited by the national parks and special protection zones throughout the FMA have been deemed to *sufficiently represent* old-growth. It is interesting to note, therefore, the claim that 'The Plan provides representative conservation of vegetation communities and significant flora and fauna *within each GRU* and therefore across the region [that is East Gippsland]' (Department of Conservation and Natural Resources, 1995, p. 13, emphases added).

With the advent of this text, the relationship between, on the one hand, *the total composition of GRUs*, and on the other, the total composition of national parks and special protection zones becomes, in effect, the central tool for decisions about land management. In other terms, what the EG FMP ensures is the privileging of the *composition* of a particular type of forest over and above its *distribution* and/or *location* across the earth (FMA). In the abscence of specific targets for each GRU, it is, for example, possible for old-growth Damp Forest to be confined to small areas within one or two GRUs instead of being allowed to flourish across multiple areas of the FMA. This decision has major consequences in terms of biodiversity management. Forests – EVCs, bodies of trees – quite literally move over time in accordance with weather patterns and climatic variations. They undergo significant alterations in their latitudes and longitudes – and such alterations can occur within decades. Accordingly, a management plan which sanctions the confining of old-growth forests to just one or two main areas runs the serious risk of major botanical and biological extinctions.

Viewed rhetorically, the relationship between, one the one hand, the EG FMA, and on the other, permanent conservation zones, is one of *synecdochal* dimensions. The 'quality' of forest conservation across the FMA is viewed in terms of the composition and size of particular parts (that is national parks and special protection zones) with the associated idea that everything occurring 'outside' these areas must to a large degree be expendable. Appendix F is headed 'Management of Ecological Vegetation Classes' (Department of Conservation and Natural Resources, 1995) and gives some idea of what can and cannot occur in respect of each EVC. Since ~~Goolengook~~ is composed of in excess of 80% Damp and Wet Forest, it is instructive to know how each of these are spoken of,

> *Damp Forest (EVC no. 29)* This tall open forest is widespread in the FMA, occupying gullies and sheltered slopes in the lowlands and foothills, expanding into more exposed situations in areas with higher elevation and rainfall ... Damp Forest is well *represented* in all major parks but not in the foothill units (which include few park areas) or on the Errinundra Tablelands. Old-growth forest is also under *represented*. Additional areas have therefore been placed in the SPZ, including old-growth and negligibly disturbed forest ... (Department of Conservation and Natural Resources, 1995, p. 112, emphases added).

> *Wet Forest (EVC no. 30)* is perhaps the best known tall forest of the region, valued for its old-growth forest characteristics, aesthetic qualities and high timber-producing capacity. ... The creation of Errinundra National Park and the Rodger extension to the Snowy River National Park in the late 1980s placed substantial areas of Wet Forest in the park system. Wet forest is less well *represented* in the Cann Foothills and west of the Snowy River, and old-growth forest is also under *represented*. Additional areas have therefore been placed in the SPZ, including old-growth forest [...] in the Goolengook River headwaters (839/1) ... (Department of Conservation and Natural Resources, 1995, p. 113, emphases added).

These passages further cement the discourse of *sufficient representation*, that is, a representation that portends to be entirely adequate to its task (that is the task of 'balancing' levels of timber harvesting and levels of biodiversity). But the surety and adequacy of such a discourse is founded on a very problematic concept of ecological sustainability. For the underlying idea is that 'good' conservation is about the management of a few privileged parts capable of standing for the complexity and variations (in hydrological flows, geological formations, altitude, age of vegetation, rate of growth and decay) of 'the whole'. And here arises a further problem. The adequacy (or so-called 'scientific validity') of the conservation targets and thresholds for the combined GRUs is dependent on the ontological primacy and legitimacy of the concept of 'wholeness'. The EG FMP is replete with synecdochal and other rhetorical manoeuvres which allow it the guise of being representative (when in fact, beyond such a guise, pass multiplicity upon multiplicity sacrificed to a questionable imposition of categories and thresholds). Without such manoeuvres the resource management strategies extant in this text would be shown to have a completely arbitrary basis as opposed to appearing to possess an *a priori* validity.

1996 (July): site of resource inventory

In July 1996, the Commonwealth government published a series of reports for the East Gippsland area as part of the Comprehensive Regional Assessment (CRA) process. Of particular interest here are the maps which accompany the *Resources and Economics Report* (Commonwealth and Victorian Regional Forest Agreement Steering Committee, 1996). For it is these which enunciate ~~Goolengook~~ in strictly molarised terms. Map 2 indicates 'current sawlog resources (excluding regrowth forest)' for each forest block across the FMA.[7] With respect to ~~Goolengook~~ FMB, seven of the nine compartments devoted to timber production are deemed 'high yielding forests' – meaning that if harvested they would yield between 5001 and 15,000 cubic metres of sawlogs at a rate of at least 50 cubic metres per hectare. Map 5 shows the projected amount of sawlog material available once logged areas again reach 'maturity'. What is interesting here – indeed one might say, what is decidedly monstrous – is that the majority of compartments of ~~Goolengook~~ FMB will each be fashioned in such a way as to yield at least 25,000 cubic metres of sawlogs at a minimum rate of 200 cubic metres per hectare. At least one compartment is expected to yield in excess of 70,000 cubic metres of sawlogs at this latter rate. Overall, forests once deemed 'medium yielding' will be transformed into 'high yielding' areas. The effect of these texts is to place ~~Goolengook~~ (and those areas surrounding it) on a hyper-industrial trajectory – a trajectory which proceeds by way of expected returns (both current and future) and the capacity to measure and quantify Nature according to a single attribute. Here, ~~Goolengook~~ is divided into its constituent economic parts, as if its body automatically and naturally had residing within it the ma(r)kings of such divisions. In these texts there are no becomings, only machines which (would) make of ~~Goolengook~~ a series of productive units.

1996 (October): site of national park management strategy

On the face of it, the inception of the Errinundra National Park Management Strategy would appear to be an incredibly important step in securing the long-term viability of the biodiversity of the EG FMA. After all, the park 'conserves one of the most significant wet forest areas in south-eastern mainland Australia, including old-growth forest, rainforest, a rich arboreal fauna and undisturbed catchments' (Victoria National Parks Service, 1996, p. v). However, despite its size (25,600 hectares) and the diversity of its terrains, this text contributes to the fragmentation of ~~Goolengook~~ and like bodies. And it does this because the urge to preserve aspects of the Errinundra Plateau involves constructing a part of the earth precisely as if it was a 'part', instead of a flow which exceeds the boundaries (roads, contour lines) ascribed by administrators (foresters, scientists, conservationists, law makers, and so on). This is not to say that having a portion of ~~Goolengook~~ and the Errinundra Plateau declared a national park is less preferable to having such areas clearfelled or intensively mined. But it is to assert that the declaration of an area as a national park is a highly problematic moment in terms of ongoing perceptions of what is, and what is not, an adequate strategy for fostering biodiversity over the longer term and over the greatest possible scale. The survival of the wet forests of Errinundra National

7 In effect, this map gives a visual basis to the information contained in the 1993 HARIS text previously cited.

Park is inextricably tied to processes and events taking place 'beyond' its borders. To put it very succinctly, forests 'within' the park do not cease at its borders. They depend on the floristic, aquatic and faunal composition of immediately adjacent areas for their ongoing vitality. And yet clearfelling can – and does – take place right up to the edge of park boundaries (indeed this was to occur in relation to ~~Goolengook~~ in 1999). The full effects of this on surrounding forest are unknown. Also unknown is the moment at which it becomes safe to talk in terms of an 'adequately protected area'. A park of nearly 26,000 hectares sounds quite large but nobody knows if this is a large enough area to sustain all the processes 'within' the park over the longer term. What is known is that this area would only sustain a dozen pairs of Powerful Owls and perhaps only contain several pairs of Spot-tailed Quolls (listed, respectively, as rare and vulnerable under the *Flora and Fauna Guarantee Act* 1988). It should also be borne in mind that the area spanned by Errinundra National Park is well under 3% of the total forested area within the EG FMA.

1996 (November): site subject to revised code of forest practices

In November of 1996 the revised Code of Forest Practices for Timber Production was released and implemented by the Department of Natural Resources and Environment. The significance of this text for ~~Goolengook~~ resides in what it does *not* do much as with what it achieves. Firstly, it fails to place ecological values and processes ahead of the need for 'continuous' timber production. The stated 'Purpose of the Code' is to,

> a) promote[ ] an internationally competitive forest industry;
> b) [be] compatible with the conservation of the wide range of environmental values associated with the forests; and
> c) promote[ ] the ecologically sustainable management of native forests proposed for continuous timber production (Department of Natural Resources and Environment, 1996, p. 2).

From this it is clear that environmental values are taken into account only where the requirements for being 'competitive' have been satisfied. On a second count, the code contains no information about penalties for non-compliance nor does it communicate the various means and levels of enforcement. This is none-too-surprising given that the text is based around the discourse of the 'goal', the 'guideline' and the 'prescription' (see Department of Natural Resources and Environment, 1996, p. 3). More accurately it is predominantly a rhetoric of 'wherever possible' that takes precedence over 'without exception'. It is a code that draws a sharp distinction between forest used for timber production and that permanently devoted to conservation – indeed its 'prescriptions' only apply to the former. As such, it is a text that continues to treat the aspects of ~~Goolengook~~ which lie 'outside' Errinundra National Park as qualitatively distinct from those which lie within it. And of course, such areas are, in a sense, distinct. But this distinction is one founded only on an *enacted location* and not upon the differences of biotic and aquatic intensities. In short, this is a code which functions more in the vein of an *axiom* since it maintains strict divisions between bodies that differ only according to what they can (now) be used for (paper, furniture, a nesting site, a carbon sink), and not what they might otherwise become.

1996 (December): site of logging reprieve

On December 24, 1996 a letter was drafted by a staff member of the Department of Natural Resources and Environment which confirmed for persons at Environment Victoria and other environmental organisations that there would be no logging in ~~Goolengook~~ in January or February of 1997 which, as the document notes, is consistent with 'the commitment to not harvest before the signature of the East Gippsland RFA'.

1997 (January): site of protester base camp

The Victorian branch of Friends of the Earth (FoE) have, with the help of Goongerah Environment Centre (GECO) and Concerned Residents of East Gippsland (CROEG) been long time campaigners against the logging of native forest. With the probability of logging beginning (resuming) at ~~Goolengook~~ in the coming months, FoE mounted a sustained campaign of resistance against such activities. An A4 Spirax notebook detailing the situation in ~~Goolengook~~ forest block was kept at the head office of FoE at Smith Street, Collingwood, Victoria. The cover of the notebook read 'EG Blockades Book: Goolengook Base Camp'. Someone had scrawled the phrase 'fuck the Dominant Paradigms' and placed the anarchist icon below it. Another had written 'No political bullshit. Thanks' down the left side of the cover. The Minister for Conservation and the Environment's phone number (Marie Tehan) was also present. Amongst other things, the first page of the book reads, 'There is currently a base camp, which will turn into a blockade if there are attempts to log the area. The base camp needs people! You need to take food, be prepared to camp out, & take whatever camping gear you might need'. At this stage, base camp was located just outside of ~~Goolengook~~ block. What is most interesting here is the use of the phrase 'base camp'. It is a phrase that had been used more than a century earlier by Spencer, Merrall and others whilst recording their journeys through the region. But whereas such persons left camp to gather various specimens or possibly discover new ones in order to then relocate to the city, the protesters' goal would be to remain at camp indefinitely. Supplies – including food, clothing, radios, materials for hindering logging machinery – would be brought to them. The modern base camp was the point of reterritorialisation not the point of dissipation. As of January 6 there were 25 persons at base camp. An entry from January 7 reported that 'someone cut a hole in the engine block [of a bulldozer] with an oxy torch!!' but that 'no one is jumping up & down about greenies having done it'. As if to pre-empt a bad situation, someone else added the words 'as yet' to this entry. January 13 brought with it the first arrest. The week of January 16 was reportedly uneventful – 'no actions this week – too wet!!!'. A note dated January 23 reads, 'The Goolengook campsite has a presence of up to 20 people working on scouting missions and fortifications at the camp site. Media is believed to be arriving on Wednesday'.

1997 (February): site subject to regional forest agreement

On February 3 1997 the Commonwealth and Victorian Governments signed the Regional Forest Agreement for East Gippsland. This had two major implications for ~~Goolengook~~. First, the agreement signalled the intent to create the ~~Goolengook~~ Flora and Fauna reserve. Second, it was (and remains) a text which sets in place for the next 20 years a particular series of thresholds governing conservation and resource use. With the stroke of a pen it cemented the benchmarks articulated by the Commonwealth in July 1995. This agreement was a victory for the science machine and its quantification of the type and extent of forest necessary to reserve to avoid an ecological collapse. ~~Goolengook~~ and, by default, the EG FMA became at such time a body divided by molar estimates, a binary body pulled in two completely different directions by the forces of excess (expendability) and rarity (preservation).

1997 (March): site of police presence

An entry from the FoE log book dated March 3 reads, 'IMPORTANT: The Goolengook camp was visited yesterday by head cop Rod Right, an unknown cop and head of DNRE Gary Featherstone. The[y] expressed their concerne [sic.] about vandalism to the road and had an issue with some spikes. It is my belief that they will probably try to bust the camp in the coming week or possibly sooner'.

1997 (April): site of arrests (round 1)

An entry from the FoE log book for April 7 indicates that two more people were arrested for locking on to a bulldozer. A note from April 10 says that 'feelings are pretty low with colds & flu. Spoke to Nick who felt that police implied that they would bust camp next week'. Communication from April 17 reads, '6 people in court – approx 15 at G'gook'. The entry for April 28 tells of declining numbers of protesters – 'apparently there are only 2 people @ base camp. Some problems in main radio link between G'gook and GECO – the radio link is not regular & this is increasing the sense of isolation'.

1997 (May): site earmarked for timber harvesting

On May 30, 1997 a form detailing a prospective forest coupe plan within ~~Goolengook~~ was completed by the relevant supervisor for the Orbost district. It showed that a gross area of 32 hectares of 'forest mixed species' located in block 839 compartment number 513/10 was 'due' for logging any time from June 4 of the said year. In all, 3072 cubic metres of sawlog material was earmarked for removal. This is less than 10% of the total weight of the wooded materials (trees) across the 32 hectares. And, moreover, in the process of extracting this small percentage every tree in the coupe would be felled (as would all undergrowth and 'extraneous' or non-productive' vegetation). The only trees to be left standing were those which the then Department of Conservation and Environment (DCE) believed were important for 'habitat protection'. Here, the instruction to the logging team leader was to leave '5 trees per 15 hectares'. Conservatively speaking, one hectare of forest mixed species contains around 100 mature eucalypts – amounting to around 1500 trees over 15 hectares. On this basis, the DCE's environmental protection regime requires that less than one tenth of 1% of such trees be reserved from logging programmes. Such a threshold necessarily entails the death of countless mammals, birds and insects alike, since the competition for remaining trees is, to say the least, overly fierce. One might ask how the process of *destroying* nearly every last vestige of habitat could ever sit consistently alongside the idea that such a process could also involve habitat *protection*. The fact that the timbers extracted from such areas are often used to provide a 'habitat' (that is in the form of scantling for houses) for a very different species (that is 'man') is something that will be discussed in the following chapter in the context of surveying matters of scale, speed and proximity. All that need be noted here is that this text is instrumental in effecting the corporeal effacement of ~~Goolengook~~ and its associated flows and intensities.

One further aspect to note about this text is the requirements relating to 'stream quality and water protection'. Here, the District Supervisor has stipulated that there be,

> 100m buffer on the goolengook [sic.]. 20 m buffers on permanent streams and 10m filter on non-permanent streams.

This instruction, perhaps more than any other, would see ~~Goolengook~~ and its associated bodies become part of the largest forest protest in Australian history. It would also ensure ~~Goolengook~~ a place in the annals of the Supreme Court of Victoria.

1997 (June): site of 'scientific lament'

On June 9, 1997 – five days after logging resumes in ~~Goolengook~~ forest block – a letter to the editor appeared in *The Age*.[8] It was signed by three of the authors of the ~~Goolengook~~ pre-logging survey which had recommended against any logging activity in the block. The text read as follows,

> CONSERVATION MUST BRIDGE THE GAPS
>
> Yes, Jill Redwood (5/6), the state of the environment in Victoria is poor indeed (on World Environment day and every other day) as Marie Tehan's environment department begins logging Goolengook, one of East Gippsland's most wonderful forests. As scientists once employed by the conservation department to survey the Goolengook area, we are appalled at the prospect of logging in this unique area. Goolengook Forest Block was studied in a series of departmental 'pre-logging surveys'. Its biological values were immense, exceeding those of virtually all other forests studied during the program: endangered plants, birds, mammals, a unique rainforest community, all within a closed and largely undisturbed catchment. Our 1991 report concluded: 'the combined flora and fauna values of the study area are exemplary' and 'the combination of particular significant biological values ... are not known from any reserve system in south-eastern Australia'. The area is listed under the National Estate and as a Nationally Significant Rainforest Site. Clearly, the entire Goolengook area should be added to the Errinundra National Park. Instead, Marie Tehan has allowed logging, and 'saved' just small, disjointed areas, protected by narrow buffers of dubious merit. To suggest that the Goolengook forest can be conserved by saving a bit of this and a bit of that is akin to suggesting that we can preserve the Sydney Harbour Bridge by saving just one of all the different types of bolts, a few pylons and a representative truss.
>
> Dr Ian Lunt, Dr Doug Robinson and Bertram Lobert

This remarkable text clearly points to the highly contested nature of ~~Goolengook~~ at this time. But what is more remarkable is the way in which politics chooses or draws a particular type of scientific machine – in this case, one which sanctions the juxtaposition of bodies demanded by governments over and above those made possible by ecological limits.

1997 (June): site of arrests (round 2)

The frequency of arrests reached something of a zenith in June. Ironically, logging started in earnest on June 5 – World Environment Day. The FoE log book shows that 12 persons were arrested on June 9 and a further four on June 11. The entry here reads, '4 people arrested this morning. People are in tree-sits and are prepared to stick it out even though clearfelling is going on all around them. 5 people are in the coup [sic.] and logging is going on while they are there. We need *no's* out there

---

8 Melbourne's/Victoria's major daily broadsheet newspaper.

in coup [sic.] and people to call DNRE Melb & Orbost stating how unacceptable this is'. The entry for Friday June 13 told of yet more arrests – one of whom was a federal member of parliament. The entry here ran, 'Forest. Bob Brown arrested. 10 More arrested. Very far from the truth of being saved. Maintain pressure until at least Next week. GECO – Noops'. On June 14, 1997, the front page of Melbourne's premier newspaper *The Age* carried the headline 'Greens leader arrested at protest'. It displayed a picture of Senator Bob Brown of the Australian Greens sitting in the back of a police wagon with one of 14 other protesters arrested on the same day. The charge was one of 'obstructing the lawful carrying out of forest operations' as listed under s.95A(1)(b) of the *Conservation Forests and Lands Act* 1987. This was by no means the first series of arrests at ~~Goolengook~~ (indeed 38 persons were taken into custody over preceding days) but it was, in many ways, the most prominent. The arrest of Senator Brown brought with it the media machine (newspaper, TV, radio, internet) and associated deterritorialisations ('RFA is a sham') and reterritorialisations (the 'smug' Senator who has 'play[ed] a cruel joke on working people who face losing their jobs'). Further arrests occurred over following days with a note from the logbook of FoE for June 16 reading, 'cops came before dawn, greenies stopped work until 1 pm; 10 arrests today, Bob Humphries was there [owner of a number of local sawmills]; some dodgy things – mud in the bulldozer, glass in the cement for the lock ons'. Four more arrests took place on June 20, 18 arrests on June 23, and four more on June 25. Over the next three years and beyond, ~~Goolengook~~ would feature in various media circles, sometimes as a site of destruction and sometimes a site of responsible management, but always as a site subject to contestation by the molar body of the conservationist as against that of the forester.

1997 (July): site of public relations exercise

On July 1 the Department of Natural Resources and Environment distributed a media release designed to quell fears that ~~Goolengook~~ and like areas were being unsustainably harvested. The Manager of the Forest Management Branch remarked, 'Fifty per cent of the entire region [that is that encompassed by the EG FMA] is within the National Reserve System, endorsed through the East Gippsland Forest Agreement which ensures a world-class reserve system has been established for East Gippsland'. Again, the rhetoric of correct and 'scientifically' derived benchmarks for conservation is present – as if one could, in the first instance know and mark out 'half' a forest, and in the second judge that this is sufficient for the replication of the diversity spawned by thousands of years of ecological becomings. But of more serious concern is the five page text which accompanied the press release – a text designed specifically to placate anyone who had concerns over logging in East Gippsland. Amongst other things it shows that of the 224,000 hectares of old-growth forest in the EG FMA, 14% or 28,555 hectares is 'available for timber production'. Within ~~Goolengook~~ forest block, the text indicates that 722 hectares out of a possible 3484 hectares of old-growth forest is open to logging (read clearfelling) (Department of Natural Resources and Environment, 1997b, p. 1). It is further noted that 'While this forest has high scenic quality, extensive areas of similar forest are represented in nearby Errinundra National Park and adjacent areas of Special Protection Zone, and the new Goolengook flora and fauna reserve' (Department of Natural Resources and Environment, 1997b, p. 2). Once again, particular areas 'within' ~~Goolengook~~ are constructed as expedient through rhetorical manoeuvring – primarily by way of metalepsis (that is a conflation of the general (National Parks) with the particular (vegetation within specific forest coupes)). Like the rationales given in previous years, location is privileged above composition. This is industry sustained not through a consideration of ecological relations and the juxtaposition of bodies, but through a belief that portions of the earth can be adequately represented and repeated by the forces traversing so-called 'like areas'.

There is another rhetorical device at work in this text and it is one that owes its prominence as much to the efforts of conservationists as forest planners and workers. On the face of it, the fact that only 8% of the old-growth forest in ~~Goolengook~~ block is open to logging looks to be a fair outcome for 'ecology'. But it should be noted that 'old-growth forest' is just one way of categorising the complexity of forces traversing terrains. Moreover it is a category which privileges the actual (being) over and above the potential (becoming). As previously mentioned, over one quarter of the forest in the EG FMA was deemed something 'less' than old-growth forest *only* on account of a lack of the visible signs of old-age within the upper most portions of particular stands of trees. This division, based solely on the privileging of *khronos* (time) over *formis* (form), exposed around 140,000 hectares of negligibly disturbed forest to timber harvesting – forest which in time would assume all the characteristics of the definition of old-growth articulated in the Woodgate text cited above. Within the present text, however, no mention is made of negligibly disturbed forest. Instead it speaks solely in terms of old-growth forest and 'other forest'. This is highly problematic given that the Department of Natural Resources and Environment's own scientists have said that at least half of ~~Goolengook~~ is constituted by forest of negligible disturbance. The effect of all this is that a substantial portion of ~~Goolengook~~ is discursively effaced from debates over what should and should not be the object of forestry debates. After years of fighting for the prominence of old-growth forest, the conservation movement(s) received in this text much of what they were looking for – namely, confirmation that most of the old-growth EVCs in ~~Goolengook~~ were safe from timber harvesting activities. And yet such a result could in no way be viewed as equivalent to saying that the ecological vitality of ~~Goolengook~~ had been ensured against irreparable damage. Indeed, nearly 1977 hectares of negligibly disturbed forest in ~~Goolengook~~ forest block is available for timber harvesting – almost three times the amount of old-growth forest available for the same purpose. It is probably fair to say that the incessant reterritorialisation of the conservation movement upon the category old-growth forest allowed equally significant areas to be given over to the chainsaw. These areas are, of course, old-growth forests by another name. Looking beyond ~~Goolengook~~ block, no less than 87% (196,993 hectares) of timber presently open to immediate harvesting within the EG FMA is constituted by negligibly disturbed forest. Comparatively speaking, old-growth forest – the forest lauded by holiday makers, conservation groups, and politicians – fares very well in terms of its conservation status with just 13% (28,555 hectares) of the currently harvestable resource constituted by such forest.[9]

1997 (July): site of arrests (round 3)

The FoE text reports 22 arrests were made for the month of July. As of July 12, the blockade had been running for 100 days.[10]

1997 (August): site of geological destruction/indigenous desecration

On August 4 forest workers used dynamite to blow apart a geological formation known as 'Egg Rocks'. Although sacred to the Bidwell people, such rocks were deemed by the Department of Natural Resources and Environment to be blocking the construction of a new logging track (for an example of such damage see Figure 4 on p. 191). On August 13, a Departmental official named Ian Miles remarked to a representative of FoE that they 'were not logging rainforest' and that 'there was nothing in the area [that is of Goolengook] that [could not] be found elsewhere'. Five arrests were reported as taking place in August. In total, 164 arrests were made between June 4 and October 4.

1997 (November): site of 'concluded' logging operations

A note in the FoE log book dated November 19 reads, 'Both contractors are finished. There is only one person at camp … People who are interested need to either help pack camp OR if there is energy we could move back on the road & set another blockade up. Remember there are more coupes & they will want to burn the ones they have logged. There's also the idea of moving back to regenerate the fucked-up mess'. Here the bodies of ~~Goolengook~~ receive a temporary reprieve from timber harvesting. ~~Goolengook~~ becomes, at such time, a body poised between two very different states of affairs – intensive industry and intensive ecology.

---

9 119,148 hectares of regrowth forest makes up the remaining forest within the net timber production area. Figures derived through cross-referencing statistics provided at Department of Conservation and Natural Resources (1995, p. 8), Commonwealth and Victorian Regional Forest Agreement (RFA) Steering Committee (1996, p. 23 and p. 25) and Department of Natural Resources and Environment (1997b, p. 1).

10 ~~Goolengook~~ was mentioned on pages 1 and 6 of *The Age*, July 21, 1997.

1997 (December): site of police publicity

The December issue of *Police Life: The Victorian Police Magazine* featured an article about the role of police in mitigating between 'greenies' and 'loggers'. The story is headed 'Peacekeepers in a war of tactics' with the by-line reading, 'when the greenies and the loggers are "at war" at ~~Goolengook~~, police from Orbost make a four-hour round trip along dirt roads, often twice a day, to restore peace' (Miller, 1997, p. 11). Several things can be noted about this line. First, the use of the word 'war' portrays the idea of their being opponents who inhabit entirely different universes. Loggers could have nothing in common with greenies because they are diametrically opposed to their cause just as greenies could never hope to have anything in common with loggers because they are striving for entirely different outcomes. The fact that both groups (which are, in any case, many groups) inhale the oxygen and drink the water made possible by ~~Goolengook~~ and like places is not mentioned. Secondly, the deployment of the word 'peace' serves an important rhetorical and political function. Police restore peace. And they do so, as Acting Senior Sergeant Terry Bradford remarks, by 'removing the greenies from their devices [so] there'll be no dramas'. Here, the notion is that peace is what occurs when loggers are allowed to 'go about their legal business' (Miller, 1997, p. 12). Clearly this is an overtly anthropocentric rendering of the term. For one might ask how much 'peace' there is for streams undergoing sedimentation and eutrophication as a result of soil erosion and the passing of heavy vehicles, or how much 'peace' there is for the arboreal species nesting in the hollows of 80-metre high trees which are felled in a matter of seconds, or how much peace there is for the Spot-tailed Quoll whose foraging grounds and habitat is steadily being depleted by timber harvesting processes. This is a version of 'peace' that rhetorically discards its ecological effects. It is therefore a peace which, far from restoring 'order' or 'serenity', instead levies untold violence upon ~~Goolengook~~ and its associated bodies.

1998 (February): site subject to Magistrates Court decision

On February 27 Senator Bob Brown and two co-defendants were acquitted in the Moe Magistrates court of the charge of 'obstruction of the lawful carrying out of forest operations'. In his decision, the Magistrate decided that although the actions of the defendants constituted an obstruction, there was no case to answer since the forest operations occurring in the relevant coupe were, in fact, unlawful. This unlawfulness derived from the fact that logging operations were deemed to have been carried out in contravention of s.15(2) of the *Heritage Rivers Act*. In simple terms, the buffer zone along the ~~Goolengook~~ River was set at 100 metres by the Department of Natural Resources and Environment where it should have in fact been at least 200 metres from each bank. In the Victorian context, it was the first time a group of protesters had formally proved that logging operations were conducted illegally. The decision was to have serious implications for the majority of individuals arrested in or near block 839, compartment 513/10. The Director of

Public Prosecutions appealed the decision and the case eventually made its way to the Supreme Court. At such time ~~Goolengook~~ became a site subject to judicial interpretation and bureaucratic wrangling.

1998 (March): site of continuing conflict

On March 21, 1998 (p. 15), *The Age* carried a story regarding the implications of Senator Brown's acquittal. It also tells of activist 'footage of a young woman protester having petrol splashed in her face and a logging contractor pursuing others with a revving chainsaw'. Gunshots were 'also said to have been fired at an environmentalist's "safe house" in the main street of Orbost'. The text also cites the words of a 'fourth generation logger' and sawmiller from Bendoc who says he is unfamiliar with the term 'biodiversity'. Instead he offers to the journalist the following remark, 'Sure when you flatten the forest you are going to destroy animals, but they've got legs, they've got wings. There is plenty of other forest, they can fly, they can walk'.

1998 (May): site subject to statutory amendment

Following the acquittal of Senator Brown and his co-defendants in the Moe Magistrates court in February, the Victorian Government moved immediately to amend the Heritage Rivers Act. Assented to on May 19, the purpose of this amendment was to reduce, for selected sections, the width of the heritage river corridor along ~~Goolengook~~ River from 200 metres to 100 metres. Sections that received such a reduction included compartment 513/10 and all related coupes adjacent to the newly prescribed buffer between points E and F on LEGL/98-37, a distance covering approximately 14 kilometres of the ~~Goolengook~~ River. The effect of this rewriting upon ~~Goolengook~~ was to give further of its terrains over to timber harvesting – terrains which included scatterings of rainforest deemed by Department of Natural Resources and Environment to be below the minimum threshold 'suitable' for conservation (that is five hectares).

1998 (May): site of forest operation zone

On May 26, 1998, in response to the interruptions to logging operations in 839, specific zones were developed and given legal basis by the *Forests (Miscellaneous) (Amendment) Regulations* 1998. Section 1 states, 'The objective of these Regulations is to amend the Forests (Miscellaneous) Regulations 1989 to regulate certain activities in state forests'. Section 14A was specifically conceived to outlaw so-called 'dragons' and tripods placed on logging roads by forest protesters. Dragons are partially buried objects made of sharp metal or the like and are designed to puncture the tyres of logging trucks. Tripods are a series of long pieces of wood (usually thin branches or saplings) tied together in a manner which allows a person to nestle at the top where the poles meet. These are usually placed on logging roads to stop trucks and vehicles associated with logging from passing in to (and therefore out of) coupes. Given that tripods can be over 20 metres high, and that police and loggers did not want to damage the tripod for fear of sustaining serious injury to those perched above, these proved to be a very effective means of holding up logging operations. The section here reads,

> ***14A. Offence to obstruct road, track or tramway in State forest***
>
> (1) A person must not in a State forest –
> (a) construct or place any object, device or other thing that
> (i) obstructs, or is designed to obstruct, passage on a road, track or tramway constructed or maintained by the Secretary; or
> (ii) damages, or is designed to damage, a road, track, or tramway or a vehicle on that road, track or tramway; or
> (b) dig a hole, pit or trench in a road, track or tramway constructed or maintained by the Secretary in a manner that prevents safe passage on such a road, track or tramway.
>
> Penalty: 20 penalty units [...]

Section 18 is headed 'Entry into forest operations zone prohibited' and reads,

> (1) A person must not enter into or remain in any forest operations zone.
>
> Penalty: 20 penalty units.
>
> (2) Sub-regulation (1) does not apply to –
> (a) an authorised officer or member of the police force acting in the course of his or her duty; or
> (b) a person who has been granted a licence or permit under section 52 of the Act that authorises the cutting, digging or taking away of forest produce from land within that zone or is an employee or agent of a licence or permit holder authorised to carry out those activities; or
> (c) a person who is acting in accordance with a written authority of the Secretary issued under regulation 19.

Section 19 runs,

> (1) The Secretary may issue an authority, in writing, to a person authorising that person to –
>
> (a) enter into a forest operations zone; or
> (b) carry out any of the activities specified in regulation 14A(1)(a)(i) and (b).
>
> (2) An authority issued under sub-regulation (1) must specify –
>
> (a) the place to which the authority applies; and

(b) the period during which the authority applies; and
(c) any distance, not exceeding 150 meters, that a person must remain away from persons or machinery engaged in, or associated with, the cutting, digging or taking away of forest produce; and
(d) the purpose for which the authority is granted.

Schedule 3 lists the various forest operations created by the legislation. The zone relevant to 839 reads,

> Goolengook River Forest Operations Zone
>
> > Goolengook River forest operations zone is the area of State forest in the Shire of East Gippsland shown by hatching on the plan set out in Part 2, excluding Greens Road and Big River Track and the State forest within 30 metres on either side of that road and track and any land that is a heritage river area within the meaning of the *Heritage Rivers Act* 1992.

Here, ~~Goolengook~~ becomes a prohibited zone – it is the space whose (forced) transformations are to be witnessed by only a select few. In a little over a year, these regulations would be repealed by the newly appointed Labor government.[11]

---

11 The following text illustrates the kind of effect the forest operations zones were to have upon persons who had ventured in the forests on entirely 'innocent' grounds,

> Monday 27 July 1998
>
> You can't go down to the woods today
>
> **By BRIAN WALTERS**
>
> IN the dark the rain kept pouring down, and as floods hit Gippsland last month, the Goolengook River was steadily rising. Andrew Picone was in his car on the wrong side of the bridge when it washed away. He was stranded.
>
> Andrew had been engaged as a volunteer in a flora and fauna survey in the Goolengook forest area. These surveys have located endangered species, helping to save areas of forest from logging.
>
> Andrew needed help, and his father, Tony, made the long drive down to help get him out. Tony asked for assistance from the Department of Natural Resources and Environment. They would not help – and then told him that there was something he should know.
>
> He was not allowed into the forest at all: it would be a criminal offence to go into the forest unless he obtained a written permit.
>
> It is true. On 1 June, with no publicity, the Victorian Government passed regulations that made it a criminal offence to enter a 'forest operations zone' – unless you are a logger, a policeman, or a person with written authorisation. These zones are very large, and are currently in East Gippsland and the Otways. One of the zones in the Otways is just north of Apollo Bay, and covers an area some five kilometres by three kilometres. Four of the East Gippsland zones are contiguous, and form a band some 50 kilometres by 15 kilometres. There are no signs or fences to mark out these areas. You are expected to get the regulations yourself and find the boundaries of these zones. If you get it wrong, you face a fine of $2000.

1998 (October): site subject to Supreme Court decision

On October 23, 1998 the Supreme Court passed judgement on the appeal of the Director of Public Prosecutions (DPP) in the case of Robert James Brown, Alistair Forbes Knight and Emma Jane Hess. In pronouncing judgement, Kellam J determined that the key issue was whether the EG FMP could be legally classified as a 'delegated

---

Many of the zones go right up to private land – as at Bonang and Combienbar. If a ball goes over the back fence, you'll need a permit to retrieve it. If your child goes wandering, you'll need a permit before going after him or her.

For many kilometres these zones border national parks. If you stray on a walk and go into a zone, you are liable to be charged.

Major logging roads are open – and 30 metres on each side of them. Go further than 30metres from the road – say for a picnic – and you'll commit an offence unless you have a written authorisation. Dead end tracks are no go zones. If you want to find that special spot, be careful you are not committing a crime.

When you apply for your permit you'll have to state your purpose for going into the forest. Is curiosity, or wonder, or a love of the bush an acceptable purpose? Why were the regulations kept so secret? Was it so that the authorities would have this charge in their back pocket as a nasty surprise for protesters?

Forest bureaucrats say we have nothing to fear. They will give permits to everyone – everyone, that is, except protesters. But this is even more alarming. If the law is really to suppress democratic dissent, why does the Government not openly say so? And why should we have to obtain written authorisation to wander in publicly owned bush – or even to protest?

Some of these zones, such as that around Bonang, have no logging scheduled within them at all. Perhaps this is an attempt to ensure the public does not see how impressive these places are so that they do not oppose future logging. Or perhaps it is an attempt to prevent volunteers like Andrew Picone from obtaining information which would oblige the authorities to desist from logging.

Department representatives also say the law has been made because protesters are costing money. This might carry more weight if the department would publicly reveal the cost of native forest logging. But the present administration has gone to extraordinary lengths to keep this secret. There is no doubt that heavy effective subsidies are involved, with taxpayers paying for roads, rehabilitation of clearfelled areas and countless other costs that the royalties for timber do not cover. The Government will not release the precise figures.

In the past the timber industry has accused conservationists of wanting to 'lock up' our forests. Now the Government, under pressure from the timber industry, has been caught with the padlock in its hands.

The bush has always been part of our heritage as Australians. But it now it seems before you can go into a forest to find a clear stream, to sit by a large tree, or just to be inspired, you must first obtain written permission.

In the end Andrew Picone and his father secured permits and retrieved the car. But in so doing, they unearthed a set of regulations that show how far the Government is prepared to go to destroy our forest heritage.

Brian Walters is a Melbourne barrister and co-founder of Wild magazine. E-mail: opinion@theage.fairfax.com.au.

instrument', and whether such an instrument could rightfully take precedence over the prescriptions laid out in the *Heritage Rivers Act* 1992. The primary question was whether Parliament intended the width of the buffer zone along the ~~Goolengook~~ River to be that 'shown bordered in blue on plan LEGL/91-10' under the said Act, or whether Parliament intended the width of the buffer zone to be that articulated on page 52 of the EG FMP in its capacity as a delegated instrument (at 2). In His Honour's words, this reduced to the following question: 'What was established as the boundary of the relevant heritage river area and was this shown to be not more than 100 metres from the river bank?' (at 4). There was much riding on this decision – not the least of which was the capacity to sustain the charge of obstructing a *lawful* forest operation in respect of more than 100 persons. With respect to the powers of the *Heritage Rivers Act*, Kellam J noted that 'Section 15 provides that the Act prevails over any other Act and that any instrument made under another Act in contravention of the Act is void' (at 3). Despite the unambiguous nature of the Act's powers, His Honour nonetheless noted that 'the determination [of the boundary dividing lands open to timber harvesting and lands within the heritage area] is, in my view, a most difficult exercise in statutory interpretation' (at 2). The respondents argued that the width of the river should be taken from the 1:100,000 scale present on plan LEGL/91-10 as this document overrode and made void any contradictory instrument or plan (section 15(1) of the *Heritage Rivers Act* attests to the prevailing nature of the Act). The appellant agreed that the scale on the said plan indicated that a buffer zone of 200 metres was to be retained in the coupe where the respondents were arrested. However, they also contended that Parliament intended for the width of this buffer should actually be given at a later date by the Forest Management Plan. The reason for this contention was that the map in question (that is LEGL/91-10) displayed, at certain points, the phrase 'Boundary is the Natural Features Zone defined in the Forest Management Plan'. These words were argued by the appellant to be the 'rubric' which should ultimately lead to and define the correct width. It was noted by the judge that these words did *not* appear adjacent to but below the relevant coupe. Counsel for the respondents submitted that at the time the Act was introduced (that is 1992) there was no forest management plan and that it was therefore improbable that Parliament intended the boundary of the heritage river zone to remain ambiguous or even unknown for the period it took to establish a management plan – in this case, a period of three years. The question for His Honour subsequently became 'whether [in trying to determine the precise width of a heritage river corridor] it is permissible to make reference to a Forest Management Plan brought into existence at later date' (at 8). In making his decision, Kellam J averted to the fact that the *Heritage Rivers Act* at Part 8 Schedule 1 expressly states that a heritage river area, is, in this instance, to be taken as 'All those pieces of land … shown bordered in blue on the plan lodged in the Central Plan Office and numbered LEGL/91-10'. In this situation, His Honour determined that these 'words … expressly define the area of the land which forms the heritage river area' and, therefore, 'that the only way to determine the extent of the heritage river area would be reference to the "land … shown bordered in blue" on the map and to the scale of the map' (at 10). Furthermore, His Honour noted that the wording of the aforementioned 'rubric' was very much of the present tense ('Boundary *is* …' as opposed to 'Boundary will be ...') – indicating, in no uncertain terms, that the width of the buffer zone was to be taken from the Act itself and not from some instrument yet to be formulated. As noted in judgement, 'In my view it cannot be that Parliament intended a two-stage definition of the boundary of a heritage river area, nor can it be that Parliament intended that the boundary of a heritage river should stay undefined for an uncertain period following the proclamation of the Act' (at 11). On this basis, the appeal was dismissed and the logging operation at block 839 compartment 513/10 reaffirmed as unlawful. Over the coming months, this decision would lead the police and DPP to drop charges against nearly 100 persons arrested in ~~Goolengook~~ at or around the said compartment.

1998 (November): site of flora and fauna reserve

The *National Parks (Amendment) Act* 1998 was assented to on November 4 of that year and gave legal standing to the ~~Goolengook~~ Flora and Fauna Reserve. Part VIII of the Act is headed 'Creation of Crown Land Reserves'. The relevant section – section 51 – reads,

> Goolengook Flora and Fauna Reserve
>
> On the commencement of section 13 of the *National Parks (Amendment) Act* 1998–
>
> (a) any part of the land shown bordered in red on the plan lodged in the Central Plan Office and numbered LEGL./98-50 that is reserved forest, ceases to be reserved forest and is deemed to be unalienated land of the crown, freed and discharged from all trusts, limitations, reservations, restrictions, encumbrances, estates and interests; and
> (b) the land shown bordered in red on that plan is deemed to be permanently reserved under the *Crown Land (Reserves) Act* 1978 for public purposes being, in particular, the purposes set out in section 4 (1) (l) (m) (n) and (o) of that Act.

The relevant sections of the *Crown Land Reserves Act* 1978 concern, 'The preservation of areas of ecological significance', 'The conservation of areas of natural interest or beauty or of scientific historic or archaeological interest', 'The preservation of species of native plants', and 'The preservation or management of wildlife or the preservation of wildlife habitat'. The area of ~~Goolengook~~ transformed here was that deemed Special Protection Zone 839/01 by the EG FMP, which in turn was a portion of the area labelled 'Site of Biological Significance 4' by the pre-logging flora and fauna survey text of 1991. Politically, the creation of this reserve was a success. But, according to well known environmental activist Michelle van Gerrevink, it is known to 'contain[ ] old clearfells, with dense, spindly stick forest. It also contains fire damaged forest [and] the boundaries [of the reserve] are [poorly positioned] – the lushest rainforest and tallest trees are up for logging while the less valuable area has been protected. There has been no consideration of edge effects such as invasion of weeds and feral animals in the planning of the reserve [and] scientific recommendations have been ignored' (http://www.green.net.au/slide/gook6.htm).

1998 (December): site of corporate concern

On December 10, 1998 an event known as 'fashion for forests' took place at The Empire, Winsdor (a suburb of Melbourne). Here, fashion icons such as Calvin Klein and Saba took to the catwalks in support of particular forests located throughout Victoria. ~~Goolengook~~ was one such forest. The idea – conceived by Emma Hess of the Wilderness Society – was to raise the profile of the logging of high conservation forests and to bring such issues to a 'niche' of society that might not normally consider such issues. As a result of the fashion machine, the bodies of ~~Goolengook~~ were reterritorialised – made to stand as a single body under immanent threat from forestry operations. A new juxtaposition of bodies – the model and the forest.

1999 (January): site for immediate timber extraction

The draft wood utilisation plan (WUP) for the Orbost Logging District was released on January 29, 1999. It showed, amongst other things, that 135 hectares of Mountain Mixed Species totalling 39,695 cubic metres was to be 'harvested' over the financial year 1999/2000. Just over 80% (32,170 cubic metres) of the material extracted from this area would be constituted by D, D+, E and 'RL' logs (where the latter signifies residual logs). Each of these categories denotes logs that have been judged by the supervising forester as 'unfit' for sawmilling but 'good enough' for pulp and paper production, or for niche timber markets where quality is not of great importance. Accordingly, marking a log with one of these grades means that trees in excess of 200 years old will be converted either into writing paper or wooden stakes for use by market gardeners as a means of propping up string beans, tomatoes and the like. Logs graded A, B, or C are logs deemed suitable for sawmilling. In this text, such logs amount to 7525 cubic metres all of which are predicted to be of C grade quality – just 18% of the total volume scheduled for removal. What is of significance here is that 60–70% of any sawlog is sacrificed during the sawmilling process in an effort to gain desired lengths and qualities of timbers. On this basis, the area of 135 hectares scheduled for felling would ultimately produce just 3000 cubic metres of merchantable timbers – timbers that could be used in construction without risk of decaying or breaking due to 'defects' or knots in the timber (such knots, of course, are indicative of trees that provided or would eventually have provided hollows for arboreal species). This incredibly low ratio of actually merchantable timber to residual logs means that around 60 areas equivalent to that just described must be felled each year in order to meet the legislated sustainable yield for the EG FMA of 174,000 cubic metres. It is little wonder that around 7500 hectares of forest are clearfelled every year across the FMA. What this text can be made to show is that 1 tonne of merchantable timber entails the removal and eventual destruction of 13 tonnes of 'other' materials (that is old or 'crooked' trees). Of course, materials such as tree ferns, rocks and soil are not included by forest administrators in their calculations of things earmarked for interruption and/or extraction. In a further demonstration of a monstrous alignment of bodies, three of the four coupes scheduled for logging are located in special management zones – that is, zones whose ecological attributes fall just behind national parks and Special Protection Zones in significance.

1999 (February): site invoked at Senate Inquiry

On Tuesday February 2, 1999 the Rural and Regional Affairs and Transport Legislation Committee met for the second consecutive day to discuss and hear comments on the Regional Forest Agreements Bill, 1998. Reference to ~~Goolengook~~ was made on two of the 224 pages of transcript of the day's proceedings. Long-time activist and spokesperson for CROEG Jill Redwood made the following remark, 'I did some sums yesterday, too. It seems that for about the amount to keep each senator here for a day you would have to log 50 hectares of forest a day, getting 9c a tonne for the pulpwood, to keep the senators sitting at this table. One wage for the two days would have saved all of the Goolengook forest, and that, by the way, had 85 per cent pulpwood that came out of it. We figured that to fund this whole RFA process, which is over $200 million, you would have to log East Gippsland 12 times over' (Rural and Regional Affairs and Transport Legislation Committee, 1999, p. 165). In reply, the Chair of the committee asked, 'Would you like us to leave?'.

1999 (April): site displaying signs of conflict

On April 14 and 15, 1999, I obtained written permission from the forester-in-charge to enter ~~Goolengook~~ River Forest Operation Zone for the purposes of 'research and leisure'. This meant that both myself and my companion had to 'remain at least 150 metres away from any person(s) or machinery engaged in, or associated with, the cutting, digging or taking away of forest produce' (*Forest (Miscellaneous) Regulations* 1989 [sic.] Regulation 19, Authority). As we journeyed from the highway onto the dirt roads that led into ~~Goolengook~~, I recall questioning how an area as beautiful and diverse as this could be given over to clearfelling – a process that would take from this block one fifth of its old-growth forests (800 hectares) and over one half of the remaining negligibly disturbed forest (1977 hectares) over the coming years. But then I realised that the area was, of course, neither beautiful nor ugly nor anything else. Instead it had become what various textual machines and the practices of particular bodies had made of it. It had, in this sense, become stratified and organised and for this reason it had become highly and repeatedly contested – usually along molar lines – as if, at some primordial level, ~~Goolengook~~ had to be *either* preserved *or* transformed. Nearly two years after the first arrests, the signs of conflict were unmistakably present in ~~Goolengook~~ block. This is no better illustrated than the brief exchange we had with a gentleman who – after reversing his vehicle half a kilometre along a narrow track to catch up with our vehicle – asked us why we were in ~~Goolengook~~ block. After showing him our permit his suspicion subsided somewhat. But just as he was leaving he said something that has remained in my mind to this day. He told me that no matter where I go I should keep in mind that this was 'a very technical area' and that 'a lot of things had happened' in recent times. Shining gums, Messmates, Slender Tree Ferns, ~~Goolengook~~ River, Freddy Creek – all technical bodies as much as ecological processes. The proliferation of ~~Goolengook~~ as a quantified and orchestrated body loomed large at this moment.

1999 (November): site subject to statutory repeal

On November 19 the Labor government repealed legislation which had previously made it illegal for persons to enter particular areas of public forest without a permit.

2000 (February): site of increased conflict

A text from the Australian Associated Press reports that in the early hours of February 22, 2000 (1.30 am) around 50 loggers attacked and beat a number of protesters in ~~Goolengook~~ block – one of whom was taken by ambulance to Orbost hospital with head injuries. Loggers contend that the fight began when 'protesters jumped on their car and tried to punch the driver'.

2000 (May): site subject of feature article

The Australian Magazine dated May 13 and 14, 2000 carried a four page feature entitled 'Log Jam'. It focused specifically on ~~Goolengook~~ and the issues which had framed the conflict there since June 1997. In an interview, former Departmental forestry officer and current chief executive of one of the largest logging companies in East Gippsland, Gary Squires, remarked that 'Every old-growth forest out there is really a regrowth forest, usually following a fire' (quoted in Lunn, 2000, p. 31). He went on to comment, 'I think of forestry in the same way as farming except you are dealing with a crop that is harvested once every 80 years, not once or twice a year. Forestry is an environmentally sound practice because trees are a renewable resource'. As expected – and in order to 'even' the debate – the text also offered the views of a protester who was present the night the ~~Goolengook~~ blockade was raided by loggers. A comment here runs, 'I'd love to see an end to old growth forest logging in Goolengook because here there are areas of both cool and [warm] temperate rainforest which are pretty unique. When you cut them down, it's lost. The new vegetation all grows back to one height and it's really just another plantation. All the diversity is gone, all the tree hollows for animals to live in are gone. I'm just here trying to show Australia it has these amazing wild, deep forests that they should be keeping so one day they have the opportunity to see them' (quoted in Lunn, 2000, p. 30). This polarisation mirrors that in evidence at the outset of Chapter 4. Here, ~~Goolengook~~ continues to be spoken and written in binary terms. One could ask what exactly has changed over the years in relation to the discursive production of this conflict. Perhaps the only aspect to differ has been the intensity and not the terms of the debate – an intensity whose only surety is the continued (re)production of the same kinds of bodies (logger/protester, forester/conservationist, old-growth/regrowth, and so on).

2000 (October): site of police raid

On October 25, 2000 an email was sent to a number of major environmental groups warning that 'Fort Goolengook' was likely to be 'busted' by police and other authorised officers in an attempt to get all protesters out of ~~Goolengook~~. It read,

> UrgentUrgentUrgentUrgentUrgentUrgent
>
> Today the Police, DNRE, Search and Rescue, Police Security and Intelligence Group came and inspected Fort Goolengook and took a lot of photos. This leads us to believe that a bust will happen tomorrow or in the next few days.
>
> Please pass this message around to as many people as you can and come out to Goolengook if you can. Numbers are low and Goolengook needs you now. The fort protects only one end of Goolengook [and so] we need to urgently set up another camp to protect the untouched Little Goolengook region where many coupes are scheduled [for logging].
>
> Everyone's help is needed[,] please come if you can.
>
> If you cannot come to Goolengook, we also need people to raise the profile of this issue in [...] Melbourne.
>
> For information call GECO 0351 540 156.

Interruption

At this point – a point where the contestations over ~~Goolengook~~ seem set to continue – it is necessary to interrupt the process of textual incorporation. There are, no doubt, many texts which have had an effect upon ~~Goolengook~~ not subject to analysis here. Where this is so – and undoubtedly it is – then such 'textual gaps' should in no way be seen as undermining efforts to write ~~Goolengook~~. Instead, they stand as evidence that the world evades all attempts to capture its dimensions. What matters therefore, is not whether 'all' of ~~Goolengook~~ has been accounted for – an impossible situation in any case – so much as the number, intensity and type of molecular becomings (the little deterritorialisations) and lines of flight (absolute deterritorialisations) which might inhere within (or might be made to flow from) such an account. More tellingly, what matters is how attempts to know, name, and lay claim to various aspects of ~~Goolengook~~ impacts on criminological conceptions of ‘nature’, ‘environmental harm’, and its regulation. This, along with other matters, will be the subject of the ensuing chapter.

PART C

Chapter 8

On the Unsaid: Text, Nature(s), Damage

> [F]orm will never inspire anything but conformities.
>
> Deleuze, *Difference and Repetition*, 1994, p. 134

My aim in this final chapter is to outline the various *modalities* which have informed pronouncements (social, legal, economic, and other) about ~~Goolengook~~ (and thus, in many senses, about Australian earth generally) over the last two centuries. As will become apparent, these modalities have chiefly to do with the way nature is *envisioned*, the way nature is *named*, the *speed* at which nature is transformed, and the *affect* (image, concept, sense) of nature subsequently produced. A discussion of these factors is critical since they influence – both implicitly and explicitly – the manner by which various disciplines talk about, construct, perform, and write Nature. I conclude the chapter with a very brief survey of the main criminological implications which may be drawn from the preceding case study.

Modalities of 'Nature'

Visions

Virilio writes, 'Sight was once a cottage industry, an "art of seeing". But today we are in the presence of a "tangible appearances business" that may well be some form of pernicious *industrialization of vision*' (1997, p. 89). This statement is highly applicable to events surrounding ~~Goolengook~~. At the turn of the twenty-first century it is no longer the envisionings of small landholders, shopkeepers, mail deliverers, or bush walkers which hold sway with respect to what can be seen in such territories. Instead, what it is possible and not possible to see at ~~Goolengook~~ has been usurped by the power residing in the arrival of successive ocular prosthetics. First came binoculars (bringing distant and hazy images into focus), then surveyor's instruments (leading to 'the gridding of nature'), then microscopes (enabling 'man' to see the very 'essence' of forests – as conglomerations of cells, lignins, fibres, and the like), then aerial photography (establishing 'beyond all doubt' the lines which divide one forest type and growth stage from another), and finally satellite imagery (contributing to the capacity to watch growth rates, effects of fire, impacts of surrounding land use, and so forth across all FMAs simultaneously and therefore across the State). These are the prosthetics (and this term should in no way be taken as denoting something artificial) which contributed to the 'industrialisation of vision'. They set in train not just a new way of viewing the landscape so much as a mode of envisioning that is central to the function of late capitalism. Exponential growth, it must be said, does not come solely by way of new relations between humans and machines. Instead, such growth – or more accurately, the speed and velocity at which growth takes place – is very much dependent on the ability to render accountable the various ways in which 'nature' can be 'seen' or *imag(in)ed*. The charting of the boundaries of forest blocks and the positioning of prospective logging roads owed as much to the capacity to see earth 'from above' (in terms of its aerial aspect) as they did the capacities associated with cartographers or bulldozers. It is never a matter, therefore, of simply seeing 'nature' (Armitage, 1997). For that matter, it is never a matter of there being simply 'nature'. Vision, just like nature, is socially and historically (not to mention industrially) situated. As Donald Lowe remarks,

> From the standpoint of the perceiver, the world unfolds different spatio-temporal horizons of familiarity and anonymity. However, the world is a cultural, historical growth and sedimentation. There are in it different epistemic orders (such as anagogy, similitude, representation-in-space, development-in-time, and synchronic system), different communications media (such as oral, chirographic, typographic, and electronic), different forms of expression (such as the novel, fictional film, the television commercial, etc.). Perception is always by means of these cultural, historical legacies (Lowe, 1982, p. 171).

Echoing these remarks, Deleuze (1988, pp. 57, 59) writes,

> [T]he conditions pertaining to visibility are not the way in which the subject sees: the subject who sees is himself a place within visibility (as in the king in classical representation, or the place of any observer in any prison system)...[E]ach historical formation sees and reveals all it can within the conditions laid down for visibility, just as it says all it can within the conditions relating to statements. Nothing is ever[ ] secret, even though nothing is ever immediately visible or directly readable.

What these passages indicate is that viewer and object are conditioned by the particular limits ascribed to vision from one episteme to the next. Hal Foster (1988) says that such limits indicate that it is more accurate to talk in terms of *visuality* rather than some ahistorical or apolitical 'envisioning' *per se*. In the present context, it is fair to say that ~~Goolengook~~ has been viewed predominantly through *the lens of modernity*. This is a lens heavily imbued by a belief in the illuminative powers of the scientific method. It is no coincidence, therefore, that the first chirographic records of ~~Goolengook~~ were those written by geologists and botanists, as opposed to, say, artists. These scientific excursions were nothing less than reconnaissance work devoted to visualising and subsequently enunciating 'nature'. More accurately, they were exercises which enabled western eyes to gaze upon and ascribe a sense of order to that which lay beyond civilisation (or 'settled districts'). In short, modernity requires a *particular way of seeing* and not merely that one sees (Berger, 1977).

For Deleuze, vision and language (if, indeed, it is possible to distinguish one from the other) have long been haunted by certain transcendental structures which limit sight. Signifier, science, ego, God, truth, rationality, cause, effect, and so on, are the horizons (idols) which govern what it has been deemed permissible to see over the last three centuries or so. The recurrence of such structures has meant that subjects do not envision an unfettered reality but instead interpret and posit the world according to the 'scopic regimes' that evolve across and within particular epistemes (for example Antiquity, Renaissance, Classicism, Modernity) (Jay, 1988; Crary, 1996). It is, of course, impossible to get permanently outside these regimes – which is to say that a 'pure' scopic moment or a 'pure' language capable of depicting the 'essence' of things does not, indeed cannot, exist. And yet what is obvious is that the texts which relay the various sightings of ~~Goolengook~~ – whether they be scientific, legal, political or industrial – do so as if precisely the opposite were so. Of course, it would be foolish to deny that ~~Goolengook~~ was looked upon differently by various groups at distinct moments. But at each point, for each lexical folding, modern visuality has functioned as a device for delimiting what might otherwise be treated as a flow of differential, acategorical forces. And how, specifically, was ~~Goolengook~~ envisioned throughout these texts? As something beautiful, something wild and something unique. But also as something banal, something in need of taming, and as something common (that is as elsewhere represented and/or repeated). What is truly remarkable is that no matter which group gazes upon ~~Goolengook~~ – explorers, foresters, conservationists – this space is, with one notable exception, always envisaged as something in need of alteration. ~~Goolengook~~, from the very 'first', is conceived either in terms of a lack that needs filling out or as a place of excess which needs to be curtailed. It is as if observing ~~Goolengook~~ is equivalent to cultivating the urge to transform its dimensions which, of course, includes the process of ascribing certain dimensions (depths, breadths, heights, objects) in the first place. Thus the 'answer' to the question, How has ~~Goolengook~~ been envisioned? must in some sense be concomitant with a fervent and ongoing instrumentalism. Here, nature is conceived either as a tool in the service of 'man', or where such service is deemed inappropriate, as some*thing* to be cast out as Other, as use*less*, as beyond redemption.

I mentioned there was one exception to the general trend whereby ~~Goolengook~~ has been envisioned as something in need of alteration or 'adjustment' (a road and mine shaft here, a bridge, fire track, kiosk, or information centre there). This exception was the period of time when ~~Goolengook~~ and places like 'it' were deemed to exist beyond the limits of civilisation (the known, the familiar) and therefore beyond the limits of modern bourgeois consciousness (encompassing the recognisable). Such terms as 'waste lands of the Crown', 'unsettled districts', and 'back country' all attest to the notion that there existed terrains whose bodies were once worthy neither of exploration nor occupation (even though they had been traversed by indigenous persons for tens of thousands of years). And yet, on the other hand, these terms belie a certain teleology, one that aligns itself to the lack spoken of earlier. For there is in these modes of envisioning a contempt for earth. There exists the assumption that that which has not or cannot be seen (with western eyes) must automatically be of little or no (ecological, cultural, social) worth. The great and tragic irony is that sooner or later the modern subject has come around to filling out lack wherever it has been deemed to have resided – whether this be in the religious beliefs of 'primitives', in the techniques of warfare engaged by developing nations, in the pedagogical and child rearing practices of the third world, or with respect to the wild and 'empty' regions of far flung lands (such as ~~Goolengook~~). What I am suggesting here is that even when ~~Goolengook~~ was envisioned as something entirely separate to the development of a nation, it was in fact being constructed as an essential component of that development. Civilisation needs something to compare and oppose itself to in order that it may know and envision itself as the inside of the outside, as the order amongst chaos, as, in short, the location for the formation of selves as against the terrains where the Other lurks or takes hold.

The question of how ~~Goolengook~~ came to be envisioned in terms of its forest(s) (as a molarised body) is an incredibly complex one. Moreover, it is a question which cannot be divorced from a consideration of the categories, speeds and affects which have infused ~~Goolengook~~ over time. It is, to be sure, a monumental socio-ethical moment wherever one ceases treating a space in terms of its differences and begins to speak of or envision it in terms of its similarities or uniformities. On March 2, 1908 – by dint of legislative decree – 'the discourse of the representative', as Deleuze (1994, p. 130) puts it, formally took hold of ~~Goolengook~~, and with it, the slow if more deliberate effacement and manipulation of its aspects continued. To say that ~~Goolengook~~ suffered irrevocable harm as of 1908 is perhaps an insufficient remark. ~~Goolengook~~ *has never suffered or endured harm*. Rather, and more controversially, it has stood as witness to those bodies which have tried to justify or dissent from the possibilities curtailed or preserved by the operation of various machines. ~~Goolengook~~ is part of the machinic interplay which sets in train a series of events which are, in turn, construed or stratified by various bodies as approximating one state of affairs over and above another. This, however, is most certainly not to say that ~~Goolengook~~ has never been envisioned in terms of the harm perpetrated upon it, across it, throughout it, and so forth. What I am suggesting is that there is always already a cost attached to our envisionings of earth because vision – our modes of seeing – can only bring bodies into 'focus' by ignoring their differences, their 'deep disparity' (Deleuze, 1990, p. 261). In the present case, such costs are borne *both* by the forest sector *and* those committed to 'conservation'. Whereas the forestry machine charts similarities (between stands of trees) in order to convert them into resource inventories, the conservation machine locates similarities (across age and disturbance history) in order to constitute a plane of authenticity.[1] The point is that both 'strategies' tend, on the whole, to be oblivious to the dangers associated with the will to representation. One might therefore ask, What would it mean to cease mapping earth? Alternatively, what kinds of possibilities might arise were earth to be conceived along the lines of a both/and ethic instead of an either/or dichotomy? Perhaps the point is not to cease mapping *per se*, but to place into critical relief

1 The 'costs' associated with the plane of authenticity will be canvassed under the section headed 'affects' in this chapter.

modern epistemologies governing the marking and management of earth – to ask which bodies and processes are rendered invisible by various units of management and at what cost such invisibility occurs.

Names

It is tempting to ask whether naming facilitates vision or whether envisioning leads to naming. But this would be to lapse into the image of thought, an image it will be recalled, constructed in linear and binary fashion. It is better, therefore, to say that naming rises up in accordance with visuality (with what it is possible to see), but that visuality at one and the same time is always already replete with a charter of names, categories, bodies, depths and limits beyond which vision is not permitted to move lest, as Foucault says, it lapses into the realm of unreason, madness, heresy. One sees (or remains within the image of thought) because one has been inculcated with a lexicon believed to be entirely sufficient to name what one gazes upon. Even when one is equivocal about what one sees, there exist a very specific series of terms for naming the unrecognisable – 'wildness', 'jungle', 'savages', 'bush country', 'strangeness', 'Otherness'. Terms such as these are all-too-frequently engaged even if the consequences of using them are rarely taken into account. Here again, the significance of the term 'waste lands of the Crown' cannot be overestimated. For this was the 'first' (European) phrase to describe the region of which ~~Goolengook~~ formed a part. Waste, it can be noted, is that which has no place. It is the body which no one desires, the thing which must be kept at bay. And, more importantly, it is that which sets in motion the discourse of the indispensable, the integral, the pure, and the proper (Douglas, 1966; Davies, 1998). In such an instance, the Crown affirms the right not only to name waste (the outside, the unfamiliar), but gives out the impression that it is waste's antithesis. The Crown – in essence, the modern State – constitutes itself as of universal value. More than this, it turns on the machine of the construction of value.[2] By this I mean the State activates the axiom through which all events must pass in order that their 'true' worth or place within the emerging 'order of things' might be definitively determined.

The State has always had the capacity to divide and conquer. However, the object of such divisions and conquests are neither the 'wills' nor 'minds' of the populous but the right to categorise territories (to be inhabited, transformed, and so on). Categories restrict movement. They control the flow and location of forces. This is why Deleuze and Guattari spend so much time talking about the effects of deterritorialisation. One can, in the present context, take this term quite literally. As of 1788 the juxtaposition of bodies and bodies without organs that had pertained in 'Australia' for in excess of 40,000 years suffered one implosion after another. The violence of this process received its momentum from, and took its form in relation

2 In recent times, of course, places once deemed 'beyond use' or value*less* – places that Massumi terms 'derelict zones' – have become key sites for the doing(s) of late capitalism (Massumi, 1992, pp. 104–5). Arguably, ~~Goolengook~~ can be conceived as one such zone.

to, something more than orthodox weaponry (blunderbusts, knives, swords, and so on). Instead, and as has all-too-often been overlooked, such violence was borne by a nomenclature which marginalised and even forced into extinction other ways of naming or bringing forth the features of the 'new' world. That ~~Goolengook~~ was once not forest, nor timber reserve, nor national park, nor impenetrable scrub but 'a place of banishment' was something inconceivable to the newly formed collective assemblages of enunciation. Such assemblages – composed not of individuals but of bodies whose speech clings doggedly to the image of thought mapped out by the Crown/Commonwealth – promulgate/d an alien lexicon. In so doing, the State has perpetrated what can only be called a discursive assault on all before it. Deleuze and Guattari (1996, p. 437) are therefore right when they assert that 'The State as apparatus of capture has a *power of appropriation*'. But what can be added here is that this appropriation is built on the (juridical) right to *(re)name* earth as much as it is upon the capacity to capture a people, their land, or their customs. Indeed, perhaps it is built on all these at once since one cannot, or presumably would not, wish to control the latter elements were it not for the fact that they so greatly conflicted with the bodies charted by the 'incoming' lexicon.

The texts discussed in previous chapters each have their own way of naming ~~Goolengook~~. There is no escaping the fact that naming is a violent activity insofar as it distributes and demarcates bodies in places once occupied only by various flows (principally that of matter-energy). This means we need to decide upon the thresholds at which a certain type of (lexical) violence will be permitted (or tolerated), rather than upon how to eradicate the violence of naming *per se*. In Deleuze and Guattari's terms, the task is to discern for what period certain types of bodies without organs can co-exist prior to the discourse of the representative rearing its head (prior, that is, to the urge to assimilate and categorise those forces which appear to exhibit the same attributes or functions). 'The question [...] is whether the pieces [composing the plane of consistency or field of immanence] can fit together, and at what price. Inevitably, there will be monstrous crossbreeds' (1996, p. 157). In the context of the folding of ~~Goolengook~~, there have been many monsters.

First and foremost in this regard is the marking of ~~Goolengook~~ as a forest management block. This is a monstrous occurrence because it is *the* molar refrain which dictates the form, function and capacities of the bodies which lie 'inside' this area. It is monstrous because it brings with it all manner of depths, heights, lengths and breadths – and the mystique of being able to statistically divide and quantify Nature – when in fact it interrupts and reconstitutes flows of matter-energy in ways which remain, to date, *un*quantifiable and beyond the limits of discourse. And it is monstrous because it ascribes ~~Goolengook~~ a spine but strictly limits the velocities (directions) it can chart. All roads (literally) lead to clearfelled bodies and, by default, monocultures in waiting.

A second monstrous becoming has to do with the declaration of the Errinundra National Park. This may come as some what of a surprise since orthodoxy dictates that such parks must *ipso facto* be beneficial to ecological processes and, therefore, reside at the opposite end of the spectrum to things terrible or monstrous. However, national parks, Special Protection Zones, conservation zones, heritage river corridors, and the like, are as much imbued and troubled by the rhetorics of similitude and the representative as general management areas or logging zones. The surveying and naming of Errinundra National Park has in no way guaranteed becomings conducive to the preservation of bodies without organs. Rather, it has ushered in a different set of stratifications and binary oppositions for the governing of Nature. Put another way, nature is not any more 'wild' or 'free' in national parks so much as it is captured in a different way by other kinds of abstract machines (those of botany, law, conservation, aesthetics, and the like). Nature is as intensively managed and surveyed within national parks (and indeed wilderness areas) as 'outside' such places. The 'problems' of fire, of disease, of litter, of sewage disposal, of road maintenance, of tourist facilities, and the like, are problems constituted by a particular brand of conservation as much as they are constituted by the pressures of industrialisation.

This is a mode of conservation that insists, firstly, on packaging nature, and, secondly, on privileging certain of its parts (those within park boundaries) above all others (those outside park boundaries). It is therefore the height of misconception to think of such places as devoid of, or divorced from, the monstrous. The obvious retort here is that it is better to 'save' some 'parts' of the environment rather than let it 'all' be given over to the 'ravages' of industry. However, one could also say that in naming certain spaces as rare, more precious, more vital than others, there also marches the problems attending the hierarchisation of earth. This hierarchisation provides the point of reterritorialisation for those supporting clearfelling regimes and the lines which divide industrial zones from conservation zones. The form of the statements which effect such a reterritorialisation are well known – 'The best timber has been locked up by (you) greenies', '60% of old-growth is in conservation reserves, what more do you want?', and so forth. It is a game of binaries (loggers/protesters, industry/conservation) rather than flows (of species, income, votes, aesthetics, leisure). And as the history of forest struggle in Australia and elsewhere has shown, it is incredibly difficult to imagine the landscape in terms of its immanence and interconnectedness where it has for over a century been (re)written in a stochastic manner (in terms of its 'significant' and 'expendable' attributes).

There are other monstrous categories lurking with respect to ~~Goolengook~~. A chief example is the division between old-growth, negligibly disturbed and regrowth forest. Indeed, it would be no exaggeration to say that recent conflict over ~~Goolengook~~ has largely been concomitant with attempts to establish the threshold at which old-growth status can be 'legitimately' and 'popularly' ascribed. These are monstrous categories in the sense that those who impose them believe there is some kind of intrinsic and timeless causal connection between word and object – between things uttered and things existing 'independently' and 'objectively' in the world. They are also monstrous because, from the perspective of State/Royal science, they perpetuate the idea that the task of conserving ecological vitalities is complete when it has, in fact, only been reconfigured. The texts which formally articulate the thresholds dividing the three aforementioned categories display, at first glance, an irrefutable logic. This runs something akin to: There are forests. Forests exhibit various growth stages. Each growth stage has the potential to be impacted either by 'human' or 'natural' processes. Typically these reduce to the effects of industrial activities (logging, mining, grazing) or to those of fire and disease. The label ascribed to a given stand or section of forest will therefore depend on two factors – *age* (denoted by the proportion of dead material in the upper-most stratum) and known or surmised *disturbance history*. In all instances, age will take precedent over disturbance history in deciding the ultimate applicability of categories. The critical point to glean from this brand of logic is that it only holds together so long as one ignores the multiplicity of alternatives with which to think through the vicissitudes of forest status. It is a logic which, although exhibiting all the classic traits of positivism – objectivity, rigidity, lucidity – is nonetheless haunted by the volatile nature of the forces it wishes to capture/represent. As hinted at in the previous chapter, there is no good reason for coding the proportion of 'dead' matter within the forest crown as that which necessarily separates old-growth from negligibly disturbed forest. Here, 'time' is the only element separating the imposition of one category as opposed to another. *Naming, therefore, both makes and interrupts time.* It violates the becomings-other normally nascent within the plane of consistency.

To be clear, this equates to a monumental *violencing*. And it is a violencing not of some eternal or immutable 'natural world' and its 'innate rhythms', but of the possibility of discovering and inventing new ways to facilitate the widest possible array of bodies without organs. A clearfelled coupe – the projected result of earmarking terrains in one fashion rather than another – draws forth no body without organs. It is a space lacking in intensity. Of course one could, and indeed the Department of Natural Resources and Environment does, attempt to conjure a monoculture of bodies in such places (all sharing the same age, disturbance history, height, density, and so on). These bodies are, no doubt, easier to name, manage, count, monitor, and sort. But their existence is also concomitant with the destruction of a diversity of life-forms and capacities still barely comprehensible to modern science and other ways of knowing. Perhaps what makes such a destruction so spectacularly banal to the majority of bureaucrats is the belief that the capacity to name earth is one and the same as the capacity to develop a profound knowledge of its flows and compositions. More specifically, the renaming or reassigning of management thresholds is taken by such agencies to be devoid of lexical violence (see Delaney, 2001).

The question which has haunted, and continues to haunt, forest administrators (and indeed those with an 'interest' in places akin to ~~Goolengook~~ generally) is classically Aristotelian. This question asks, What is x?, meaning, in this context, What is a forest? More specifically, At what point is it reasonable to begin talking of one forest type over and above another? Further, Which forests 'deserve' to remain free from intensive industrial activity and which should be held over for logging and the like? These are Aristotelian in composition insofar as they seek to derive a response on the basis of the calculation and demarcation of essences. Here, the essence of a forest has for well over a century been written in terms of its morphology – in terms of its 'undeniable' and 'calculable' structure(s). The catch-cry has been something similar to, 'Uncover the morphology in order to name the collections of attributes one gazes upon'. Naming forest types, therefore, is everywhere permeated by the discourse of the representative and the recognisable,

> Nature is conceived as an enormous mimesis: either in the form of a chain of beings perpetually imitating one another, progressively and regressively, and tending toward the divine higher term they all imitate by graduated resemblance, as the model for and principle behind the series ... (Deleuze and Guattari, 1996, pp. 234–35).

Deleuze and Guattari urge that we need to get rid of the tree in our heads in order to create the space to think rhizomatically. In like fashion it could be said that we need to discursively expunge the trees from forest management areas in order to free up the modes of representation which have for so long dominated the way we speak about various terrains ('This is a mountain ash forest', 'This is a stand of shining gum', 'This is an area dominated by messmate', and so on). Of course, the point is not that such areas are non-existent, that they lack material force. Rather, the critical matter is that the attributes of such areas always already exceed the molar categories of 'forest type', and even the higher resolution categories of 'ecological vegetation class', or 'stand' conceived by administrators. Names, it must be said, simultaneously render visible and invisible. For this reason, the ascription of categories is inherently laden with politico-ethical overtones since each curtails in advance the existence of other bodies – bodies which are subsequently made to fall 'outside' orthodox or so-called 'normal' discursive moments or cognitive frames.

The management of ~~Goolengook~~ – which is, importantly, concomitant with the regulation of those bodies drawn by particular machines over time – is and always has been about the violence of representation. From an administrative point of view it has been vital that all 'formal' attempts to delineate ~~Goolengook~~ in one fashion rather than another are conceived as both entirely natural and wholly benign. The problem, however, is that ~~Goolengook~~ resists all attempts to code its aspects (whether this be the rigid codes levied through law and science or the more supple codes pronounced by sightseers, bush walkers, and the like). The 'reality' of the bodies configured by molar machines is premised upon the idea that there is an isomorphic relation between words and things. Nietzsche and many others have challenged the correspondence theory of truth which proposes that categorising the world (through the auspices of positivism) is equivalent to unveiling the essence of things. In a brilliant critique of this idea, Deleuze writes of the fundamental *aporia* that has existed, and will continue to do so, between naming and knowing, or between representation and truth. As he remarks,

> All differences are borne by individuals, but they are not all individual differences. Under what conditions does a difference become regarded as individual? The problem of classification was clearly always a problem of ordering differences. However, plant and animal classifications show that we can order differences only so long as we are provided with a multiple network of continuity of resemblance. The idea of a continuity among living beings was never distinct from that of classification, much less opposed to it. It

> was not even an idea supposed to limit or nuance the demands of classification. On the contrary, it is the prerequisite of any possible classification (1994, p. 247).

This tension between having to order difference whilst maintaining a continuity of resemblance is, in many senses, the point at which environmental conflict emerges. The problem is that there are, in fact, no individual differences and no single field of resemblance. However, this has not prevented modern systems of land management acting to the contrary. Indeed, the naming of forest types, species conservation thresholds, national parks, and the like proceeds precisely according to this logic. Again, as Deleuze puts it,

> We invoke a field of individuation or individuating difference as the condition of the organisation and determination of species. However, this field of individuation is posited only formally and in general: it seems to be 'the same' for a given species, and to vary in intensity from one species to another. It seems, therefore, to depend upon the species and the determination of species, and to refer us once more to differences borne by the individual, not to individual differences. In order for this difficulty to disappear, the individuating difference must not only be conceived within a field of individuation in general, but must itself be conceived as an individual difference. The form of the field must be necessarily and in itself filled with individual differences (1994, pp. 251–52).

The primary – and one might say, critical – consequence of constructing a field of individuation (equivalent in many ways to the plane of organisation) is that it enables administrators to classify the world according to the distribution and repetition of so-called like groups rather than, as would seem preferable, in terms of the differences borne by individuals. This is, to be clear, an incredibly important moment in the lexical folding and demarcation of Nature. For at this point the guiding objective of environmental administrators becomes the location and categorisation of a delimited series of attributes common to a field (of species, of classes, of types) as opposed to establishing categories on the basis of the relations pertaining between individuals and their associated becomings. Here, Deleuze suggests that there has perhaps been a serious misinterpretation of Darwin's work. As he states,

> Darwin's great novelty [...] was that of inaugurating the thought of individual difference. The leitmotiv of *The Origin of the Species* is: we do not know what individual difference is capable of! We do not know how far it can go, assuming that we add to it natural selection. Darwin's problem is posed in terms rather similar to those employed by Freud on another occasion: it is a question of knowing under what conditions small, unconnected or free-floating differences become appreciable, connected and fixed (1994, p. 248).

Can it really be said that we have the knowledge sufficient to discern such conditions? I would argue that we do not but that present environmental regulations (whether those concerned with forestry, mining, waste management, or whatever) function as if such knowledge exists and that it exists unproblematically.

At the most basic level, forest administrators – and this includes the botanists, hydrologists, and ecologists employed to enunciate Royal science – do not have the lexicon with which to adequately describe the relations pertaining between the forces occupying even the smallest of terrains. But, and somewhat predictably, forestry officials cannot afford to admit this fact – that management is a machine whose effects are levied without regard for the differences borne by individuals (and the significance of such differences for ecological renewal). To admit as much would mean the sudden and dramatic demise of modern forest management principles premised as they are on the notion that great sections of forest can be clearfelled without serious consequence since there also exist, when all is said and done, other sections 'just like' them (whether these be extant in national parks or in state forest more generally). There is, then, a line of thought which environmental regulators want at all costs to keep at bay: namely, that 'The great taxonomic units – genera, families, orders and classes – no longer provide a means of understanding difference by relating it to such apparent conditions as resemblances, identities, analogies and determined oppositions' (Deleuze, 1994, p. 248). And it is at this point that a discussion of the issue of speed becomes vital. For the envisioning and naming of earth has everything to do with how and at what rate bodies move through, above, or across various of its elements.

Speeds

Without the advent of and changes in speed, ~~Goolengook~~ would, in all probability, exhibit an entirely different range of bodies and intensities. Speed, and more accurately, alterations in the velocities associated with various abstract machines, have irrevocably transformed ~~Goolengook~~ and the wider terrains within which it is situated. Virilio remarks that 'Every society is founded on a relation of speed. Every society is dromocratic' (Virilio and Lotringer, 1997, p. 49). What this means is that every social formation reckons with movement and is, therefore, imbued by a 'logic(s) of the race' – a logic of modes and rates of movement. For Virilio, variants of speed remained fairly constant until the mid-nineteenth century. Here, the chief role of politics was to administer mechanisms capable of inducing modes of constraint and capture, or a great slowing down of bodies/populations. The state deployed instruments in keeping with a general philosophy of 'the brake' (that is 'laws', 'taxes', 'ramparts', 'interdictions', and so on) (Virilio and Lotringer, 1997, pp. 50–51). But after such a time, the limits of speed (and concomitantly the focus of the state) underwent a massive deterritorialisation. '[S]uddenly, there's the great revolution that others have called the Industrial Revolution or the Transportation Revolution. I call it a dromocratic revolution because what was invented was not only […] the possibility of multiplying similar objects […], but especially a means of fabricating speed with the steam engine, then the combustion engine. And so [society] pass[ed] from the age of brakes to the age of the accelerator. In other words, power will be invested in acceleration itself' (Virilio and Lotringer, 1997, p. 51). One of the most important forms of power, of course, is the ability to occupy and traverse space. In this regard, the industrial revolution was more than just a qualitative change in the juxtaposition of 'man' to matter-energy. It was, more significantly, a moment which heralded the transition 'from geopolitics to chronopolitics' (Virilio, 1999, p. 18). Put differently, industrialisation transformed time (the way bodies situated themselves with respect to time) as much as it transformed relations of economic production (the ways bodies were positioned with respect to the means of production). The question posed by the modern state is: How fast (speed) and in what direction (velocity) can bodies move? This can be contrasted against the question posed since antiquity: namely, How might bodies best be restrained?

The state is first and foremost concerned with the movement of bodies and their associated speeds.[3] 'The question of speed is central. It pertains to the question of economy. Not only is speed a threat, insofar as it is capitalised and tyrannical, but it is also life itself. Speed and wealth go hand in hand' (Virilio, 1999, pp. 13–14). Speed is the key to colonisation since it places people in far flung lands and lends to various armies the capacity to mount all manner of defences/attacks. More than this, technologies of speed facilitate the laying bare of 'impenetrable' terrains – at least, this is the teleology frequently associated with them. Revolutions in speed enable a reconfiguration of the relationship between, on the one hand, 'man', time, and distance, and on the other, the object or 'bounty' reached through such a reconfiguration (which is, more accurately, more in the order of a *recalibration*). Virilio remarks, 'We generally distinguish three types of distance. Space-distance is the day of walking, or the kilometer [...]; then time-distance, the kilometer/hour; and finally speed-distance, which is the mach. Movement is no longer indexed according to metrics, but to the speed of sound' (Virilio and Lotringer, 1997, p. 64). In relation to ~~Goolengook~~, it is the second type of distance that has most relevance. There could be no thought of intensively logging East Gippsland until the problem of distance had been overcome (which, at one and the same time, means to reckon with matters of political economy). The completion of the Melbourne to Orbost railway, the invention of the footed track, the deployment of the oscillation ring, and the adaptation of the rotating blade were all linked by their ability to increase the speed at which humans (read *men*) could access and transform 'nature'. To this list should also be added the invention of the light aircraft engine which has dramatically

3 Speed – and the teleology supposedly embedded within certain of its manifestations – was certainly of key relevance to the former federal Minister for Forestry and Conservation, Wilson Tuckey. In an effort to marginalise the concerns of many 'green' groups, he once remarked to the effect that 'Old trees have to make way for young trees, like older workers have to make way for younger workers'. The underlying message here is that 'nature' has its (time) limits – and that sooner or later certain of its processes of diminution must be given a 'helping hand' (especially where this process threatens to interrupt or delay the interests of capital. In the same interview, Tuckey quipped that 'A tree in Styx Valley [a location in Tasmania containing some of the tallest forests in the southern hemisphere] was logged and it fell apart when it hit the ground because it was rotten. Bugs had eaten it out. It needed to make way for new trees' ('Spitting Chips', *Lateline*, ABC TV, March 9, 1999). Here, the Minister invokes an overtly molar view of death and decay – that such processes must have, somehow, a final or absolute point where they cease being 'productive'. Such a conception, of course, usefully obscures the biological, hydrological and aesthetic role played by 'rotten' trees.

altered not only the techniques used to 'regenerate' coupes but the speed and scale at which this occurs.

Changes in technology did not simply enable the faster transformation of 'nature'. Instead, alterations in speed set up a new relation between observer and observed – meaning that 'nature' was seen, enunciated, and categorised in ways concomitant with the rate at which it was traversed. As Virilio puts it, 'Speed enables you to see. It does not simply allow you to arrive at your destination more quickly, rather it enables you to see and foresee. To see, yesterday with photography and cinema, and to foresee today with electronics, the calculator and the computer. Speed changes the world vision [*Weltanschauung*]' (1999, p. 21). And again, 'All speed illuminates [...] When one is on a jet or on a train, one sees the world in a different light, so to speak. It's not the problem of light source, but of relation to the world. The world flown over is a world produced by speed. It's a representation' (Virilio and Lotringer, 1997, p. 85). In the present context, one could say that there is a completely different sense of Nature to be had through walking as opposed to commandeering an animal or driving a motorised vehicle (or indeed piloting a plane). But, in ecological terms (and against romantic ideals) the former is by no means automatically 'better' than the latter. One would perhaps have thought that traversing the forests of East Gippsland by foot would have given naturalists and even speculators/industrialists the sense that such forests are worth preserving on account of their geographical range and diversity. However, the opposite proved to be so. Specifically, it was the fact that such forests seemed to 'stretch on for eternity' that led directly to the notion that they must be inexhaustible and therefore ripe for exploitation. Here the speeds associated with walking resulted in the largest possible intervals being levied between forms (forests/plains/towns). It was as if Nature existed as a set of partitioned zones – 'this is forest', 'this is where open terrain begins', 'this is the edge of town' – and that such zones were extensive rather than intensive in composition. The speeds associated with walking help to conjure an idea of Nature as limitless, harsh, dense and resolute and, concomitantly, as that which could resist and recover from all manner of impacts.

At the opposite end of the spectrum (speedometer), one would perhaps also have thought that the advent of chainsaws, railways, trucks and planes would have enabled 'man' to literally see the geographical limits of forested terrains and that this would give rise to appropriate resource utilisation principles. But instead, the technologies of speed (in the main the combustion engine and its associated reterritorialisations) led to the idea that since nature could be viewed and traversed 'in its entirety' that this must somehow be concomitant with the capacity to know and manage its various parts. Here, speed brings with it (the idea of) total control and absolute knowledge – an omnipotence and omniscience with respect to earth. The increased ability to grid and monitor Nature – that is, the supposed capacity to name and surveil 'all' its aspects – has arguably produced the situation where administrators are unable (or unwilling) to distinguish adverse and rapid changes in biodiversity from what are typically taken to be world's best practice in environmental management. Modern principles of forest administration plug nature into a speed machine the likes of which have not been seen before. Areas which were once subject to geological rhythms now develop according to industrial velocities. Forests have, in effect, become crops to be harvested every 80 years or so in quantities dictated by markets and electoral politics. The consequences of such a programme can be viewed in terms of the spectre of what Virilio calls the *specific accident*,

> We are forced to expand the question of technology not only to the substance produced but also to the accident produced. The riddle of technology … is also the riddle of the accident. … In classic Aristotelian philosophy, substance is necessary and the accident is relative and contingent. Every technology produces, provokes, programs a specific accident. For example: when they invented the railroad, what did they invent? An object that allowed you to go fast, which allowed you to progress – a vision *a la* Jules Verne, positivism, evolutionism. But at the same time they invented the railway catastrophe. The invention of the boat was the invention of ship wrecks. The invention of the steam engine and the locomotive was the invention of derailments. The invention of the highway was the invention of three hundred cars colliding in five minutes. The invention of the airplane was the invention of the plane crash. I believe that from now on, if we wish to continue with technology (and I don't think there will be a neolithic regression), we must think about both the substance and the accident – substance being both the object and its accident. The negative side of technology and speed was censored (Virilio and Lotringer, 1997, pp. 37–8).

Perhaps the only thing separating the specific accidents listed above from those which may or may not be seen to operate with respect to forest management is, simply, time. More accurately, the key factor here is the speed of absolute loss and the capacity to recognise when one is on the path to such a loss. There is, to be sure, good evidence to suggest that clearfelling has as its necessary consequence the depletion of biodiversity (if not the eutrophication of inland rivers, the release of carbon into the atmosphere, and a decrease in soil fertility). However, no one can *definitively* name the specific accident associated with current logging and conservation programmes and this, it may be said, is one of the main 'sources' of forest conflict. As such, the politics and (re)presentation(s) of speed remain predominately on the side of Royal/State science (that is those who set conservation thresholds and logging quotas) (see Deleuze and Guattari, 1996, pp. 361–74).[4] Most old-growth forests are in the vicinity of 350 years old and have evolved in the context of geological time scales measuring in excess of 10,000 years. The result here is that time (or its failure to rapidly pass) beats any and all 'green' protestations. This should come as little surprise since what 'environmentalists' are battling is not so much the power of unions, the ineptitudes of law, or the demands from overseas markets, but *the problems associated with having to (empirically) demonstrate the*

---

4 Clearfelling, for instance, has only been operative in East Gippsland since the late 1960s. Accordingly, anyone who opposes current logging techniques finds themselves in the invidious position of being unable to categorically say one way or the other what the *long term* effects of clearfelling will be (since the technology has, at most, only been extant for around half a century).

long term consequences of an event prior to the long term having transpired. Even if one were able to fast forward 300 years to view such consequences, the conflict surrounding forest use would in all likelihood persist since the task of how best to name what one sees would have to be reckoned with (leading, one would suspect, to a proliferation of discourses pitting the 'authentic' forest body against the copy). The question, therefore, would seem to turn on the probable rather than definitive ecological effects of forest administration, of the moment where absolute loss looks more, rather than less, likely. From previous chapters, it is clear that administrators (at least those who control policy in the most direct of ways) believe the speed of forest transformation to be satisfactory if not unproblematic – that clearfelling up to one third the area of East Gippsland over the next 60 or so years can only lead to (economic) gains not (biotic) losses.

Another aspect in need of clarification here is the relationship between speeds (the rate at which bodies move across earth) and scales (the units deployed in an effort to contain, mark off, catalogue, and manage certain of earth's dimensions). Without the capacity to traverse lands and consume resources at particular speeds, the issue of scale would be of little import. However, in the present context this is far from being the case. Indeed, the composition of the speeds and scales associated with ~~Goolengook~~ speak directly to the intensity of the conflict that has surrounded, and continues to surround, this space. What is manifestly clear is that there exists an inverse relationship between speed and the size of the management units which 'govern' ~~Goolengook~~ and nature generally. More simply, units of management generally become smaller in line with increases in the speed with which territories are (or can be) traversed. One notable exception to this rule is the period spanning 18,000 BCE (foot-speed) to 1770 (wind-speed) where the relevant scale moved from tribal area to sub-continental (eastern third of Australia). But from shortly after 1788 it was the speed (and strength) of the horse which helped usher in the change from district (60 million acres) in 1836, to pastoral lease (tens of thousands of acres) in 1848, to Parish (measured in terms of chains or one mile intervals) in 1888. Between 1916 and 1928, the convergence of the horse and the locomotive (combined with the speeds associated with the rotating blade) heralded the advent of the (Orbost) forest district. This was, it should be noted, the first occasion whereby ~~Goolengook~~ was formally enunciated in terms of 'merchantable timber' and 'principal tree species'. However, it was the collective effect of the 1939 fires and the postwar construction boom (and not some 'innate greed' or 'lust to dominate nature') which opened the way for further changes in the capacity to access and transform the terrains of East Gippsland.

In 1972, with the combustion engine firmly encased in the dozer and the articulated trailer (not to mention the chainsaw) the key unit of management reduced in size once again to that of the forest management block. But even here, as if to attest to the 'frontier-like' dimensions of ~~Goolengook~~ and its surrounding areas, it was necessary to combine legwork (the speed of the foot) with that of the combustion engine in its various deterritorialised forms. Such a combination allowed the aspects of ~~Goolengook~~ to be enunciated according to the dictates of the

'Division of Economics and Marketing'. Further segmentations of ~~Goolengook~~ also occurred around this time. Specifically, ~~Goolengook~~ (coded as 17122 – denoting forest district and block number) was divided into 15 compartments encompassing 181 forest stands. These stands would be further divided into the much smaller unit of the coupe wherever logging was scheduled to take place. It is no coincidence that aerial shots of ~~Goolengook~~ and surrounding regions were becoming more regular at this time. These led to the idea that ~~Goolengook~~ could be managed not so much from the ground up but from the sky downward. Wide-angle lenses deployed at various altitudes would make apparent the 'natural' segmentations (rivers, ridges, valleys) that traversed ~~Goolengook~~ and 'like' areas. What better way to divide ~~Goolengook~~(ature) into its constituent parts than to mimic its geographical 'differences' (from the vantage point of the sky, and, later, space). Here, as 'man' moves by way of the aeroplane further and faster away from ~~Goolengook~~, the units deployed to manage such terrain(s) become smaller and smaller. One could even say that leaving earth has become equivalent to a more intense colonising (striating) of its aspects.

The final matter in need of comment concerns the relationship between transformations in speed and the frequency (and focus) of the texts which speak of ~~Goolengook~~. In the first 50 years of European occupation, and under the speed of horsepower, there were just five texts which transformed ~~Goolengook~~, and they did so only in the most general of ways. Over the next half century (1848–91), 13 texts emerged which enunciated ~~Goolengook~~. Here, around 1856, the first *direct* chirographic reference to ~~Goolengook~~ occurred describing it in terms of 'dense scrub' and 'bush country'. Three decades later in 1887 – the time of the steamship and the horse-drawn buggy – the area was still recorded as 'entirely unexplored'. Indeed, it wasn't until the early 1890s that Europeans began to keep more comprehensive notes about ~~Goolengook~~ and surrounding territories, and this mainly in the context of marking survey lines for the Parishes of ~~Goolengook~~, Noonga, Bungywarr, Goongerah and Kuark. Over the next 80 years (1891–1972), a further eight texts emerged, the majority of which appeared prior to the advent of the combustion engine, the portable rotating blade, and the dozer, but after the arrival of the locomotive. The first of these, in 1908, supplied ~~Goolengook~~ with the category 'protected forest' and enunciated this space as containing, in very general terms, 'timber'. In 1959, the *Forests Act* outlined in greater detail the meaning of the term 'forest' and 'forest produce'. In 1960 – around the time that dozers and articulated vehicles began their reign in East Gippsland – portions of ~~Goolengook~~ were incorporated into Victoria's body of 'permanently reserved forest'. Finally, in 1972, and just ahead of the great rush of texts to come, ~~Goolengook~~ was inscribed by the boundaries of a forest management block. In all, there were a mere 25 texts which configured ~~Goolengook~~ in one way or another over the 200-year period spanning 1770 to 1972. From this time on, however, a very different story emerged. Specifically, in just a quarter of a century (1977 to 2000) no less (and undoubtedly more) than 55 texts emerged to enunciate or build ~~Goolengook~~ in various ways. Two thirds (n=32) of these emerged subsequent to the publication of the Woodgate study in 1994 and the release of the EG FMP in 1995. Here, ~~Goolengook~~ was subject to a greater number of codings and to a more intense plotting of various bodies across its terrains than had previously ever been the case. Road construction, in particular, brought with it a greater capacity to explore, measure, document, and mark ~~Goolengook~~. Each machine – conservation, industrial, scientific – coded and recoded what could rightfully be said to exist within ~~Goolengook~~'s borders, and each perceived that it had discovered the 'Truth' of this space, its very essence, its enduring quality (for example, untold diversity of bird and animal species, mineral deposits lying in wait, untapped timbers, pockets of rainforest overlap, and so on). One could not imagine a greater contrast between those 'early' texts which cast ~~Goolengook~~ as 'wasteland' (1788), 'worthless' (1872), 'entirely unexplored' (1887), and 'wild district' (1889), as against those of the late twentieth century which wrote ~~Goolengook~~ as containing 'sites of national biological significance' (1991), as exhibiting 'high yielding forests' (1996), as subject to juridical proceedings (1998), as the object of legislative decree to keep, ironically, bodies *away* from its terrains (1998), as an event mentioned at a Senate Inquiry (1999), and as a site subject to police raids (2000).

This proliferation of texts speaks, quite obviously, to the highly contested nature of ~~Goolengook~~ – a contestation inconceivable even just half a century ago. But what has occurred here is, arguably, emblematic of the kinds of battles which have emerged in the last few decades concerning particular portions of earth. In Australia such battles have included attempts to dam the Gordon below Franklin and the actual damming of Lake Pedder in Tasmania, uranium mining in Kakadu National Park in the Northern Territory, heap-leach/cyanide mining in the Box Ironbark forests of northern Victoria, salt mining in Shark Bay world heritage area in Western Australia, attempts to mine magnesium in Yumbarra National Park in South Australia, the refusal to curtail native vegetation clearance practices in Queensland (which has, per capita, one of the highest clearance rates in the world), and many others. Each of these sites of contestation has something in common with ~~Goolengook~~ – and it is not merely that they have an 'environmental' focus. Rather, each is linked to the other by the effects of speed, or, more accurately, by particular ways of moving across and transforming earth. To revert to ~~Goolengook~~, the conflict is not over 'Goolengook' so much as what, precisely, the disappearance (and preservation) of its aspects symbolises or means for various groups. Speed is central to the debate because there is a link between how fast we go, what we see, and what we can know. Presently, there is good evidence to suggest that we are in the midst not of some 'green' revolution or backlash but of what Virilio terms a *gray ecology* (1997, pp. 58–68),

> Alongside the pollution of substances that make up our environment, which ecologists are always [talking] about, surely we should also be able to detect the sudden pollution of distances and lengths of time that is degrading the expanse of our habitat. Being eternally preoccupied by the pollution of nature, are we not deliberately overlooking this pollution of life-size that reduces to nothing earth's scale and size? (Virilio, 1997, p. 58, emphases removed).

There is a direct if little theorised relationship between the rate at which we transform Nature and the number and kind of textual foldings levied with respect to various terrains. In general, the number and range of texts increases in line with the pollution or invasion of the world by speed. More than this, variances in speed impact the *resolution* at which earth is examined and enunciated. Over the course of the last century – as territories have become subject to increased ways and speeds of movement – the units associated with forest management and ecology have become smaller and smaller. But whereas the ecological machine aims to write the world at higher and higher resolutions, it could be said that the forestry machine strives to ward off attempts to apply such envisionings (and the bodies subsequently 'seen' or brought into being) to 'its' domain. This helps to explain, for instance, the reaction of forestry personnel to the recent discovery that Wet Forest in the central highlands of Victoria is in fact floristically *distinct* to Wet Forest exhibited at East Gippsland. Such knowledge has been viewed by forest administrators as an obstacle to scheduled harvesting programmes rather than as something to be lauded. It would seem, therefore, that in order to 'successfully' and repeatedly destroy 'a' forest, one must resist obtaining too fine a knowledge of such bodies. A question to be asked here is, What would happen to the forestry machine were the mapping of terrains to be undertaken at smaller and smaller resolutions? Would it not begin to collapse under its own logic or (delimited) mode of envisioning?

Perhaps, then, conflict over ~~Goolengook~~ is in fact a conflict concerning the correct alignment or proximity of bodies which disparate groups believe should pertain in particular regions. Perhaps it is *a conflict which turns on how best to manage distance* (between one body and the next) and, relatedly, how best to manage those bodies which reside in 'far flung' places. Moreover, perhaps it is *a conflict concerning the resolutions that should or should not be deployed in efforts to name earth* and manage its so-called 'natural resources'. Perhaps also it is a conflict which represents a limit case – in the sense that mining the depths of the deepest ocean or the surface of Mars might also represent such cases. 'Goolengook' has evolved to embody the notion that something distant and deterritorialised has value precisely on these counts alone – that there is untold worth in places which fit the equation: earth minus human interruptions. Here, the battle is no longer over timber or tree ferns or arboreal species, but over the capacity to preserve remote, difficult, and largely inaccessible places. To lose these, one could argue, would be paramount to suffering a permanent state of spatial and temporal nausea, or, as Virilio calls it, an omnipresent 'dromospheric pollution' (1999, p. 59).

Affects

The combined result of envisioning, categorising and transforming Nature at various speeds, brings about new relations between bodies. For Deleuze and Guattari, as for Spinoza before them, these bodies exist in an *affective* state of one kind or another. Paul Patton writes,

> Affects can be either active or reactive and … Deleuze relies upon this distinction to classify the different ways in which a body can act upon others and the ways it can be acted upon: 'to incite, provoke or produce … constitute active affects, while to be incited, or provoked, to be induced to produce, to have a 'useful' effect, constitute reactive affects […] (Patton, 2000, p. 78).

Here, the critically important distinction is made between forces (texts) which separate, as against those which do not separate, a body from what it can do. Using such a division it can be said that the texts which make of ~~Goolengook~~ one body or another are reactive in the extreme. Even the jottings of Edwin Merrall in 1887 which, at one point, 'innocently' describe ~~Goolengook~~ as 'a native crystal palace' and as exhibiting a 'sassafras jungle', must be seen as ascribing ~~Goolengook~~ forms and functions that have no 'actual' basis. ~~Goolengook~~ is indeed a space replete with affective bodies insofar as each enters into relations with all kinds of other bodies – loggers, police, protesters, bulldozers, trucks, scientific calculations, to name several. But the fact is that ~~Goolengook~~ is *made* to enter into such relations. It is, in other words, '*induced to produce*', it is *forced* to perform, to display its 'beauty' and its 'ruggedness', to offer up timber, aesthetic experiences, and scientific data in place of becomings-immanent. Deleuze and Guattari remark, 'We know nothing about a body until we know what it can do, in other words, what its affects are, how they can or cannot enter into composition with other affects, with the affects of another body, either to destroy that body or to be destroyed by it, either to exchange actions and passions with it or to join with it in composing a more powerful body' (1996, p. 257). The term 'power' should not be viewed in the sense of 'domination' or 'control'. Instead, as Massumi notes, there are two distinct terms for power in French – *puissance* and *pouvoir*. The first 'refers to a range of potential. It has been defined by Deleuze as a "capacity for existence", "a capacity to affect or be affected", a capacity to multiply connections that may be realised by a given "body" to varying degrees in varying situations … Here, *puissance* pertains to the virtual (the plane of consistency) [whereas] *pouvoir* [relates] to the actual (plane of organisation)' (Massumi in Deleuze and Guattari, 1996, p. xvii).

To compose a more powerful body, therefore, is to create conditions whereby each body retains its capacity to enter into affective relations of the *active* kind – conditions, in other words, where 'uses', 'values', and (corporate/state) 'inducements to produce' are least in number. The bodies extracted from ~~Goolengook~~ – or from what is now a plane of organisation (called, most commonly, 'Goolengook forest block 839') – are reactive bodies par excellence. They are bodies entirely separated from what they might otherwise be capable of doing. These are the bodies which manifest themselves in the form of woodchips, copying paper, tomato stakes, forklift pallets, scantling, and perhaps, every so often, as a piece of furniture for 'niche' markets. Monstrous crossbreeds. It is not that such bodies cease being affective for clearly they enter into new relations with all kinds of other bodies – humans, laser beams, desks, trucks, trains, board rooms, lounge rooms, gardens, snails, insecticides – the list is endless. But these new relations are 'sustained' at the expense of combinations of flows, speeds and intensities whose affects are yet to be adequately understood. This new juxtaposition of bodies, in short, has arisen prior to the development of a nomenclature/knowledge capable of relaying the significance and composition of the plane of consistency.

Here we arrive at the crux of the matter. For the penultimate series of questions that need to be asked are as follows. First, what kind of body emerges as a result of the operation of particular machines (texts)? Second, how is such a body positioned or aligned with respect to other bodies? And third, which kinds of alignments allow for the maximum possible variation in the type and intensity of bodies given to reside within and across territories (homes, workplaces, schools, government departments, water catchments, forests)? Most bodies/institutions have not adequately posed and replied to such questions for to do so would be to unearth the absurdity attached to privileging the (use) value of tomato stakes above the integrity of ecosystems that have evolved over millennia. There is a kind of warped fetishism in operation here – one where although the product does not entirely disguise the relations of production that surround its manufacture (since most know of the link between, for instance, copying paper and old-growth destruction), it nonetheless proceeds to take on a life of its own independent of such relations. This is the point at which a machinic philosophy – one based around flows, interruptions, and the modes and durations of reterritorialisation – comes into its own, so to speak. Although we are 'human beings', we are at one and the same time stratifications of matter-energy (stardust, sunlight and water). Our existence is, therefore, truly/literally of cosmic proportions. Deleuze (1990) once wrote that a camel passed through his mouth each time he uttered its name. In the same way, a hyper-stratified portion of ~~Goolengook~~ is summoned forth whenever and wherever our bodies copy paper, engage a builder, maintain gardens, load freight, sit on a couch, and so on. There is, accordingly, a need for each to become more highly attuned to the *proximity* of our own bodies to the forces which simplify and fragment the world. Arguably, no ethical distinction should be made between bodies who knowingly use wood products derived from areas such as ~~Goolengook~~ as against bodies who sign off on the coupe plans which facilitate the removal of 'timber'. One might go a little further and say that no distinction should be drawn between these latter bodies and those which champion national parks or conservation reserves. This is, to be sure, an extreme position. But it is one premised on the conviction that 'better' (a *more powerful body* of) socio-ecological relations cannot emerge from the same kinds of binary imaginings that have guided (Australian) governments over the last century or so ('this is where we will dig, cut, transform, put down roots'/'this is where we will not').

The principles governing the regulation of ~~Goolengook~~ (and indeed like areas across/beneath/above the globe) cling doggedly to the idea of an Outside – of a place which, as if indifferent to Nietzsche's thought, will not (cannot) return to haunt us (pollute us, poison us). The 'legitimacy' and cogency of environmental regulations are, therefore, sustained not via some inherent rigor or congruence between science, law, politics and nature, but by way of a generalised yet simultaneously personalised *affect* – an affect which portends to conjure an unproblematic alignment of bodies and capacities but on closer inspection may well be ushering in diminutions and transformations of the most dangerous kind. Such an affect – such a reactive state of affairs – concerns itself more with the relationship spanning electorates and governments than the long-term viability of, for instance, Spotted Quolls, Powerful Owls, or 'negligibly disturbed' stands of messmate. The task for policy makers has thus become one of how best to (re)present varieties of loss (and gain). Borrowing from Virilio, there exists the urgent need to become cognisant of the bodies which orchestrate this 'aesthetics of disappearance'. The bodies in question here are not simply those which operate within the confines of an office, a family, an industry, or a classroom, so much as the body which leaves its trace – however benign or destructive – *at all times and in all places* (whether it be a bush walker defined by the food wrapper dropped or left behind, or a mining company defined by the effects of cyanide in the water-table).

As mentioned at the outset of this study, schizoanalysis has an abiding interest in the body as it affects and is affected by multiple machines. This means that bodies undertaking even the most routine activities (watering the garden, making a cup of tea, buying a shirt, watching TV, driving to a friend's house, or watching a bird gather twigs for its nest) should be considered as immersed in machinic interactions of the richest kind involving multiple disconnections and reconnections of various flows, intensities and speeds. For instance, in the first example (watering a garden), an aesthetic-assemblage is made possible by flows of water which depend on intensities of rain which depends on the speed and scale of the removal of biomass (forests, vegetation). In the second (making a cup of tea), a drinking-assemblage emerges from flows of electricity or gas which depend on the speed and scale of the removal of earthly compounds which in turn depends on intensities of knowledge and flows of labour (planting, tending and harvesting the tea leaves). In the third (buying a shirt), a fashion-assemblage is produced via flows of cotton which depend on flows of water (irrigation) which often interrupt the intensity (quantities) and speeds (maturity) of native fish which in turn impacts on the flow of money available to freshwater fisher-persons.[5]

5 To continue, in the fourth (watching TV), a viewer-assemblage is sculptured from intensities of colour and light which rely on flows of electricity and petrochemicals (plastic components) which in turn rely on intensities (polymers) produced in a laboratory. In the fifth (driving to a friend's house), a visitor-assemblage is crafted from intensities of aluminium and steel (body of car, engine), flows of rubber and petrochemicals (tyres, fuel), speeds and intensities of sand (windows, mirrors) all existing within flows of traffic and bitumen which in turn are made possible by varying intensities of knowledge (mathematics, engineering), flows of labour (assembly line workers) and assemblages of desire (the manufactured passion for greater speed and mobility). In the final example (watching a bird gather materials for its nest), an observer-assemblage is made possible by the speeds and intensities of wind and rain (ensuring that the twigs have not been blown or washed away), intensities of light (allowing the eye to observe the bird), flows of reproduction (the biological urge to produce offspring) and flows of dead biomass (sticks).

These examples demonstrate that bodies form and move through multiple machinic assemblages from moment to moment and that these assemblages (and their socio-ecological effects) are levied across multiple levels of the mechanosphere (or within a multiplicity of other machinic assemblages). This means that 'environmental damage' cannot be reduced to the collective actions of bodies located within the molar (rigid, segmented, binary) machines of economy, bureaucracy, patriarchy, corporations, politics, pedagogy or law. Rather it is equally the case that the production of anti-ecological flows finds its footing in molar assemblages of a different kind as well. Leisure-assemblages (speedboat racing, formula one), engagement-assemblages (consuming industrially made gold, silver or diamond), music-assemblages (petro-chemicals and polymers in compact discs), dining-assemblages (consuming fish caught in drift-nets or on long-lines, eating the flesh of hoofed animals), artist-assemblages (polymers and toxic chemicals in paints) are all examples of molarised machinic assemblages which leave indelible yet arguably *illegible* marks on the earth (insofar as we have yet to learn to adequately read and write their effects).[6] Isn't it precisely now – in an era where the 'ideal subject' is a body that has been successfully, and, some might say, willingly, folded along the striated lines of credit and the eight hour working day, who actively practices the art of (c)overt pollution on themselves and other species, and who desires the longevity of striated spaces (nuclear family, schools, capital, bureaucracy, government, police, prisons) – isn't it precisely now against the backdrop of an 'integrated world capitalism' (Guattari, 1989; Guattari and Alliez, 1996) that a philosophy of flows, speeds and intensities is most needed to chart new interfaces between 'culture' and 'environment'?

(Some) criminological implications (toward the acategorical)

At first glance, criminology may appear to be decidedly absent from much of the study. But as a discipline concerned with the movements (licit/illicit), intensities and durations of various bodies (of harm, of liability, of intent) it should be apparent that 'the objects of criminology' (Cohen, 1988) are, in one form or another, present throughout. This is certainly not to imply that criminologists have some 'inherent' or long-standing interest in environmental damage. Indeed, as shown in Chapter 2, criminological concern for the 'environment' is a relatively rare and recent event (but see Goff and Geis, 1993; Edwards et al., 1996; Beirne, 1998; Halsey and White, 1998; Williams, 1998; A-Khavari, England and Godden, 1999; Halsey, 1997a, 1997b, 1999; Seis, 1999). Nonetheless, the question I want now to pose and respond to is this: What do the vicissitudes of ~~Goolengook~~ mean for (ecologically oriented) criminological thought? At least four points come to mind.

First, as event, ~~Goolengook~~ assists criminology to know something of the socio-ecological costs of attempting to categorise the acategorical, and by default, the costs of attempting to regulate forces which never arrive on time or remain in (one) place.

6 In conversation, Peter Rush, August, 1997.

The world flows and flees in spite of the bodies imposed by law, by science, by public opinion, or by any other field designed to contain or control 'things'. Because of this, criminology needs to move beyond binary conceptions of the socio-ecological terrain. To do so would help defuse the rhetorics of similitude (and its associated adverse impacts) and enable the differences borne between and across bodies to be valued anew.

Second, criminology needs to come to grips with the role of language in framing and dealing with environmental problems. Until it does this – until, that is, criminology develops a critical understanding of how various discourses frame 'harm' as other than criminal (most usually, as normal, necessary, accidental, incidental, or non-existent) – it will continue to be an (unwitting) apologist for the countless micro-violences levied against earth from moment to moment. An important step toward recognising or naming these violences would be, as previously discussed, to foster an understanding of the various modalities (visions, categories, speeds and affects) which inform those texts which speak, or, as the case may be, do *not* speak, of 'environmental' regulatory matters.

Third, the machinic production of ~~Goolengook~~ enables criminology to see how bodies which appear unified, manifest, and unambiguous are necessarily traversed by the most heterogeneous elements. Accordingly, if criminologists wish to learn something (more) of the processes which lead to environmental damage it is necessary to tease the multiple from the unitary, and to follow the (molar and molecular) lines which arise to the ends of the earth.

Fourth, and finally, criminology would do best to accept that there is no such thing as 'the environment' and, therefore, that there can be no such thing as laws and regulations which speak directly and essentially of 'nature'. The latter waxes and wanes in accordance with the intensity of texts which ascribe forms and functions to (parts of) earth. Here it becomes necessary to speak in terms of the machines which make of the plane of immanence a plane of organisation, and the capacities curtailed or promoted through writing bodies (forests, trees, rivers) in molar fashion. Rather than persisting with the search for 'essential attributes' or trying to predict events ahead of time, criminologists may benefit more from becoming acquainted with the lines of deterritorialisation and reterritorialisation apt to transform bodies. In sum, criminology should work to shake off its unerring belief in the legitimacy and ontological consistency of the representations of 'nature' presently informing its corpus.

Conclusion

In their final collaborative work entitled *What is Philosophy?*, Deleuze and Guattari remark,

> Chaos [i.e. the plane of consistency] is defined not so much by its disorder as by the infinite speed with which every form taking shape in it vanishes. It is a void that is not a nothingness but a *virtual*, containing all possible particles and drawing out all possible forms, which spring up only to disappear immediately, without consistency or reference, without consequence. Chaos is an infinite speed of birth and disappearance (1994b, p. 118).

As should be apparent, Deleuze and Guattari were particularly interested in the way various discourses confront or deal with 'chaos' – the outside, the unsaid, the remainder. The task of philosophy, they argue, is (or should be) to invent concepts which allow the maximum possible chaos – a chaos that would 'retain infinite speeds while gaining consistency …' through ways of thinking, living and communicating that express the individuality and interrelatedness of events (1994b, p. 118). Philosophy, in other words, should involve a continuous experimentation with the Real. This can be sharply contrasted against the molarised worlds reproduced by discourses which rely so heavily upon the ontological certainty of their subjects and objects. Deleuze and Guattari reserve particular scorn for the so-called scientific method,

> Science approaches chaos in a completely different, almost opposite way: it relinquishes the infinite, infinite speed, in order to gain *a reference able to actualise the virtual*… In the case of science it is like a freeze-frame. It is a fantastic *slowing down*, and it is by slowing down that matter, as well as the scientific thought able to penetrate it with propositions, is actualised … To slow down is to set a limit in chaos to which all speeds are subject, so that they form a variable determined as abscissa, at the same time as the limit forms a universal constant that cannot be gone beyond … (Deleuze and Guattari, 1994b, p. 118).

This passage well describes what has transpired over the course of this book. Indeed, to a very large extent, the articulation of the phylum of ~~Goolengook~~ throughout this work can be seen as an attempt to interrupt the plane of reference drawn by various machines (scientific, legal, political, and other). It is an attempt, in other words, to render a 'fantastic slowing down' of events common to a specific geopolitical terrain. *But* unlike the molar discourses of science or law, my intention has *not* been to posit or locate the existence of immutable bodies or a finite set of possibilities within each 'frame' (each text, each fold). Instead, I have attempted to show the volatility and contingency of the Real as it resides within various texts. Accordingly, it is the permanent presence of the possible and not merely the weight of actual that has been the key focus of this study. In short, if the various dimensions of ~~Goolengook~~ have been dramatically slowed down this is only in order to show that there exist a preponderance of trajectories and speeds beyond those typically associated with post-industrial times and constraints.

In 1770 ~~Goolengook~~ was transformed into an outpost of the British empire. More than two centuries later, it became a site subject to police raids. The common trait is that both of these events display all the hallmarks of an invasion – the former receiving its momentum from the juridical imposition of particular bodies of words upon new lands, the latter proceeding by way of the dispatchment of bodies into contested territories. Here, as in all instances, there is a reciprocal relationship between texts and bodies. At stake in this book has been the capacity to write the machines which invade the plane of consistency and in so doing extract molar bodies of various kinds (Nature, Forest, Man, Species) at the expense of difference and vitality. Also in question has been the ability to write such machines without having to ascribe humanity an enduring ontological place – a place that has historically taken as its starting point the dichotomy human/nonhuman.[1] The undeniable politico-ethical strength of a schizoanalytic of environmental regulation is that it views *all* bodies as conduits for the varying flows, speeds and intensities of the cosmos, and, therefore, as sites for the possible diminution of human-induced environmental damage. If the world is thought of in terms of a never-ending flow of non-stratified matter-energy then each body or assemblage becomes a zone of intensity capturing and giving form to such matter-energy in specific ways.

Environmental regulation (no less than environmental conflict) is and always has been about monitoring and controlling the flows, speeds and intensities of matter (organic and inorganic) and energy (kinetic and potential) which pass through and across particular kinds of bodies (atmospheric, aquatic, terrestrial). Conversely, and relatedly, environmental regulation is and always has been a technique used to control and segregate the flows, speeds and intensities of each body as it passes through and across designated zones of matter and energy. As I have attempted to illustrate, the bodies in question here go far beyond the 'human' subject. Of equal importance are the bodies of expertise, forest blocks, endangered species, snig tracks, coupes, heritage rivers, national parks, and so forth. The key question emerging from this book for environmental administrators is this: By what criteria and to what effect do various collective assemblages portend to 'accurately' represent or administer the bodies of Nature? For Deleuze and Guattari, the only means of reply is to study the composition and intensity of the lines traversing the cosmos from one moment to the next – lines of molarity (becomings-the-same, reaction, obedience), lines of molecularity (becomings-other, action, minor dissent), and lines of flight (becomings-immanent, conspicuous dissent, hyper-creativity). Although Goolengook forest block is, in one sense, a remarkably small territory (equivalent in area to Manhattan), the

1 In conversation, Peter Rush, August, 1997.

plane of consistency – the free uninterrupted flow of matter-energy coursing through it – is literally of cosmic proportions. The task for regulators, criminologists and like groups is to see to it that this plane is populated by something more than forms and functions. How might this be accomplished?

As Deleuze and Guattari urge, the first step involvs engaging with the plane of consistency. Playing, in other words, with the idea of flows, speeds and intensities in order to escape the image of thought which governs what it is possible and not possible to do and say with respect to 'the environment'. Relatedly, conjure an image of the acategorical (even as it keeps slipping away, for it surely will) in order to understand anew the ethical weight which arrives with speaking and naming earth. A second tactic would involve thinking in terms of lines rather than structures. That is, consider the idea that molarity (identity) equates more often than not to a truncation of the possibilities associated with particular terrains. Conversely, experiment with the Real in order to maximise the molecular and supermolecular aspects of events. A third strategy would be to give serious consideration to the juxtaposition of bodies which result from the operation of texts. Indeed, all events should be approached as texts to be pulled this way and that rather than as objective instruments or data waiting to be received. Relatedly, realise that although there are no limits to the juxtaposition and ordering of bodies, there are, nonetheless, consequences and effects. It is the machines (political, scientific, legal, economic) which portray these consequences and effects as knowable and/or controllable that need to be exposed for what they are – the impossible masquerading as the attainable.

A fourth course of action would see all bodies out into critical relief (especially so-called 'human' bodies). Conceive bodies as projects in-the-making and as conduits for the flows of commodification which reach across and irrevocably transform the planet. Think about the body as one's first and last means of resisting the forces establishing a becoming-the-same from one territory to the next. Think, in other words, of the epidermis not as a container but as a membrane whose aspects are infused not just by sunlight, sound, water, and so forth but by the decisions reached on climate change, corporate investment, trade subsidies, export volumes, the value of the dollar, and the like around the globe. Treat the body as the politico-ecologically interested force par excellence. In terms of instituting meaningful change, put faith in one's own body (which is, in any case, always already subject to someone else's desires, knowledges, capacities) *before* one puts faith in bodies of laws and regulations. A fifth condition of re-engagement would be to know that socio-environmental conflict will always be present in one form or another. What counts is maintaining enough room on the plane of reference (filled as it is with subjects, objects and Truth) such that no single solution holds sway for any length of time. To run contrary to this would be to invite the forces of fascism into the discourse(s) of environmental harm and its possible renewal. These forces, are, of course, ever-present. But the *proliferation and diversification of environmental strategies* may help limit their impact on day to day struggles. As Guattari writes, 'Rather than looking for a stupefying and infantilising consensus, it will be a question in the future of cultivating a dissensus and the singular production of existence' (2000, p.

50). In simpler terms, 'We must ward off, by every means possible, the entropic rise of a dominant subjectivity' (Guattari, 2000, p. 68).

A sixth and final (although there can be no final) point for commentators to keep in mind when dealing with the problematics of nature would be to connect the process of mapping to the 'wider' expanses of ethics, politics and law. Know that each of these and other 'spheres' exists only insofar as they are produced and reproduced by collective assemblages of enunciation. Further, know that since the nature of an assemblage is to incessantly fuse with and alter the composition of other assemblages (the botany assemblage opening onto the fashion assemblage, the logging assemblage opening onto the juridical assemblage) that one is never totally removed from 'the action'. Accordingly, mapping the earth is not something which can be said to occur in another place at another time on behalf of other groups or species. Instead, the consequences of mapping 'distant' terrains and naming 'unremarked' bodies bear upon the here and now. *Mapping always already has an ethical and social dimension to its aspects*. This is why it is not enough to merely become acquainted with the machines plugged into one's own body. Instead, it is equally vital to develop a knowledge of how and where to plug one's body into the machine or machines deemed capable of delivering the desired socio-ecological effect(s).

In concluding (which is simultaneously a beginning of sorts), it is important to return to a key question posed at the outset of this study: namely, Of what is ~~Goolengook~~ capable subsequent to the production of the different texts which (re)align its body/bodies? In light of foregoing analyses, it is possible to see that this becomes a question concerning the vicissitudes of ~~Goolengook~~ not 'Goolengook'. *Goolengook is the body one must destroy in order to wrestle other becomings and possibilities from its aspects*. The body of Goolengook, in other words, can do little other than fill out one side of the binary oppositions underpinning debates about forest conflict (trees versus jobs, science versus public opinion, and so on). But to ask, What can ~~Goolengook~~ do?, is to pose a very different question. Here, responses are (or should be) unconstrained by the image of thought – by what it is to speak rationally, normally, predictably, responsibly of 'nature'. To ask what ~~Goolengook~~ can do is to immediately embark upon an encounter with the plane of immanence. And this, in short, is to reinstate the unsettling but productive force associated with the acategorical.

Clearly, the range of responses to the question, 'What can ~~Goolengook~~ do?', will always be dependent on the proclivity of 'human' bodies to conceptualise their modes of envisioning, categorising, consuming and affecting as impacting more than their immediate surrounds or circumstances. Bodies are *ex*tensive (in the sense that they irrevocably act and draw vitality from 'distant' worlds) as well as *in*tensive (in the sense that each has its own immediate 'needs', rhythms, and durations). The challenge, it would seem, is to conceive the micro as inescapably macro in both composition and effect. The great strength of a schizoanalytic view of environmental law/regulation, is that it requires each body to consider the way it invites or participates in its own *reactive* state of affairs. As one commentator has remarked,

> The politics that emerges from Deleuze's analysis is a micropolitics situated on many levels ... For Deleuze, what must be understood is not – or better, not only – how I am oppressed by external circumstances, but the ways in which I participate in, foster, and desire oppression even in trying to escape or overturn it. The most insidious dangers of social oppression are not the horrors done to me against my will – though they are bad enough – but the horrors I am made to desire. The great political discovery of Deleuze ... is this: what keeps us all from becoming revolutionaries is not that we are fooled, but that we have come to desire what oppresses us (May, 1991, p. 31).

Here, the rewriting of spaces such as ~~Goolengook~~ necessarily equates to rewriting the capacities and co-ordinates of our own bodies as well. This is a process that need have very little to do with criminalising this or that practice and far more to do with a reconceptualisation of bodies, their mixtures, and the machines which attempt to hypostatise their aspects. Michel Tournier – the subject of one of Deleuze's early essays – once observed, 'That was what other people were: the possible obstinately passing for the real' (quoted in Deleuze, 1990, p. 309). Might this sentiment not also hold true for the machines which name, divide, measure and otherwise give form and function to the plane of consistency? In short, might these words not hold good with respect to Nature? If so, the object of future socio-ecological struggles should not – indeed cannot – be the 'environment' or 'humanity', but the techniques and processes which govern their image(s) and frame the limits of the possible.

References

Acampora, R. (1994), 'Using and Abusing Nietzsche for Environmental Ethics', *Environmental Ethics*, Vol. 16, No. 2, pp. 187–94.

A-Khavari, A., England, P. and Godden, L. (eds) (1999), 'Special Issue: Interdisciplinary Perspectives on Environmental Law', *Griffith Law Review*, Vol. 8, No. 2.

Ansell-Pearson, K. (1999), *Germinal Life: The Difference and Repetition of Deleuze*, London: Routledge.

Arendt, H. (1959), *The Human Condition*, Chicago: University of Chicago Press.

Armitage, J. (1997), 'Accelerated Aesthetics', *Angelaki*, Vol. 2, No. 3, pp. 199–208.

Auchmuty, J.J. (1976), '1810–30', in F. Crowley (ed.), *A New History of Australia*, Adelaide: Griffin Press, pp. 45–81.

Auditor-General of Victoria (1993), *Special Report no. 22, Timber Industry Strategy*, Melbourne: L.V. North, Government Printer.

Australian Bureau of Agricultural and Resource Economics (2001), *Australian Forest and Wood Products Statistics*, Canberra: ABARE, March/June quarters.

Australian Heritage Commission and Department of Natural Resources and Environment (1996), *Comprehensive Regional Assessment, East Gippsland: National Estate Report July 1996*, Canberra: Joint Commonwealth and Victorian Regional Forest Agreement (RFA) Steering Committee.

Bahro, R. (1984), *From Red to Green*, London: Verso and NLB.

Barbier, E. (1989), 'The Contribution of Environmental and Resource Economics to an Economics of Sustainable Development', *Development and Change*, Vol. 20, pp. 429–59.

Barde, J. and Pearce, D. (eds) (1991), *Valuing the Environment*, London: Earthscan.

Barnett, H. (1999), 'The Land Ethic and Environmental Crime', *Criminal Justice Policy Review*, Vol. 10, No. 2, pp. 161–92.

Barry, A., Osborne, T. and Rose, N. (eds) (1996), *Foucault and Political Reason: Liberalism, Neo-Liberalism and Rationalities Government*, Chicago: University of Chicago Press.

Barthes, R. (1993), *Mythologies*, London: Vintage.

Bate, J. (1991), *Romantic Ecology*, London: Routledge.

Bauman, Z. (1988), 'Is there a Postmodern Sociology', *Theory, Culture and Society*, Vol. 5, pp. 217–37.

Bauman, Z. (1991), *Modernity and the Holocaust*, Ithaca: Cornell University Press.

Bauman, Z. (1995), *Postmodern Ethics*, Oxford: Blackwell Publishers.

Bauman, Z. (2000), 'Social Issues of Law and Order', *British Journal of Criminology*, Vol. 40, No. 2, pp. 205–21.

Beck, U. (1992), *Risk Society*, London: Sage.

Becker, H. (1963), *Outsiders*, New York: Free Press.

Beirne, P. (ed.) (1998), 'Special Issue: For a Green Criminology', *Theoretical Criminology*, Vol. 2, No. 2.

Belsey, C. (2002) *Poststructuralism: A Very Short Introduction*, New York: Oxford University Press.

Benton, T. (1989), 'Marxism and Natural Limits', *New Left Review*, No. 178, pp. 51–86.

Benton, T. (1992), 'Ecology, Socialism and the Mastery of Nature: A Reply to Reiner Grundmann', *New Left Review*, pp. 55–74.

Benton, T. (1998), 'Rights and Justice on a Shared Planet: More Rights or New Relations', *Theoretical Criminology*, Vol. 2, No. 2, pp. 149–76.

Berger, J. (1977), *Ways of Seeing*, London: Penguin.

Bernard, J.R.L. (ed.) (1989), *The Pocket Macquarie Dictionary*, Sydney: The Jacaranda Press.

Birch, T.H. (1990), 'The Incarceration of Wilderness: Wilderness Areas as Prisons', *Environmental Ethics*, Vol. 12, pp. 3–26.

Birkeland, J. (1993), 'Eco-feminism: Linking Theory and Practice', in G. Gaard (ed.), *Ecofeminism: Women, Animals, Nature*, Philadelphia: Temple University Press, pp. 13–59.

Blondel, E. (1991), *Nietzsche: The Body and Culture*, Stanford: Stanford University Press.

Bookchin, M. (1986), *The Modern Crisis*, Philadelphia: New Society Publishers.

Bookchin, M. (1987), 'Social Ecology versus "Deep Ecology": A Challenge for the Ecology Movement', *The Raven Anarchist Quarterly*, Vol. 1, No. 3, pp. 219–50.

Box, S. (1983), *Power, Crime and Mystification*, London: Tavistock.

Brown, R.H. (1995), 'Rhetoric, Textuality, and the Postmodern Turn in Sociological Theory', in S. Seidman (ed.), *The Postmodern Turn: New Perspectives on Social Theory*, Cambridge: Cambridge University Press, pp. 229–41.

Bruner, M. and Oelschlaeger, M. (1994), 'Rhetoric, Environmentalism, and Environmental Ethics', *Environmental Ethics*, Vol. 16, pp. 377–96.

Cache, B. (1995), *Earth Moves*, Cambridge: Massachusetts Institute of Technology.

Carrington, K. (1994), 'Postmodernism and Feminist Criminologies: Disconnecting Discourses?', *International Journal of the Sociology of Law*, Vol. 22, pp. 261–77.

Carron, L.T. (1985), *A History of Forestry in Australia*, Rushcutters Bay: Pergamon Press.

Carson, R. (1956), *The Sea Around Us*, Mitcham: Penguin.

Carson, R. (1965), *Silent Spring*, Ringwood: Penguin.

Castillina, L. (1985), 'Why "Red" Must be "Green" Too', in Nikolic, M. (ed.) *Socialism on the Threshold of the Twenty-first Century*, London: Verso.

Chawla, S. (1991), 'Linguistic and Philosophical Roots of Our Environmental Crisis', *Environmental Ethics*, Vol. 13, No. 3, pp. 253–62.
Cheney, J. (1989), 'Postmodern Environmental Ethics: Ethics as Bioregional Narrative', *Environmental Ethics*, Vol. 11, No. 2, pp. 117–34.
Clark, J. (ed.) (1990), *Renewing the Earth: The Promise of Social Ecology*, London: Merlin Press.
Cohen, S. (1988), *Against Criminology*, New Brunswick: Transaction Books.
Collingwood, R.G. (1960), *The Idea of Nature*, London: Oxford University Press.
Commonwealth of Australia (1992), *National Forest Policy Statement*, Canberra: Commonwealth of Australia.
Conley, V. (1997), *Ecopolitics: The Environment in Poststructuralist Thought*, London: Routledge.
Cornish, H. (1975) [1880], *Under the Southern Cross*, Ringwood: Penguin.
Crary, J. (1996), *Techniques of the Observer: On Vision and Modernity in the Nineteenth Century*, Cambridge: MIT Press.
Darier, E. (ed.) (1999), *Discourses of the Environment*, Oxford: Blackwell Publishers.
Davies, J. (2002), 'To Fight Environmental Crime, Together, and Win', *The Journal of the Australian Federal Police: Platypus Magazine*, No. 74, pp. 20–8.
Davies, M. (1994), *Asking the Law Question*, Sydney: Law Book Company.
Davies, M. (1998), 'The Proper Discourses of Purity', *Law and Critique*, Vol. 9, pp. 147–73.
De Landa, M. (1997), *A Thousand Years of Nonlinear History*, New York: Zone Books.
Delaney, D. (2001), 'Semantic Ecology and Lexical Violence: Nature at the Limits of Law', *Law, Text, Culture*, Vol. 5, No. 2, pp. 77–112.
Deleuze, G. (1971) 'Codes', lecture 16th November 1971, www.webdeleuze.com/sommaire.html, English translation.
Deleuze, G. (1983), *Nietzsche and Philosophy*, New York: Columbia University Press.
Deleuze, G. (1986), *Cinema 1: The Movement Image*, H. Tomlinson and B. Habberjam (trans.), Minneapolis: University of Minnesota Press.
Deleuze, G. (1987), *Dialogues*, London: Athlone.
Deleuze, G. (1988), *Foucault*, Minneapolis: University of Minnesota Press.
Deleuze, G. (1990), *The Logic of Sense*, New York: Columbia University Press.
Deleuze, G. (1992), *Expressionism in Philosophy: Spinoza*, New York: Zone Books.
Deleuze, G. (1994), *Difference and Repetition*, New York: Columbia University Press.
Deleuze, G. (1995), 'Foucault and the Prison', in B. Smart (ed.), *Michel Foucault: Critical Assessments, Politics, Ethics and Truth*, London: Routledge, pp. 266–71.
Deleuze, G. and Guattari, F. (1986), *Kafka: Toward a Minor Literature*, Minneapolis: University of Minnesota Press.

Deleuze, G. and Guattari, F. (1994a), *Anti-Oedipus: Capitalism and Schizophrenia*, Minneapolis: University of Minnesota Press.

Deleuze, G. and Guattari, F. (1994b), *What is Philosophy?*, London: Verso.

Deleuze, G. and Guattari, F. (1996), *A Thousand Plateaus: Capitalism and Schizophrenia*, Minneapolis: University of Minnesota Press.

del Frate, A.A. and Norberry, J. (eds) (1993), *Environmental Crime, Sanctioning Strategies and Sustainable Development*, UNICRI/AIC: Rome/Canberra.

Department of Conservation, Forests and Lands (1989), *Code of Forest Practices for Timber Production*, Victoria: Department of Conservation, Forests and Lands.

Department of Conservation and Natural Resources (1993a), *Statement of Resources, Uses and Values: East Gippsland Forest Management Area*, East Melbourne: Department of Conservation and Natural Resources.

Department of Conservation and Natural Resources (1993b), *Hardwood Timber Resources in the East Gippsland Forest Management Area: Areas and Volumes Report*, Resource Assessment Report No. 93/01, Melbourne: Department of Conservation and Natural Resources.

Department of Conservation and Natural Resources (1995), *Forest Management Plan for the East Gippsland Forest Management Area*, East Melbourne: Department of Conservation and Natural Resources.

Department of Natural Resources and Environment (1996), *Code of Practice: Code of Forest Practices for Timber Production, Revision No. 2*, East Melbourne: Department of Natural Resources and Environment.

Department of Natural Resources and Environment (1997a), *Victoria's Biodiversity: Sustaining Our Living Wealth*, East Melbourne: Department of Natural Resources and Environment.

Department of Natural Resources and Environment (1997b), 'East Gippsland's Forests', East Melbourne, Media Release, July.

Derrida, J. (1992), 'Force of Law: The "Mystical Foundation of Authority"', in G. Carlson, D. Cornell and M. Rosenfeld (eds), *Deconstruction and the Possibility of Justice*, New York: Routledge.

Devall, B. and Sessions, G. (1985), *Deep Ecology: Living as if Nature Mattered*, Salt Lake City: Gibbs Smith.

Dobson, A. (1990), *Green Political Thought*, London: Unwin Hyman.

Douglas, M. (1966), *Purity and Danger: An Analysis of Concepts of Pollution and Taboo*, London: Routledge and Kegan Paul.

Doyle, R. (1997), *On Beyond Living: Rhetorical Transformations of the Life Sciences*, Stanford: Stanford University Press.

Dunkley, G. (1992), *The Greening of the Red: Sustainability, Socialism and the Environmental Crisis*, Leichardt: Pluto Press.

Dunlop, E.W. and Pike, W. (1965), *Australia: Colony to Nation*, 2nd edition, Sydney: New Century Press.

Eckersley, R. (1992), *Environmentalism and Political Theory: Toward an Ecocentric Approach*, London: UCL Press.

Edwards, S., Edwards, T. and Fields, C. (eds) (1996), *Environmental Crime and Criminality: Theoretical and Practical Issues*, New York: Garland Publishing.

Environment Australia (1998), *National Pollutant Inventory Guide*, Canberra: Environment Australia.

Environment Protection Authority (1994), *Environment Protection Authority Annual Report 93/94*, Melbourne: EPA.

Environment Protection Authority (1995), *Environment Protection Authority Annual Report 94/95*, Melbourne: EPA.

Environment Protection Authority (1996), *Environment Protection Authority Annual Report 95/96*, Melbourne: EPA.

Environment Protection Authority (1997), *Environment Protection Authority Annual Report 96/97,* Melbourne: EPA.

Ewald, F. (1995), 'Bio-Power', in B. Smart (ed.), *Michel Foucault: Critical Assessments*, Vol. 5, Sec. 2, 'Relations of Power and Knowledge', London: Routledge, pp. 281–84.

Featherstone, M. (1991), 'The Body in Consumer Culture', in M. Featherstone, M. Hepworth and B. Turner (eds), *The Body: Social Process and Cultural Theory*, London: Sage, pp. 170–96.

Featherstone, M. (1993), *Consumer Culture and Postmodernism*, London: Sage.

Ferguson, K.V.M. (1957), *Handbook of Forestry in Victoria*, prepared for The Forests Commission of Victoria, Miscellaneous Publication No. 7, Melbourne: Government Printer.

Flannery, T. (1994), *The Future Eaters: An Ecological History of the Australian Lands and Peoples*, Catswood, NSW: Reed Books.

Forbes, S.J., Gullan, P.K. and Walsh, N.G. (1981), *Sites of Botanical Significance in East Gippsland*, Environmental Studies Division Paper, No. 322, Victoria: Ministry for Conservation.

Forests Commission of Victoria (1928), *Handbook of Forestry in Victoria*, Melbourne: Government Printer.

Forests Commission of Victoria (1943), *Summary of Evidence presented before the Rural Reconstruction Commission of the Ministry of Post-war Reconstruction by A.V. Gailbraith*, Miscellaneous Publication No. 2, August, Melbourne: Government Printer.

Forests Task Force (1995), *Deferred Forest Areas: Victoria*, Canberra: Department of Prime Minister and Cabinet.

Forsyth, J. (1998), 'Anarchy in the Forests: A Plethora of Rules, an Absence of Enforceability', *Environmental and Planning Law Journal*, Vol. 15, No. 5, pp. 338–49.

Foster, H. (ed.) (1988), *Vision and Visuality*, Seattle: Bay Press.

Foucault, M. (1971), 'A Conversation with Michel Foucault', *Partisan Review*, Vol. 38, No. 2, pp. 192–201.

Foucault, M. (1977), *Discipline and Punish*, Ringwood: Penguin.

Foucault, M. (1980a), *Language, Counter-Memory, Practice: Selected Essays and Interviews by Michel Foucault*, edited and introduced by Donald F. Bouchard, New York: Cornell University Press.

Foucault, M. (1980b), *Power/Knowledge: Selected Interviews and Other Writings 1972–1977*, edited by Colin Gordon, New York: Pantheon Books.

Foucault, M. (1982), 'Afterword: The Subject and Power', in H.L. Dreyfus and P. Rabinow (eds), *Michel Foucault: Beyond Structuralism and Hermeneutics*, Chicago: University of Chicago Press.

Foucault, M. (1990), 'Nietzsche, Freud, Marx', in G. Ormiston and A. Schrift (eds), *Transforming the Hermeneutic Context: From Nietzsche to Nancy*, Albany, NY: State University of New York Press.

Foucault, M. (1991a), *Remarks on Marx*, New York: Semiotext(e).

Foucault, M. (1991b), 'On the Genalogy of Ethics: An Overview of Work in Progress', in P. Rabinow (ed.), *The Foucault Reader: An Introduction to Foucault's Thought*, Penguin: London.

Foucault, M. (1997), *The Order Things: An Archaeology of the Human Sciences*, London: Routledge.

Fox, W. (1989), 'The Deep Ecology-Ecofeminism Debate and its Parallels', *Environmental Ethics*, Vol. 11, pp. 5–25.

Frank, A. (1995), 'For a Sociology of the Body: An Analytical Review', in M. Featherstone, M. Hepworth and B. Turner (eds), *The Body: Social Process and Cultural Theory*, London: Sage, pp. 36–102.

Frawley, K.J. (1993), 'Logging Practices and Forest Cutting Practices', in J. Dargavel and S. Feary (eds), *Australia's Ever-Changing Forests II*, Canberra: Australian Forest History Society/Centre for Resource and Environmental Studies, pp. 143–64.

Fuller, G. (2000), 'The Textual Politics of Good Intentions: Critical Theory and Semiotics', in A. Lee and C. Poynton (eds), *Culture and Text: Discourse and Methodology in Social Research and Cultural Studies*, St. Leonards: Allen and Unwin, pp. 81–98.

Gaard, G. (1993a), 'Living Interconnectedness with Animals and Nature', in G. Gaard (ed.), *Ecofeminism: Women, Animals, Nature*, Philadelphia: Temple University Press, pp. 1–12.

Gaard, G. (1993b), 'Ecofeminism and Native American Cultures: Pushing the Limits of Cultural Imperialism', in G. Gaard (ed.), *Ecofeminism: Women, Animals, Nature*, Philadelphia: Temple University Press, pp. 295–314.

Gare, A. (1995), *Postmodernism and the Environmental Crisis*, New York: Routledge.

Goff, C. and Geis, G. (eds) (1993), 'The Environment and Social Justice', *The Journal of Human Justice*, Vol. 5, No. 1.

Goffman, I. (1963), *Stigma*, Prentice Hall: Englewood Cliffs.

Grabosky, P. (1994), 'Green Markets: Environmental Regulation by the Private Sector', *Law and Policy*, Vol. 16, No. 4, pp. 420–48.

Grabosky, P. and Braithwaite, J. (1986), *Of Manners Gentle: Enforcement Strategies of Australian Business Regulatory Agencies*, Melbourne: Oxford University Press.

Grabosky, P. and Gant, F. (2000), *Improving Environmental Performance, Preventing Environmental Crime*, Research and Public Policy Series, No. 27, Canberra: AIC.

Groombridge, N. (1998), 'Masculinities and Crimes Against the Environment', *Theoretical Criminology*, Vol. 2, No. 2, pp. 249–68.

Grundmann, R. (1991), 'The Ecological Challenge to Marxism', *New Left Review*, No. 187, pp. 103–20.

Guattari, F. (1988), 'Three Ecologies', paper delivered at *Psychoanalytic Forum*, 26 November 1988, London: ICA Video (No 404).

Guattari, F. (1989), 'The Three Ecologies', *New Formations*, Vol. 8, pp. 131–47.

Guattari, F. (1995), *Chaosmosis*, Sydney: Power Publications.

Guattari, F. (1996a), *Soft Subversions*, New York: Semiotext(e).

Guattari, F. (1996b), *The Guattari Reader*, edited by G. Genosko, Oxford: Blackwell.

Guattari, F. (2000), *The Three Ecologies*, London: Athlone Press.

Guattari, F. and Alliez, E. (1996), *Communists Like Us*, New York: Semiotext(e).

Gunningham, N., Norberry, J. and McKillop, S. (eds) (1995), *Environmental Crime*, Conference Porceedings Series, No. 26, Canberra: AIC.

Hallman, M. (1991), 'Nietzsche's Environmental Ethics', *Environmental Ethics*, Vol. 13, No. 2, pp. 99–125.

Halsey, M. (1997a), 'Environmental Crime: Towards an Eco-Human Rights Approach', *Current Issues in Criminal Justice*, Vol. 8, No. 3, pp. 217–42.

Halsey, M. (1997b), 'The Wood for the Paper: Old-growth Forest, Hemp and Environmental Harm', *Australian and New Zealand Journal of Criminology*, Vol. 30, No. 2, pp. 121–48.

Halsey, M. (1999), 'Environmental Discontinuities: The Production and Regulation of an Eco-experience', *Criminal Justice Policy Review*, Vol. 10, No. 2, pp. 213–55.

Halsey, M. and White, R. (1998), 'Crime, Ecophilosophy and Environmental Harm', *Theoretical Criminology*, Vol. 2, No. 3, pp. 345–72.

Harari, J. (1979), 'Critical Factions/Critical Fictions', in J. Harari (ed.), *Textual Strategies: Perspectives in Poststructuralist Criticism*, New York: Cornell University Press, pp. 17–72.

Hayden, P. (1997), 'Gilles Deleuze and Naturalism: A Convergence with Ecological Theory and Politics', *Environmental Ethics*, Vol. 19, No. 2, pp. 185–204.

Henry, S. and Milovanovic, D. (1996), *Constitutive Criminology: Beyond Postmodernism*, London: Sage.

Historical Subcommittee of Centenary Celebrations Council (1934), *Victoria the First Century: An Historical Survey*, Melbourne: Robertson and Mullens.

Howard, T. (2000), 'Liability of Directors for Environmental Crime: The Anything-but-Level Playing Field in Australia', *Environmental and Planning Law Journal*, Vol. 17, No. 4, pp. 250–71.

JANIS (1995), *Broad Criteria for the Establishment of Comprehensive, Adequate and Representative Forest Reserve System in Australia*, Canberra: Joint ANZECC-MCFFA National Forest Policy Statement Implementation Sub-committee.

Jay, M. (1988), 'Scopic Regimes of Modernity', in H. Foster (ed.), *Vision and Visuality*, Seattle: Bay Press, pp. 3–28.

Kofman, S. (1991), 'Descartes Entrapped', in E. Cadaua, P. Connor, and J.L. Nancy (eds), *Who Comes After the Subject?*, New York: Routledge, pp. 178–97.

Lacan, J. (1968), *The Language of the Self*, Baltimore: The Johns Hopkins University Press.

Lakoff, G. and Johnson, M. (1980), *Metaphors We Live By*, Chicago: University of Chicago Press.

Land Conservation Council (1977), *Land Conservation Council Final Recommendations, East Gippsland Study Area*, Melbourne: Victorian Government Printing Office.

Land Conservation Council (1986), *Final Recommendations, East Gippsland Area Review*, Victoria: Land Conservation Council.

Land Conservation Council (1991), *Rivers and Streams, Special Investigation: Final Recommendations*, Melbourne: Department of Conservation and Environment.

Land Conservation Council (1997), *Annual Report 1996–97*, Victoria: Land Conservation Council.

Lane, P. (1998), 'Ecofeminism Meets Criminology', *Theoretical Criminology*, Vol. 2, No. 2, pp. 235–48.

Lash, S., Szerszynski, B. and Wynne, B. (eds) (1996), *Risk, Environment and Modernity*, London: Sage.

Lecercle, J-J. (2002), *Deleuze and Language*, Houndmills: Palgrave Macmillan.

Leff, E. (1993), 'Marxism and the Environmental Question: From the Critical Theory of Production to an Environmental Rationality for Sustainable Development', *Capitalism, Nature, Socialism*, Vol. 4, no. 1, pp. 44–66.

Lemert, E. (1967), *Human Deviance, Social Problems and Social Control*, Englewood Cliffs: Prentice Hall.

Leopold, A. (1970), *A Sand County Almanac*, New York: Ballantine Books.

Levi-Strauss, C. (1963), *Structural Anthropology*, New York: Basic Books.

Litfin, K. (1994), *Ozone Discourses*, New York: Columbia University Press.

Lobert, B.O., Gillespie, G.R., Lunt, I.D., Peacock, R.J. and Robinson, D. (1991), *Ecological Survey Report no. 35 Flora and Fauna of the Goolengook Forest Block, East Gippsland, Victoria*, East Melbourne: Department of Conservation and Environment.

Lowe, D.M. (1982), *History of Bourgeois Perception*, Sussex: Harvester Press.

Luke, T. (1995), 'On Environmentality: Geo-Power and Eco-Knowledge in the Discourses of Contemporary Environmentalism', *Cultural Critique*, Fall, pp. 57–81.

Luke, T. (1997), *Ecocritique*, Minneapolis: University of Minnesota Press.
Lunn, S. (2000), 'Log Jam', *The Australian Magazine*, May 13 and 14, pp. 28–31.
Luzon, M. (1992), 'Political Ecological Considerations in Marx', *Capitalism, Nature, Socialism*, Vol. 3, No. 1, pp. 37–48.
Lynch, M. (1990), 'The Greening of Criminology: A Perspective for the 1990s', *The Critical Criminologist*, Vol. 2, pp. 11–12.
Lynch, M. and Stretsky, P. (2003), 'The Meaning of Green: Contrasting Criminological Perspectives', *Theoretical Criminology*, Vol. 7, No. 2, pp. 217–38.
Markham, A. (1994), *A Brief History of Pollution*, New York: St Martin's Press.
Marx, K. (1977), *Economic and Philosophic Manuscripts of 1844*, Moscow: Progress Publishers.
Marx, K. (1988), *Selected Writings*, edited by David McLellan, Oxford: Oxford University Press.
Massumi, B. (1992), *A User's Guide to Capitalism and Schizophrenia*, Cambridge, MA: Massachusetts Institute of Technology.
Massumi, B. (1996), 'The Autonomy of Affect', in P. Patton (ed.), *Deleuze: A Critical Reader*, Sydney: Blackwell, pp. 217–39.
May, T. (1991), 'The Politics of Life in the Thought of Gilles Deleuze', *SubStance*, No. 66, pp. 24–35.
May, T. (1997), *Reconsidering Difference*, University Park, PA: Pennsylvania State University Press.
McDowell, D. (1997), *Wildlife Crime Policy and the Law: An Australian Study*, Canberra: Australian Government Printing Service.
McKinty, J.M. (1969), 'Forestry in East Gippsland', *Royal Society of Victoria Proceedings*, East Gippsland Symposium, Vol. 82, Part 1, pp. 129–39.
McRae, C.F. (1976), 'Exploration, Early Settlement and Agricultural Development', in C.F. McRae (ed.), *Land to Pasture: Environment, Land Use and Primary Production in East Gippsland*, Bairnsdale: Department of Agriculture, pp. 53–68.
Merchant, C. (1992), *Radical Ecology: The Search for a Livable World*, New York: Routledge.
Merrall, E. (1888), 'An Unknown Portion of Victoria', *Transactions and Proceedings of the Royal Geographical Society of Australasia (Victorian Branch)*, Part 1, Vol. 5, March, pp. 9–13.
Meyer, M. (1989), 'Toward and Anthropology of Rhetoric', in M. Myer (ed.), *From Metaphysics to Rhetoric*, London: Kluwer Publications, pp. 111–35.
Mies, M. and Shiva, V. (1993), *Ecofeminism*, Melbourne: Spinifex.
Miller, M. (1997), 'Peacekeepers in a War of Tactics', *Police Life: The Victorian Police Magazine*, December Issue, Melbourne: Publications Unit, Victoria Police, pp. 10–12.
Moulds, F. (1991) *The Dynamic Forest: A History of Forests and Forest Industries in Victoria*, Richmond, Victoria: Lynedoch Publications.
Naess, A. (1973), 'The Shallow and the Deep, Long-Range Ecology Movement: A Summary', *Inquiry*, Vol. 16, pp. 95–100.

Naess, A. (1989), *Ecology, Community, and Lifestyle*, Cambridge: Cambridge University Press.

Naffine, N. (1990), *Law and the Sexes*, Sydney: Allen and Unwin.

Nast, H. and Pile, S. (1998), 'EverydayPlacesBodies', in H. Nast and S. Pile (eds), *Places Through the Body*, London: Routledge, pp. 405–16.

National Forest Conservation Reserves, Commonwealth Proposed Criteria: A Position Paper, July 1995.

National Greenhouse Gas Inventory Committee (1997), *National Greenhouse Gas Inventory 1995*, Canberra: Environment Australia.

Nelken, D. (ed.) (1994), *The Futures of Criminology*, London: Sage.

Nietzsche, F. (1968), *The Will to Power*, New York: Vintage Books.

Nietzsche, F. (1969), *Thus Spoke Zarathustra*, London: Penguin.

Nietzsche, F. (1974), *The Gay Science, With a Prelude in Rhymes and an Appendix of Songs*, W. Kaufmann (trans., ed.), New York: Random House.

Nietzsche, F. (1979), *Ecce Homo*, London: Penguin.

Nietzsche, F. (1990a), *Twilight of the Idols/The Anti-Christ*, London: Penguin.

Nietzsche, F. (1990b), *Beyond Good and Evil*, London: Penguin.

Nietzsche, F. (1991), *Human, All Too Human*, Cambridge: Cambridge University Press.

Nietzsche, F. (1992), *Philosophy and Truth: Selections from Nietzsche's Notebooks of the Early 1870s*, D. Breazeale (trans., ed.), New Jersey: Humanities Press International.

Nietzsche, F. (1994), *Philosophy in the Tragic Age of the Greeks*, Washington, D.C.: Regnery.

Norris, K.C. and Mansergh, I.M. (1981), *Sites of Zoological Significance in East Gippsland*, Environmental Studies Series Report, No. 321, Victoria: Ministry for Conservation.

O'Bryan, D. (1983), *Pioneering East Gippsland*, Gisborne, Victoria: D. O'Bryan.

Olsen, F. (1990), 'The Sex of Law', in D. Kairys (ed.), *The Politics of Law*, New York: Pantheon Books, pp. 453–67.

O'Riordan, T. (1976), *Environmentalism*, London: Pion.

Paehlke, R. and Torgerson, D. (eds) (1990), *Managing Leviathan: Environmental Politics and the Administrative State*, London: Belhaven.

Parkes, G. (1999), 'Staying Loyal to the Earth: Nietzsche as Ecological Thinker', in J. Lippet (ed.), *Nietzsche's Futures*, New York: St. Martin's Press, pp. 167–88.

Parsons, H.L. (ed.) (1977), *Marx and Engels on Ecology*, Westport: Greenwood Press.

Patton, P. (2000), *Deleuze and the Political*, New York: Routledge.

Pavlich, G. (1999), 'Criticism and Criminology: In Search of Legitimacy', *Theoretical Criminology*, Vol. 3, No. 1, pp. 29–51.

Pavlich, G. (2000), 'Forget Crime: Accusation, Governance and Criminology', *Australian and New Zealand Journal of Criminology*, Vol. 33, No. 2, pp. 136–52.

Pavlich, G. (2001) 'Critical Genres and Radical Criminology in Britain', *British Journal of Criminology*, Vol. 41, No. 1, pp. 150–67.

Peace, A. (1997), 'Governing the Environment: The Programs and Politics of Environmental Discourse', in C. O'Farrell (ed.), *Foucault: The Legacy*, Brisbane: Queensland University of Technology, pp. 530–45.

Pearce, D. (ed.) (1991), *Blueprint 2: Greening the World Economy*, London: Earthscan.

Pearce, D., Markandya, A. and Barbier, E. (1989), *Blueprint for a Green Economy*, London: Earthscan.

Pearce, F. and Tombs, S. (1998) *Toxic Capitalism: Corporate Crime and the Chemical Industry*, Brookfield, VT: Ashgate.

Peers, J.G. (1885), *Reports of the Mining Registrars for the Quarter Ended 30th June,* Appendix B, pp. 70–1.

Pepper, D. (1993), *Eco-Socialism: From Deep Ecology to Social Justice*, New York: Routledge.

Pepper, P. and De Araugo, T. (1985), *The Kurnai of East Gippsland*, Melbourne: Hyland House.

Plumwood, V. (1986), 'Eco-Feminism: An Overview and Discussion of Positions and Arguments', *Australasian Journal of Philosophy*, supplement to Vol. 64, pp. 120–38.

Rabinow, P. (ed.) (1991), *The Foucault Reader*, London: Penguin.

Rajchman, J. (1998), *Constructions*, Cambridge: Massachusetts Institute of Technology.

Raskin, P.D. and Bernow, S.S. (1991), 'Ecology and Marxism: Are Green and Red Complementary', *Rethinking Marxism*, Vol. 4, No. 1, pp. 87–103.

Resource Assessment Commission (1989), *Issues for Inquiries*, Canberra: Pirie Printer Sales.

Resource Assessment Commisssion (1992), *Forest and Timber Inquiry Final Report: Overview*, Canberra: Australian Government Printing Service.

Rose, N. (1999), *Governing the Soul: The Shaping of the Private Self*, 2nd edition, London: Free Association Books.

Rural and Regional Affairs and Transport Legislation Committee (1999), *Reference: Regional Forest Agreements Bill 1998*, Tuesday 2nd February 1999, Melbourne, Proof Committee Hansard, Commonwealth of Australia.

Russell, L. (1998), '"Mere Trifles and Faint Representations": The Representations of Savage Life Offered by Eliza Fraser', in J. McNiven, L. Russell and K. Schaffer (eds), *Constructions of Colonialism: Perspectives on Eliza Fraser's Shipwreck*, London: Leicester University Press, pp. 51–62.

Rutherford, P. (1997), 'Policing Nature: Ecology, Natural Science and Biopolitics', in C. O'Farrell (ed.), *Foucault: The Legacy*, Brisbane: Queensland University of Technology, pp. 546–62.

Salleh, A. (1997), *Ecofeminism as Politics: Nature, Marx and the Postmodern*, London: Zed Books.

Saussure, F. de (1966), *Course in General Linguistics*, New York: McGraw Hill.

Schwendinger, H. and Schwendinger, J. (1975), 'Defenders of Order or Guardians of Human Rights?', in I. Taylor, P. Walton and J. Young (eds), *Critical Criminology*, London: Routledge and Kegan Paul.

Scotts, D. (1991), 'Old-growth Forests: Their Ecological Characteristics and Value to Forest-Dependent Vertebrate Fauna of South-East Australia', in D. Lunney (ed.), *Conservation of Australia's Forest Fauna*, Sydney: Surrey Beatty, pp. 147–61.

Seddon, G. (1997), *Landprints: Reflections on Place and Landscape*, Cambridge: Cambridge University Press.

Seidman, S. (1994), 'Introduction', in S. Seidman (ed.), *The Postmodern Turn*, Melbourne: Cambridge University Press, pp. 1–26.

Seis, M. (1993), 'Ecological Blunders in US Clean Air Legislation', *Journal of Human Justice*, Vol. 5, No. 1, pp. 58–81.

Seis, M. (ed.) (1999), 'Special Issue: Environmental Justice Policy', *Criminal Justice Policy Review*, Vol. 10, No. 2.

Shank, G. (ed.) (2002), 'Special Issue: Globalisation and Environmental Harm', *Social Justice*, Vol. 29, No. 1/2.

Shaw, A.G.L. (1976) '1788–1810', in F. Crowley (ed.), *A New History of Australia*, Adelaide: Griffin Press, pp. 1–44.

Shiva, V. (1988), *Staying Alive: Women, Ecology and Development*, London: Zed Books.

Shiva, V. (1993), 'Homeless in the Global Village', in M. Mies and V. Shiva (eds) *Ecofeminism*, Melbourne: Spinifex, pp. 98–107.

Simington, F. (1997), 'Sensory Speculations: Visual Discourse and the Vision of Visuality', *Social Semiotics*, Vol. 7, No. 3, pp. 307–21.

Sontheimer, S. (ed.) (1991), *Women and the Environment: A Reader*, London: Earthscan.

South Australian Government (1996), *A Greener South Australia*, statement on the environment, The Hon. Dean Brown, Premier of South Australia.

Spencer, B. and French, C. (1889), 'Trip to Croajingolong', *Victorian Naturalist*, Vol. 6, May–June, pp. 1–38.

Spinoza, B. de (1996), *Ethics*, London: Penguin.

State of the Environment Advisory Council (1996), *Australia: State of the Environment 1996*, Executive Summary, Collingwood: CSIRO Publishing.

Sutherland, E. (1949), *White Collar Crime*, New York: Dryden Press.

Tappan, P. (1947), 'Who is the Criminal?', *American Sociological Review*, Vol. 12, pp. 96–102.

Tranter, K. (1999) 'Return to Green Foundations: Liberation and Survival', *Griffith Law Review*, Vol. 8, No. 2, pp. 280–316.

Tobias, M. (ed.) (1985), *Deep Ecology*, San Diego: Avant Books.

Turner, B. (1995), 'Recent Development in the Theory of the Body', in M. Featherstone, M. Hepworth and B. Turner (eds), *The Body: Social Process and Cultural Theory*, London: Sage, pp. 1–35.

Turner, H.G. (1973) [1904], *History of the Colony of Victoria from its Discovery to its Absorption into the Commonwealth of Australia in Two Volumes, Vol. 1, A.D. 1797–1854*, Melbourne: Heritage Publications.

United Nations Environment Programme (2002), *Global Environment Outlook 3: Past Present and Future Perspectives*, UNEP: Nairobi.

Vaillancourt, J. (1992), 'Marxism and Ecology: More Benedictine than Franciscan', *Capitalism, Nature, Socialism*, Vol. 3, No. 1, pp. 19–35.

Vance, L. (1993), 'Ecofeminism and the Politics of Reality', in G. Gaard (ed.), *Ecofeminism: Women, Animals, Nature*, Philadelphia: Temple University Press, pp. 118–45.

Victoria (1874), 'Papers relating to Forest Conservancy', presented to both Houses of Parliament by His Excellency's Command, in M. Carver, *Forestry in Victoria 1838-1919*, Melbourne: Department of Sustainability and Environment, Vol. D.

Victoria National Parks Service (1996), *Errinundra National Park Management Plan*, East Melbourne: Department of Natural Resources and Environment.

Victoria (1918), Parliamentary Debates, Session 1918, Legislative Council and Legislative Assembly, Vol. CLI, 16th December 1918.

Victorian Government (1986), *Timber Industry Strategy*, Government Statement No. 9, Melbourne: Government Printer.

Victorian Environment Protection Authority (1998), *Zeroing in on Waste: Pathways to Cleaner Production for Victorian Industries*, Melbourne: Environment Protection Authority, Publication 537.

Victorian Forests Commission (1977), *Forests and Man*, Melbourne: Forests Commission of Victoria.

Victorian Year Book 1902, Melbourne: Government Printer.

Victorian Year Book 1907–8, Melbourne: Government Printer.

Victorian Year Book 1924–5, Melbourne: Government Printer.

Vincent, A. (1993), 'The Character of Ecology', *Environmental Politics*, Vol. 2, No. 2, pp. 248–76.

Virilio, P. (1986), *Speed and Politics*, New York: Semiotext(e).

Virilio, P. (1997), *Open Sky*, London: Verso.

Virilio, P. (1999), *Politics of the Very Worst*, New York: Semiotext(e).

Virilio, P. (2000), *Paul Virilio: From Modernism to Hypermodernism and Beyond*, edited by John Armitage, London: Sage.

Virilio, P. and Lotringer, S. (1997), *Pure War*, New York: Semiotext(e).

Walters, R. (2004) 'Criminology and Genetically Modified Food', *British Journal of Criminology*, Vol. 44, No. 2, pp. 151–167.

Ward, R. (1965), *Australia*, North Sydney: Ure Smith.

Weisberg, B. (1971), *Beyond Repair: The Ecology of Capitalism*, Boston: Beacon Press.

Williams, C. (ed.) (1996), 'Special Issue: Environmental Victims', *Social Justice*, Vol. 23, No. 4.

Woodgate, P., Peel, W.D., Ritman, K.T., Coram, J.E., Brady, A., Rule, A.J. and Banks, J.C.G. (1994), *A Study of the Old-Growth Forests of East Gippsland*, Victoria: Department of Conservation and Natural Resources.
World Commission on Environment and Development (1987), *Our Common Future*, Oxford: Oxford University Press.
Wynne, B. (1996), 'May the Sheep Safely Graze?: A Reflexive View of the Expert-Lay Knowledge Divide', in S. Lash, B. Szerszynski and B. Wynne (eds), *Risk, Environment and Modernity*, London: Sage, pp. 44–83.
Young, A. (1996a), *Imagining Crime*, London: Sage.
Young, A. (1996b), 'In the Frame: Crime and the Limits of Representation', *Australian and New Zealand Journal of Criminology*, Vol. 29, No. 2, pp. 81–101.
Young, A. (2004) *Judging the Image: Art, Value, Law*, New York: Routledge.

Index

Aboriginal Australians 98–9, 101, 112, 134, 191
  Bulmer on 116–17
  'Egg Rocks' 113n19, 213
  naming of Goolengook 123–4
  see also Indigenous peoples
abundance 165–6, 200
activists 77–8
  see also protesters
Adamson, Joy 25n3
administrative borders 112–13, 143
aesthetics 163–4
affects 11, 246–50
Alexander, John Junior 107–8, 109n15, 110n16, 111n16
Amending Land Act (1865) 111
anarchism 31, 49
androcentrism 22, 27, 42
Ansell-Pearson, K. 79
anthropocentrism 4, 39, 214
  criminological thought 42, 43–5, 49, 54
  liberal ecology 17
aporia 34, 64, 69, 237
arborescence 34, 35, 68, 70, 78
Aristotle 61, 69
arrests 208, 210–11, 213, 220
articulated vehicles 149, 150–1
assemblages 4, 60, 91–2, 100, 254
  of enunciation 56, 59, 74, 84, 234, 256
  flows 121, 122, 249
  industrial-exploratory machine 123, 124
  machinic 75, 78n7, n8, 151, 250
  mining 129, 134
  Nature 80
  textual machines 49
  writing 124
  see also bodies
Audas, J.W. 143–4
The Australian Conservation Foundation 23
authenticity 93, 232
axiomisation 90, 136
Barnett, H. 45–8
Bauman, Zygmunt 14, 34, 64
Beauglehole, A.C. 164–5
beauty 46, 47, 48
Beauvoir, Simone de 22
becoming-other 4, 6, 34, 87, 141
  philosophy of flows 64
  plane of consistency 236
  see also Other
Bemm River 98, 102n6, 109, 131, 172–3, 184, 189
Bendoc 119n22, 122–3, 130
Benton, Ted 48–50
Bidwell people 98, 101, 112, 134, 191
  Bulmer on 116, 117
  'Egg Rocks' 113n19, 213
  naming of Goolengook 123
binary schemas 5, 7, 35, 43, 235
  criminology 56, 251
  ethnographic Other 117
  forest conflict 224, 256
  see also dialectical models; dichotomies
biocentrism 28, 29, 45–8, 49
biodiversity 92, 93, 159, 179n2, 215
  adverse changes in 241
  clearfelling impact on 242
  Ecological Vegetation Classes 200, 203
  Errinundra National Park 205
  global depletions 41
  old-growth forest 195, 196
  salmon migration 32
  sites of biological significance 188
biological significance 127, 186–9, 199, 220
  see also botanical significance; zoological significance
biotic communities 46
Birkeland, J. 24
Black Watch Creek 118–22, 123–4, 128, 129
  CRAE Report 182–3
  geodetic surveys 131, 132–3
Black-Allan line 112
Blair, Tony 68

Blondel, E. 87
bodies 4, 91–2, 93, 255, 256–7
  affective 247–8
  deterritorialisation of 199
  environmental crime 55
  formation of 97
  geodetic surveys 132
  heterogeneous elements 251
  molarisation of 134
  monoculture of 236
  multiplicity 77
  plane of reference 157
  of representation 146
  resolution 164
  reterritorialisation of 199
  schizoanalysis 249
  socius concept 73, 74
  speeds 239, 240
  stochastic modelling 35
  texts relationship 86, 87, 254
  without organs 64, 146, 162, 233, 234, 235
  see also assemblages
Bola Creek 182–3
Bookchin, Murray 31, 33–4
botanical exploration 126–30
botanical significance 165–7, 173–4
  see also biological significance
Boulder Flat (Burtons) 125
boundaries 108, 112–13, 143, 180n2, 219–20
Bradford, Terry 214
British Empire 99, 254
Brown, Bob 211, 214, 215, 218
buffer zones 176, 185, 209, 214, 215, 219–20
bulldozers 149–50
Bulmer, John 116–17
Bush, George W. 68

cadastral plans 133–4
Cann Run 102–3, 105n9, 107–10, 125
capitalism 12, 73, 91n5, 250
  deep ecology 29
  'derelict zones' 233n2
  ecomarxism 4, 18, 19, 20, 35
  green criminology 51
  liberal ecology 16
  mode of envisioning 230
CAR *see* Comprehensive, Adequate and Representative reserve system
Carrington, K. 13
Carron, L.T. 148
carrying capacity 105–6
Carson, Rachel 25n3
categories 83–4, 194–7, 233, 235, 237–8
caterpillar tracks 150
cattle 105–6, 115, 138n2, 139
chainsaws 149, 151
chaos 76–7, 253
Chernobyl 22, 77
China 20
chirographic machine 6, 87
chlorofluorocarbons 77
Christianity 116
civilisation 116, 117, 232
class 17, 24, 51
clearfelling 158–9, 163, 167, 169, 222, 239
  buffer zones 185
  chainsaws 149
  depletion of biodiversity 242
  ecological integrity 47
  economic gains from 243
  Errinundra National Park 206
  habitat destruction 81
  hectares cleared per year 221
  old-growth forest 196
  'permanent forest' 155
  supporters of 235
  see also logging
Clements, Ruth 25n3
Code of Forest Practices for Timber Production 179–81, 206–7
Cohen, Stanley 51
colonialism 99, 100, 117
communism 18, 20–1
Comprehensive, Adequate and Representative (CAR) reserve system 197, 199
Comte, Auguste 12, 13, 31
Concerned Residents of East Gippsland (CROEG) 207, 222
conservation 77, 142, 143–5, 235
  abundance concept 166
  CAR system 197, 199
  Forest Management Areas 203–4
  geographic representation units 202–3
  hydrological 183–6

Land Conservation Council report 163, 175, 176
old-growth forest 213
'rare'/'common' dichotomy 183
Conservation Forests and Lands Act (1987) 211
conservation movement 212
constructionism 52–3
consumers 4, 17, 35, 69, 91n5, 181n2
content 88–9
Cook, James 99
Cornish, H. 99
corporate concern 221
corporate perspective 50, 51
correspondence theory of truth 237
crime
definition of 43–4, 54, 55, 56
eco-critical approach 45–6
leakages 72n3
criminology 4–5, 7, 41–56, 250–1
anthropocentrism 43–5
biocentrism 45–8
constitutive 54–5
critical 45–6, 48, 53–4
ecocentrism 45, 48–53
green 4–5, 42, 50–3
critical criminology 45–6, 48, 53–4
Croajingolong 112–13, 122, 124, 147, 152
biological exploration 126, 129–30
clearfelling 149
East Gippsland Forest Management Area 172
forests 140–1
National Park 176
new mode of envisioning 151
watersheds 128
CROEG *see* Concerned Residents of East Gippsland
Crown Land (Reserves) Act (1978) 220
cyanide 183

Damp Forest 194, 200, 202, 203, 204
dams 17, 42, 245
Darwin, Charles 12, 238
Davies, J. 43
DCE *see* Department of Conservation and Environment
deconstruction 52, 56
deep ecology 4, 15, 28–31, 35, 37
Deferred Forest Areas (DFAs) 197
deforestation 41–2, 77, 143–4
see also clearfelling; logging
Deleuze, Gilles 3–4, 5, 7, 59–61, 68–80, 248
affects 246, 247
arborescence 35, 68
assemblages 91–2
becoming 82
body without organs 64
capitalism 29
chaos 253
classification 237–8, 239
desire 23, 75–6
deterritorialisation 79n9, 233
differences 27
discourse 87
ecology as an affect of modernity 11
envisioning 230, 232
flow 76–7
fold concept 92
form and content 88, 229
gender politics 24
immanent conception of the world 28
lines of molarity 254
machines 57, 90–1, 97
maps 85n3
micropolitics 257
molar refrains 177
multiplicity 77–80
naming 85
Nature 161, 237
nomadism 30
phylogenetic lineage 84
plane of consistency 27, 71–3, 255
plane of reference 157
schizoanalysis 69–71
signs 57–8
socius 73–5
Spinoza 6
the state 21, 133, 134, 234
statements 89
striated space 126, 133
subjectivity 26
totality 24–5
town/country relationship 132
trees 11
will to power 65–6, 141
'dense scrub' 107, 244

Department of Conservation and Environment (DCE) 37, 209
Department of Conservation and Natural Resources 37–8, 199–200, 202, 203, 204, 211–12
depasturing 100–3, 107–10, 113–16
Derrida, Jacques 52n10, 86n4
Descartes, René 12, 13, 146
desire 4, 23, 24, 57, 65, 75–6
deterritorialisation 46, 71n3, 86n4, 124, 153, 224
 alluvial mining 121
 bodies 92
 CAR system 199
 criminology 251
 effects of 233
 geodetic surveys 134
 jointed track 150
 locomotives 144
 machinic incisions 117
 multiplicities 78, 79
 pastoral sites 104, 106
 roads 130
 'sawmilling species' 149
 seasons 151
 signs 57
 speeds 239
 towns 132
DFAs *see* Deferred Forest Areas
dialectical models 52, 53
dialectics 27, 39
dichotomies 4, 35, 36, 93, 117
 green criminology 51
 social/natural world 28
 species of commercial value 146
 universal/particular 159
 see also binary schemas
difference 5, 7, 27, 71, 83
 ethic of 92
 individual 238, 239
 modernist ecologies 36
 molarity 91
 Nature 48
 Nietzsche on 66
 poststructuralism 58
 production of 159
Dionysian forces 64, 65
discourse 36, 146, 159
 discursive formation 87
 discursive practices 19
 universality 55
'dislocated ecology' 179n2
distance 240, 246
distorted speech patterns 39
disturbance categories 194–5, 196, 201, 212–13, 236
domination 4, 35, 39
Durkheim, Émile 12, 13
dykes 190

East Gippsland
 Aboriginal occupation 98
 botanical significance 165–7, 173–4
 bulldozers 150
 bushfires 147–9
 flora 143, 145
 Forest Management Area 171–2, 190–2, 194–6, 197–206, 208, 211–13
 Forest Management Plan 177, 189, 198–204, 218–19
 forest operation zones 217n11
 forest reserves 144
 habitat loss 77n6
 Land Conservation Council reports 161–4, 185
 logging 119n22, 169, 190–2, 242n4, 243
 National Parks (Amendment) Act 178
 pastoral industry 115
 Regional Forest Agreement 208
 resource inventory 204–5
 'scrub-dwellers' 116
 sites of biological significance 187–9
 sustainable yield 182, 192
 textual reproduction of 164
 vegetation 164–5, 194–7
 Wet Forests 246
 zoological significance 168
 see also Goolengook
Eckersley, R. 31
eco-critical criminology 45–6, 48
ecocentrism 45, 48–53
ecofeminism 4, 15, 22–8, 35, 36–7
ecological renewal 17–18, 34, 49
Ecological Vegetation Classes (EVCs) 194–7, 199–201, 202–3, 204, 212

ecomarxism 4, 15, 18–21, 35, 36
  see also Marxism
economic growth 39
economic sphere 51–2
ecosystemic integrity 46, 47, 48
Edgeworth, R.L 150
'Egg Rocks' 113n219, 213
Ellery, Mount 120, 123, 124, 128
  pastoral run demarcation 113n19, 114n19
  renaming of 115
  views from 174
Engels, Friedrich 19, 20
Environment Protection Agencies (EPAs) 17, 44n2
environmental activists 77–8
  see also protesters
environmental damage
  bodies 254
  categorical accounts of 5
  communist states 20–1
  criminological thought 41, 53
  discursive limits of 60
  ecofeminism 22, 23
  ecomarxism 18
  green criminology 51–2
  human/social dimensions of 68
  Land Conservation Council report 177
  liberal ecology 15–16, 18
  modernist accounts of 4, 35
  modernity 12
  molar assemblages 250
  naming of 7
  pleasure gained from 52
  state permission 45
  see also deforestation
envisioning 5, 6, 110, 153, 165, 229–33
  Croajingolong 151
  depasturing 100–1, 107
  forest management blocks 157
  movement of bodies 239
  'sawmilling species' 149
EPAs *see* Environment Protection Agencies
epistemology 4, 26, 233
Errinundra National Park 177, 178, 180n2, 191, 212
  biological/botanical significance 173–4, 188
  Cutting Areas Review Committee 171
  'Essentially Natural Catchments' 186
  logging 192
  Management Strategy 205–6
  as monstrous becoming 234–5
  Natural Features Zone 185
  'permanent forest' 155
  Wet Forest 204
Errinundra Plateau 115, 123, 171, 173, 187, 205
Errinundra (Yerungunderah) Valley 123, 124, 125
'Essentially Natural Catchments' 185–6
ethics 46n4, 48, 256
Eurocentrism 28, 99
EVCs *see* Ecological Vegetation Classes
event, forest conflict as 3, 6, 82, 87
Everett, Arthur 111
Ewald, F. 13
Export Control Act (1982) 168–9
expressions 121
exteriority 141
Exxon Valdez 77

fascism 33, 48, 50, 51n9, 67–8, 255
femininity 22
feminism 4, 15, 22–8, 35, 36–7, 49
fires 115–16, 138n2, 147–9
fishing 17, 42
flows 61, 64, 84, 92, 235
  desire 75
  discontinuities 121–2
  environmental regulation 254
  machinic interactions 249
  modernist ecologies 36
  multiplicities 76–7
FMAs *see* forest management areas
FMBs *see* forest management blocks
FMP *see* Forest Management Plan
FoE *see* Friends of the Earth
fold concept 60, 92–3, 141
footed wheel 150
Forbes, S.J. 165–7
forest management areas (FMAs) 171–2, 186, 190–2, 194–6, 197–206, 208, 211–13
forest management blocks (FMBs) 155–9, 161, 188, 190, 234
Forest Management Plan (FMP) 177, 189, 198–204, 218–19

forest operation zones 215–17, 222
'forest produce' 136–8, 139, 140, 152–3
foresters 69–70
Forests Act (1907) 135–41, 142
Forests Act (1918) 142
Forests Act (1958) 142n6, 152–5, 163, 170, 173, 244
Forests Commission 142–3, 145, 147, 148, 152
Forests (Miscellaneous) (Amendment) Regulations (1998) 215–17
Forests (Timber Harvesting) Act (1990) 181–2
form 88–9, 229
Fossey, Diane 25n3
Foster, Hal 230
Foucault, Michel 1, 11, 12n1, 30, 233
  biopolitics 134
  categories 83
  fascism 33, 50
  knowing subject 20
  panopticism 70
  pleasure 23
  rationality 19
  representation 146
  the state 21
  subjectivity 26
Fox, W. 31
French, Charles 126
French, Marilyn 22
Friends of the Earth (FoE) 23, 207, 208, 210–11

Gaard, G. 24
Galileo 12
gardens 179n2
GECO *see* Goongerah Environment Centre
gender 17, 22–8, 29, 50, 51
genealogies 31
General Management Zone (GMZ) 198, 199
'generalised accident' 77n6
geodetic surveys 112, 113, 126, 130–4
geographic representation units (GRUs) 202–3, 204
geology 129
GMZ *see* General Management Zone
gold 118–22, 123–4, 129, 182, 190
Goolengook 3–4, 6, 63, 82–5, 93–4, 253–7
  becoming contested 161–225, 245
  becoming forest 135–59
  becoming known 97–130
  building 86–7
  correspondences 81
  criminology 250–1
  envisioning 229–33
  as event 82
  maps of 62, 127
  naming 85–6, 123–4, 233–7
  plane of consistency 254–5
  protesters 3, 207–8, 210–11, 213, 214–17, 222–3
  representing 88–9
  selecting texts 88
  speeds 239–46
  textual machines 91, 92, 93
  see also East Gippsland
Goongerah Environment Centre (GECO) 207, 208, 211
Goongerah Run 113–15, 116n21
gray ecology 245
'green' concept 42–3
green criminology 4–5, 42, 50–3
Green, Jack 115
Greenpeace 23
GRUs *see* geographic representation units
Guattari, Felix 3–4, 5, 59, 59–61, 68–80
  affects 246, 247
  arborescence 35, 68
  assemblages 91–2
  becoming 82
  body without organs 64
  capitalism 29
  chaos 253
  desire 23, 75–6
  deterritorialisation 233
  discourse 87
  dissensus 255–6
  ecosophical territories 93
  flow 76–7
  fold concept 92
  form and content 88
  gender politics 24
  immanent conception of the world 28
  lines of molarity 254

machines 57, 90–1, 97
maps 85n3
molar refrains 177
multiplicity 77–80
Nature 237
'new aesthetic paradigm' 84
nomadism 30
phylogenetic lineage 84
plane of consistency 27, 71–3, 255
plane of reference 157
schizoanalysis 69–71
signs 57–8
socius 73–5
the state 21, 133, 134, 234
striated space 126, 133
totality 24–5
town/country relationship 132
trees 11
will to power 141
Gullan, P.K. 165–7

Habermas, Jürgen 55
haecceities 124
Harari, J. 58, 59
hardwood resources 190–3
harm 2, 3, 41, 43, 232
biocentric perspectives 46, 48
criminological thought 45, 53, 55, 251
enforcement bodies 44
green criminology 51
modernist conception of 42
Henry, Stuart 49, 54–5, 56
Heritage Rivers Act (1992) 189–90, 214, 215, 217, 220–1
Hess, Emma 218, 221
Hibbard, William 103–4, 105n9
hierarchies 4, 27, 29, 31, 35, 39
Hobbes, Thomas 13
Holderlin, Friedrich 72–3
housing 147
Howard, John 68
human nature 49, 54
humanity 12, 46, 50, 54
Hume, David 13
hydrological conservation 183–6

illegal activities 43–4
image of thought 59–60
indexes 97
Indigenous peoples 29–30, 106, 213
see also Aboriginal Australians
individuation 238
industrial revolution 239–40
industrialisation 29
inequalities 49, 52
instrumental rationality 13–14, 33
integrity 46, 47, 48
intensities 97, 106, 111, 141, 249
bodies 92
environmental regulation 254
plane of consistency 72
interconnectedness 28, 29
Irigaray, L. 28

justice 3, 47–8, 50–1, 52–3

Knight, Alistair Forbes 218
knowledge 57, 158–9

land 76
Land Conservation Act (1970) 172
Land Conservation Council 161–4, 173–7, 183–6
language 55, 66–7, 251
law 3, 7, 77, 256
environmental crimes 43
ethics relationship 46n4
rule of 72n3
leakages 71n3
legislation
Amending Land Act (1865) 111
Conservation Forests and Lands Act (1987) 211
Crown Land (Reserves) Act (1978) 220
depasturing 100–1
Export Control Act (1982) 168–9
Forests Act (1907) 135–41, 142
Forests Act (1918) 142
Forests Act (1958) 142n6, 152–5, 163, 170, 173, 244
Forests (Miscellaneous) (Amendment) Regulations (1998) 215–17
Forests (Timber Harvesting) Act (1990) 181–2
Heritage Rivers Act (1992) 189–90, 214, 215, 217, 220–1
Land Acts 130n26, 137n2, 138n2, 139
Land Conservation Act (1970) 172

National Parks Act (1975) 175
National Parks (Amendment) Act (1988) 178
National Parks (Amendment) Act (1998) 220
National Parks (Miscellaneous Amendments) Act (1991) 183
Soil Conservation and Land Utilisation Act (1958) 172
State Forests Act (1876) 117n22
Victoria establishment 106
see also regulation
Leopold, Aldo 45–6
liberal ecology 4, 15–18, 35, 36, 43
liberalism 17, 33, 66
licensing 119n22, 138n2, 139–40
Lobert, Bertram 210
Lock, John 113
Locke, John 13
logging 21, 41–2, 190–3, 221–2
ecological integrity 47
'Essentially Natural Catchments' 186
forest management blocks 156, 158
Forest Management Plan 201, 203
gold mining 122n23
Land Conservation Council report 162, 175, 176
media release 211–12
national parks 180n2
new technologies 149–51
protests against 3, 207–8, 210–11, 213, 214–17, 222–3
sites of biological significance 187
unlawful nature of 220
woodchips 168–9
see also clearfelling; deforestation; timber
Lowe, Donald 230
Lowland Forest 194, 200
Lunt, Ian 210
Lynch, M. 50–3

machines 4, 78n7, 90–1, 117, 255, 256
academic 124
aesthetic 163–4
bodies 92
conservation 232
forestry 232, 246
geodetic 112, 133
industrial-exploratory 123, 124
naming 97–8
overcoding 159, 199
pastoral 106
plane of consistency 71–2, 254, 257
plane of immanence 251
resource inventory maps 205
social heritage 129
socius 74, 75
textual 49, 90, 91, 93–4
machinic thought 5, 57, 69–71, 78n7, 79, 84
McKinty, J.M. 119n22
McRae, C.F. 150
Man 12–13, 18, 19, 20, 31
Mansergh, I.M. 168
maps 85n3, 111, 141
'Forests of Victoria' 164
geodetic co-ordinates 113
Port Phillip District 105
resource inventory 204–5
sites of biological significance 127
species of commercial value 145–6
market failure 16
market forces 43
Marx, Karl 12, 13, 18, 19, 78n7
Marxism 51, 70, 78n7
see also ecomarxism
masculinity 22, 23
Massumi, B. 23–4, 74, 233n2, 247
materialism 18
May, T. 257
meaning 87, 89
mecanosphere (socius) 60, 70, 73–5, 76, 141
machinic assemblages 250
Nature as other 93
nonmolarizing 24
strata 92
Melbourne 119n22, 124, 140, 144, 151n11, 179n2, 240
Merchant, Carolyn 22, 25n3, 31n5
Merrall, Edwin 122–6, 130, 207, 247
metalepsis 177, 212
micropolitics 4–5, 51, 92, 257
see also schizoanalysis
Mies, M. 22, 25–6, 27
Miles, Ian 213
Milovanovic, Dragon 49, 54–5, 56
mimesis 53, 167, 193, 237
mineralisation 193

mining
- contestations over 245
- CRAE Report 182–3
- gold 118–22, 129
- Land Conservation Council reports 175, 186

mission statements 37–8

modernism
- biocentrism 46
- conception of harm 42
- ecocentrism 50
- ecological perspectives 7, 13, 14–15, 24, 35–7, 39
- green criminology 52
- machinic thought opposition to 57, 90
- social ecology 34
- 'words'/'things' relationship 53

modernity 11, 12–14, 15, 34
- chaos 76–7
- lens of 230
- rhetoric of 50
- schizoanalysis 73
- signifier/signified 58
- values 55

molarity 75, 86, 89, 91, 158, 255
- assemblages 250
- bodies 92, 134
- Land Conservation Council report 162
- lines of 254
- molar blockages 71n3
- molar politics 145, 153
- schizoanalysis 73
- socius concept 74

molecularity 89, 91, 92, 134, 255
- lines of 254
- molecular politics 153
- Nature 75

money 76

moralisation 91

morality 46n4

Mount Ellery 120, 123, 124, 128
- pastoral run demarcation 113n19, 114n19
- renaming of 115
- views from 174

multiplicity 77–80, 86, 180n2, 204
- Goolengook as 83, 126
- instantaneous apprehension of 59

Naess, Arne 30

naming 2, 6, 85–6, 123, 233–9
- environmental damage 7
- forest management blocks 157
- machines 97–8
- Nature 39, 83

national parks 114, 178, 179n2, 234–5
- boundaries 180n2
- Ecological Vegetation Classes 203
- 'Essentially Natural Catchments' 186
- extension of 183
- management strategy 205–6
- *see also* Errinundra National Park

National Parks Act (1975) 175

National Parks (Amendment) Act (1988) 178

National Parks (Amendment) Act (1998) 220

National Parks (Miscellaneous Amendments) Act (1991) 183

Natural Features Zones 174, 176, 177, 185, 219

Nature 2, 3, 61, 257
- biocentrism 47, 48
- criminological thought 53–4, 251
- deep ecology 28, 29–30, 37
- diversity 161
- ecofeminism 22, 23, 25–6, 27, 28, 36
- ecomarxism 18, 19, 20
- envisioning 5, 6, 39, 83, 230
- liberal ecology 36
- machinic thought 57
- Man's relationship to 13
- micropolitical forces 5
- mimesis 237
- modernist ecology 7, 12, 14–15
- molar 75, 79
- molecular 75, 76
- multiplicity 78–9, 80
- naming 39, 83
- national parks 235
- Nietzsche 64, 67, 97
- as Other 37, 42, 93, 231
- Parks Victoria advertisements 179n2, 180n2
- plane of consistency 5, 73
- preservation strategies 181n2
- regulation 50

scientific method 14
social ecology 31, 32–3
speeds of traversing 241
texts 86
transformation of 39, 83, 241, 246
New South Wales (NSW) 99–100, 101, 106, 112, 126, 157
Nietzsche, Friedrich 1, 11, 24, 61, 64–8, 248
Aristotle's law of contradiction 69
correspondence theory of truth 237
environmental damage 12
good and evil 5, 57
logical discourse 87
Man 12
Nature 97
plane of consistency 72–3
'return to nature' 30
similarity 193
socius 74n5
subjectivity 26
unity 81
values 55
will to power 65–6, 134
nihilism 13, 56, 59
nomadism 30, 133
norms 46
Norris, K.C 168
NSW *see* New South Wales

old-growth forest 187, 194–7, 200–3, 211–13, 223, 235–6, 242
Orbost 122–3, 126, 128, 141, 142–3
forest management blocks 155–6, 157, 158
mining track 130
railway 144, 151n11, 240
timber resources 190
Orwell, George 50
O'Shea, John 108, 109, 110n15
Other 29, 33, 35, 232
commodification of the 67
Indigenous peoples 116–17
Nature as 37, 42, 93, 231
see also becoming-other
'overmature' (OM) forest 192, 201

Papua New Guinea 30, 31
Parks Victoria 179n2, 180n2
pastoral runs 101–6, 107–10, 113–16
'pathos of distance' 66
patriarchy 4, 22, 26, 35, 39
Patterson, G.W. 190
Patton, Paul 246–7
Pavlich, G. 56n15, n16
peace 214
Peers, John Grimes 118–22, 130
permanence 155
Phillip, Arthur 99, 100n2
phylum 84, 106, 112, 115
Picone, Andrew 217n11, 218n11
plane of consistency 5, 27, 56, 60, 71–3, 83
becoming-other 236
blockages 78
categorisation 234
chaos of 76
definitions 55n13
Goolengook 254–5
machines 254, 257
maps 85n3
Nature 80
puissance 247
plane of immanence 153, 251, 256
plane of reference 56, 153, 157, 255
Plato 34
pleasure 23, 52
police 208, 214, 224
politics
assemblages of enunciation 256
molar 145, 153
Nietzsche 67
scientific machines 210
pollution 16, 245
Port Phillip District 100, 101, 104n8, 105, 106
positivism 13, 53, 236, 237
postmodernism 13, 54, 55
poststructuralism 5, 15, 24, 87
criminological thought 54
machinic thought 57, 90
Nietzsche 67
structuralism contrast with 58–9
power 4, 47, 54, 55
green criminology 50, 51, 52
machinic thought 57
puissance/pouvoir distinction 247
preservation strategies 181n2
processuality 65, 68, 69, 73n4
protected forests 135, 136, 139, 140, 153

protesters 3, 69–70, 207–8, 210–11, 213–17, 222–3
see also activists
public interest 110
public relations 211–12

race 17, 50, 51
railways 144
Rajchman, J. 93
rationality
ecomarxism 19
instrumental 13–14, 33
as masculine trait 22, 29
social ecology 33, 34
recreation 163, 174, 175, 176, 185
Redwood, Jill 25n3, 210, 222
Reed, Hamilton 113
Regan, Tom 48
Regional Forest Agreements (RFAs) 197, 208, 222
regulation
affects 248–9
Benton 49, 50
categories 83
green criminology 51
image of thought 60
logging 118n22
machinic thought 5
modernist ecology 4, 14–15
schizoanalysis 254, 256–7
see also legislation
regulatory capture 39, 51, 60
representation 5, 58, 68, 87, 88–9, 232
bodies of 146
geographic representation units 202–3, 204
sufficient 204
violence of 237
reserved forest 135, 138n2, 139, 140, 145
Crown Lands 154–5, 220
Dedication Schedules 170
forest produce 152
resource consumption 17
reterritorialisation 124, 129, 221, 235
CAR system 199
conservation movement 212
criminology 251
geodetic surveys 134
machinic incisions 117
modes and durations of 248
signs 57
tree species 149
RFAs see Regional Forest Agreements
rights 3, 49, 50
risk 39
roads 130, 132, 150, 176, 190, 245
Robinson, Doug 210
Romanticism 29–30
Rousseau, Jean-Jacques 13
ruptures 71n3
Russell, L. 117
Russia 20
Ryan, Joanne 25n3

Salleh, A. 26
saw mills 138n2, 140–1, 151
scale 243
schizoanalysis 68, 69–71, 73, 78n7
bodies 249, 254, 256–7
deep ecology 31
Goolengook 82, 83
science 7, 13, 14, 77
biocentrism 46, 47
ecomarxism 19–20
liberal ecology 16
machinic thought 57
social ecology 33, 37
scientific method 14, 46, 47, 142, 230, 253
'scopic regimes' 231
Seidman, S. 13
Self 117
self-realisation 28, 29
'semi-trailers' 151
semiotics 35
Shiva, V. 26, 27
Shrubby Dry Forest 194, 196, 200, 202
signifier/signified 57–8, 77, 78n7, 87
signs 57–8, 90, 146
simulacrum 93
Singer, Peter 48
SMZ see Special Management Zone
social class 17, 24, 51
social ecology 4, 15, 31–4, 35, 37
social heritage machine 129
social relations
arborescent model of 35
biocentrism 46
green criminology 52

processual conception of 69
social ecology 31
socialism 18, 49
society 12–13, 14, 61
contradictions of 70
processual conception of 69
socius concept 74
sociology 13
socius (mecanosphere) 60, 70, 73–5, 76, 141
machinic assemblages 250
Nature as other 93
nonmolarizing 24
strata 92
Soil Conservation and Land Utilisation Act (1958) 172
soil degradation 42
Special Management Zone (SMZ) 198, 199, 222
Special Protection Zone (SPZ) 197–8, 199, 203, 204, 212, 220
'specific accident' 77n6, 242
speeds 111, 112, 141, 239–46
bodies 92
environmental regulation 254
flow of matter-energy 122
Spencer, Baldwin 126–30, 207
Spinoza, Benedict de 6, 55, 72–3, 246
SPZ *see* Special Protection Zone
Squires, Gary 223
stability 46, 47, 48
the state 20, 21, 44–5, 134, 233
control 153
discursive assault of the 234
green criminology 51
limits of speed 239
territorial boundaries 133
State Forests Act (1876) 117n22
Steinem, Gloria 22
Stevenson, John 107
strata 92
Stretsky, P. 50–3
striated spaces 104, 126, 133
Stringybark trees 111, 112, 164
structuralism 57, 58, 59, 90
subjectivity 4, 13, 20, 21, 68
capitalist societies 73
Derrida 52n10
ecocentrism 49
ecofeminism 26
leakages 71n3
machinic thought 57
poststructuralism 58–9
processual conception of 69
social ecology 33
supermolecularity 24, 89, 91, 92, 153, 255
Supreme Court decision 218–20
sustainability 2, 3, 20, 60–1
ecofeminism 23
liberal ecology 18
modernist ecologies 15
regulation 50
scientific method 46, 47
sufficient representation 204
sustainable development 16–17, 34, 71n3
Sutherland, Edwin 46, 48
Sydenham Run 109n14
synedoche 159, 167, 177, 203, 204

'Tasmanian Tiger' 1–2
technology 149–51, 164, 240–1, 242, 243
Tehan, Marie 81, 207, 210
teleology 28, 34, 116
texts 6, 89, 93, 224, 231, 255
affective bodies 247
bodies relationship 86–7, 254
machines 91, 97, 98
modalities 251
selecting 88
transformations in speed 244–5, 246
visual factors 163
Thales 5, 61
thylacine ('Tasmanian Tiger') 1–2
timber 111–12, 152, 190–3, 248
bushfire impact on 147, 148–9
Code of Forest Practices for Timber Production 179–81, 206–7
definition of 136
Errinundra National Park 171
forest regulation 118n22, 137n2, 139–40, 142, 154–5, 181–2
geographic representation units 202
Land Conservation Council report 162, 175, 177
licensing system 119n22
protected sites 189
resource inventory maps 205

sawlogs 169–70, 171–2, 221
sawmills 140–1
Special Protection Zones 198
wood utilisation plan 221–2
see also clearfelling; logging
time 158, 236, 242
Tournier, Michel 257
transience 66
Tranter, K. 16
trees 11, 34, 111–12, 180
commercial value 145–6
definition of 136
geodetic surveys 131, 133
'rotten' 240n3
'sawmilling species' 148–9
see also vegetation
truth effects 20
Tuckey, Wilson 240n3
Turner, B. 13–14
Tyers, Charles J. 108n13

United Nations Development Programme 41
United Nations Environment Programme 41
units of management 143, 233, 243–4, 246
'unsettled districts' 101, 102, 103, 231

values 6, 49, 55–6, 163, 210
Land Conservation Council reports 176, 177, 184–5
sites of biological significance 188
van Gerrevink, Michelle 220
Vance, L. 27
vegetation 164, 168, 180
Ecological Vegetation Classes 194–7, 199–201, 202–3, 204, 212
native clearance practices 245
sites of biological/botanical significance 165–7, 174, 187
see also trees
Victoria
bushfires 147–9
Code of Forest Practices for Timber Production 179–81
creation of state 106
Croajingolong County 112
Dedication Schedules 170–1
departmental name changes 37–8
dislocated ecology 178n2
District of Port Phillip 101
environmental crimes 44n2
forest products 152
forest regulation 117n22, 135–41, 142
'Forests of Victoria' map 164
geodetic survey 130–1
hydrological conservation 183–4, 186
Land Acts 130n26
national parks 114
NSW border 113
pollution 16n2
sites of biological significance 186–9
Wet Forests 246
see also East Gippsland
violencing 236
Virilio, Paul
'aesthetics of disappearance' 249
'dromospheric pollution' 246
ecological dilemmas 29
gray ecology 245
'specific accident' concept 77n6, 242
speed 239–40, 241
vision 144–5, 229
vision 144–5, 229–33
see also envisioning

Walsh, N.G. 165–7
Walters, Brian 217n11
war 148, 151–2
Waring, Marilyn 22
waste 15
'waste lands' 99–100, 101, 231, 233
water 61–4, 131, 172–3
buffer zones 209, 214, 215, 219–20
Code of Forest Practices for Timber Production 179–80
Heritage Rivers Act 189–90, 214, 215, 217, 220–1
hydrological conservation 183–6
Land Conservation Council reports 175, 176
Weber, Max 12, 13
Wet Forest 194, 200, 202, 204, 205–6, 246
'wholeness' 204
The Wilderness Society 23, 221
wildlife 125–6, 129–30, 163, 187
Code of Forest Practices for Timber Production 180

Crown Land (Reserves) Act 220
Errinundra National Park 206
habitat destruction 81, 209
illegal trade in 43
sites of zoological significance 168
will to power 65–6, 134, 141
women 22–8, 36–7, 68
wood 79n8
wood utilisation plan (WUP) 221–2
woodchips 36–7, 168–9
Woodgate, P. 136n2, 143n7, 151n11
forest categories 195, 196, 197, 200–1
timber licensing system 119n22
words 1, 5, 47, 53, 146
constitutive criminology 55
expressions 121
fluidity of 110
machines 91
socius concept 73, 74
work 76
World Bank 41
World Commission on Environment and Development 16
World Resources Institute 41, 47n5
WUP *see* wood utilisation plan

zoological significance 168
see also biological significance